NOV 16 2007

John Walkenbach's Favorite
Excel® 2007 Tips & Tricks

DATE DUE

John Walkenbach's Favorite Excel® 2007 Tips & Tricks

John Walkenbach

BICENTENNIAL
1807
WILEY
2007
BICENTENNIAL

Wiley Publishing, Inc.

John Walkenbach's Favorite Excel® 2007 Tips & Tricks

Published by
Wiley Publishing, Inc.
111 River Street
Hoboken, NJ 07030-5774
www.wiley.com

Copyright © 2007 by Wiley Publishing, Inc., Indianapolis, Indiana

Published by Wiley Publishing, Inc., Indianapolis, Indiana

Published simultaneously in Canada

For general information on our other products and services, please contact our Customer Care Department within the U.S. at 800-762-2974, outside the U.S. at 317-572-3993, or fax 317-572-4002.

For technical support, please visit www.wiley.com/techsupport.

Wiley also publishes its books in a variety of electronic formats. Some content that appears in print may not be available in electronic books.

Library of Congress Control Number: 2007926382

ISBN: 978-0-470-13766-6

Manufactured in the United States of America

10 9 8 7 6 5 4 3 2 1

WILEY

About the Author

John Walkenbach is a leading authority on spreadsheet software, and principal of J-Walk and Associates Inc., an Arizona-based consulting firm that specializes in spreadsheet application development. John is the author of about 50 spreadsheet books, and has written more than 300 articles and reviews for a variety of publications, including *PC World, InfoWorld, PC Magazine, Windows,* and *PC/Computing.* He also maintains a popular Internet Web site (The Spreadsheet Page, `www.j-walk.com/ss`), and is the developer of the Power Utility Pak, an award-winning add-in for Microsoft Excel. John graduated from the University of Missouri and earned master's and PhD degrees from the University of Montana.

Acknowledgments

Writing a book that contains Excel tips was much more difficult than I originally thought it would be. The challenge is deciding on what exactly constitutes a tip. If I present a technique that you didn't know about, you may consider it to be a valuable tip. But if you're already familiar with the technique, it's *not* a tip.

I decided to select my tips based on a specific Excel user — a person who really exists but who will remain nameless. This person uses Excel on a regular basis but has never bothered to take the time to dig in and learn how to work more efficiently. I think this target reader has a lot in common with millions of other Excel users. If that's the case, most of them will find this book to be very useful. So, thanks to my anonymous target reader.

I must also acknowledge the world-famous Excel virtuoso Nick Hodge. Over the years, I've mentioned many people in my Acknowledgments sections, but none has responded more enthusiastically than Nick Hodge — who, by the way, holds the European record for having the thickest wallet. Adding his name to this section virtually guarantees a dozen additional sales in the UK.

Finally, thanks are due to the people behind the scenes at Wiley who converted my Microsoft Word files into a tangible book. First, thanks to Greg Croy, my acquisitions editor. This book was Greg's idea, and I'm glad that he chose me to be the author. I also appreciate the help and guidance of Paul Levesque. He and the other editors made many helpful suggestions, which I've incorporated into these pages.

Contents at a Glance

Contents

Part III: Formatting 107

Part IV: Basic Formulas and Functions   155

Part V: Useful Formula Examples   205

Part VII: Charts and Graphics   289

Part IX: Working With Files   **375**

Part X: Printing   **401**

Part XI: Spotting, Fixing, and Preventing Errors   427

Part XII: Basic VBA and Macros   445

Introduction

Excel is a very popular program. Millions of people throughout the world use it on a regular basis. But it's a safe bet that the vast majority of users have yet to discover some of the amazing things this product can do. If I've done my job, you'll find enough useful information in this book to help you use Excel on a new level.

This is the second edition of this book, and I added about 50 new tips (and deleted some that no longer apply to Excel 2007). In addition, I beefed up many of the old tips based on feedback from readers of the first edition.

What You Should Know

This book isn't a beginner's guide to Excel. Rather, it's a book for those who already use Excel but realize that they have a lot more to learn. This book is filled with tips and tricks that I've learned over the years, and I'm certain that about 99 percent of all Excel users will find something new and useful in these pages.

If you have absolutely no experience with Excel, this book might not be the best choice for you. To get the most out of this book, you should have some background in using Excel. Specifically, I assume that you know how to accomplish the following tasks with Excel:

- Create workbooks, insert worksheets, save files, and perform other basic tasks.
- Navigate through a workbook.

- Use the Excel Ribbon and dialog boxes.
- Use basic Windows features, such as file management and copy-and-paste techniques.

What You Should Have

To use this book, you need a copy of Microsoft Excel 2007 for Windows. No exceptions. Excel 2007 is so radically different from previous versions that you will probably be very confused if you're using an older version of Excel.

As far as hardware goes for the computer you use to run Excel, the faster, the better. And, of course, the more memory in your system, the happier you'll be.

Conventions in This Book

Take a minute to skim this section and learn some of the typographic conventions used throughout this book.

Formula Listings

Formulas usually appear on a separate line in monospace font. For example, I might list the following formula:

```
=VLOOKUP(StockNumber,PriceList,2,False)
```

Excel supports a special type of formula known as an *array formula*. When you enter an array formula, press Ctrl+Shift+Enter (not just Enter). Excel encloses an array formula in curly braces to remind you that it's an array formula.

 NOTE
Do not type the curly braces for an array formula. Excel puts them in automatically.

VBA Code Listings

This book also contains examples of VBA code. Each listing appears in a monospace font; each line of code occupies a separate line. To make the code easier to read, I usually use indentation on specific lines. Although indentation is optional, it helps to delineate statements that go together.

If a line of code doesn't fit on a single line in this book, I use the standard VBA line continuation sequence: a space followed by an underscore character, to indicate that the line of code extends to the next line. For example, the following two lines comprise a single VBA statement:

```
If Right(cell.Value, 1) = "!" Then cell.Value _
    = Left(cell.Value, Len(cell.Value) - 1)
```

You can enter this code either exactly as shown, on two lines, or on a single line without the trailing underscore character.

Key Names

Names of keys on the keyboard appear in normal type: for example Alt, Home, PgDn, and Ctrl. When you should press two or more keys simultaneously, the keys are connected with a plus sign: "Press Ctrl+G to display the Go To dialog box."

The Ribbon

Excel 2007 features a brand-new user interface. Menus and toolbars have been replaced by a tab-and-Ribbon interface.

When you need to select a command by using the Ribbon, I describe the command by using the tab name, the group name, and the command name: for example, "Choose Home ⇨ Alignment ⇨ Wrap Text." This command translates to "Click the Home tab, locate the Alignment group, and then click the Wrap Text button."

Some commands use a drop-down Ribbon control. For example: Home ⇨ Styles ⇨ Conditional Formatting ⇨ New Rule. In this case, you need to click the down-pointing arrow on the Conditional Formatting control in order to access the New Rule command.

Many commands begin with the word Office. There is no Office tab. Rather, this refers to the round logo in the upper left corner of the Excel window (the Office Button).

Functions, Procedures, and Named Ranges

The names of the Excel worksheet functions appear in all uppercase, like so: "Use the SUM function to add the values in column A."

Macro and VBA procedure names appear in normal type: "Execute the InsertTotals procedure." I often use mixed upper- and lowercase to make these names easier to read. Named ranges appear in italic: "Select the *InputArea* range."

Unless you're dealing with text inside quotation marks, Excel isn't sensitive to case. In other words, both the following formulas produce the same result:

```
=SUM(A1:A50)
=sum(a1:a50)
```

Excel, however, converts the characters in the second formula to uppercase.

Mouse Conventions

The mouse terminology in this book is all standard fare: pointing, clicking, right-clicking, dragging, and so on. You know the drill.

What the Icons Mean

Throughout this book, icons appear in the left margin to call your attention to points that are particularly important.

NOTE
I use Note icons to tell you that something is important — perhaps a concept that can help you master the task at hand or something fundamental for understanding subsequent material.

CAUTION
I use Caution icons when the operation I'm describing can cause problems if you're not careful.

CROSS-REFERENCE
I use the Cross-Reference icon to refer you to other tips that have more to say on a particular topic.

NEW
This icon indicates a feature new to Excel 2007.

Entering VBA Code

Some of these tips and tricks involve *Visual Basic for Applications (VBA)*, a programming language built into Excel. You use the following basic procedure to enter a VBA procedure into a workbook:

1. Press Alt+F11 to activate the VBA editor window.

2. Click your workbook's name in the Project window. If the Project window isn't visible, press Ctrl+R to display it.

3. Choose Insert ⇨ Module to add a VBA module to the project. A code window appears.

4. Type the code in the code window.

When your workbook contains VBA code, you must save it as a macro-enabled workbook. These workbooks have the *.xlsm extension.

When a workbook contains VBA code, you might receive a warning when you open the workbook. This warning depends on your security settings. To view or change your security settings, display the Trust Center dialog box:

1. Choose Office ⇨ Excel Options.

2. In the Excel Options dialog box, click the Trust Center tab.

3. Click the Trust Center Settings button.

4. In the Trust Center dialog box, click the Macro Settings tab.

I recommend the default setting: Disable All Macros with Notification. When this setting is in effect, you have the option to enable or disable macros in every workbook you open. The exception is when the workbook is opened from a trusted location. Specify trusted locations on the Trusted Locations tab of the Trust Center dialog box.

How This Book Is Organized

To provide some semblance of order, I grouped these tips and tricks into 13 parts:

- Part I: Basic Excel Usage
- Part II: Data Entry
- Part III: Formatting
- Part IV: Basic Formulas and Functions
- Part V: Useful Formula Examples
- Part VI: Conversions and Mathematical Calculations
- Part VII: Charts and Graphics
- Part VIII: Data Analysis and Lists
- Part IX: Working with Files
- Part X: Printing Tips
- Part XI: Spotting, Fixing, and Preventing Errors
- Part XII: Basic VBA and Macros
- Part XIII: Sources for Excel Information

How to Use This Book

This book really isn't intended to be read from cover to cover, as you would read a novel — but I'm sure that some people will do so. More likely, you'll want to use it as a reference book and consult it when necessary. If you're faced with a challenging task, you might want to check the index first, to see whether the book specifically addresses your problem. The order of the parts and tips is arbitrary. Most readers will probably skip around and pick up useful tidbits here and there.

About the Power Utility Pak Offer

Toward the back of this book is a coupon that you can redeem for a discounted copy of my award-winning Power Utility Pak — a collection of useful Excel utilities, plus many new worksheet functions. I developed version 7 of this product exclusively for Excel 2007.

You can also use this coupon to purchase the complete VBA source code for a nominal fee. Studying the code is an excellent way to pick up some useful programming techniques. You can take the product for a test drive by downloading the trial version from my Web site at `www.j-walk.com/ss`.

 NOTE
Power Utility Pak version 7 requires Excel 2007 for Windows.

Reach Out

I'm always interested in getting feedback on my books. The best way to provide this feedback is by e-mail. Send your comments and suggestions to `john@j-walk.com`.

Unfortunately, I cannot reply to specific questions. Posting your question to one of the Excel newsgroups is, by far, the best way to get assistance. See Tip 219 for more information.

Also, when you're out surfing the Web, don't overlook my Web site (The Spreadsheet Page) at `www.j-walk.com/ss`.

Now, without further ado, it's time to turn the page and expand your horizons.

Part I

Basic Excel Usage

In this part, you'll find tips and tricks covering some of the fundamental uses of Excel, from selecting cells and navigating sheets in a workbook to hiding rows and columns, as well as working with the Quick Access Toolbar and changing Excel's color scheme.

Tips and Where to Find Them

Understanding Excel Versions

If you're reading this book, you should be using Excel 2007 — which is radically different from all other Excel versions.

I've found that most users don't even know which version of Excel they use. Here's how to find out your Excel version, plus additional information.

If Excel has a menu titled Help, click it and then choose About. If Excel does *not* have a menu titled Help, then you're using Excel 2007. Follow these steps to find out more:

1. Choose Office ⇨ Excel Options.

2. In the Excel Options dialog box, click the Resources tab.

3. On the Resources tab, click the About button.

Figure 1-1 shows that I'm using version 12.0, also known (officially) as Microsoft Office Excel 2007. Most people just call it Excel 2007. Notice the decimal places after the version number? That represents the *build* of the product. In my case, I'm using build 4518. I don't know what the 1014 means.

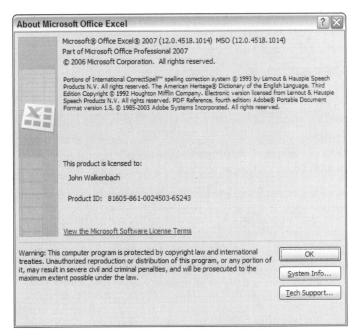

Figure 1-1: This dialog box displays the Excel version.

So, who cares which version of Excel you use? Most of the time, nobody cares. As long as your version does what you want it to do, the version makes no difference. But if you share your workbooks with other users, the version may be very important.

Suppose that you use Excel 2007 and you give a co-worker (who uses Excel 2000) a copy of a workbook. If you happened to use a feature that was introduced in Excel 2002, Excel 2003, or Excel 2007, your co-worker may not be able to work with your file in the way you intended. In fact, if you saved the file in one of the new Excel 2007 file formats, she may not even be able to *open* the file.

NOTE

Microsoft provides the free add-on Office 2007 Compatibility Pack. This download gives previous versions of Office support for the new Office 2007 file formats. Therefore, you can share Excel 2007 files with users of Excel 2000, Excel 2002, and Excel 2003. Note, however, that this add-on doesn't endow the older versions with any new features. It just allows the software to open and save the files.

For the record, the following table shows the major version numbers of Excel.

Version	Released	Comments
1	1985	The first version of Excel was for the Apple Macintosh.
2	1987	The first Windows version was labeled 2 to correspond to the Macintosh version. Because Windows was not widely used, this version included a runtime version of Windows.
3	1990	This version included toolbars, drawing capabilities, outlining, add-in support, 3D charts, and many more new features.
4	1992	The first "popular" version of Excel. It included quite a few usability features.
5	1993	Excel 5, a major upgrade, included multisheet workbooks and support for VBA.
7*	1995	This version, known as Excel 95, was the first major 32-bit version of Excel. Feature-wise, it was similar to Excel 5.
8	1997	This version, known as Excel 97, was the first version to support conditional formatting and data validation. It also incorporated new menus and toolbars. VBA programmers found quite a few enhancements, including a completely new VBA editor, UserForms, class modules, and more.
9	1999	This version, known as Excel 2000, could use HTML as a native file format and (for the first time) supported COM add-ins. It also featured a self-repair capability, an enhanced Clipboard, and pivot charts. VBA programmers could use modeless UserForms, and several new VBA functions were introduced.

Version	Released	Comments
10	2001	Known as Excel 2002 (or Excel XP), this version is part of Office XP. It has a long list of new features, but most of them are of little value to the majority of users. Perhaps this version's most significant feature is its ability to recover your work when Excel crashes.
11	2003	Officially known as Microsoft Office Excel 2003, this version's new features are improved support for XML, a new list range feature, Smart Tag enhancements, and corrected statistical functions.
12	2007	As I write this book, the current version is officially known as Microsoft Office Excel 2007. This version has many new features, including new file formats, a revamped user interface, support for much larger worksheets, a handy page layout view, document themes, new conditional formatting options, much better-looking charts, a new table feature, a few new worksheet functions, and much more.

* Excel 6 doesn't exist. Beginning with Excel 7, the version numbering was changed so that all Microsoft Office applications had the same version number.

If you must share a workbook with someone using a version before Excel 2007, save the file as an XLS file by choosing the Excel 97–2003 Workbook option in the Save As dialog box. *Pay attention* to the results of the Compatibility Checker, which appears automatically whenever you save your file in this older format. This useful dialog box, shown in Figure 1-2, identifies potential problems when your workbook is used by someone who has an Excel version earlier than Excel 2007.

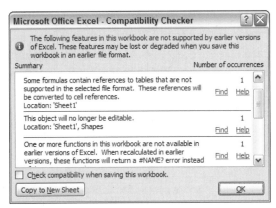

Figure 1-2: The Compatibility Checker helps identify potential compatibility problems.

You can display the Compatibility Checker dialog box at any time by choosing Office ⇨ Prepare ⇨ Run Compatibility Checker.

Maximizing Ribbon Efficiency

When you first fired up Excel 2007, you probably noticed that the commands at the top of the window are different — *very* different — from other versions. Since the beginning of time, all Windows programs have had a similar user interface that consists of menus and toolbars. The Office 2007 designers went out on a limb and came up with a radically different user interface: the Ribbon.

The words along the top (Home, Insert, and Page Layout, for example) are known as *tabs*. Click a tab, and the Ribbon changes to display a new set of commands, arranged in groups. (For example, the Home tab has groups labeled Clipboard, Font, Alignment, and more).

Using the Ribbon is straightforward enough. Somewhat ironically, new users will adapt much more quickly to the Ribbon than experienced users will. Long-time Excel users will spend a considerable amount of time scratching their heads and trying to figure out where their favorite commands now live.

The following tips help you get the most out of the new Ribbon user interface:

- Don't be afraid to click on the stuff you find on the Ribbon. This advice applies especially if you're an experienced user who is trying to adapt to the new user interface. Everything you do can be undone by clicking Undo (located on the Quick Access Toolbar, which is on the left side of the Excel title bar by default).

- To get more screen real estate, enter "Hide the Ribbon mode." You can hide the Ribbon by double-clicking any of the tabs. When you need to access a command, just click the tab, and the Ribbon comes back to life. The Ribbon disappears again when you finish. To leave this mode and return to normal, just double-click a tab. You can also enable and disable Hide the Ribbon mode by pressing Ctrl+F1.

- Access the Ribbon from the keyboard. Although the Ribbon appears to be mouse-centric, it's quite functional from the keyboard. See Tip 11 for some keyboard access tips.

- Note that the appearance of the commands on the Ribbon varies, depending on the width of the Excel window. When the window is too narrow to display the entire Ribbon, the commands adapt and may seem to be missing. But the commands are still available. Figure 2-1 shows the Home tab of the Ribbon when the Excel window is at three different widths. In the first view, all controls are fully visible. When the Excel window is made narrower, some descriptive text disappears, but the icons remain. When the window is made very narrow, some groups display a single icon. However, if you click the icon, all the group commands are available to you.

- Take advantage of contextual tabs on the Ribbon. In some cases, the Ribbon displays new, *contextual* tabs. For example, when you select a chart, you see three new tabs: Design, Layout, and Format. Notice that these new tabs contain a description on the Excel title bar (when a chart is selected, the description reads Chart Tools). Selecting any of the following elements also results in the display of contextual tabs: a table, a pivot table, a drawing (a shape or WordArt), a picture (a photo or clip art), a header or footer (in Page Layout view), or a SmartArt diagram. You can, of course, continue to use all the other tabs when a contextual tab is displayed.

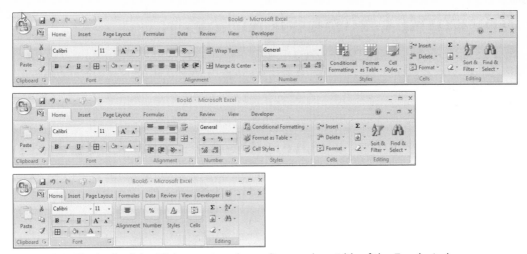

Figure 2-1: The look of the Ribbon varies, depending on the width of the Excel window.

- Right-click just about anything on-screen to get a context-sensitive shortcut menu. It's one element of the old user interface that's still in place. And, if you're trying to decrease your mouse dependence, you can also press Shift+F10 to display the shortcut menu for the selected item (cell, range, or chart element, for example).

- Right-click certain items in Excel to take advantage of the mini Toolbar, displayed above the shortcut menu (see Figure 2-2). This toolbar contains formatting tools that may save you a trip to the Ribbon. When I started using Excel 2007, I just ignored the mini Toolbar, but I soon realized that it's a very handy tool.

- Don't ignore the Quick Access Toolbar (QAT). This part of the new user interface is the only interface element that you (the user) can customize. Check out Tip 10 to find out how easy it is to customize it.

- Finally, keep in mind that Excel has additional commands that aren't even on the Ribbon. If you come up empty-handed after performing an exhaustive Ribbon search for the old text-to-speech commands, for example, don't despair: You need to add those commands yourself, by customizing the QAT (see Tip 10).

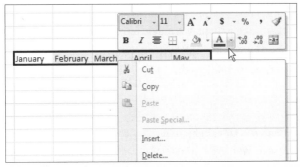

Figure 2-2: The mini Toolbar is easy to ignore, but it can save lots of trips to the Ribbon.

Selecting Cells Efficiently

Many Excel users think that the only way to select a range of cells is to drag over the cells with the mouse. Although selecting cells with a mouse works, it's rarely the most *efficient* way to accomplish the task. The answer, of course, is to use your keyboard to select ranges.

Selecting a Range by Using the Shift and Arrow Keys

The simplest way to select a range is to press (and hold) Shift and then use the arrow keys to highlight the cells. For larger selections, you can use PgDn or PgUp while pressing Shift to move in larger increments.

You can also use the End key to quickly extend a selection to the last non-empty cell in a row or column. To select the range B3:B8 (see Figure 3-1) by using the keyboard, move the cell pointer to B3 and then press the Shift key while you press End followed by the down arrow key. Similarly, to select B3:D3, press the Shift key while you press End, followed by the right-arrow key.

	A	B	C	D	E	F	G	H	I
1									
2									
3		1	2	3					
4		4	5	6					
5		7	8	9					
6		10	11	12					
7		13	14	15					
8		16	17	18					
9									
10									
11									
12									
13									
14									

Sheet1

Figure 3-1: A range of cells.

Selecting the Current Region

Often, you need to select a large rectangular selection of cells — the *current region*. To select the entire block of cells, move the cell pointer anywhere within the range and press Ctrl+Shift+8.

NEW

If the active cell is within an Excel 2007 table (created by choosing Insert ⇨ Tables ⇨ Table), you can press Ctrl+A to select the cells (but not the header row or total row) within the table. Press Ctrl+A again to select the entire table (including the header row and total row). Press Ctrl+A a third time to select the entire worksheet.

Selecting a Range by Shift+Clicking

When you're selecting a very large range, using the mouse may be the most efficient method — but dragging is not required. Select the upper-left cell in the range. Then scroll to the lower-right corner of the range, press Shift, and click the lower-right cell.

Selecting Noncontiguous Ranges

Most of the time, your range selections are probably simple rectangular ranges. In some cases, you may need to make a multiple selection — a selection that includes nonadjacent cells or ranges. For example, you may want to apply formatting to cells in different areas of your worksheet. If you make a multiple selection, you can apply the formatting in one step to all selected ranges. Figure 3-2 shows an example of a multiple selection.

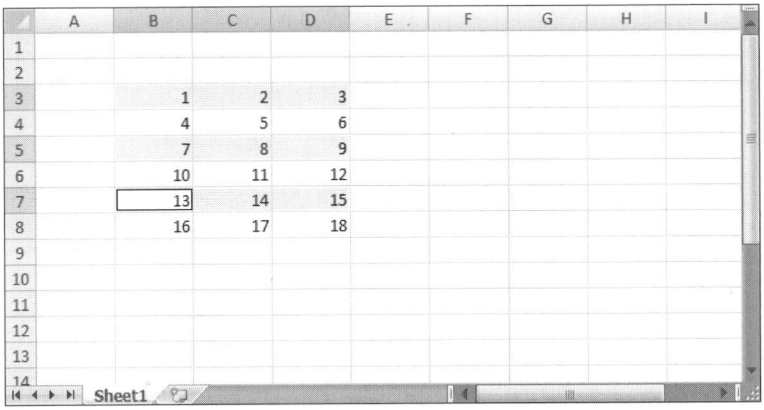

Figure 3-2: A multiple selection that consists of noncontiguous ranges.

You can select a noncontiguous range by using either the mouse or the keyboard.

Press Ctrl as you click and drag the mouse to highlight individual cells or ranges.

From the keyboard, select a range as described previously (by using the Shift key). Then press Shift+F8 to select another range without canceling the previous range selection. Repeat this action as many times as needed.

Selecting Entire Rows

To select a single row, click a row number along the left of the worksheet. Or, select any cell in the row and press Shift+spacebar.

To select multiple adjacent rows, click and drag in the row number area. Or, select any cell in the first (or last) row, press Shift+spacebar, and use the arrow keys to extend the selection down (or up).

To select multiple nonadjacent rows, press Ctrl while you click the row numbers for the rows you want to include.

Selecting Entire Columns

To select a single column, click a column letter along the top of the worksheet. Or, select any cell in the column and press Ctrl+spacebar.

To select multiple adjacent columns, click and drag in the column letter section. Or, select any cell in the first (or last) column, press Ctrl+spacebar, and use the arrow keys to extend the selection to the right (or left).

To select multiple nonadjacent columns, press Ctrl while you click the column letters for the columns you want to include.

Selecting Multisheet Ranges

In addition to two-dimensional ranges on a single worksheet, ranges can extend across multiple worksheets to be three-dimensional ranges.

Figure 3-3 shows a simple example of a multisheet workbook. The workbook has four sheets, named Totals, Marketing, Operations, and Manufacturing. The sheets are laid out identically.

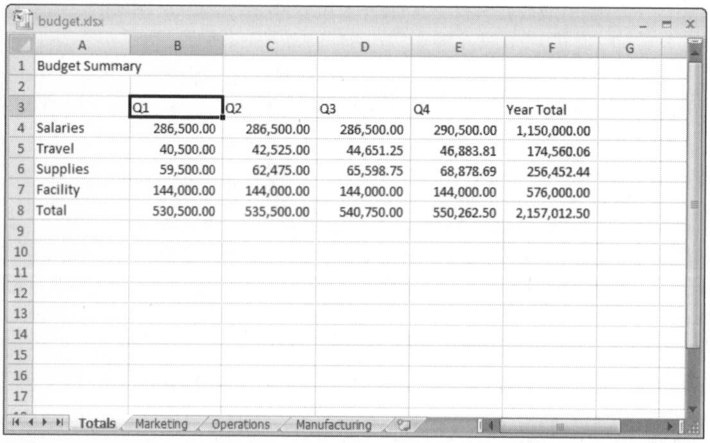
budget.xlsx

	A	B	C	D	E	F
1	Budget Summary					
2						
3		Q1	Q2	Q3	Q4	Year Total
4	Salaries	286,500.00	286,500.00	286,500.00	290,500.00	1,150,000.00
5	Travel	40,500.00	42,525.00	44,651.25	46,883.81	174,560.06
6	Supplies	59,500.00	62,475.00	65,598.75	68,878.69	256,452.44
7	Facility	144,000.00	144,000.00	144,000.00	144,000.00	576,000.00
8	Total	530,500.00	535,500.00	540,750.00	550,262.50	2,157,012.50

Totals / Marketing / Operations / Manufacturing

Figure 3-3: Each worksheet in this workbook is laid out identically.

Assume that you want to apply the same formatting to all sheets — for example, you want to make the column headings bold with background shading. Selecting a multisheet range is the best approach. When the ranges are selected, the formatting is applied to all sheets.

In general, selecting a multisheet range is a simple two-step process:

1. Select the range in one sheet.
2. Select the worksheets to include in the range.

NOTE
To select a group of contiguous worksheets, press Shift and click the sheet tab of the last worksheet that you want to include in the selection. To select individual worksheets, press Ctrl and click the sheet tab of each worksheet that you want to select. When you make the selection, the sheet tabs of the selected sheets appear with a white background, and Excel displays [Group] on the title bar.

When you finish working with the multisheet range, click any sheet tab to leave Group mode.

Part I

Making "Special" Range Selections

As you use Excel, you'll probably wonder how you can locate specific types of cells in your worksheets. For example, wouldn't it be handy to be able to locate every cell that contains a formula, or perhaps all cells whose values depend on the current cell?

Excel provides an easy way to locate these and many other special types of cells.

The key to many types of special selections is the Go To Special dialog box. Choose Home ⇨ Find & Select ⇨ Go To Special to display the Go To Special dialog box, as shown in Figure 4-1. Another way to open the Go To Special dialog box is to press F5 and then click the Special button in the Go To dialog box.

Figure 4-1: Use the Go To Special dialog box to select specific types of cells.

After you make your choice in the Go To Special dialog box, Excel selects the qualifying subset of cells in the current selection. Usually, this results in a multiple selection. If no cells qualify, Excel lets you know with the message No cells were found.

NOTE

If you bring up the Go To Special dialog box when only one cell is selected, Excel bases its selection on the entire active area of the worksheet. Otherwise, the selection is based on the selected range.

Table 4-1 summarizes the options available in the Go To Special dialog box.

TABLE 4-1   GO TO SPECIAL OPTIONS

Option	What It Selects
Comments	Only the cells that contain cell comments.
Constants	All non-empty cells that don't contain formulas. This option is useful if you have a model set up and you want to clear out all input cells and enter new values. The formulas remain intact. Use the check boxes under the Formulas option to choose which cells to include.
Formulas	Cells that contain formulas. Qualify this choice by selecting the check box for the type of result: Numbers, Text, Logicals (the logical values TRUE or FALSE), or Errors.
Blanks	All empty cells.
Current Region	A rectangular range of cells around the active cell. This range is determined by surrounding blank rows and columns. You can also use the Ctrl+Shift+8 shortcut key combination.
Current Array	The entire array (used for multicell array formulas).
Objects	All graphical objects on the worksheet.
Row Differences	If one row is selected, cells that are different from the active cell. If more than one row is selected, the same comparison is done, but the comparison cell for each row is the cell in the same column as the active cell.
Column Differences	If one column is selected, cells that are different from the active cell. If more than one column is selected, the same comparison is done, but the comparison cell for each column is the cell in the same rows as the active cell.
Precedents	Cells that are referred to in the formulas in the active cell or selection (limited to the active sheet). You can select either direct precedents or precedents at any level.
Dependents	Cells with formulas that refer to the active cell or selection (limited to the active sheet). You can select either direct dependents or dependents at any level.
Last Cell	The lower-right cell in the worksheet that contains data or formatting.
Visible Cells Only	Only visible cells in the selection. This option is useful when dealing with outlines or a filtered list.
Conditional Formats	Cells that have a conditional format applied (by using the Home ⇨ Styles ⇨ Conditional Formatting command).
Data Validation	Cells that are set up for data entry validation (by using the Data ⇨ Data Tools ⇨ Data Validation command). The All option selects all cells of this type. The Same option selects only the cells that have the same validation rules as the active cell.

Part I

NOTE

When you select an option in the Go To Special dialog box, be sure to note which sub-options become available. For example, when you select the Constants option, the Formulas suboptions become available to help you further refine the results. Likewise, the Dependents suboptions also apply to Precedents, and the Data Validation suboptions also apply to Conditional formats.

CROSS-REFERENCE

For information about selecting cells based on their content, see Tip 19.

Undoing, Redoing, and Repeating

This tip describes three procedures that every Excel user needs to understand. These procedures help you recover from mistakes and improve your editing efficiency.

Undoing

Just about every command in Excel can be reversed by using the Undo command. In Excel 2007, the Undo command is located on the Quick Access Toolbar (QAT), which is normally displayed on the left side of the Excel title bar. You can also press Ctrl+Z to undo your actions.

Choose Undo after issuing a command in error and it's as though you never issued the command. You can reverse the effects of the last 100 commands that you executed by selecting Undo multiple times.

Some actions, however, can't be reversed. Anything that you do by using the Office button — for example, saving a workbook — is not undoable.

 NEW
Undoing 100 actions is new to Excel 2007. In previous versions, the Undo list was limited to 16 actions.

If you click the arrow on the right side of the Undo button, you see a description of the recent commands that can be reversed (see Figure 5-1).

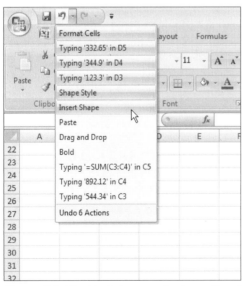

Figure 5-1: The Undo button displays a list of recent actions that can be undone.

NOTE

Keep in mind that the effect of executing a macro cannot be undone. In fact, running a macro wipes out all the Undo information. This serious weakness in Excel isn't present in Microsoft Word. However, at least Excel 2007 fixed another Undo-related problem. In previous versions, saving your workbook destroyed the Undo information. Fortunately, that's no longer the case.

Redoing

The Redo button (located to the right of the Undo button on the QAT) essentially undoes the Undo command. If you undo too much, you can click the Redo button (or press Ctrl+Y or F4) to repeat commands that have been undone.

Repeating

You can repeat a command by pressing Ctrl+Y or F4. This command simply repeats the last action — unless the last operation was an Undo operation. In this case, the Undo is undone (as described in the previous section).

Repeating a command can be a great timesaver. Here's an example of how useful the Repeat command can be. You may apply lots of formatting (for example, font size, bold formatting, background color, and borders) to a cell by using the Format Cells dialog box. After you close the dialog box, it's a snap to apply that same formatting to other cells or ranges by pressing Ctrl+Y. Or, you may need to insert blank rows at certain locations in your worksheet. Issue the Home ➪ Cells ➪ Insert ➪ Insert Sheet Rows command one time. Then move the cell pointer to the next row to be inserted and press Ctrl+Y to repeat the row insertion command.

Excel also has a Repeat button, but it's not normally available. You can, however, add this button to your QAT:

1. Right-click the QAT and choose Customize Quick Access Toolbar to display the Customize tab of the Excel Options dialog box.

2. In the Excel Options dialog box, select Popular Commands from the drop-down list on the right.

3. In the list of commands, select Repeat.

4. Click Add to add the selected command to the QAT.

5. Click OK to close the Excel Options dialog box.

Why add the Repeat button to your QAT, when pressing Ctrl+Y is so easy? One reason is that you can hover your mouse pointer over the button and Excel displays a description of what will be repeated (see Figure 5-2). Another reason is that the Repeat button is disabled if the most recent command cannot be repeated — a visual cue that may prevent you from trying to repeat something that can't be repeated.

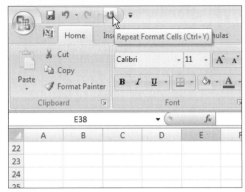

Figure 5-2: After you add the Repeat button to the QAT, a ToolTip describes the task (if any) that will be repeated.

NOTE

Unfortunately, repeating an operation is unreliable in Excel 2007 — at least in the initial release. In fact, it's seriously broken. In some situations, you may find that pressing Ctrl+Y has no effect (when it should have an effect). At other times, you may find that pressing Ctrl+Y repeats the command that you issued *before* the previous command.

Part I

Discovering Some Useful Shortcut Keys

Excel has no shortage of shortcut keys. Your productivity is sure to increase if you take the time to learn the shortcut keys for commands that you use frequently. In the following table, I list some of the most useful shortcut keys. This list is certainly not an exhaustive one — it describes just the commands that I find most useful.

Shortcut	What You Can Do with It
F11	Create a new chart on a separate chart sheet (of the default chart type) by using data in the selected range
Alt+F1	Create a new, embedded chart (of the default chart type) by using the data in the selected range
F5	Display the Go To dialog box
Alt	Display the keytips for the Ribbon commands so that you can access the commands by using letters on the keyboard
Shift+F2	Edit the comment in the active cell or insert a comment if the cell doesn't have one
Shift+F10	Display the shortcut menu for the selected item
Ctrl+F6	Activate the next window
Ctrl+PgUp	Activate the previous sheet in the workbook
Ctrl+PgDn	Activate the next sheet in the workbook
Alt+Ctrl+V	Display the Paste Special dialog box
Alt+=	Perform the equivalent of clicking the AutoSum button
Ctrl+B	Make the selected cells bold
Ctrl+C	Copy the selected cells
Ctrl+D	Fill down
Ctrl+F	Display the Find dialog box
Ctrl+H	Display the Replace dialog box
Ctrl+I	Make the selected cells italic
Ctrl+N	Create a new default workbook
Ctrl+R	Fill to the right
Ctrl+S	Save the active workbook

Shortcut	What You Can Do with It
Ctrl+V	Paste a copied or cut item in the selected cell
Ctrl+X	Cut the selected cells
Ctrl+Y	Repeat the last repeatable command
Ctrl+Z	Undo the last action

Part I

Navigating Sheets in a Workbook

As you know, a single workbook can contain multiple worksheets. The sheet tabs at the bottom of the Excel window identify the worksheets. All Excel users know that they can activate a different sheet by clicking its sheet tab. If the tab for the sheet you want isn't visible, you can use the tab scroll controls to the left of the first sheet tab to scroll the tabs left or right (see Figure 7-1).

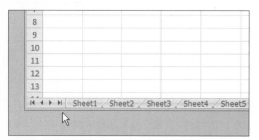

Figure 7-1: Use these controls to scroll the sheet tabs to the left or right.

You can also reduce the width of the horizontal scroll bar to reveal more sheet tabs. Just click the vertical bar on the left side of the scroll bar and drag it to the right.

Another way to activate a sheet is to right-click the tab scroll controls. This action displays a pop-up list of sheet names (see Figure 7-2). Just click a name, and you're there. If not all the sheet names are listed, click the More Sheets item at the bottom, and a dialog box that lists the sheet names appears. Just double-click a sheet name to activate that sheet.

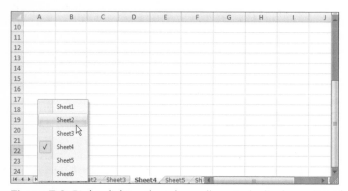

Figure 7-2: Right-clicking the tab scroll controls displays a list of sheet names.

In many cases, the most efficient way to activate a different sheet is to avoid the mouse and use the keyboard. Surprisingly, many users don't know about two useful keyboard commands:

- **Ctrl+PgDn:** Activates the next sheet
- **Ctrl+PgUp:** Activates the previous sheet

I use these keys 90 percent of the time — but then again, I avoid using a mouse whenever I can.

Part I

Resetting the Used Area of a Worksheet

When you press Ctrl+End, Excel activates the lower-right cell in the used area of the worksheet. In some cases, you find that the lower-right cell in the worksheet is an empty cell — not the *real* last cell. In other words, Excel sometimes loses track of the used area of your worksheet. For example, you may find that a workbook's file size seems much too large. It's possible that Excel has misidentified the used area, and is storing a large number of empty cells.

First, try saving the workbook. After the workbook is saved, Excel may correctly identify the last cell. If Excel still doesn't identify the last cell, it's probably because you deleted data but left the formatting in the cells. To force Excel to identify the real used area, you need to delete the columns to the right of your data and then delete the rows below your data.

For example, assume that the real last cell in your workbook is G25 but pressing Ctrl+End takes you to some other cell — M50, for example.

To delete those formatted cells, follow these steps:

1. Select all columns to the right of column G. To do this, activate any cell in column H, and then press Ctrl+spacebar followed by Shift+End and then the right-arrow key.

2. Select Home ⇨ Cells ⇨ Delete ⇨ Delete Sheet Columns. Or, right-click any column header and choose Delete.

3. Select all rows below row 25. To do this, activate any cell in row 26, and then press Shift+spacebar followed by Ctrl+End and then the down-arrow key.

4. Select Home ⇨ Cells ⇨ Delete ⇨ Delete Sheet Row. Or, right-click any column header and choose Delete.

5. Save your workbook, and Excel resets the last cell.

After performing these steps, pressing Ctrl+End takes you to the *real* last cell.

Understanding Workbooks versus Windows

One of the most common questions asked in the Excel newsgroups is "Why is Excel displaying two copies of my workbook?" Then the Excel users go on to describe the symptoms: The filename is followed by a colon and a number (for example, `budget.xlsx:2`).

Normally, a workbook is displayed in a single window within Excel. However, you can create multiple windows for a single workbook by using the View ⇨ Window ⇨ New Window command.

Most people who ask this question in the newsgroups have probably issued the New Window command accidentally. What they're really asking for is a way to close the additional window (or windows). That's an easy problem to solve: Just click the X on the title bar of the unwanted windows. Or, press Ctrl+F4 to close the window. After you close all extra windows, the title bar no longer displays the window number.

By the way, the multiple window configuration is saved with the workbook, so when you open the file later, the multiple windows are still displayed.

Although many people are confused about multiple windows, there are at least two good reasons why you might want your workbook to display in two or more windows:

- You can view two worksheets in the same workbook simultaneously. For example, you can display Sheet1 in the first window and Sheet2 in the second window and then tile the two windows so that both are visible. The View ⇨ Window ⇨ Arrange All command is useful for tiling windows. This statement also applies to chart sheets. If you have a chart on a chart sheet, you can arrange the windows so that you can see the chart along with its data.

- You can view cells and their formulas at the same time. Create a second window, and then press Ctrl+` to display the formulas. Tile the two windows so that you can view the formulas and their results side by side (see Figure 9-1).

 NOTE

When you need to compare information in two worksheets (or the same worksheet in two windows), try the View ⇨ Window ⇨ View Side by Side command. It makes it easy to compare two worksheets because Excel automatically scrolls the second window to keep them synchronized. To use this feature with a single workbook, first create a second window by choosing the View ⇨ Window ⇨ New Window command.

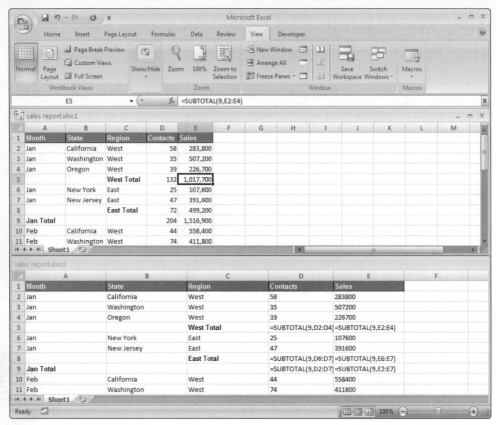

Figure 9-1: Displaying two windows for a workbook lets you view the cells and their formulas.

Customizing the Quick Access Toolbar

In previous versions of Excel, you can fairly easily modify the user interface. You can create custom toolbars that contain frequently used commands, and you can even remove menu items that you never use. In earlier versions of Excel, you can also display any number of toolbars and move them wherever you like. For users who have moved up to Excel 2007, those days are over.

With the introduction of the new Ribbon-based user interface in Office 2007, user customization is severely curtailed. Although it's possible to modify the Ribbon, it's a rather complicated process, and it's not something a casual user would do. In Office 2007, user interface customization is limited to the Quick Access Toolbar, or QAT — and that's the topic of this tip.

If you find that you continually need to switch Ribbon tabs because a frequently used command never seems to be on the Ribbon that's displayed, this tip is for you.

About the QAT

The QAT is always visible, regardless of which Ribbon tab is selected. After you customize the QAT, your frequently used commands are always one click away.

 NOTE
The only situation in which the QAT is not visible is in Full Screen mode, which is enabled by choosing View ➪ Workbook Views ➪ Full Screen. To cancel Full Screen mode (and restore the Ribbon and QAT), right-click any cell and choose Close Full Screen, or press Escape.

By default, the QAT is located on the left side of the Excel title bar, and it includes the following three tools:

- **Save:** Saves the active workbook.
- **Undo:** Reverses the effect of the last action.
- **Redo:** Reverses the effect of the last undo.

If you prefer, you can move the QAT below the Ribbon: Right-click the QAT and choose Show Quick Access Toolbar Below The Ribbon. Moving the QAT below the Ribbon eats up some additional vertical space on your screen. In other words, you see one or two fewer rows of your worksheet if you move the QAT from its default location.

Commands on the QAT always appear as small icons, with no text. When you hover your mouse pointer over an icon, you see the name of the command and a brief description.

As far as I can tell, there is no limit to the number of commands that you can add to your QAT. But regardless of the number of icons, the QAT always displays a single line of icons. If the number of icons exceeds the Excel window width, it displays an additional icon at the end: More Controls. Click the More Controls icon, and the hidden QAT icons appear in a pop-up window.

Adding New Commands to the QAT

You can add a new command to the QAT in three ways:

- Click the QAT drop-down control, which is located on the right side of the QAT (see Figure 10-1). The list contains several commonly used commands. Select a command from the list, and Excel adds it to your QAT.

- Right-click any control on the Ribbon, and choose Add To Quick Access Toolbar. The control is added to your QAT, after the last control.

- Use the Customize tab of the Excel Options dialog box. A quick way to access this dialog box is to right-click any Ribbon control and choose Customize Quick Access Toolbar.

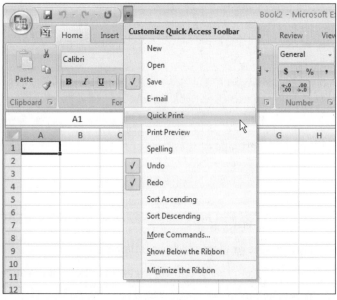

Figure 10-1: The QAT drop-down menu is one way to add a new command to the QAT.

Figure 10-2 shows the Customize tab of the Excel Options dialog box. The left side of the dialog box displays a list of Excel commands, and the right side shows the commands that are now on the QAT. Above the command list on the left is a drop-down control that lets you filter the list. Select an item for the drop-down list, and the list displays only the commands for that item.

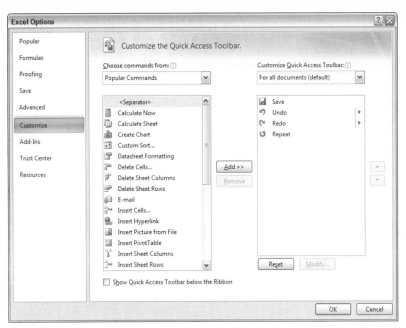

Figure 10-2: Use the Customization tab in the Excel Options dialog box to customize the QAT.

Some of the items in the drop-down control are described in this list:

- **Popular Commands:** Displays commands that Excel users commonly use
- **Commands Not In The Ribbon:** Displays a list of commands that you cannot access from the Ribbon
- **All Commands:** Displays a complete list of Excel commands
- **Macros:** Displays a list of all available macros
- **Office Menu:** Displays the commands available on the Office menu
- **Home Tab:** Displays all commands that are available when the Home tab is active

In addition, the drop-down list contains an item for every other tab.

To add an item to your QAT, select it from the list on the right and click Add. Notice that some commands in the list on the left display icons. The icon tells you what form the command will take: a drop-down list, a split button, an edit control, or a Ribbon group. If the command doesn't display an icon, it's a button control.

If you add a macro to your QAT, you can click the Modify button to change the text and choose a different icon for the macro.

The only time you ever need to use the Customize tab of the Excel Options dialog box is when you want to add a command that's not on the Ribbon or add a command that executes a macro. In all other situations, it's much easier to locate the command on the Ribbon, right-click the command, and choose Add To Quick Access Toolbar.

Only you can decide which commands to put on your QAT. In general, if you find that you use a particular command frequently, it should probably be on your QAT. For example, when I work on a chart, I like to use the Chart Elements control to make it easy to select chart elements. That control is located in the Chart Tools ⇨ Format tab and the Chart Tools ⇨ Layout tab, but not in the Chart Tools ⇨ Design tab. Putting a copy of this control on my QAT saves me many keystrokes on every chart I work on.

Performing Other QAT Actions

Here are some other things you can do with your QAT:

- **Rearrange the QAT icons:** If you want to change the order of your QAT icons, you can do so on the Customization tab of the Excel Options dialog box. Select the command and then use the up- and down-arrow buttons on the right to move the icon.

- **Remove QAT icons:** The easiest way to remove an icon from your QAT is to right-click the icon and choose Remove from Quick Access Toolbar. You can also use the Customization tab of the Excel Options dialog box. Just select the command in the list on the right and click the Remove button.

- **Reset the QAT:** If you want to return the QAT to its default state, display the Customization tab in the Excel Options dialog box and click the Reset button. All your customizations disappear, and the QAT then displays its three default commands.

Accessing the Ribbon from Your Keyboard

At first glance, you may think that the Ribbon is completely mouse-centric. After all, none of the commands has the traditional underlined letter to indicate the Alt+keystrokes. In fact, the Ribbon is very keyboard friendly. The trick is to press the Alt key (or slash key) to display the pop-up *keytips:* Each Ribbon control has a letter (or series of letters) that you type to issue the command.

By the way, you don't have to hold down the Alt key as you type the keytip letters.

Figure 11-1 shows how the Home tab looks after I press the Alt key to display the keytips. If you press one of the keytips, the screen then displays more keytips. For example, to use the keyboard to align the cell contents to the left, press Alt followed by H (for Home) and then AL (for Align Left). If you're a keyboard fan (like I am), after just a few times you memorize the keystrokes required for common commands that you use frequently.

Figure 11-1: Pressing Alt displays the keytips.

After you press Alt, you can also use the left- and right-arrow keys to scroll through the tabs. When you reach the proper tab, press the down-arrow key to enter the Ribbon. Then use the left- and right-arrow keys to scroll through the Ribbon commands. When you reach the command you need, press Enter to execute it. This method isn't as efficient as using keytips, but it's an easy, mouse-free way to take a quick look at the available commands.

Customizing the Default Workbook

When you create a new Excel workbook, you get a standard default workbook. What if you don't like that workbook? For example, you may prefer a workbook with only one worksheet. Or, maybe you don't like the default font or font size. Perhaps you prefer to have the gridlines hidden in your worksheets. Or, maybe you have a standard header that you always use on printed pages.

As it turns out, Excel gives you quite a bit of control in this area. It's relatively simple to create an entirely different default workbook. The trick is creating a custom template file named `book.xltx` and then saving that file to the proper location on your hard drive.

NOTE

If all you care about is changing the number of worksheets in a new workbook, that change is very easy to make, and a template is not required. Choose Office ⇨ Excel Options, and click the Popular tab. Then change the setting for the option labeled Include This Many Sheets. I always keep it set to 1. (After all, I can easily add more sheets, if needed.)

To create a new default workbook template, all you need to do is customize a blank workbook exactly as you like it. Here's a list of some of the items you can change:

- **Number of sheets:** Add or delete sheets as you like. You can also change their names.

- **Styles:** Use the Style Gallery (Home ⇨ Styles) to customize styles. By default, all cells use the Normal style, so if you want to change the default font in any way (including fill color, number format, font, and borders), modify the Normal style. To change the Normal style, right-click its name in the Style Gallery and choose Modify. Then make the changes in the Style dialog box.

- **Print settings:** Use the commands on the Page Layout tab to specify print-related settings. For example, you can include header or footer information or adjust the margins.

- **Column widths:** If you don't like the default column widths, change them.

- **Graphics:** You can even insert a graphical object or two — for example, your company logo or a picture of your cat.

When the new default workbook is set up to your specifications, choose Office ⇨ Save As. In the Save As dialog box, follow these steps:

1. Select Template (*.xltx) in the Save As Type drop-down list. If your template contains any VBA macros, select Excel Macro-Enabled Template (*.xltm).

2. Name the file `book.xltx` (or `book.xltm` if it has macros).

3. Make sure that the file is saved to your XLStart folder. Excel proposes that you save the file in your Templates folder, but it must be saved in your XLStart folder.

NOTE

If you're using Windows XP, the XLStart folder may be located in either of these directories:

```
C:\Documents and Settings\<username>\Application Data\
Microsoft\Excel\XLStart
C:\Program Files\Microsoft Office\Office12\XLStart
```

If you're using Windows Vista, the directory is:

```
C:\Users\<username>\AppData\Roaming\Microsoft\Excel\XLStart
```

After you save the file, you can close it. Now, every time you start Excel, the blank workbook that's displayed will be based on the template you created. In addition, when you press Ctrl+N, the new workbook will be created from your template.

If you ever need to bypass your new default workbook and start with one of the normal Excel default workbooks, choose Office ⇨ New and choose the Blank Workbook item.

Part I

Using Document Themes

Over the years, I've seen hundreds of Excel workbooks that were created by others. A significant percentage of these workbooks have one thing in common: They are ugly!

In an effort to help users create more professional-looking documents, the Office 2007 designers incorporated the concept of Office *document themes*. Using themes is an easy (and almost foolproof) way to specify the colors and fonts and a variety of graphical effects in a document. Best of all, changing the entire look of your document is a breeze. A few mouse clicks is all it takes to apply a different theme and change the look of your workbook.

Importantly, the concept of themes is incorporated into other Office 2007 applications. Therefore, a company can now easily create a standard look for all its documents.

Elements within Excel that are controlled by themes are:

- Cells and ranges that use theme colors (as opposed to standard colors)
- Tables
- Charts
- Pivot tables
- Shapes
- SmartArt
- WordArt
- Sheet tab colors (see Tip 14)

Figure 13-1 shows a worksheet that contains a SmartArt diagram, a table, a chart, and a range formatted using the Heading 1 named style. These items all use the default formatting, which is known as Office Theme.

Figure 13-1: The elements in this worksheet use default formatting.

Figure 13-2 shows the same worksheet after applying a different document theme. The different theme changes the fonts, colors (which may not be apparent in the figure), and graphical effects for the SmartArt diagram.

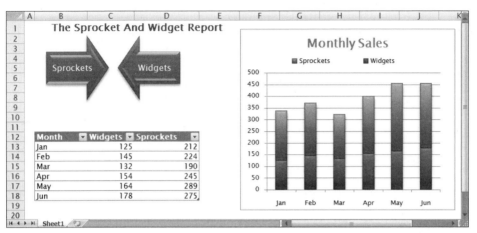

Figure 13-2: The worksheet, after applying a different theme.

Applying a Theme

Figure 13-3 shows the theme choices that appear when you choose Page ⇨ Layout ⇨ Themes. This display is a "live preview" display. As you move your mouse over the theme choices, the active worksheet displays the theme. When you see a theme you like, click it to apply the theme to all worksheets in the workbook.

A theme applies to the entire workbook. You cannot use different themes on different worksheets within a workbook.

When you specify a particular theme, you find that the gallery choices for various elements reflect the new theme. For example, the chart styles that you can choose from vary, depending on which theme is active.

Because themes use different fonts and font sizes, changing to a different theme can affect the layout of your worksheet. For example, after you apply a new theme, a worksheet that printed on a single page may spill over to a second page. Therefore, you may need to make some adjustments after you apply a new theme.

Customizing a Theme

Notice that the Page Layout ⇨ Themes group contains three other controls: Colors, Fonts, and Effects. You can use these controls to change just one of the three components of a theme. For example, if you like the Urban theme but prefer different fonts, apply the Urban theme and then specify your preferred font set by using the Page Layout ⇨ Themes ⇨ Font control.

Part I

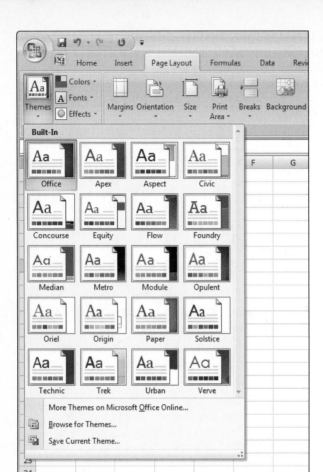

Figure 13-3: The built-in Excel theme choices.

Each theme uses two fonts (one for headers and one for the body), and in some cases, these two fonts are the same. If none of the theme choices is suitable, choose Page Layout ⇨ Themes ⇨ Font ⇨ Create New Theme Fonts to specify the two fonts you prefer (see Figure 13-4). When you use the Home ⇨ Fonts ⇨ Font control, the two fonts from the current theme are listed first in the drop-down list.

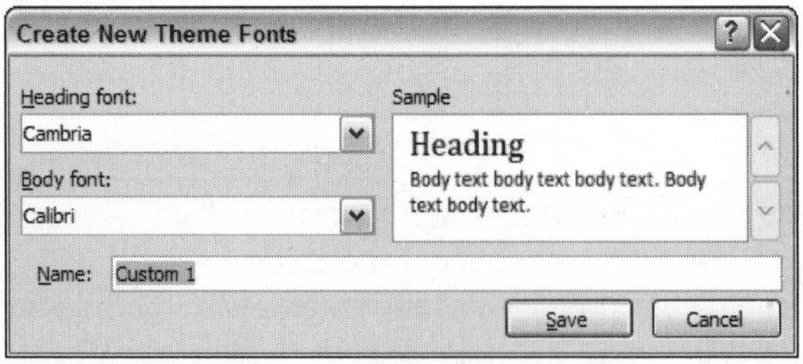

Figure 13-4: Use this dialog box to specify two fonts for a theme.

Use the Page Layout ⇨ Themes ⇨ Colors control to select a different set of colors. And, if you're so inclined, you can even create a custom set of colors by choosing Page Layout ⇨ Themes ⇨ Colors ⇨ Create Theme Colors. This command displays the dialog box shown in Figure 13-5. Note that each theme consists of 12 colors. Four of the colors are for text and backgrounds, six are for accents, and two are for hyperlinks. As you specify different colors, the Preview panel in the dialog box is updated.

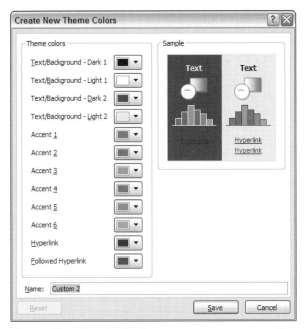

Figure 13-5: If you're feeling creative, you can specify a set of custom colors for a theme.

Theme effects operate on graphical elements, such as SmartArt, shapes, and charts. You can't customize theme effects.

If you customize a theme by using different fonts or colors, you can save the new theme by choosing Page Layout ⇨ Themes ⇨ Save Current Theme. Your customized themes appear in the theme list in the Custom category. Other Office 2007 applications, such as Word and PowerPoint, can use these theme files.

Changing the Sheet Tab Appearance

Many users don't realize it, but they can change the appearance of the sheet tabs displayed in a workbook. This tip describes how to change the size of the text and the color of the sheet tabs.

Changing the Sheet Tab Color

If your workbook has many sheets, you may find it helpful to color-code the sheet tabs. For example, you may use red tabs for sheets that need to be checked and use green tabs for sheets that have already been checked.

To change the color of a sheet tab, right-click the tab, and then select Tab Color from the shortcut menu. You can then pick a background color from the palette. To change the color of multiple sheet tabs at one time, press Ctrl while you click the sheet tabs. Then right-click and change the color. If you select a color from the Theme Colors section of the palette, the tab color changes if you apply a different document theme (see Tip 13).

When the colored tab sheet is active, the text appears underlined with that color. When the sheet is not active, the entire background of the sheet tab is displayed in that color.

Changing the Sheet Tab Text Size

If you find that the text displayed in your sheet tabs is too small (or too large), you can change the size of the text — but you have to make a system-wide change.

The text size on the Excel sheets tabs is determined by a Windows systemwide setting. To change it, open the Windows Display Properties dialog box. The easiest way to do this is to right-click on your desktop and choose Properties from the shortcut menu. In the Display Properties dialog box that appears, follow these steps (which assume that you're using Windows XP):

1. Click the Appearance tab in the Display Properties dialog box.
2. Click the Advanced button to display the Advanced Appearance dialog box (see Figure 14-1).
3. Choose Scrollbar from the Item drop-down list.
4. Adjust the Size setting, and then click OK.

Be aware that this setting affects the size of the scroll bars in all your applications.

Figure 14-1: Use the Advanced Appearance dialog box to change the text size in the Excel sheet tabs.

Part I

Hiding User Interface Elements

Excel has various options that enable you to hide quite a few elements in order to customize your workspace. In some cases, you can change the display options in more than one place. For each of the elements listed in this section, I show you the easiest Hide method possible.

From the Ribbon

Change the following settings by using controls on the Ribbon:

- **Ruler:** When your worksheet is in Page Layout view, use View ⇨ Show/Hide ⇨ Ruler to toggle the display of the rulers at the top and left sides of the window. Turning off the rulers gives you slightly more screen real estate.

- **Gridlines:** When View ⇨ Show/Hide ⇨ Gridlines is not checked, cell gridlines are not displayed. If you format ranges by using cell borders, turning off the gridlines makes the borders more prominent.

- **Message Bar:** The message bar appears directly above the formula bar and (as far as I can tell) is present only if you open a workbook that triggers a security warning. Turn off the message bar display by choosing View ⇨ Show/Hide ⇨ Message Bar.

- **Formula Bar:** The formula bar, located just below the Ribbon, displays the contents of the selected cell. To see more of your worksheet, turn it off by choosing View ⇨ Show/Hide ⇨ Formula Bar.

- **Row & Column Headers:** If this setting is turned off (by choosing View ⇨ Show/Hide ⇨ Heading), you don't see the row (numbers) and column (letters) headers.

- **Comments:** If you use cell comments, you can choose to display a comment indicator (or not) or display the comment and indicator. I use the second option, Comment Indicator Only. These choices are on the Review ⇨ Comments tab.

From the Keyboard

Modify the items below by using the keyboard.

- **The Ribbon:** Press Ctrl+F1 to turn the Ribbon display off or on. In previous versions of Excel, Ctrl+F1 toggles the Task pane.

- **Outline symbols:** This option is relevant only if you added a worksheet outline (by using the Data ⇨ Outline ⇨ Group command). If you don't like seeing the Outline symbols, you can turn them off. Or, you can press Ctrl+8 to toggle the display of the Outline symbols.

From the Excel Options Dialog Box

You change the following settings from the Advanced tab in the Excel Options dialog box. To display this dialog box, choose Office ⇨ Excel Options. Then click the Advanced tab.

- **Windows in Taskbar:** This option is in the Display section of the Advanced tab in the Excel Options dialog box. When the Show All Windows in the Taskbar option is turned on, each workbook appears as a separate icon on the Windows taskbar. It's too much clutter for my taste, so I keep it turned off.

- **Objects:** This setting refers to graphical objects embedded in your sheets (including charts). You may want to hide these objects if you have many of them and your system performance is suffering. To hide all objects in the workbook, use the For Objects Show options, located in the Display Options for This Workbook section of the Advanced tab in the Excel Options dialog box.

- **Page Breaks:** After you print or preview a document, Excel displays dotted line page breaks in the worksheet. You can turn them off, if you like. Use the Show Page Breaks check box in the Display Options for This Worksheet section of the Advanced tab in the Excel Options dialog box.

- **Zero Values:** Sometimes, you may prefer to hide all zero cells and show a blank cell instead. Control this option by using the Show a Zero in Cells That Have Zero Value check box in the Display Options For This Worksheet section of the Advanced tab in the Excel Options dialog box.

- **Scroll Bars:** You can hide the horizontal and vertical scroll bars for a workbook. Go to the Display Options for This Workbook section on the Advanced tab of the Excel Options dialog box, and use the two check boxes labeled Show Horizontal Scroll Bar and Show Vertical Scroll Bar.

- **Sheet Tabs:** To hide the sheet tab, go to the Display Options for This Workbook section on the Advanced tab of the Excel Options dialog box, and remove the check mark from the Show Sheet Tabs check box. With no sheet tabs, you can use Ctrl+PgUp and Ctrl+PgDn to activate a different sheet.

A Setting That Requires a Macro

Turning off the display of one user interface element now requires a macro.

The status bar, at the bottom of the Excel window, displays a variety of information. In previous versions of Excel, the user could turn the status bar display on or off. Excel 2007 requires a VBA macro to toggle the status bar display:

```
Sub ToggleStatusBar()
  With Application
     .DisplayStatusBar = Not .DisplayStatusBar
  End With
End Sub
```

Part I

Hiding Columns or Rows

If you have data in a column or row that you don't want to see, you can hide the column or row. Doing this is often useful if you have formulas that provide intermediate calculations and you don't want them to appear in a report. Or, you may just want to hide unused rows and columns so that you can focus only on the used area of the sheet.

NOTE

Formulas that refer to data in hidden rows or columns continue to function normally. An exception is the SUBTOTAL function. If the first argument for SUBTOTAL is greater than 100, the SUBTOTAL function ignores the data in the hidden rows or columns. Refer to the Help system for information about the arguments for SUBTOTAL. (It does lots more than just sum.)

Hiding

To hide one or more columns, use any of these techniques:

- Select a cell in the column (or columns) to be hidden. Then choose Home ⇨ Cells ⇨ Format ⇨ Hide & Unhide ⇨ Hide Columns.

- Select entire columns, and then right-click and choose Hide from the shortcut menu.

- Select a cell in the column (or columns) to hide, and press Ctrl+0 (that's a zero).

To hide one or more rows, use any of these methods:

- Select a cell in the row(or rows) to be hidden. Then choose Home ⇨ Cells ⇨ Format ⇨ Hide & Unhide ⇨ Hide Rows.

- Select entire rows, and then right-click and choose Hide from the shortcut menu.

- Select a cell in the row (or rows) to be hidden, and press Ctrl+9.

Unhiding

That which is hidden also needs to be unhidden.

To unhide one or more hidden columns, use any of these techniques:

- Select a range that consists of cells to the left and to the right of the hidden columns. Then choose Home ⇨ Cells ⇨ Format ⇨ Hide & Unhide ⇨ Unhide Columns.

- Select entire columns to the left and to the right of the hidden columns, and then right-click and choose Unhide from the shortcut menu.

- Select a range that consists of cells to the left and to the right of the hidden columns, and press Ctrl+Shift+0 (that's a zero).

To unhide one or more hidden rows, use any of these methods:

- Select a range that consists of cells above and below the hidden rows. Then choose Home ⇨ Cells ⇨ Format ⇨ Hide & Unhide ⇨ Unhide Rows.

- Select entire rows above and below the hidden rows, and then right-click and choose Unhide from the shortcut menu.

- Select a range that consists of cells above and below the hidden rows, and press Ctrl+Shift+9.

Part I

Hiding Cell Contents

Excel doesn't provide a direct way to hide the contents of cells (without hiding entire rows and columns), but you can fake it in a few ways:

- Use a special custom number format. Select the cell or cells to be hidden, press Ctrl+1 and click the Number tab in the Format Cells dialog box. Select Custom from the Category list, and then, in the Type field, enter ;;; (three semicolons).
- Make the font color the same as the background color.
- Add a shape to your worksheet and position it over the cell or cells to be hidden. You should make the shape the same color as the cell background and (probably) remove the borders.

All these methods have problems: The cell's contents are still displayed on the formula bar when the cell is selected. If you don't want to see the cell contents on the formula bar after you use one of those methods, you can either hide the formula bar or perform these additional steps:

1. Select the cells.
2. Press Ctrl+1, and then click the Protection tab in the Format Cells dialog box.
3. Select the Hidden check box and click OK.
4. Choose Review ➪ Protect Sheet.
5. In the Protect Sheet dialog box, add a password if desired, and click OK.

Keep in mind that when a sheet is protected, you can't change any cells unless they are not locked. By default, all cells *are* locked. You change the locked status of a cell by using the Protection tab in the Format Cells dialog box.

Taking Pictures of Ranges

Excel 2007 makes it easy to convert a range of cells into a picture. The picture can either be a "dead" image (it doesn't change if the original range changes) or a "live" picture (which reflects changes in the original range). The range can even contain objects, such as charts.

Creating a Static Image of a Range

To create a snapshot of a range, start by selecting a range of cells, and then press Ctrl+C to copy the range to the Clipboard. Then choose Home ⇨ Clipboard ⇨ Paste ⇨ As Picture ⇨ Paste As Picture. The result is a graphical image of the original range. When you select this image, Excel displays its Picture Tools context menu — which means that you can apply some additional formatting to the picture.

Figure 18-1 shows a range of cells (B2:E9), along with a picture of the range after I applied one of the built-in styles from the Picture Tools ⇨ Format ⇨ Picture Styles gallery.

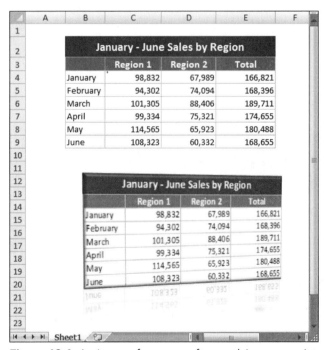

Figure 18-1: A picture of a range, after applying some picture formatting.

Creating a Live Image of a Range

To create an image that's linked to the original range of cells, select the cells and press Ctrl+C to copy the range to the Clipboard. Then choose Home ➪ Clipboard ➪ Paste ➪ As Picture ➪ Paste Picture Link. Excel pastes a picture of the original range, and the picture is linked — if you make changes to the original, those changes are shown in the linked picture.

Notice that when you select the linked picture, the formula bar displays the address of the original range. You can edit this range reference to change the cells that are displayed in the picture. To "de-link" the picture, just delete the formula on the formula bar.

You can also cut and paste this picture to a different worksheet, if you like. That makes it easy to refer to information on a different sheet. Unfortunately, Excel doesn't allow much formatting of this picture. You can change its size by dragging a corner, but none of the standard picture formatting commands is available.

Figure 18-2 shows a linked picture of a range placed on top of a shape, which has lots of interesting formatting capabilities. Placing a linked picture on top of a shape is a good way to make a particular range stand out.

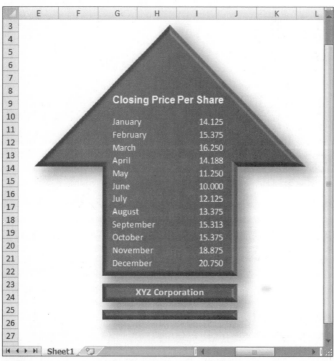

Figure 18-2: A linked picture of a range, placed on top of a shape.

Performing Inexact Searches

If you have a large worksheet with lots of data, locating what you're looking for can be difficult. The Excel Find and Replace dialog box is a useful tool for locating information, and it has a few features that many users overlook.

Access the Find and Replace dialog box by choosing Home ➪ Editing ➪ Find & Select ➪ Find (or pressing Ctrl+F). If you're replacing information, you can use Home ➪ Editing ➪ Find & Select ➪ Replace (or Ctrl+H). The only difference is which of the two tabs is displayed in the dialog box. Figure 19-1 shows the Find and Replace dialog box after clicking the Options button, which expands the dialog box to show additional options.

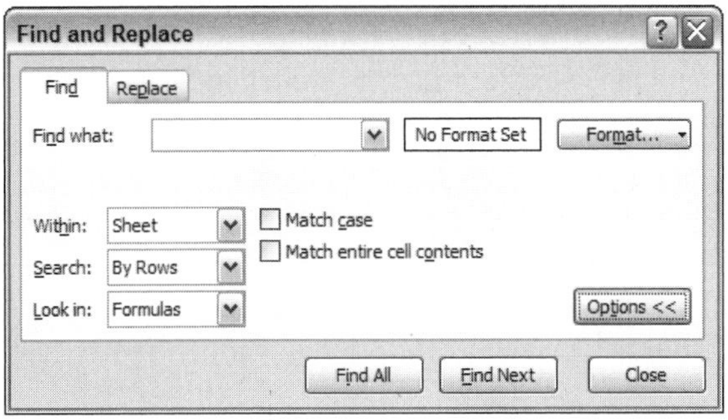

Figure 19-1: The Find and Replace dialog box, with the Find tab selected.

In many cases, you want to locate "approximate" text. For example, you may be trying to find data for a customer named Stephen R. Rosencrantz. You can, of course, search for the exact text: *Stephen R. Rosencrantz*. However, there's a reasonably good chance that the search will fail. The name may have been entered differently, as Steve Rosencrantz or S.R. Rosencrantz, for example. It may have even been misspelled as Rosentcrantz.

The most efficient search for this name is to use a wildcard character and search for st*rosen* and then click the Find All button. In addition to reducing the amount of text that you enter, this search is practically guaranteed to locate the customer, if the record is in your worksheet. The search may also find some records that you aren't looking for, but that's better than not finding anything.

The Find and Replace dialog box supports two wildcard characters:

- ? matches any single character.
- * matches any number of characters.

Wildcard characters also work with values. For example, searching for 3* locates all cells that contain a value that begins with 3. Searching for 1?9 locates all three-digit entries that begin with 1 and end with 9.

NOTE

To search for a question mark or an asterisk, precede the character with a tilde character (~). For example, the following search string finds the text *NONE*:

~*NONE~*

If you need to search for the tilde character, use two tildes.

If your searches don't seem to be working correctly, double-check these three options (which sometimes have a way of changing on their own):

- **Match Case:** If this check box is selected, the case of the text must match exactly. For example, searching for smith does not locate Smith.

- **Match Entire Cell Contents:** If this check box is selected, a match occurs if the cell contains only the search string (and nothing else). For example, searching for Excel doesn't locate a cell that contains Microsoft Excel.

- **Look In:** This drop-down list has three options: Values, Formulas, and Comments. If, for example, Values is selected, searching for 900 doesn't find a cell that contains 900 if that value is generated by a formula.

Remember that searching operates on the selected range of cells. If you want to search the entire worksheet, select only one cell.

Also, remember that searches do not include numeric formatting. For example, if you have a value that uses currency formatting so that it appears as $54.00, searching for $5* doesn't locate that value.

Working with dates can be a bit tricky because Excel offers many ways to format dates. If you search for a date by using the default date format, Excel locates the dates even if they're formatted differently. For example, if your system uses the m/d/y date format, the search string 10/*/2005 finds all dates in October 2005, regardless of how the dates are formatted.

You can also use an empty Replace With field. For example, to quickly delete all asterisks from your worksheet, enter ~* in the Find What field and leave the Replace With field blank. When you click the Replace All button, Excel finds all the asterisks and replaces them with nothing.

Replacing Formatting

A useful, but often overlooked, Excel feature is the ability to search for (and replace) cell formatting. For example, if you have cells that use the 14-point Calibri font, it's a simple matter to change the formatting in all those cells to something else.

The process isn't as intuitive as it could be, so I walk you through the steps. Assume that your worksheet contains many cells that are formatted with a yellow background and in 14-point Calibri in bold. Furthermore, assume that these cells are scattered throughout the workbook. The goal is to change all those cells so that they're displayed with 16-point Cambria in bold, with white text on a black background.

To change the formatting by searching and replacing, follow these steps:

1. Click on any single cell, and choose Home ⇨ Editing ⇨ Find & Select ⇨ Replace (or press Ctrl+H) to display the Find and Replace dialog box. If you want to limit the searching to a particular range, select the range rather than a single cell.

2. In the Find and Replace dialog box, make sure that the Find What and Replace With fields are blank.

3. Click the upper Format button (the one beside the Find What field) to display the Find Format dialog box.

4. You can use the Find Format dialog box to specify the formatting you're looking for, but it's much easier to click the arrow on the Format button and click Choose Format from Cell. Then click on a cell that already has the formatting you want to replace.

5. Click the lower Format button (the one beside the Replace With field) to display the Find Format dialog box again.

6. You can use the Choose Format from Cell option and specify a cell that contains the replacement formatting. Or, use the tabs in the Find Format dialog box to specify the desired formatting. In this example, click the Font tab and select Cambria, size 16, bold style, and white color. On the Patterns tab, choose black as the cell shading color. At this point, the Find And Replace dialog box should resemble Figure 20-1.

7. In the Find and Replace dialog box, click the Replace All button.

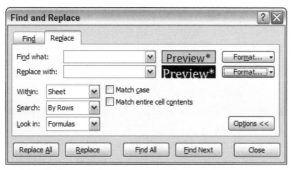

Figure 20-1: The Replace tab in the Find and Replace dialog box.

NOTE

If you use the Choose Format from Cell option in Step 4, you may find that not all occurrences of the formatting are replaced — usually because one or more aspects of the formatting do not match. For example, if you click on a cell that has General number formatting, it doesn't replace cells that have Date number formatting. The solution is to click the Format button to display the Find Format dialog box and then click the Clear button in each dialog box tab in which the formatting is not relevant.

In some cases, you may prefer to simply select the cells with a particular format. To do so, perform Steps 1 through 4 in the preceding step list. Then click the Find All button. The dialog box expands to display information about the qualifying cells (see Figure 20-2). Click on the bottom part of the dialog box, and then press Ctrl+A to select all qualifying cells.

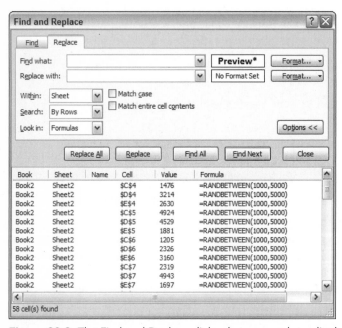

Figure 20-2: The Find and Replace dialog box expands to display a list of all matching cells.

When these cells are selected, you can then format them any way you like. Note that you can widen the columns in the list of found cells (by dragging a column border), and you can also sort the list by clicking a column header.

NOTE

Conspicuously absent from the Find and Replace dialog box is the ability to search for cells by their styles. Despite the fact that Excel 2007 places increased emphasis on cell styles, it's not possible to find all cells that use a particular style and apply a different style to those cells. You can find and replace the formatting, but the cell style does not change.

Changing the Excel Color Scheme

One of the new features in Office 2007 is the ability to change the color scheme of the applications. You do this in the Excel Options dialog box. Choose Office ➪ Excel Options, and then click the Popular tab. Use the Color Scheme drop-down list to select your color choice: Blue, Sliver, or Black (see Figure 21-1). When you change the color scheme, your choice affects all other Microsoft Office 2007 applications.

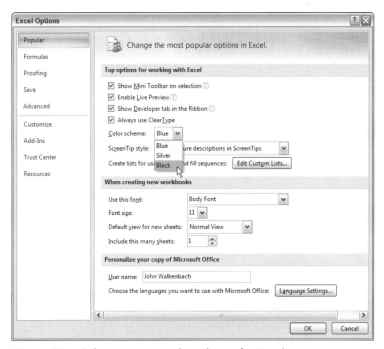

Figure 21-1: Selecting a new color scheme for Excel.

You may find that a particular color scheme is easier on the eyes. Or, you may just want an occasional change of scenery. Unfortunately, the three choices are all there is — what you see is what you get. You cannot customize the color schemes in any way, and (as far as I know) third-party developers cannot even create new color schemes.

CROSS-REFERENCE
Don't confuse color schemes with document themes (another new Office 2007 feature). The document theme feature is an entirely different concept, and these two features are not related. See Tip 13 for more about document themes.

Limiting the Usable Area in a Worksheet

Have you ever wanted to restrict access to a certain range within a worksheet? For example, you may want to set up a worksheet so that only cells in a particular range can be activated or modified. This tip describes two ways to accomplish this task: by using the ScrollArea property and by using worksheet protection.

Setting the ScrollArea Property

A worksheet's ScrollArea property determines which range is visible. Figure 22-1 shows a worksheet. The instructions that follow restrict the usable area of the worksheet to the range C6:F13.

	A	B	C	D	E	F	G	H
1								
2								
3								
4								
5								
6			January - June Sales by Region					
7				Region 1	Region 2	Total		
8			January	98,832	67,989	166,821		
9			February	94,302	74,094	168,396		
10			March	101,305	88,406	189,711		
11			April	99,334	75,321	174,655		
12			May	114,565	65,923	180,488		
13			June	108,323	60,332	168,655		
14								
15								
16								
17								

Sheet1 / Sheet2 / Sheet3

Figure 22-1: You can restrict the usable area of a worksheet to a particular range.

Here's how to do it:

1. First, make sure that the Developer tab of the Ribbon is displayed. (By default, this tab is not displayed.) To turn on the Developer tab, access the Excel Options dialog box (choose Office ⇨ Excel Options), click the Popular tab, and select the Show Developer Tab in the Ribbon check box.

2. Choose Developer ⇨ Controls ⇨ Properties to display the Properties window (see Figure 22-2).

3. In the Properties window, enter C6:F13 in the ScrollArea field and press Enter. You can't point to the range; you must enter the range address manually.

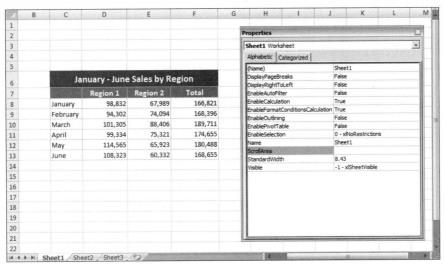

Figure 22-2: Use the Properties window to control some properties of the worksheet.

After performing these steps, you find that you cannot activate any cell outside the specified range. Also, some commands no longer work. For example, you cannot select entire rows and columns. Note that the scroll area is limited to a single contiguous range of cells.

There's a problem: The ScrollArea property isn't persistent. In other words, if you save your file, close it, and then open it again, the ScrollArea is reset and you're free to select any cell you like. One solution is to write a simple VBA macro that is executed when the workbook is opened. To add this type of macro, follow these instructions:

1. Make sure that the workbook window is not maximized. One way to do this is to press Ctrl+F5.

2. Right-click the workbook's title bar and choose View Code from the shortcut menu. This action displays the ThisWorkbook code module for the workbook.

3. Enter the following VBA code in the ThisWorkbook code module:

```
Private Sub Workbook_Open()
    Worksheets("Sheet1").ScrollArea = "C6:F13"
End Sub
```

4. Press Alt+F11 to return to Excel.

5. Save the workbook, close it, and reopen it. If your workbook has an XLSX extension, you need to save it as a macro-enabled workbook (with an XLSM extension).

When the workbook is opened, the Workbook_Open procedure is executed automatically, and the ScrollArea property is set.

Part I

⚠ **CAUTION**
This method is by no means a foolproof way to prevent users from accessing parts of a workbook. Nothing can prevent a savvy user from using the Properties window to delete the contents of the ScrollArea field. Or, when the workbook is open, the user can choose to disable macros for the workbook. Another way to bypass the Workbook_Open macro is to press Shift while the file opens.

Using Worksheet Protection

The second method of limiting the usable area of a worksheet relies on unlocking cells and protecting the workbook:

1. Select all cells that you want to be accessible. They can be single cells or any number of ranges.

2. Press Ctrl+1 to display the Format Cells dialog box.

3. In the Format Cells dialog box, click the Protection tab and remove the check mark from the Locked check box.

4. Choose Review ⇨ Protect Sheet to display the Protect Sheet dialog box.

5. In the Protect Sheet dialog box, remove the check mark from the Select Locked Cells check box (see Figure 22-3).

Figure 22-3: Use the Protect Sheet dialog box to prevent the user from selecting locked cells.

6. If desired, specify a password that will be required in order to unprotect the sheet, and then click OK.

After you perform these steps, only the unlocked cells (those you selected in Step 1) are accessible.

 CAUTION

Worksheet passwords are not at all secure. In fact, it's a trivial matter to crack such a password. Therefore, worksheet protection is more of a convenience feature than a security feature.

Part I

Using an Alternative to Cell Comments

As you probably know, you can attach a comment to any cell by using the Review ➪ Comments ➪ New Comment button (or, by right-clicking the cell and choosing Insert Comment from the shortcut menu). Use Review ➪ Comments ➪ Show All Comments to toggle the display of comments. The Excel Options dialog box has additional comment viewing options, found in the Display section of the Advanced tab. A user can choose to hide all comments and comment indicators — which means that your comments will never be seen.

This tip describes how to use Excel's Data Validation feature to display a pop-up message whenever a cell is activated. It's a good way to ensure that your "comment" will always be seen, regardless of the user's comment viewing setting.

Follow these steps to add a message to a cell:

1. Activate the cell that you want to display the pop-up message.
2. Select Data ➪ Data Tools ➪ Data Validation to display the Data Validation dialog box.
3. In the Data Validation dialog box, click the Input Message tab.
4. (Optional) In the Title field, enter a title for your message.
5. Enter the message itself in the Input Message box.
6. Click OK to close the Data Validation dialog box.

After you perform these steps, the message appears whenever the cell is activated (see Figure 23-1 for an example). You can also click and drag the message to a different location, if it's in your way.

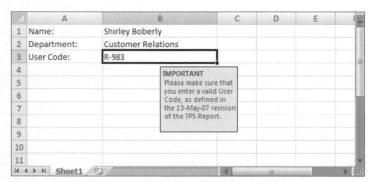

Figure 23-1: This pop-up message was created by using Excel's Data Validation feature.

Understanding the Excel Help System

With every new release of Office, it seems that Microsoft revamps the Help system. Office 2007 is no exception. The new Help system (officially known as the Help Viewer) is radically different from the previous one, and in fact uses completely different technology.

A new aspect of Office 2007 is its Supertip feature. When you hover your mouse over a command on the Ribbon, you see a pop-up description of what that command does. Figure 24-1 shows an example of a Supertip.

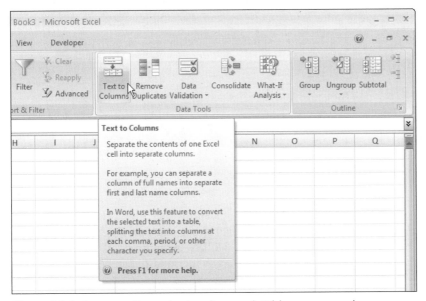

Figure 24-1: A pop-up Supertip describes each Ribbon command.

But the real Help content is found in the Help Viewer window. The following notes help familiarize you with the Excel 2007 Help system:

- The Excel 2007 Help system has a single entry point (no more Help menu, with various options). To display Excel Help, press F1 or click the round question mark icon below the Excel title bar.

- The Help content resides in two places: on your hard drive and on a Microsoft Web server. The lower-right corner of the Help window displays the status in a button: either Offline (shows content only from your computer) or Connected to Office Online (shows content from the Web). You can change the status by clicking the button and making your choice. In some cases, using the Online option gives you more up-to-date information.

- Connecting to Office Online displays additional content that's not available when you choose the Offline option. Specifically, you can search for templates or training materials. Figure 24-2 shows the option in the drop-down Search button list.

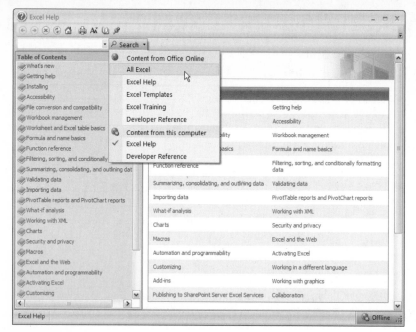

Figure 24-2: Specifying where to search for help.

- When you're connected to Office Online, you can identify the URL for the Help topic and send it to someone else. To do so, right-click the current Help topic and choose Properties. The Properties dialog box displays the URL of the Help topic. Select the URL text with your mouse, and press Ctrl+C to copy it. The URL can be opened with any Web browser.

- It took me a long time to figure this one out: You can determine which buttons appear on the toolbar in the Help window. Click the tiny icon on the right side of the toolbar and select Add or Remove buttons. You see the list shown in Figure 24-3.

- Context-sensitive help is spotty. For example, if an Excel dialog box is displayed, pressing F1 (or clicking the question mark icon on the dialog box title bar) displays the Help window. In some cases, the Help information relates to what you're doing (for example, the Name Manager dialog box). In other cases, you're presented with the opening screen of the Excel Help system (for example, when the Sort dialog box is displayed). In the latter case, you can use the Search box to find the information that should have been displayed for you automatically.

- You have no way to display the Office Help window if an Office application is not running. In previous versions of Office, you could double-click a *.CHM help file, and the help file would be displayed. That's no longer possible in Office 2007 because of the new Help system technology that's used.

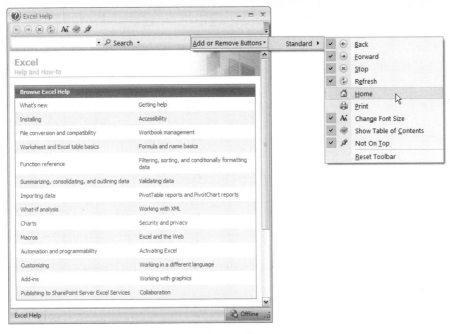

Figure 24-3: Configuring the Help window toolbar.

- If you're a VBA programmer, you can write a macro to display a particular help topic. To do so, you need to know the topic ID. Locate the Help topic that you want to display, and then right-click and choose Copy Topic ID. For example, the topic ID for the topic Overview of Formulas is HP10081865. The following VBA procedure, when executed, displays that Help topic:

```
Sub ShowFormulaOverview()
  Application.Assistance.ShowHelp ("HP10081865")
End Sub
```

NOTE

Unfortunately, displaying a Help topic by using VBA works only if the user's Help system is in Offline mode. If the user's Help system is connected to Office Online, attempting to display a Help topic shows only the opening screen. Unfortunately, VBA has no way to determine which mode is being used.

Making a Worksheet "Very Hidden"

You probably already know how to hide a worksheet: Just right-click the sheet tab and choose Hide Sheet from the shortcut menu. And, of course, it's just as easy to *unhide* a sheet: Right-click any sheet tab and choose Unhide from the shortcut menu. (You see a list of all hidden sheets.)

To make it more difficult for the casual user to unhide a hidden sheet, make the worksheet "very hidden." Here's how to do it:

1. First, make sure that the Developer tab of the Ribbon is displayed. (By default, this tab is not displayed.) To turn on the Developer tab, open the Excel Options dialog box (choose Office ⇨ Excel Options), click the Popular tab, and select the Show Developer Tab in the Ribbon check box.

2. Activate the sheet you want to hide.

3. Click Developer ⇨ Controls ⇨ Properties to display the Properties window (see Figure 25-1).

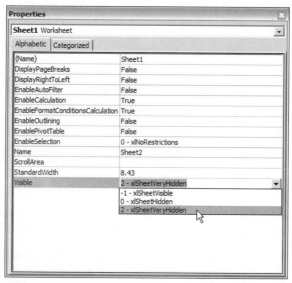

Figure 25-1: Use the Properties window to make a worksheet very hidden.

4. In the Properties window, click the Visible property to display a down-arrow button; click the button to display a drop-down list and select 2 -xlSheetVeryHidden.

After performing these steps, you find that you cannot unhide the sheet by using any Excel command. In fact, you cannot even unhide the sheet by using the Properties window. The Properties window shows the properties of the active sheet. When a sheet is hidden, it's never the active sheet.

Is the sheet is hidden forever? Nope. To make the very hidden sheet visible again, you use a simple VBA macro. The macro listed here unhides Sheet2 of the active workbook (change the sheet name as appropriate):

```
Sub UnhideSheet()
    Worksheets("Sheet2").Visible = True
End Sub
```

CAUTION

Making a worksheet very hidden is not a security feature. Anyone who really wants to know what resides on a very hidden sheet can easily find out by using the UnhideSheet macro.

Part I

Disabling Hyperlink Warnings

As you probably know, Excel lets you insert a hyperlink into a cell. A hyperlink can activate a different sheet or a different workbook, or it can execute an external program. For
example, if a cell contains a hyperlink to an MP3 music file, clicking the hyperlink plays
the song on the default music player.

Hyperlinks are great — until you start using them. Unless the hyperlink goes to a location
in the same workbook, you see the warning message shown in Figure 26-1. If you click 20
hyperlinks, you see the message 20 times. You even see the message if the hyperlink
points to an Excel workbook that's in a trusted location. And there is no direct way to turn
it off!

Figure 26-1: Clicking a hyperlink may display this message.

You can avoid seeing this annoying message — but you need to make a modification to the
Windows Registry:

1. Close Excel.

2. Click the Windows Start button, and then choose Run.

3. In the Open dialog box, type **regedit** and then click OK. This command launches the
   Registry Editor.

4. In the Registry Editor, locate the following Registry subkey and click it:

   `HKEY_CURRENT_USER\Software\Microsoft\Office\12.0\Common`

5. Choose Edit ➪ New ➪ Key.

6. Type **Security**, and then press Enter to name the key.

7. With the Security key selected, choose Edit ➪ New ➪ DWORD Value.

8. Type **DisableHyperlinkWarning**, and then press Enter to name the entry.

9. Double-click the DisableHyperlinkWarning entry to display the Edit DWORD Value
   dialog box.

10. In the Edit DWORD Value dialog box, click the Decimal option, and type **1** in the Value data field.

11. Click OK to enter the value.

Figure 26-2 shows the Registry Editor after I made the change.

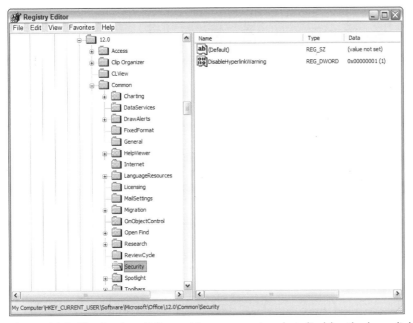

Figure 26-2: The Registry Editor, with a new setting that disables the hyperlink warning message.

After performing these steps, restart Excel. The new setting takes effect. By the way, this change affects all Microsoft Office 2007 applications.

Even after making this change, you may still get a warning when you click a hyperlink for a certain type of file. For example, after I made this modification, I still saw a warning when I clicked a hyperlink for an MP3 music file. I had to make *another* change for this particular file type:

1. Double-click the My Computer icon to open an Explorer window.

2. Choose Tools ➪ Folder Options.

3. Click the File Types tab.

4. In the Register File Types list, select the extension for the type of file that's generating a hyperlink warning (for example, MP3).

5. Click Advanced to display the Edit File Type dialog box.

6. Remove the check mark from the Confirm Open After Download option, and click OK.

7. Click Close to close the Folder Options dialog box.

You may need to repeat these steps for other file types. Eventually, Excel will be an environment free of hyperlink warnings.

Part **II**

Data Entry

In this part, you'll find tips related to entering data into an Excel workbook. Entering data into an Excel worksheet is easy, but there's an excellent chance that the tips here will improve your overall efficiency.

Tips and Where to Find Them

Understanding the Types of Data

Whenever you enter something into a cell in a worksheet, Excel goes to work and makes one of the following decisions regarding the type of data you entered:

- You entered a value.

- You entered a date or time.

- You entered some text.

- You entered a formula.

If you understand how Excel interprets the data you enter into a cell, you can save yourself a bit of frustration when Excel's decision about what you entered doesn't correspond to what you had in mind.

Entering Values

Any cell entry that consists of numerical digits is considered a *value*. Values can also include a few special characters:

- **Negative sign:** If a negative sign (–) precedes the value, Excel interprets it as a negative number.

- **Plus sign:** If a plus sign (+) precedes the value, Excel interprets it as a positive number (and does not display the plus sign).

- **Percent sign:** If a percent sign (%) follows the numbers, Excel interprets the value as a percentage and automatically applies percent numeric formatting.

- **Currency symbol:** If your system's currency symbol (for example, a dollar sign) precedes the numbers, Excel interprets the entry as a monetary value and automatically formats it as currency.

- **Thousands separator:** If the number includes one or more of your system's thousands separators (for example, a comma), Excel interprets the entry as a number and also applies numeric formatting to display the thousands separator symbol. Note that the thousands separator must be in the appropriate position. For example, if the comma is your system's thousands separator, Excel interprets 4,500 as a value but does not interpret 45,00 as a value.

- **Scientific notation:** If the value contains the letter E, Excel attempts to interpret it as scientific notation. For example, 3.2E5 is interpreted as 3.2×10^5.

Entering Dates and Times

Excel treats dates and times as special types of numeric values. Typically, these values are formatted so that they appear as dates or times because humans find it much easier to understand these values if they appear in the correct format.

Excel handles dates by using a serial number system. The earliest date that Excel under-stands is January 1, 1900. This date has a serial number of 1. January 2, 1900, has a serial number of 2, and so on. This system makes it easy to deal with dates in formulas. For example, you can enter a formula to calculate the number of days between two dates.

 NOTE

The date examples in this book use the U.S. English system. Depending on your regional settings, entering a date in a format such as June 1, 2008, might be interpreted as text rather than as a date. In this case, you need to enter the date in a format that corre-sponds to your regional date settings — for example, 1 June, 2008.

The following table provides a sampling of the date formats that Excel recognizes. After entering a date, you can format it to appear in a different date format by using the Number tab of the Format Cells dialog box.

Date Entered in Cell	Excel's Interpretation (U.S. Settings)
6-26-08	June 26, 2008
6-26-2008	June 26, 2008
6/26/08	June 26, 2008
6/26/2008	June 26, 2008
6-26/08	June 26, 2008
June 26, 2008	June 26, 2008
Jun 26	June 26 of the current year
June 26	June 26 of the current year
6/26	June 26 of the current year
6-26	June 26 of the current year

Excel is smart, but not perfect, about recognizing dates you enter. For example, Excel does not recognize any of the following entries as dates: June 1 2008, Jun-1 2008, and Jun-1/2008. Rather, it interprets these entries as text. If you plan to use dates in formulas, make sure that the date you enter is recognized as a date; otherwise, your formulas will produce incorrect results.

A common problem is that Excel interprets your entry as a date when you intended to enter a fraction. For example, if you enter the fraction 1/5, Excel interprets it as January 5 of the current year. The solution is to precede the fraction with an equal sign.

When you work with times, Excel simply extends its date serial number system to include decimals. In other words, Excel works with times by using fractional days. For example, the date serial number for June 1, 2008, is 39600. Noon on June 1, 2008 (halfway through the day), is represented internally as 39600.5 because the time fraction is simply added to the date serial number to get the full date-and-time serial number.

Again, you normally don't have to be concerned about these serial numbers (or fractional serial numbers, for times). Just enter the time into a cell in a recognized format.

The following table shows some examples of time formats that Excel recognizes.

Entered into a Cell	Excel's Interpretation
11:30:00 am	11:30 AM
11:30:00 AM	11:30 AM
11:30 pm	11:30 PM
11:30	11:30 AM
13:30	1:30 PM

These examples don't have days associated with them, so they're represented internally as values less than 1. In other words, Excel is using the nonexistent date January 0, 1900. You also can combine dates and times, however, as shown in the following table.

Entered into a Cell	Excel's Interpretation
6/26/08 11:30	11:30 AM on June 26, 2008
6/26/08 12:00	Noon on June 26, 2008
6/26/2008 0:00	Midnight on June 26, 2008

When you enter a time that exceeds 24 hours, the associated date for the time increments accordingly. For example, if you enter the following time into a cell, it's interpreted as 1:00 AM on January 1, 1900:

```
25:00:00
```

The day section of the entry increments because the time exceeds 24 hours. Keep in mind that a time value without a date uses January 0, 1900, as the date.

Entering Text

If Excel can't interpret your cell entry as a value, a date, a time, or a formula, it goes into the catchall category of text.

A single cell can hold a massive amount of text — about 32,000 characters. However, you'll see that Excel has lots of limitations when you use large amounts of text in a cell. In fact, it can't even display all the characters.

Entering Formulas

Normally, you signal that you're entering a formula by beginning the cell entry with an equal sign (=). However, Excel also accepts a plus sign or a minus sign. And (to accommodate old Lotus 1-2-3 users), if your formula begins with a worksheet function, Excel also accepts an ampersand (@). However, as soon as you press Enter, the ampersand is replaced with an equal sign.

Formulas can contain these elements:

- Mathematical operators, such as + (for addition) and * (for multiplication)
- Parentheses
- Cell references (including named cells and ranges)
- Values or text
- Worksheet functions (such as SUM or AVERAGE)

If the formula you entered isn't syntactically correct, Excel might propose a correction. Keep in mind that the suggested Excel corrections aren't always right.

Moving the Cell Pointer after Entering Data

By default, Excel automatically moves the cell pointer to the next cell down when you press Enter after entering data into a cell. To change this setting, use the Excel Options dialog box (choose Office ⇨ Excel Options). The setting you're looking for is on the Advanced tab of the Excel Options dialog box, in the Editing Options section (see Figure 28-1).

The check box that controls this behavior is labeled After Pressing Enter, Move Selection. When that check box is enabled, you can also specify the direction in which the cell pointer moves (down, left, up, or right).

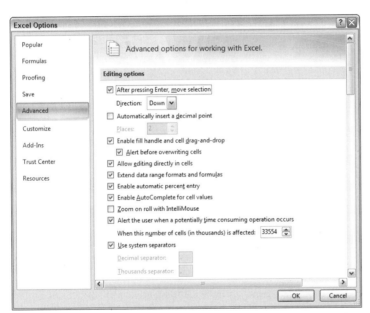

Figure 28-1: Use the Advanced tab in the Excel Options dialog box to specify where to move the cell pointer after you press Enter.

Your choice is completely a matter of personal preference. I prefer to keep this option turned off and use the arrow keys rather than press Enter. Not surprisingly, these directional keys send the cell pointer in the direction that you indicate. For example, if you're entering data in a row, press the right-arrow (⇨) key rather than Enter. The other arrow keys work as expected, and you can even use the PgUp and PgDn keys.

Part II

Selecting a Range of Input Cells before Entering Data

Here's a tip that most Excel users don't know about: When a range of cells is selected, Excel automatically moves the cell pointer to the next cell in the range when you press Enter.

The next cell is determined by the Direction setting on the Advanced tab of the Excel Options dialog box (see Tip 28).

For example, if the Direction setting is Down (or if the Move Selection option isn't enabled), it works like this: If the selection consists of multiple rows, Excel moves down the column; when Excel reaches the end of the selection in the column, it moves to the first selected cell in the next column. To skip a cell, just press Enter without entering anything. To go backward, press Shift+Enter. If you prefer to enter the data by rows rather than by columns, press Tab rather than Enter.

Using AutoComplete to Automate Data Entry

Excel's AutoComplete feature makes it very easy to enter the same text into multiple cells. With AutoComplete, you type the first few letters of a text entry into a cell and Excel automatically completes the entry, based on other entries that you already made in the column. In addition to reducing typing, this feature ensures that your entries are spelled correctly and are consistent.

Here's how it works. Suppose that you're entering product information in a column. One product is named Sugar-Free Snaphylytes. The first time that you enter Sugar-Free Snaphylytes into a cell, Excel remembers it. Later, when you start typing the words `Sugar-Free Snaphylytes` into that column, Excel recognizes the word by the first few letters and finishes typing it for you. Just press Enter and you're done.

AutoComplete also changes the case of letters for you automatically. If you start entering `sugar` (with a lowercase *s*) in the second entry, Excel makes the *s* uppercase, to be consistent with the previous entry in the column.

If the column contains entries that match on the first few characters, Excel doesn't display a suggestion until your entry matches one of them uniquely. For example, if the column also contains a product named Sugar-Free Marpinettes, AutoComplete doesn't kick in until you type either the first letter of Snaphylytes or the first letter of Marpinettes.

NOTE

You also can access a mouse-oriented version of AutoComplete by right-clicking the cell and choosing Pick from List from the shortcut menu. Excel then displays a drop-down list that has all the entries in the current column, and you just click the one you want. See Figure 30-1.

You can even access the drop-down list from the keyboard: Press Shift+F10 to display the shortcut menu, and then press **k** (the hotkey for Pick from List). Use the arrow keys to make your selection, and then press Enter.

Keep in mind that AutoComplete works only within a contiguous column of cells. If you have a blank row, for example, AutoComplete looks only at the cell contents below the blank row.

If you find the AutoComplete feature distracting, you can turn it off, on the Advanced tab of the Excel Options dialog box (choose Office ➪ Excel Options). The setting, labeled Enable AutoComplete for Cell Values, is in the Editing Options section.

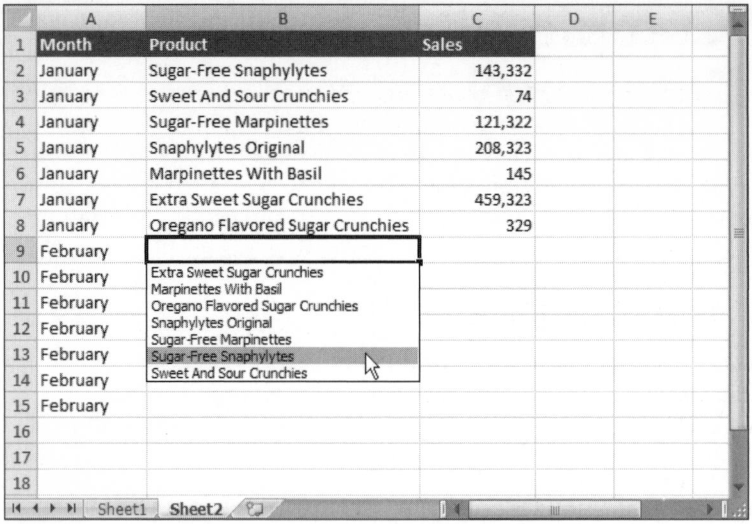

	A	B	C	D	E
1	Month	Product	Sales		
2	January	Sugar-Free Snaphylytes	143,332		
3	January	Sweet And Sour Crunchies	74		
4	January	Sugar-Free Marpinettes	121,322		
5	January	Snaphylytes Original	208,323		
6	January	Marpinettes With Basil	145		
7	January	Extra Sweet Sugar Crunchies	459,323		
8	January	Oregano Flavored Sugar Crunchies	329		
9	February				
10	February	Extra Sweet Sugar Crunchies			
11	February	Marpinettes With Basil			
12	February	Oregano Flavored Sugar Crunchies			
13	February	Snaphylytes Original			
14	February	Sugar-Free Marpinettes			
15	February	Sugar-Free Snaphylytes			
16		Sweet And Sour Crunchies			
17					
18					

Sheet1 Sheet2

Figure 30-1: Right-clicking a cell and choosing Pick From List from the shortcut menu displays a list of column entries.

Removing Duplicate Rows

A longstanding item on the Excel wish list is the ability to automatically delete duplicate rows in a worksheet. In Excel 2007, Microsoft has made that particular wish come true.

Figure 31-1 shows a range of data after it was converted to a table using Insert ⇨ Tables ⇨ Table. Notice that this table has some duplicate rows.

	A	B	C
1	Name	Birthday	Location
2	Deborah Dennis	June 12	Eastern Region
3	Ashley Armstrong	May 1	Eastern Region
4	Brenda Logan	February 16	Eastern Region
5	Ashley Armstrong	May 1	Eastern Region
6	Deanna Freeman	September 28	Eastern Region
7	Betty Mann	July 11	Eastern Region
8	Dawn Johnson	September 3	Eastern Region
9	Hilda King	January 5	Eastern Region
10	Ellen Hill	April 29	Central Region
11	Brenda Logan	February 16	Eastern Region
12	Maxine Brown	April 20	Central Region
13	Joann Jackson	June 3	Central Region
14	Maxine Brown	April 20	Central Region
15	Lakenya Cruz	August 12	Central Region
16	Mary Johnson	September 1	Western Region
17	Lakenya Cruz	August 12	Central Region
18	Michelle Ross	October 12	Western Region
19	Carmen Johnson	November 11	Western Region
20			

Sheet1

Figure 31-1: The goal is to remove all duplicate rows from this table.

Start by selecting any cell in your table. Then choose Table Tools ⇨ Design ⇨ Tools ⇨ Remove Duplicates. Excel responds with the dialog box shown in Figure 31-2. The dialog box lists all columns in your table. Select the check boxes for the columns that you want to be included in the duplicate search. Most of the time, you select all the columns — which means that a duplicate is defined as having the same data in *every* column.

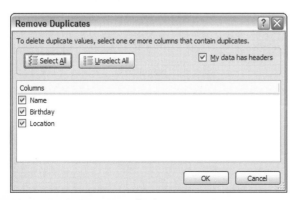

Figure 31-2: Removing duplicate rows is easy.

Click OK, and Excel weeds out the duplicate rows and displays a message that tells you how many duplicates it removed (see Figure 31-3).

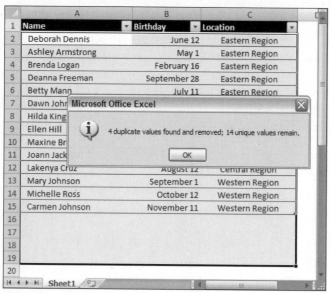

Figure 31-3: Excel tells you the result of deleting duplicate rows.

NOTE

If your data is not in a table, use the Data ⇨ Data Tools ⇨ Remove Duplicates command to display the Remove Duplicates dialog box.

CAUTION

You must understand that duplicate values are determined by the value *displayed* in the cell — not necessarily by the value stored in the cell. Assume that two cells contain the same date: One date is formatted to display as 5/15/2008, and the other is formatted to display as May 15, 2008. When removing duplicates, Excel considers these dates to be different.

Keeping Titles in View

A common type of worksheet contains a table of data with descriptive headings in the first row. As you scroll down the worksheet, the first row scrolls off the screen, so you can no longer see the column descriptions.

Excel 2007 eliminates this age-old spreadsheet problem and takes care of the details automatically — but only if your data is in the form of a table (created with Insert ➪ Tables ➪ Table). Figure 32-1 shows a table that has been scrolled down. Normally, the column headers are scrolled out of view. But, when you're working with a table, Excel displays the column headers where the column letters normally appear.

Agent	Date Listed	Area	List Price	Bedrooms	Baths	SqFt	Type	Pool
10 Romero	4/4/2007	N. County	$799,000	6	5	4,800	Single Family	FALSE
11 Hamilton	2/24/2007	N. County	$425,900	5	3	2,414	Single Family	TRUE
12 Randolph	4/24/2007	N. County	$405,000	2	3	2,444	Single Family	TRUE
13 Adams	4/21/2007	S. County	$208,750	4	3	2,207	Single Family	TRUE
14 Shasta	3/24/2007	N. County	$398,000	4	2.5	2,620	Single Family	FALSE
15 Kelly	6/9/2007	N. County	$389,500	4	2	1,971	Single Family	FALSE
16 Shasta	8/17/2007	N. County	$389,000	4	3	3,109	Single Family	FALSE
17 Adams	6/6/2007	N. County	$379,900	3	2.5	2,468	Condo	FALSE
18 Adams	2/8/2007	N. County	$379,000	3	3	2,354	Condo	FALSE
19 Robinson	3/30/2007	N. County	$379,000	4	3	3,000	Single Family	FALSE
20 Barnes	6/26/2007	S. County	$208,750	4	2	1,800	Single Family	FALSE
21 Bennet	5/12/2007	Central	$229,500	4	3	2,041	Single Family	FALSE
22 Bennet	5/9/2007	Central	$549,000	4	3	1,940	Single Family	TRUE
23 Shasta	7/15/2007	N. County	$374,900	4	3	3,927	Single Family	FALSE
24 Lang	5/3/2007	N. County	$369,900	3	2.5	2,030	Condo	TRUE
25 Romero	1/28/2007	N. County	$369,900	4	3	1,988	Condo	FALSE
26 Bennet	6/26/2007	S. County	$229,900	3	2.5	1,580	Single Family	TRUE

Figure 32-1: The column headers for this table are displayed where the column letters normally appear.

Note that the column headers are visible only when a cell within the table is selected.

If your data isn't in the form of a table, you have to resort to the old-fashioned method: Freeze panes. This method keeps the headings visible while you're scrolling through the worksheet.

To freeze the first row, choose View ➪ Window ➪ Freeze Panes ➪ Freeze Top Row. Excel inserts a dark horizontal line to indicate the frozen row. To freeze the first column, choose View ➪ Window ➪ Freeze Panes ➪ Freeze First Column.

If you want to free more than one column or one row, move the cell pointer to the cell below and to the right of where you want the freeze to occur. Then choose View ➪ Window ➪ Freeze Panes ➪ Freeze Panes. For example, if you want to freeze the first two rows and the first column, move the cell pointer to cell B3 before you issue the command. To freeze the first three rows (but not any columns), select cell A4 before you issue the Freeze Panes command.

Part II

Some navigation keys operate as though the frozen rows or columns don't exist. For example, if you press Ctrl+Home while the worksheet has frozen panes, the cell selector moves to the upper left unfrozen cell. Similarly, the Home key moves to the first unfrozen cell in the current row. You can move into the frozen rows or columns by using the direction keys or your mouse.

To remove the frozen panes, choose View ➪ Window ➪ Freeze Panes ➪ Unfreeze Panes.

Automatically Filling a Range with a Series

If you need to fill a range with a series of values, one approach is to enter the first value, write a formula to calculate the next value, and copy the formula. For example, Figure 33-1 shows a series of consecutive numbers in column A. Cell A1 contains the value 1, and cell A2 contains this formula, which was copied down the column:

```
=A1+1
```

	A	B	C	D	E	F
1	1					
2	2					
3	3					
4	4					
5	5					
6	6					
7	7					
8	8					
9	9					
10	10					
11	11					
12	12					
13	13					
14						

Sheet1

Figure 33-1: Excel offers an easy way to generate a series of values like these.

A simpler approach is to let Excel do the work by using the handy Autofill feature:

1. Enter **1** into cell A1.

2. Enter **2** into cell A2.

3. Select A1:A2.

4. Move the mouse cursor to the lower right corner of cell A2 (the cell's *fill handle*). Then when the mouse pointer turns into a black plus sign, drag down the column to fill in the cells.

NOTE

This behavior can be turned on and off. If cells don't have a fill handle, choose Office ⇨ Excel Options and click the Advanced tab in the Excel Options dialog box. Select the check box labeled Enable Fill Handle and Cell Drag-And-Drop.

Part II

The data entered in Steps 1 and 2 provide Excel with the information it needs to determine which type of series to use. If you entered 3 into cell A2, the series would then consist of odd integers: 1, 3, 5, 7, and so on.

Here's another Autofill trick: If the data you start with is irregular, Excel completes the Autofill action by doing a linear regression and fills in the predicted values. Figure 33-2 shows a worksheet with some monthly sales values for January through July. If you use Autofill after selecting C2:C8, Excel extends the best fit linear sales trend and fills in the missing values. Figure 33-3 shows the predicted values, along with a chart.

	A	B	C	D	E
1		Month	Sales		
2		Jan	12.46		
3		Feb	16.45		
4		Mar	24.52		
5		Apr	19.34		
6		May	31.44		
7		Jun	27.34		
8		Jul	31.55		
9		Aug			
10		Sep			
11		Oct			
12		Nov			
13		Dec			
14					
15					

Figure 33-2: Use Autofill to perform a linear regression and predict sales values for August through December.

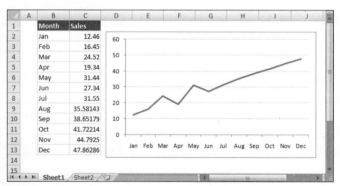

Figure 33-3: The sales figures, after using Autofill.

Autofill also works with dates and even a few text items — day names and month names. The following table lists a few examples of the types of data that can be Autofilled.

First Value	Autofilled Values
1	2, 3, 4, and so on
Sunday	Monday, Tuesday, Wednesday, and so on
Quarter-1	Quarter-2, Quarter-3, Quarter-4, Quarter-1, and so on
Jan	Feb, Mar, Apr, and so on
January	February, March, April, and so on
Month 1	Month 2, Month 3, Month 4, and so on

You can also create your own lists of items to be Autofilled. To do so, open the Excel Options dialog box and click the Popular tab. Then click the Edit Custom Lists button to display the Custom Lists dialog box. Enter your items in the List Entries box (each on a new line). Then click the Add button to create the list. Figure 33-4 shows a custom list of region names that use Roman numerals.

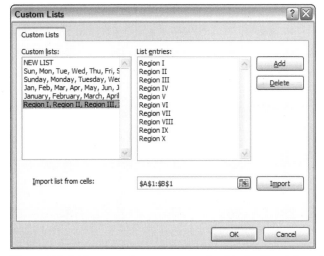

Figure 33-4: These region names work with the Excel Autofill feature.

For more control over what happens when using Autofill, using the right mouse button to click and drag the fill handle. When you release the button, you see a shortcut menu with some options (see Figure 33-5). The items that are available on the shortcut menu depend on the type of data selected. For example, if the first cell in the series contains a date, the date-related options are enabled.

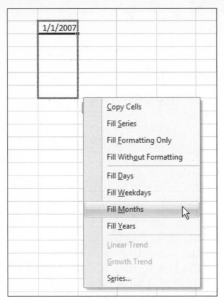

Figure 33-5: The shortcut menu for Autofill.

Working with Fractions

Although most users work with decimal values, some types of data are normally displayed as fractions, not as decimals. This tip describes how to enter noninteger values as fractions.

To enter a whole number and a fraction into a cell, leave a space between the whole number and the fraction. For example, to display 6⅞, type **6 7/8** and then press Enter. When you select the cell, 6.875 appears on the formula bar, and the cell entry appears as a fraction.

If you have only a fraction (for example, ⅛), you must enter a zero first, like this: **0 1/8** — otherwise, Excel likely assumes that you're entering a date. When you select the cell and look at the formula bar, you see 0.125. In the cell, you see 1/8.

If the numerator is larger than the denominator, Excel converts it to a whole number and a fraction. For example, if you enter **0 65/8**, Excel converts it to 8 1/8.

After you enter a fraction, take a look at the number format for the cell. You see that Excel automatically applied one of its Fraction number formats (see Figure 34-1).

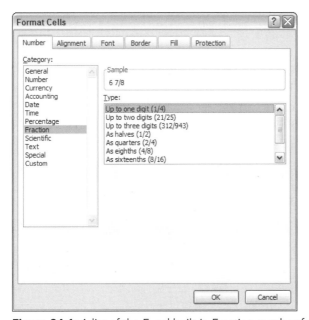

Figure 34-1: A list of the Excel built-in Fraction number formats.

Figure 34-2 shows a worksheet that displays fractional data. The values in column C are expressed in fourths, eighths, and 16ths, and the values in column D are all in 16ths.

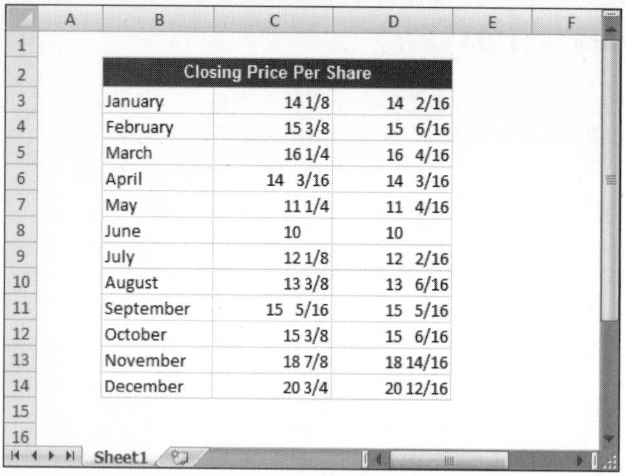

	A	B	C	D	E	F
1						
2		Closing Price Per Share				
3		January	14 1/8	14 2/16		
4		February	15 3/8	15 6/16		
5		March	16 1/4	16 4/16		
6		April	14 3/16	14 3/16		
7		May	11 1/4	11 4/16		
8		June	10	10		
9		July	12 1/8	12 2/16		
10		August	13 3/8	13 6/16		
11		September	15 5/16	15 5/16		
12		October	15 3/8	15 6/16		
13		November	18 7/8	18 14/16		
14		December	20 3/4	20 12/16		
15						
16						

Sheet1

Figure 34-2: Displaying values as fractions.

If none of the built-in Fraction number formats meets your needs, you might be able to cre-ate a custom number format. Press Ctrl+1, and in the Format Cells dialog box, click the Number tab. In the Category list, click Custom, and then enter a number format string in the Type field. For example, enter the following Number format string in the Type field to display a value in 32nds:

```
# ??/32
```

The following number format string displays a value in terms of fractional dollars. For example, the value 154.87 is displayed as 154 and 87/100 Dollars.

```
0 "and "??/100 "Dollars"
```

The following example displays the value in 16ths, with a quotation mark appended to the right. This format string is useful when you deal with inches (for example, $\frac{3}{16}$").

```
# ??/16\"
```

Resizing the Formula Bar

In previous versions of Excel, editing a cell that contains a lengthy formula or lots of text often obscures the worksheet. Figure 35-1 shows Excel 2003 when a cell that contains lengthy text is selected. Notice that many of the cells are covered up by the expanded formula bar. Excel 2007 finally addresses this problem, with a resizable formula bar.

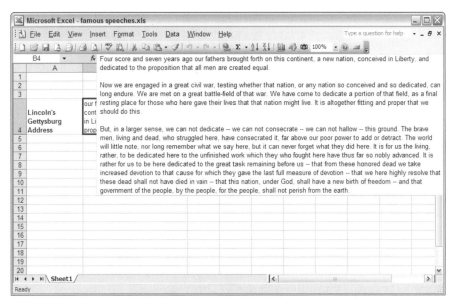

Figure 35-1: In previous versions, editing a lengthy formula or a cell that contains lots of text often obscures the worksheet.

The Excel 2007 formula bar displays a small vertical scroller on the right, but it might not be obvious that you can drag the bottom border of the formula bar to change its height. Figure 35-2 shows an example of the resized formula bar. As you can see, increasing the height of the formula bar doesn't obscure the information in the worksheet.

The ability to change the height of the formula bar is a relatively minor change, but it can be very helpful — if you know that it exists.

Excel 2007 also has a new shortcut key: Ctrl+Shift+U. Pressing this key combination toggles the height of the formula bar to show either one or two rows.

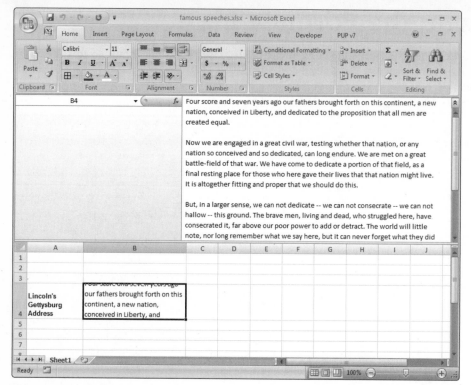

Figure 35-2: Changing the height of the formula bar makes it much easier to edit lengthy formulas, and you can still view all cells in your worksheet.

Proofing Your Data with Audio

Excel 2002 introduced a handy feature: text-to-speech. In other words, Excel is capable of speaking to you. You can have this feature read back a specific range of cells, or you can set it up so that it reads the data as you enter it.

In Excel 2007, however, this feature appears to be missing in action. You can search the ribbons all day and not find a trace of the text-to-speech feature. Fortunately, it's still available — you just need to spend a few minutes to make it available. To put the text-to-speech icons on your Quick Access Toolbar (QAT):

1. Right-click the Quick Access Toolbar, and then choose Customize Quick Access Toolbar from the shortcut menu. Excel displays the Customize tab of the Excel Options dialog box.

2. Click the drop-down list on the left, and choose Commands Not in the Ribbon.

3. Scroll down the list, and you find five items that begin with the word *Speak.* Select each one, and then click Add.

4. Click OK to close the Excel Options dialog box.

After you perform these steps, the Quick Access Toolbar displays five new icons.

To read a range of cells, select the range first and then click the Speak Cells button. You can also specify the orientation (By Rows or By Columns). To read the data as it's entered, click the Speak On Enter button.

Some people (myself included) find the voice in this "love it or hate it" feature much too annoying to use for any extended period. And, if you enter the data at a relatively rapid clip, the voice simply cannot keep up with you.

You have a small bit of control over the voice used in the Excel text-to-speech feature. To adjust the voice, open the Windows Control Panel and display the Speech Properties dialog box (see Figure 36-1). You can choose a different voice and also adjust the speed. Click the Preview Voice button to help make your choices.

Figure 36-1: Use the Speech Properties dialog box to adjust the voice.

Controlling Automatic Hyperlinks

One of the most common Excel questions is "How can I prevent Excel from creating automatic hyperlinks?"

Normally, Excel watches you type, and if it looks at all like you're typing an e-mail address or a Web URL, the entry is converted into a hyperlink. Sometimes that capability is helpful, but sometimes it's not. For example, if you enter `Meeting@4:00 pm` into a cell, Excel erroneously considers that bit of text to be an e-mail address and dutifully creates a hyperlink.

Overriding an Automatic Hyperlink

To override a single automatic hyperlink, just click Undo (or press Ctrl+Z). The hyperlink disappears, but the text you entered remains intact. Another option is to precede the entry with an apostrophe so that it's evaluated as plain text.

Turning Off Automatic Hyperlinks

If you never want to create automatic hyperlinks, here's how to turn off this feature (it's not exactly intuitive):

1. Choose Office ⇨ Excel Options to display the Excel Options dialog box.

2. Click the Proofing tab.

3. Click the AutoCorrect Options button to display the AutoCorrect dialog box (see Figure 37-1).

Figure 37-1: Use the AutoCorrect dialog box to turn off automatic hyperlinks.

Part II

4. Click the AutoFormat As You Type tab, and deselect the Internet and Network Paths with Hyperlinks check box.

Removing an Existing Hyperlink

To remove a hyperlink from a cell (but keep the cell's contents), right-click the cell and choose Remove Hyperlink from the shortcut menu.

Note that the Remove Hyperlink shortcut menu item appears only when a single cell is selected. Amazingly, Excel provides no direct way to remove hyperlinks from more than one cell at a time.

Removing Hyperlinks by Using VBA

To quickly remove all hyperlinks on a worksheet, you can use a simple VBA statement. The following instructions use the Immediate window in the VBA Editor, so the macro isn't stored in your workbook.

1. Activate the worksheet that contains the hyperlinks to be deleted.

2. Press Alt+F11 to activate the VBA Editor.

3. In the VBA Editor, choose View ⇨ Immediate Window (or press Ctrl+G).

4. Type this command in the Immediate Window (and then press Enter):

```
Cells.Hyperlinks.Delete
```

Entering Credit Card Numbers

If you've ever tried to enter a 16-digit credit card number into a cell, you might have discovered that Excel always changes the last digit to a zero. Why? The reason is that Excel can handle only 15 digits of numerical accuracy.

If you need to store credit card numbers in a worksheet, you have two options:

- Precede the credit card number with an apostrophe. Excel then interprets the data as a text string rather than as a number.

- Preformat the cell or range by using the Text number format. Select the range, choose Home ➪ Number, and then select Text from the Number Format drop-down control.

This tip, of course, also applies to other long numbers (such as part numbers) that aren't used in numeric calculations.

Part II

Using the Excel Built-In Data Entry Form

When entering data into an Excel list, some people prefer to use a dialog box — also known as the Excel data entry form. Before you can use this form, you have to set up the column headers in your worksheet. You might or might not have some data below the column headers. Alternatively, you can designate the data range as a table, by choosing Insert ⇨ Tables ⇨ Table.

To be able to use the data entry form in Excel 2007, you need to do a bit of prep work because the Data Form command doesn't appear on the Ribbon. Here's how to add the command to the Quick Access Toolbar (QAT):

1. Right-click the Quick Access Toolbar and choose Customize Quick Access Toolbar from the shortcut menu. Excel displays the Customize tab of the Excel Options dialog box.

2. In the drop-down list on the left, choose Commands Not in the Ribbon.

3. In the list box on the left, choose Form, and then click the Add button.

4. Click OK to close the Excel Options dialog box.

After you perform these steps, your QAT includes a new icon that, when clicked, displays the data entry form.

Activate any cell within your list and choose the Form command from your QAT. You see a dialog box similar to the one shown in Figure 39-1. (The fields shown in the dialog box vary, depending on your column headers.)

Figure 39-1: The Excel data entry form.

NOTE

If the number of columns in your list exceeds the limit of your display, the dialog box contains two columns of field names. If your list consists of more than 32 columns, however, the Form command doesn't work. You must forgo this method of data entry and enter the information directly into the cells.

When the Data Form dialog box appears, the first record (if any) in the list is displayed. Notice the indicator in the upper right corner of the dialog box; this indicator tells you which record is selected and the total number of records in the list.

To enter a new record, click the New button to clear the fields. Then you can enter the new information into the appropriate fields. Press Tab or Shift+Tab to move among the fields. When you click the New (or Close) button, the data that you entered is appended to the bottom of the list. You also can press Enter, which is equivalent to clicking the New button. If your list contains any formulas, they're also entered automatically into the new record in the list for you.

NOTE

If your list is named Database, Excel automatically extends the range definition to include the new row or rows that you add to the list by using the Data Form dialog box. Note that this method works only if the list has the name Database; no other name works. Use the Formulas ⇨ Define Names ⇨ Define Name command to name the range. If your list is in a table (created using Insert ⇨ Tables ⇨ Table), the table will be expanded automatically when you add new data.

You can use the Data Form dialog box for more than just data entry. You can edit existing data in the list, view data one record at a time, delete records, and display records that meet certain criteria.

The dialog box contains a number of additional buttons:

- **Delete:** Deletes the displayed record.

- **Restore:** Restores any information that you edited. You must click this button before you click the New button.

- **Find Prev:** Displays the previous record in the list. If you entered a criterion, this button displays the previous record that matches the criterion.

- **Find Next:** Displays the next record in the list. If you entered a criterion, this button displays the next record that matches the criterion.

- **Criteria:** Clears the fields and lets you enter a criterion on which to search for records. For example, to locate records that have a salary greater than $50,000, enter **>50000** into the Salary field. Then you can use the Find Next and Find Prev buttons to display the qualifying records.

- **Close:** Closes the dialog box (and enters any data that you were entering).

Part II

NOTE

If you like the idea of using a data entry dialog box — but don't care much for the Excel implementation — try out my Enhanced Data Form. This add-in, which provides a much more versatile data entry form, is available for downloading at my Web site:

`http://j-walk.com/ss.`

Customizing and Sharing AutoCorrect Entries

Most users have encountered the Excel AutoCorrect feature — often accidentally. For example, if you enter (c) into a cell, Excel automatically "corrects" it by substituting a copyright symbol ©. Excel also corrects some spelling errors, and other common mistakes, such as starting a word with two initial uppercase letters.

NOTE

To override an AutoCorrection, press Ctrl+Z while you're entering information into the cell. For example, if you need to enter (c) rather than a copyright symbol, type a space after the (c). Excel makes the autocorrection, but you can override it by pressing Ctrl+Z. If you press Ctrl+Z after you make the cell entry, the entire contents of the cell are deleted.

Fortunately, the AutoCorrect feature is highly customizable, and you can turn it off completely if you find it annoying. You might find it worth the effort to spend some time configuring AutoCorrect so that it works best for you. Figure 40-1 shows the AutoCorrect dialog box. To display this dialog box, choose Office ⇨ Excel Options. Click the Proofing tab and then click the AutoCorrect Options button. Or, just press Alt+T,A.

Figure 40-1: Use the AutoCorrect dialog box to customize the Excel AutoCorrect settings.

To add an AutoCorrect shortcut, type the shortcut text in the Replace field (for example, **msft**), and type the text that it will expand to in the With field (for example, **Microsoft Corporation**). To remove an existing shortcut, locate it in the list and click the Delete button.

Part II

The AutoCorrect shortcuts that you create in Excel are used in other Microsoft Office applications (and vice versa). The shortcut definitions are stored in the file named *.acl. Its location varies, and its exact name depends on the language version of Office. If you use the U.S. English language version of Office, the file is named mso1033.acl and the location is probably

```
C:\Documents and Settings\<username>\Application Data\Microsoft\Office
```

If you create some custom AutoCorrect shortcuts that you want to share with a colleague, you just make a copy of your *.acl file and place it in her directory. Be aware that replacing the *.acl file wipes out any custom AutoCorrect shortcuts that your colleague might have created. You have no way to merge two *.acl files.

Restricting Cursor Movement to Input Cells

A common type of worksheet uses two types of cells: input cells and formula cells. The user enters data into the input cells, and the formulas calculate and display the results.

Figure 41-1 shows a simple example. The input cells are in the range C4:C7. These cells are used by the formulas in C10:C13. To prevent the user from accidentally typing over formula cells, it's useful to limit the cursor movement so that the formula cells can't even be selected.

	A	B	C	D	E	F	G
1		Mortgage Loan Worksheet					
2							
3		Input Cells					
4		Purchase Price:	$325,000				
5		Down Payment:	10%				
6		Loan Term (Months):	360				
7		Interest Rate (APR):	6.50%				
8							
9		Result Cells					
10		Loan Amount:	$292,500				
11		Monthly Payment:	$2,054				
12		Total Payments:	$739,520				
13		Total Interest:	$447,020				
14							
15							

Sheet1

Figure 41-1: This worksheet has input cells at the top and formula cells below.

Part II

Setting up this sort of arrangement is a two-step process: Unlock the input cells, and then protect the sheet. The following specific instructions are for the example shown in the figure:

1. Select C4:C7.

2. Press Ctrl+1 to display the Format Cells dialog box.

3. In the Format Cells dialog box, click the Protection tab and deselect the Locked check box. (By default, all cells are locked.) Click OK.

4. Choose Review ➪ Changes ➪ Protect Sheet.

5. In the Protect Sheet dialog box, deselect the Select Locked Cells check box, and make sure that the Select Unlocked Cells check box is selected.

6. If you want, specify a password that will be required to unprotect the sheet.

7. Click OK.

After you perform these steps, only the unlocked cells can be selected. If you need to make any changes to your worksheet, you need to unprotect the sheet first, by choosing Review ⇨ Changes ⇨ Unprotect Sheet.

Although this example used a contiguous range of cells for the input, that isn't necessary for the steps to work. The input cells can be scattered throughout your worksheet.

 NOTE

Protecting a worksheet with a password isn't a security feature. This type of password is easily cracked.

Controlling the Office Clipboard

You're undoubtedly familiar with the Windows Clipboard. When you copy (or cut) something (such as text or a graph), the information is stored on the Clipboard. Then the information can be pasted somewhere else.

In Office 2000, Microsoft introduced the Office Clipboard. Why another Clipboard? The simple answer is because the Office Clipboard is more versatile than the Windows Clipboard. It enables you to store as many as 24 copied items. The Windows Clipboard, on the other hand, can hold only a single item. When you copy or cut something, the previous Windows Clipboard contents are wiped out. The downside to the Office Clipboard is that it works only in Microsoft Office applications (Word, Excel, PowerPoint, Access, and Outlook).

If the Office Clipboard doesn't seem to be working, you can display it by clicking the dialog box launcher in the Home ➪ Clipboard group. The dialog box launcher is the smaller icon to the right of the Clipboard group name. Clicking this dialog box launcher toggles the display of the Office Clipboard.

Every time you copy (or cut) something, the Office Clipboard displays a portion of the information (see Figure 42-1). After you stored 24 items, newly added items replace older items. To paste the information, just select the paste location and click the item in the Office Clipboard.

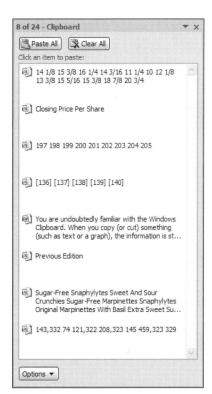

Figure 42-1: The Office Clipboard can store up to 24 items.

Part II

CAUTION

For Excel users, the Office Clipboard has a serious limitation that makes it almost worthless: It cannot hold formulas! If you copy a range of formulas to the Office Clipboard and then paste the data elsewhere, you find that the formula results (not the formulas themselves) are pasted. In a few situations, this behavior can be advantageous. In the vast majority of cases, you want to copy and paste formulas, not their values.

Although the Office Clipboard can be useful, a significant number of users find it annoying. To control some aspects of the Office Clipboard, click the Options button at the bottom of the Clipboard task pane (see Figure 42-2). Normally, the Office Clipboard is displayed automatically whenever you copy two pieces of information. To prevent this from happening, deselect the Show Office Clipboard Automatically check box.

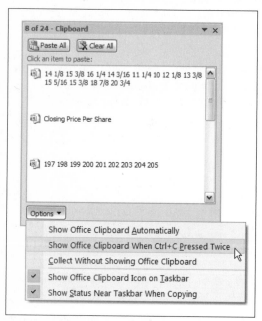

Figure 42-2: Options available for the Office Clipboard.

Creating a Drop-Down List in a Cell

Most Excel users probably believe that some type of VBA macro is required in order to display a drop-down list in a cell. You can easily display a drop-down list in a cell — and macros are *not* required.

Figure 43-1 shows an example. Cell B2, when selected, displays a down arrow. Click the arrow, and you get a list of items (in this case, month names). Click an item, and it appears in the cell. The drop-down list can contain text, numeric values, or dates. Your formulas, of course, can refer to cells that contain a drop-down list. The formulas always use the value that's displayed.

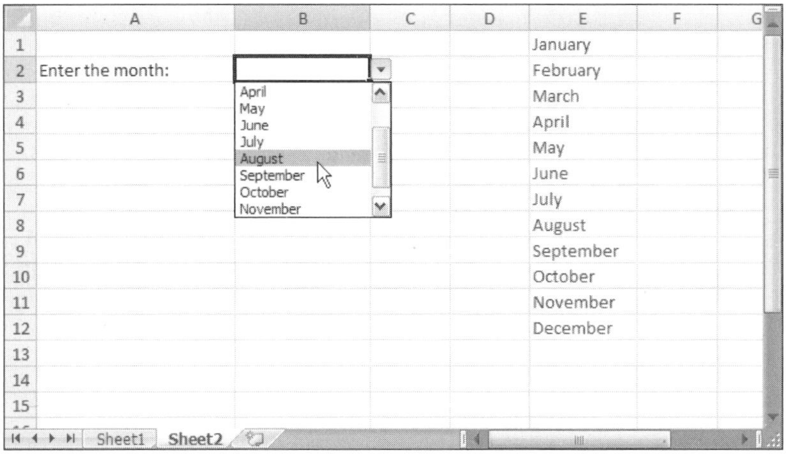

Figure 43-1: Creating a drop-down list in a cell is easy and doesn't require macros.

The trick to setting up a drop-down list is to use data validation. The following steps describe how to create a drop-down list of items in a cell:

1. Enter the list of items in a range. In this example, the month names are in the range E1:E12.

2. Select the cell that will contain the drop-down list (cell B2, in this example).

3. Choose Data ⇨ Data Tools ⇨ Data Validation.

4. In the Data Validation dialog box, click the Settings tab.

5. In the Allow drop-down list, select List.

6. In the Source box, specify the range that contains the items. In this example, the range is E1:E12.

7. Make sure that the In-Cell Dropdown option is checked (see Figure 43-2), and click OK.

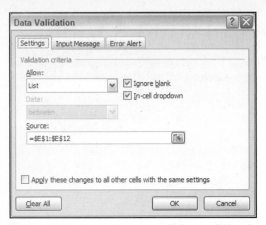

Figure 43-2: Using the Data Validation dialog box to create a drop-down list.

If your list is short, you can avoid Step 1. Rather, just type your list items (separated by commas) in the Source box in the Data Validation dialog box.

Normally, the list of items must be on the same worksheet as the cell that contains the drop-down list. You can get around this limitation if you provide a name for the range that contains the list. For example, you can choose Formulas ⇨ Defined Names ⇨ Define Name to define the name MonthNames for E1:E12. Then, in the Data Validation dialog box, enter **=MonthNames** in the Source box.

Part

Formatting

Excel has lots of formatting options to make your work look good. In this part, you'll find tips that cover formatting numbers, dates, times, text, and many other aspects of Excel.

Tips and Where to Find Them

Quick Number Formatting

As you probably know, a value in a cell can be displayed in many different ways. Excel provides a few common number-formatting options in the Home ⇨ Number group of the Ribbon. For complete control over number formatting, press Ctrl+1 to display the Format Cells dialog box, and then click the Number tab.

Many common number formats can be applied without using the Format Cells dialog box. If you use any of these number formats regularly, you can save some time by using the keyboard shortcuts shown in Table 44-1. Note that, on most keyboards, the third key in these Ctrl+Shift shortcuts is located on the top row of your keyboard.

TABLE 44-1   SHORTCUT KEYS TO APPLY NUMBER FORMATTING

Shortcut Keys	Format That the Shortcut Applies
Ctrl+Shift+` (the accent/tilde key above Tab)	General number format (removes any other number formatting)
Ctrl+Shift+1	Number format with two decimal places, thousands separator, and minus sign (–) for negative values
Ctrl+Shift+2	Time format with the hour and minute and AM or PM
Ctrl+Shift+3	Date format with the day, month, and year
Ctrl+Shift+4	Currency format with two decimal places (and negative numbers displayed in parentheses)
Ctrl+Shift+5	Percentage format with no decimal places
Ctrl+Shift+6	Exponential Number format with two decimal places

Part III

Using the Mini Toolbar

One of the new user interface elements in Excel 2007 is the *Mini toolbar.* This little pop-up toolbar appears whenever you right-click an object (a range of cells, a chart legend, or a shape, for example). The Mini toolbar appears above the shortcut menu and contains icons that are normally found on the Home tab (see Figure 45-1). Using the Mini toolbar is especially useful if you need to apply some formatting and the Home tab isn't selected.

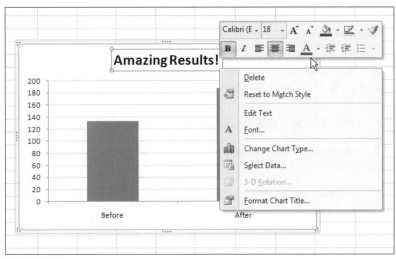

Figure 45-1: A Mini toolbar appears above the shortcut menu whenever you right-click an object.

NOTE

The Mini toolbar is a mouse-only user interface element. You cannot use any of the Mini toolbar commands from the keyboard.

The icons displayed on the Mini toolbar vary a bit, depending on the element that's selected. And, if you right-click an object that cannot display text (for example, a column in a chart), the Mini toolbar doesn't even appear. In Word 2007, the Mini toolbar is available when you make a selection (right-click not required) and is semitransparent, becoming less transparent when you move your mouse toward it. This type of behavior doesn't occur in Excel.

The main problem with the Mini toolbar is remembering to use it. When I first started using Excel 2007, I tended to just ignore the Mini toolbar. But after I got in the habit of using it, I realized that it really is a convenient feature. If you disagree, and want to prevent the Mini toolbar from appearing, open the Excel Options dialog box (choose Office ⇨ Excel Options), click the Popular tab, and remove the check mark from the Show Mini Toolbar on Selection option.

By the way, if you want to customize the Mini toolbar by adding new commands, you're out of luck. You cannot modify the Mini toolbar. What you see is what you get.

Finally, a bit of trivia. When Office 2007 was being developed, the original term for Mini toolbars was *floaties*. That term still survives in the Excel object model. The VBA statement to turn off the Mini toolbar display is

```
Application.ShowSelectionFloaties = False
```

Creating Custom Number Formats

Although Excel provides a good variety of built-in number formats, you might find that none of them suits your needs. In such a case, you can probably create a custom number format. You do this on the Number tab of the Format Cells dialog box (see Figure 46-1). The easiest way to display this dialog box is to press Ctrl+1. Or, click the dialog box launcher in the Home ⇨ Number group. (The dialog box launcher is the small icon to the right of the word *Number.*)

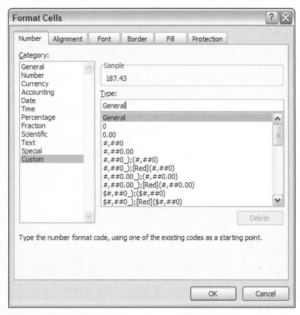

Figure 46-1: Create custom number formats on the Number tab of the Format Cells dialog box.

Many Excel users — even advanced users — avoid creating custom number formats because they think that the process is too complicated. In reality, custom number formats tend to *look* more complex than they are.

You construct a number format by specifying a series of codes as a number format string. To enter a custom number format, follow these steps:

1. Press Ctrl+1 to display the Format Cells dialog box.

2. Click the Number tab and select the Custom category.

3. Enter your custom number format in the Type field.

   See Tables 46-1 and 46-2 for examples of codes you can use to create your own, custom number formats.

4. Click OK to close the Format Cells dialog box.

Parts of a Number Format String

A custom format string enables you to specify different format codes for four categories of values: positive numbers, negative numbers, zero values, and text. You do so by separating the codes for each category with a semicolon. The codes are arranged in four sections, separated by semicolons:

```
Positive format; Negative format; Zero format; Text format
```

The following general guidelines determine how many of these four sections you need to specify:

- If your custom format string uses only one section, the format string applies to all values.
- If you use two sections, the first section applies to positive values and zeros, and the second section applies to negative values.
- If you use three sections, the first section applies to positive values, the second section applies to negative values, and the third section applies to zeros.
- If you use all four sections, the last section applies to text stored in the cell.

The following example of a custom number format specifies a different format for each of these types:

```
[Green]General;[Red]-General;[Black]General;[Blue]General
```

This example takes advantage of the fact that colors have special codes. A cell formatted with this custom number format displays its contents in a different color, depending on the value. When a cell is formatted with this custom number format, a positive number is green, a negative number is red, a zero is black, and text is blue. By the way, using the Excel conditional formatting feature is a much better way to apply color to cells based on their content.

 NOTE

When you create a custom number format, don't overlook the Sample box in the Number tab of the Format Cells dialog box. This box displays the value in the active cell by using the format string in the Type field. Be sure to test your custom number formats by using the following data: a positive value, a negative value, a zero value, and text. Often, creating a custom number format takes several attempts. Each time you edit a format string, it's added to the list. When you finally get the correct format string, open the Format Cells dialog box one more time and delete your previous attempts.

Custom Number Format Codes

Table 46-1 briefly describes the formatting codes available for custom formats.

TABLE 46-1 CODES USED TO CREATE CUSTOM NUMBER FORMATS

Code	What It Does
General	Displays the number in General format
#	Serves as a digit placeholder that displays only significant digits and does not display insignificant zeros
0 (zero)	Serves as a digit placeholder that displays insignificant zeros if a number has fewer digits than there are zeros in the format
?	Serves as a digit placeholder that adds spaces for insignificant zeros on either side of the decimal point so that decimal points align when formatted with a fixed-width font; also used for fractions that have varying numbers of digits
.	Displays the decimal point
%	Displays a percentage
,	Displays the thousands separator
E- E+ e- e+	Displays scientific notation
$ – + / ( ) : space	Displays this character
\	Displays the next character in the format
*	Repeats the next character to fill the column width
_ (underscore)	Leaves a space equal to the width of the next character
"text"	Displays the text inside the double quotation marks
@	Serves as a text placeholder
[color]	Displays the characters in the specified color and can be any of the following text strings (not case sensitive): Black, Blue, Cyan, Green, Magenta, Red, White, or Yellow
[COLOR n]	Displays the corresponding color in the color palette, where n is a number from 0 to 56
[condition value]	Enables you to set your own criteria for each section of a number format

Table 46-2 describes the codes used to create custom formats for dates and times.

TABLE 46-2 CODES USED IN CREATING CUSTOM FORMATS FOR DATES AND TIMES

Code	What It Displays
m	The month as a number without leading zeros (1–12)
mm	The month as a number with leading zeros (01–12)
mmm	The month as an abbreviation (Jan–Dec)
mmmm	The month as a full name (January–December)
mmmmm	The first letter of the month (J–D)
d	The day as a number without leading zeros (1–31)
dd	The day as a number with leading zeros (01–31)
ddd	The day as an abbreviation (Sun–Sat)
dddd	The day as a full name (Sunday–Saturday)
yy or yyyy	The year as a two-digit number (00–99) or as a four-digit number (1900–9999)
h or hh	The hour as a number without leading zeros (0–23) or as a number with leading zeros (00–23)
m or mm	The minute as a number without leading zeros (0–59) or as a number with leading zeros (00–59)
s or ss	The second as a number without leading zeros (0–59) or as a number with leading zeros (00–59)
[ ]	Hours greater than 24 or minutes or seconds greater than 60
AM/PM	The hour using a 12-hour clock, or no AM/PM indicator if the hour uses a 24-hour clock

CROSS-REFERENCE

For more tips that deal with custom number formatting, see Tip 47, Tip 48, and Tip 49.

Part III

Using Custom Number Formats to Scale Values

If you deal with large numbers, you might prefer to display them scaled to thousands or millions rather than display the entire number. For example, you may want to display a number like 132,432,145 in millions: 132.4.

The way to display scaled numbers is to use a custom number format. The actual number, of course, will be used in calculations that involve that cell. The formatting affects only how the number is displayed. To enter a custom number format, press Ctrl+1 to display the Format Cells dialog box. Then click the Number tab and select the Custom category. Put your custom number format in the Type field.

Table 47-1 shows examples of number formats that scale values in millions.

TABLE 47-1   EXAMPLES OF DISPLAYING VALUES IN MILLIONS

Value	Number Format	Display
123456789	#,###,,	123
1.23457E+11	#,###,,	123,457
1000000	#,###,,	1
5000000	#,###,,	5
−5000000	#,###,,	−5
0	#,###,,	(blank)
123456789	#,###.00,,	123.46
1.23457E+11	#,###.00,,	123,457.00
1000000	#,###.00,,	1.00
5000000	#,###.00,,	5.00
−5000000	#,###.00,,	−5.00
0	#,###.00,,	.00
123456789	#,###,,"M"	123M
1.23457E+11	#,###,,"M"	123,457M
1000000	#,###,,"M"	1M
−5000000	#,###,,"M"	−5M
123456789	#,###.0,,"M"_);(#,###.0,,"M)";0.0"M"_)	123.5M
1000000	#,###.0,,"M"_);(#,###.0,,"M)";0.0"M"_)	1.0M

Value	Number Format	Display
−5000000	#,###.0,,"M"_);(#,###.0,,"M)";0.0"M"_)	(5.0M)
0	#,###.0,,"M"_);(#,###.0,,"M)";0.0"M"_)	0.0M

Table 47-2 shows examples of number formats that scale values in thousands.

TABLE 47-2   EXAMPLES OF DISPLAYING VALUES IN THOUSANDS

Value	Number Format	Display
123456	#,###,	123
1234565	#,###,	1,235
−323434	#,###,	−323
123123.123	#,###,	123
499	#,###,	(blank)
500	#,###,	1
500	#,###.00,	.50

Table 47-3 shows examples of number formats that display values in hundreds.

TABLE 47-3   EXAMPLES OF DISPLAYING VALUES IN HUNDREDS

Value	Number Format	Display
546	0"."00	5.46
100	0"."00	1.00
9890	0"."00	98.90
500	0"."00	5.00
−500	0"."00	−5.00
0	0"."00	0.00

Part III

Using Custom Date and Time Formatting

When you enter a date into a cell, Excel formats the date by using the system short-date format. You can change this format by opening the Windows Control Panel and selecting Regional Settings.

Excel provides many useful built-in date and time formats, accessible in the Date and Time categories on the Number tab of the Format Cells dialog box. Table 48-1 shows some other date and time formats that you might find useful. The Value column in the table shows the date-and-time serial number.

TABLE 48-1   EXAMPLES OF TIME AND DATE NUMBER FORMATS

Value	Number Format	Display
39598	mmmm d, yyyy (dddd)	May 30, 2008 (Friday)
39598	"It's" dddd!	It's Friday!
39598	dddd, mm/dd/yyyy	Friday, 05/30/2008
39598	"Month: "mmm	Month: May
39598	General (m/d/yyyy)	39598 (5/30/2008)
0.345	h "Hours"	8 Hours
0.345	h:mm o'clock	8:16 o'clock
0.345	h:mm a/p"m"	8:16 am
0.345	h "hours and" m "minutes"	8 hours and 16 minutes
0.78	h:mm a/p".m."	6:43 p.m.

Examining Some Useful Custom Number Formats

This tip provides some useful examples of custom number formats.

CROSS-REFERENCE

See Tip 46 for the steps to enter a custom number format in the Format Cells dialog box as well as a list of the number format codes.

Hiding Zeros

In the following number format string, the third element of the string is empty, which causes zero value cells to be displayed as blank:

```
General;General;;@
```

This format string uses the General format for positive and negative values. You can, of course, substitute any other format codes.

Displaying Leading Zeros

To display leading zeros, create a custom number format that uses the 0 character. For example, if you want all numbers to be displayed with ten digits, use the following number format string; values with fewer than ten digits are displayed with leading zeros:

```
0000000000
```

In the following example, the format string uses the repeat-character code (an asterisk) to apply leading zeros to fill the entire width of the cell:

```
*00
```

Two zeros are required because the first one represents the character to be repeated, and the second one represents the value to be displayed.

Formatting Percentages

Using a percent symbol (%) in a format string displays the cell in Percentage format. Note that the percent sign also appears on the formula bar.

The following format string formats values less than or equal to 1 in Percentage format (values greater than 1 and text are formatted using the General format):

```
[<=1]0.00%;General
```

Part III

When you mix cells with Percentage and General formatting in a column, you might prefer to see the nonpercent values indented from the right so that the values line up properly. To do so, apply the following number format to nonpercent cells. This format string uses an underscore followed by the percent symbol. The result is a space equal to the width of the percent symbol:

```
#.00_%
```

Displaying Fractions

Excel supports quite a few built-in fraction number formats. (Select the Fraction category from the Number tab of the Format Cells dialog box to see available formats.) For example, to display the value .125 as a fraction with 8 as the denominator, select As Eighths (⅛) from the Type list.

You can use a custom format string to create other fraction formats. For example, the following format string displays a value in 50ths:

```
# ??/50
```

The following format string displays a value in terms of fractional dollars. For example, the value 154.87 is displayed as 154 and 87/100 Dollars:

```
0 "and "??/100 "Dollars"
```

The following example displays the value in sixteenths, with a quotation mark appended to the right. This format string is useful when you deal with inches (for example, ³⁄₁₆").

```
# ??/16\"
```

Repeating Text

The number format string displays the contents of the cell three times. For example, if the cell contains the text *Budget,* the cell displays Budget Budget Budget:

```
;;;@ @ @
```

Displaying a Negative Sign on the Right

The following format string displays negative values with the negative sign to the right of the number. Positive values have an additional space on the right, so both positive and negative numbers align properly on the right:

```
0.00_-;0.00-
```

Formatting Based on the Cell's Value

Conditional formatting refers to formatting that is applied based on the contents of a cell. The Excel Conditional Formatting feature provides the most efficient way to perform conditional formatting, but you also can use custom number formats. Keep in mind that this type of number formatting has nothing to do with the Excel Conditional Formatting feature.

 NOTE

Conditional number formatting is limited to three conditions — two of them explicit and the third one implied (that is, everything else). The conditions are enclosed in square brackets and must be simple numeric comparisons.

The following format string uses a different format, depending on the value in the cell. This format string essentially separates the numbers into three groups: less than or equal to 4, greater than or equal to 8, and other:

```
[<=4]"Low"* 0;[>=8]"High"* 0;"Medium"* 0
```

The following number format string displays values less than 1 with a cent symbol on the right (for example, .54¢). Otherwise, values are displayed with a dollar sign (for example, $3.54). Notice, however, that the decimal point is present when the value is displayed with a cent symbol. I'm not aware of any way to eliminate the decimal point.

```
[<1].00¢;$0.00_¢
```

The following number format is useful for telephone numbers. Values greater than 9999999 (that is, numbers with area codes) are displayed as (xxx) xxx-xxxx. Other values (numbers without area codes) are displayed as xxx-xxxx.

```
[>9999999](000) 000-0000;000-0000
```

For zip codes, you might want to use the following format string. It displays zip codes by using five digits. But if the number is greater than 99999, it uses the ZIP+4 format (xxxxx-xxxx).

```
[>99999]00000-0000;00000
```

Coloring Values

Custom number format strings can display the cell contents in various colors. The following format string, for example, displays positive numbers in red, negative numbers in green, zero values in black, and text in blue:

```
[Red]General;[Green]-General;[Black]General;[Blue]General
```

Part III

The following example shows another format string that uses colors. Positive values are displayed normally; negative numbers and text cause Error! to be displayed in red.

```
General;[Red]"Error!";0;[Red]"Error!"
```

Using the following format string, values that are less than 2 are displayed in red. Values greater than 4 are displayed in green. Everything else (text or values between 2 and 4) is displayed in black.

```
[Red][<2]General;[Green][>4]General;[Black]General
```

As shown in the preceding examples, Excel recognizes color names such as [Red] and [Blue]. It also can use other colors from the color palette, indexed by a number. The following format string, for example, displays the cell contents by using the sixteenth color in the color palette:

```
[Color16]General
```

NOTE

You cannot use normal cell formatting commands to change the text color of cells that have been colored by a number format string.

Suppressing Certain Types of Entries

You can use number formatting to hide certain types of entries. For example, the following format string displays text but not values:

```
;;
```

This format string displays values (with one decimal place) but not text or zeros:

```
0.0;-0.0;;
```

This format string displays everything except zeros (values are displayed with one decimal place):

```
0.0;-0.0;;@
```

You can use the following format string to completely hide the contents of a cell:

```
;;;
```

Note that when the cell is activated, however, the cell's contents are visible on the formula bar.

Updating Old Fonts

When you install Office 2007, several new fonts are added to your system, and these new fonts are used when you create a new workbook. The exact fonts that are used as defaults vary, depending on which document theme is in effect.

CROSS-REFERENCE

See Tip 13 for more information about using document themes.

If you use the default Office theme, a newly created Excel 2007 workbook uses two new fonts: Cambria (for headings) and Calibri (for body text). When you open a workbook that was saved in a previous version of Excel, the old fonts are not updated. The difference in appearance between a worksheet that uses the old fonts and a worksheet that uses the new fonts is dramatic. When you compare an Excel 2003 worksheet with an Excel 2007 worksheet, the latter is much more readable and seems less cramped.

To update the fonts in a workbook that was created in a previous version of Excel, follow these steps:

1. Press Ctrl+N to create a new, blank workbook.

2. Activate the workbook whose fonts will be updated.

3. Choose Home ⇨ Styles, and click the bottom arrow of the scroller on the right side of the Style Gallery. When the gallery expands, choose Merge Styles.

4. In the Merge Styles dialog box, select the workbook that you created in Step 1, and click OK.

5. Excel asks whether you want to merge styles that have the same names. Reply by clicking the Yes button.

This procedure works with all cells except those that have additional formatting, such as a different font size, bold, italic, colored text, or a shaded background. To change the font in these cells, follow these steps:

1. Select any single cell.

2. Choose Home ⇨ Editing ⇨ Find & Select ⇨ Replace to display the Find and Replace dialog box. Or, press Ctrl+H.

3. Make sure that the Find What and Replace With boxes are empty.

4. Click the upper Format button to display the Find Format dialog box.

5. Click the Font tab. In the Font list, select the name of the font that you're replacing (probably Arial), and then click OK to close the Find Format dialog box.

Part III

6. Click the lower Format button to display the Replace Format dialog box.

7. Click the Font tab. In the Font list, select the name of the font that will replace the old font (probably Calibri), and then click OK to close the Replace Format dialog box.

8. In the Find and Replace dialog box, click Replace All to replace the old font with the new font.

Understanding the New Conditional Formatting Features

Conditional formatting enables you to apply cell formatting selectively and automatically, based on the contents of the cells. For example, you can specify that all negative values in a range have a light yellow background color. When you enter or change a value in the range, Excel examines the value and checks the conditional formatting rules for the cell. If the value is negative, the background is shaded. If not, no formatting is applied.

Looking at What's New with Conditional Formatting

Excel 2007 includes some significant enhancements to the conditional formatting feature:

- Many conditional formatting rules that previously required a formula are now built in.

- In the past, it was far too easy to accidentally wipe out conditional formatting by copying and pasting a range of cells to cells that contain conditional formatting. This problem has been corrected in Excel 2007.

- You're no longer limited to using three conditional formatting rules per cell. In fact, you can specify any number of rules.

- In the past, if more than one conditional formatting rule evaluated to true, only the first conditional format was applied. In Excel 2007, all the format rules are applied. For example, you might have a cell with two rules: One rule makes the cell italic, and another rule makes the background color green. If both conditions are true, both formats are applied. When conflicts arise (for example, red background versus green background), the first rule is used.

- Excel 2007 allows number formatting to result from conditional formatting.

- In previous versions, a conditional formatting formula could not reference cells in a different worksheet. Excel 2007 removes that restriction.

Here's the most interesting change: Excel 2007 includes conditional formatting visualizations based on a range of data.

Part III

Visualizing Data with Conditional Formatting

In this section, I present a quick overview of the data-visualization conditional formatting features: data bars, color scales, and icon sets.

DATA BARS

Using the data bars conditional formatting can sometimes serve as a quick alternative to creating a chart. Figure 51-1 shows a two-column table of data (in the range B2:C14), with data bars applied in the second column. The figure also shows a bar chart created from the same data. The bar chart takes about the same amount of time to create and is a lot more flexible. For a quick and dirty chart, though, data bars are a good option — especially when you need to create several charts of this type.

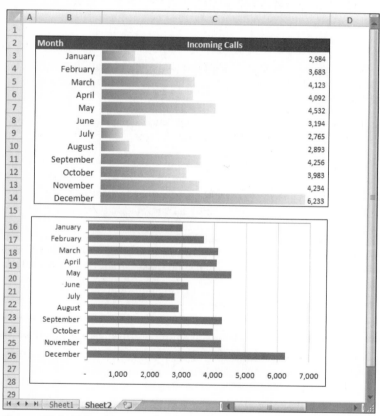

Figure 51-1: This table uses data bars conditional formatting.

COLOR SCALES

The color scale conditional formatting option varies the background color of a cell based on the cell's value, relative to other cells in the range. Figure 51-2 shows a range of cells that use color scale conditional formatting. The figure depicts the number of employees on each day of the year. This 3-color scale uses red for the lowest value, yellow for the midpoint, and green for the highest value. Values between those ranges are displayed by using a color within the gradient. The grayscale figure doesn't do justice to this example. The effect is much more impressive when you view it in color.

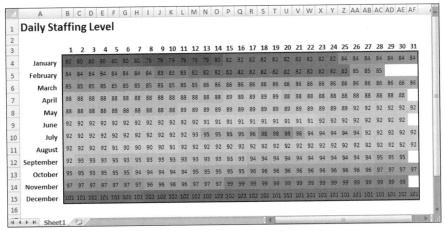

Figure 51-2: This range uses color scale conditional formatting.

ICON SETS

The third new conditional formatting option displays an icon in the cell. Which icon is displayed depends on the value of the cell, relative to other cells. Excel provides 17 icon sets to choose from (and you can't create your set of icons). The number of icons in the sets ranges from three to five.

Figure 51-3 shows an example that uses the icon set named 3 Arrows. The symbols graphically depict the change between two test scores. If the change is greater than or equal to five, an up arrow is displayed. If the change is less than –5, a down arrow is displayed. All other change vales are depicted by a right-pointing arrow.

Part III

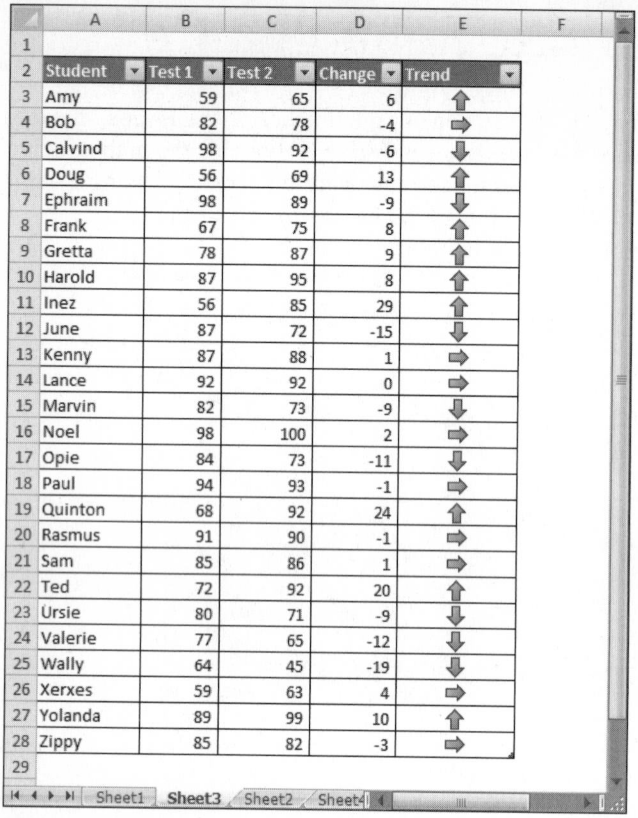

	A	B	C	D	E	F
1						
2	Student	Test 1	Test 2	Change	Trend	
3	Amy	59	65	6	⬆	
4	Bob	82	78	-4	➡	
5	Calvind	98	92	-6	⬇	
6	Doug	56	69	13	⬆	
7	Ephraim	98	89	-9	⬇	
8	Frank	67	75	8	⬆	
9	Gretta	78	87	9	⬆	
10	Harold	87	95	8	⬆	
11	Inez	56	85	29	⬆	
12	June	87	72	-15	⬇	
13	Kenny	87	88	1	➡	
14	Lance	92	92	0	➡	
15	Marvin	82	73	-9	⬇	
16	Noel	98	100	2	➡	
17	Opie	84	73	-11	⬇	
18	Paul	94	93	-1	➡	
19	Quinton	68	92	24	⬆	
20	Rasmus	91	90	-1	➡	
21	Sam	85	86	1	➡	
22	Ted	72	92	20	⬆	
23	Ursie	80	71	-9	⬇	
24	Valerie	77	65	-12	⬇	
25	Wally	64	45	-19	⬇	
26	Xerxes	59	63	4	➡	
27	Yolanda	89	99	10	⬆	
28	Zippy	85	82	-3	➡	
29						

Sheet1　**Sheet3**　Sheet2　Sheet4

Figure 51-3: This range uses an icon set.

Showing Text and a Value in a Cell

If you need to display a number and text in a single cell, Excel provides three options:

- Concatenation
- The TEXT function
- A custom number format

Assume that cell A1 contains a value, and in a cell somewhere else in your worksheet you want to display the word *Total:* along with that value. It looks something like this:

```
Total: 594.34
```

You could, of course, put the word *Total* in the cell to the left. This section describes the three methods for accomplishing this task using a single cell.

Using Concatenation

The following formula concatenates the text *Total:* with the value in cell A1:

```
="Total: "&A1
```

This solution is the simplest, but it has a problem. The result of the formula is text, so that cell cannot be used in a numeric formula.

Using the TEXT Function

Another solution uses the TEXT function, which displays a value by using a specified number format:

```
=TEXT(A1,"""Total: ""0.00")
```

The second argument for the TEXT function is a number format string — the same type of string that you use when you create a custom number format. Besides being a bit unwieldy (because of the extra quotation marks), this formula suffers from the same problem mentioned in the previous section: The result is not numeric.

Using a Custom Number Format

If you want to display text and a value — and still be able to use that value in a numeric formula — the solution is to use a custom number format.

To add text, just create the number format string as usual and put the text within quotation marks. For this example, the following custom number format does the job:

```
"Total: "0.00
```

Even though the cell displays text, Excel still considers the cell contents to be a numeric value.

Merging Cells

Merging cells is a simple concept: Join two or more cells into a single cell. To merge cells, just select them and click Home ➪ Alignment ➪ Merge & Center. Excel combines the selected cells and displays the contents of the upper left cell, centered.

Merging cells is usually done as a way to enhance the appearance of a worksheet. Figure 53-1, for example, shows a worksheet with four sets of merged cells: C2:I2, J2:P2, B4:B8, and B9:B13. The merged cells in column B also use vertical text.

		Week 1							Week 2						
		1	2	3	4	5	6	7	8	9	10	11	12	13	14
Group 1		64	68	23	61	87	71	55	75	21	22	71	95	20	25
		90	15	77	34	79	33	69	63	20	90	78	97	3	95
		49	41	17	66	68	45	87	22	46	5	83	62	30	81
		54	70	91	42	86	34	27	79	11	80	17	85	57	83
		28	7	68	54	29	91	49	50	79	53	92	25	75	27
Group 2		65	6	23	67	57	70	10	12	16	94	68	5	71	66
		63	16	24	47	77	15	68	96	29	24	2	78	95	79
		12	11	46	21	56	14	41	69	71	30	25	19	95	44
		18	14	58	39	58	17	46	5	68	74	60	97	61	14
		19	46	66	18	10	28	31	52	61	78	88	19	25	77

Figure 53-1: This worksheet has four sets of merged cells.

Remember that merged cells can contain only one piece of information: a single value, a chunk of text, or a formula. If you attempt to merge a range of cells that contains more than one non-empty cell, Excel prompts you with a warning that only the data in the upper-leftmost cell will be retained.

To unmerge cells, just select the merged area and click the Merge and Center button again.

Notice that the Merge and Center button is a drop-down menu. If you click the arrow, you see three additional commands:

- **Merge Across:** Lets you select a range and then creates multiple merged cells — one for each row in the selection.
- **Merge Cells:** Works just like Merge and Center, except that the content of the upper left cell is not centered. (It retains its original horizontal alignment.)
- **Unmerge Cells:** Unmerges the selected merged cell.

Part III

Formatting Individual Characters in a Cell

Excel cell formatting isn't an all-or-none proposition. In some cases, you might find it helpful to be able to format individual characters within a cell.

NOTE
This technique is limited to cells that contain text. It doesn't work if the cell contains a value or a formula.

To apply formatting to characters within a text string, select those characters first. You can select them by clicking and dragging your mouse on the formula bar. Or, double-click the cell and then click and drag the mouse to select specific characters directly in the cell. A more efficient way to select individual characters is to press F2 first and then use the arrow keys to move between characters and use the Shift+arrow keys to select characters.

When the characters are selected, use formatting controls to change the formatting. For example, you can make the selected text bold, italic, or a different color or even apply a different font. If you right-click, the Mini toolbar appears, and you can use those controls to change the formatting of the selected characters.

Figure 54-1 shows a few examples of cells that contain individual character formatting.

Figure 54-1: Examples of individual character formatting.

Unfortunately, two useful formatting attributes are not available on the Ribbon or on the Mini toolbar: superscript and subscript formatting. If you want to apply superscripts or subscripts, open the Font tab in the Format Cells dialog box. Just press Ctrl+1 after you select the text to format.

 NOTE

My Power Utility Pak add-in includes a handy tool that simplifies individual character formatting, including superscript and subscript formatting. You can use the coupon in the back of this book to order a discounted copy.

Part III

Displaying Times That Exceed 24 Hours

There's nothing really special about a time value. An Excel time value is a normal number that is formatted to display as a time. For example, 0 represents 12:00 a.m., 0.50 represents noon (halfway through the day), and 0.75 represents 6:00 p.m.

Because time values are numbers, you can add them together. Figure 55-1 shows a worksheet that sums several time values. The formula in cell B8 is a simple SUM formula:

```
=SUM(B3:B7)
```

	A	B	C
1			
2	Date	Hours Worked	
3	Jan 15	8:30	
4	Jan 16	4:00	
5	Jan 17	8:00	
6	Jan 18	6:30	
7	Jan 19	4:00	
8	Total	7:00	
9			
10			
11			

Sheet1 / Sheet2

Figure 55-1: Summing time values might not display the correct result.

As you can see, the formula is returning an incorrect result. Because a day has only 24 hours, Excel normally ignores hours that exceed 24 hours. To force Excel to display times that exceed 24 hours, you modify the number formatting.

In this example, Excel uses the following number format:

```
h:mm
```

To display the correct value, place square brackets around the h part:

```
[h]:mm
```

Figure 55-2 shows the worksheet after making this number format change.

	A	B	C
1			
2	Date	Hours Worked	
3	Jan 15	8:30	
4	Jan 16	4:00	
5	Jan 17	8:00	
6	Jan 18	6:30	
7	Jan 19	4:00	
8	Total	31:00	
9			
10			

Sheet1 Sheet2

Figure 55-2: Adjusting the number format causes the cell to display the correct value.

Fixing Non-Numeric Numbers

If you import data from other sources, you might have discovered that Excel sometimes does not import values correctly. Specifically, you might find that Excel is treating your numbers as text. For example, you might sum a range of values and find that the SUM formula returns 0 — even though the range apparently contains values.

To force Excel to change these non-numeric numbers to actual values, follow these steps:

1. Activate any empty cell on your worksheet.

2. Press Ctrl+C to copy the empty cell.

3. Select the range that contains the problematic values.

4. Choose Home ⇨ Clipboard ⇨ Paste Special to display the Paste Special dialog box.

5. In the Paste Special dialog box, select the Add operation.

6. Click OK.

Excel adds nothing to these values, but in the process it coerces those cells to be actual values.

Adding a Frame to a Range

Excel 2007 adds lots of new graphical formatting effects: shadows, glow, and reflection, for example. These effects apply only to graphical objects, such as pictures, shapes, and charts.

If you need to make a range of cells stand out, you can insert a shape to serve as a frame. The shape must be transparent (or semitransparent), but you can apply effects. Use the Insert ➪ Illustrations ➪ Shape command to add a shape to your worksheet.

Figure 57-1 shows an example of a range that has a transparent rectangular shape superimposed on top of it. I applied some bevel effects and a shadow to the shape to make it resemble a matted picture frame that's floating above the worksheet. The shape in the figure uses a thick compound line style, a beveled top, and a shadow.

Sales by Month			
	2005	2006	2007
January	9,734,332	12,522,502	14,245,218
February	10,226,605	13,314,689	15,064,235
March	10,793,048	14,142,956	14,451,391
April	11,023,358	13,462,616	14,359,866
May	11,273,246	13,680,815	14,225,800
June	11,114,539	14,422,329	14,818,541
July	11,528,714	13,823,182	15,257,542
August	11,315,482	14,344,295	14,915,996
September	12,110,386	14,174,612	15,814,095
October	11,531,682	13,957,137	15,298,068
November	12,286,175	13,286,430	15,165,121
December	12,537,364	13,933,378	15,674,083

Figure 57-1: A transparent shape on top of a range.

For maximum flexibility in formatting a shape, use the Format Shape dialog box rather than the Ribbon commands. To display this dialog box, select the shape and press Ctrl+1.

Part III

Dealing with Gridlines, Borders, and Underlines

If you need to draw attention to or delineate cells in a worksheet, one way to do it is with lines. Excel provides three options:

- Worksheet gridlines
- Cell borders
- Cell underlining

Worksheet gridlines is an all-or-none setting. Turn gridlines on or off for the active worksheet by using the View ➪ Show/Hide ➪ Gridlines check box. Normally, worksheet gridlines are not printed, but if you want the gridlines to appear on your printed output, use the Page Layout ➪ Sheet Options ➪ Gridlines Print check box.

Cell borders can be applied to individual cells or to a range of cells. The Borders control in the Home ➪ Font group provides the most common cell border options, but for complete control, use the Border tab of the Format Cells dialog box, which is shown in Figure 58-1. (Press Ctrl+1 to display the Format Cells dialog box.) This dialog box gives you control over border color, line style, and location (for example, horizontal borders only) and works with the selected cell or range.

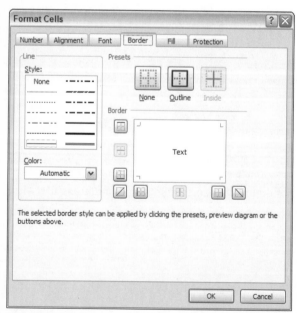

Figure 58-1: For optimal control over cell borders, use the Format Cells dialog box.

Cell underlining is completely independent of gridlines and cell borders. Excel provides four different types of underlining:

- Single
- Double
- Single accounting
- Double accounting

The Underline control in the Home ⇨ Font group lets you choose from single or double underlining. To apply the other two types of underlining, you must select the underline type from the Underline drop-down list on the Font tab of the Format Cells dialog box.

How is the accounting underlining different from normal underlining? The difference is subtle. When accounting underlining is applied to a cell that contains text, the complete width of the cell is underlined. In addition, the underline appears slightly lower in the accounting underline formats, making the underlined data more legible.

Figure 58-2 shows all four types of underlining for text (column A) and for values formatted as currency. Worksheet gridlines are turned off to make the underlining more visible.

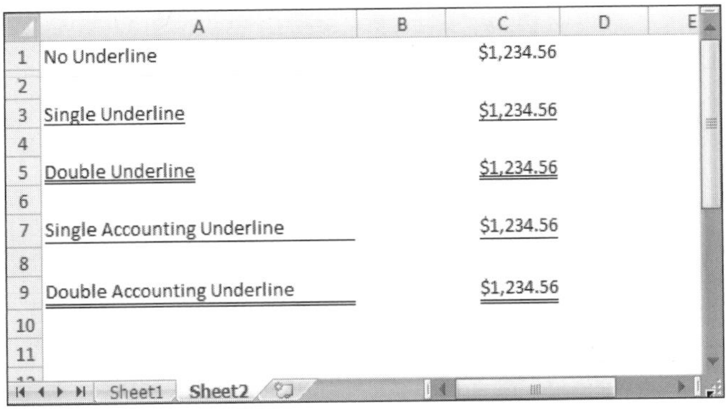

Figure 58-2: Examples of four types of underlining.

Part III

Inserting a Watermark

A *watermark* is an image (or text) that appears on each printed page. A watermark can be a faint company logo or a word, such as *DRAFT*. Excel doesn't have an official command to print a watermark, but you can add a watermark by inserting a picture in the page header or footer. Here's how to do it:

1. Note the location on your hard drive of the image you want to use for the watermark.

2. Choose View ⇨ Workbook Views ⇨ Page Layout View, to enter Page Layout View.

3. Click the center section of the header.

4. Choose Header & Footer Tools ⇨ Header & Footer Elements ⇨ Picture to display the Insert Picture dialog box.

5. Using the Insert Picture dialog box, locate and select the image you picked in Step 1. Click Insert to insert the image.

6. Click outside the header to see your image.

7. To center the image vertically on the page, click the center section of the header, and press Enter a few times before the &[Picture] code. Experiment to determine the number of extra lines to insert.

8. If you need to adjust the image (for example, to make it lighter), click the center section of the header and then choose Header & Footer Tools ⇨ Header & Footer Elements ⇨ Format Picture. Use the Image controls on the Picture tab of the Format Picture dialog box to adjust the image. You might need to experiment with the settings to make sure that the worksheet text is legible.

Figure 59-1 shows an example of a header image (a graphic of the word *draft*) used as a watermark. You can create a similar effect with plain text in the header, but Excel doesn't let you display the text at an angle.

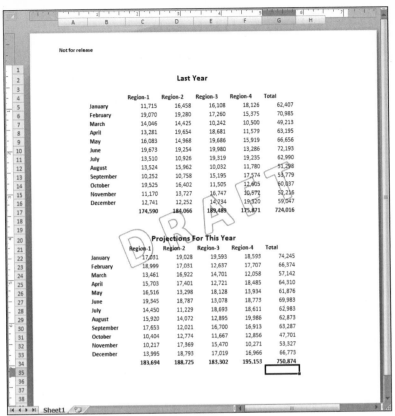

Figure 59-1: Displaying a watermark on a page.

Wrapping Text in a Cell

If you need to enter a lot of text into a cell, you have two choices:

- Allow the text to spill over into the adjacent cell on the right.
- Allow the text to wrap so that it's displayed on multiple lines within the cell.

If the cell to the right isn't empty, the text appears to be cut off if you don't wrap it. Figure 60-1 illustrates how different types of wrapped and unwrapped text can look.

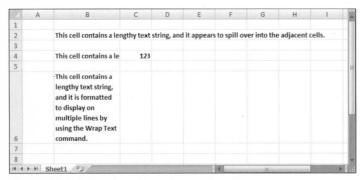

Figure 60-1: Examples of lengthy text in cells.

Cell B2 contains the default formatting. Because the cells to the right are empty, the entire chunk of text is visible.

Cell B4 contains the same text as B2, but the text appears to be cut off because cell C4 isn't empty.

Cell B6 uses the Wrap Text option, which is available in the Home ➪ Alignment group.

If you change the column width of a cell that uses Wrap Text, you find that the row height doesn't change to compensate. For example, if you reduce the column width, some of the text might not be displayed. If you increase the column width, you see extra white space in the cell. To fix the row height after changing the column width, choose Home ➪ Cells ➪ Format ➪ AutoFit Row Height.

To force a line break in a cell, press Alt+Enter. If the cell isn't already formatted with Wrap Text, pressing Alt+Enter applies Wrap Text formatting automatically.

Another way to handle lengthy text is to put it in a text box (see Figure 60-2). Add a text box by choosing Insert ➪ Text ➪ Text Box, and then just start typing. A *text box* is just a shape with text, so you can format it any way you like. And, of course, you can position it without respect to cell boundaries. To insert a line break in a text box, press Ctrl+Shift+Enter.

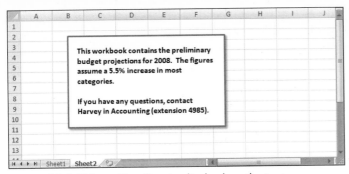

Figure 60-2: Using a Text Box to display lengthy text.

Seeing All Characters in a Font

You probably have dozens of fonts installed on your system. Here's a quick way to view the characters available in any font.

Start with a new worksheet, and then follow these steps:

1. Enter this formula into cell A1:

   ```
   =CHAR(ROW())
   ```

2. Copy cell A1 down the column to cell A255.

3. Click the Column A header to select the entire column.

4. Choose a font from the Font drop-down list in the Home ⇨ Font group.

5. Scroll down the worksheet to see the various characters in the selected font.

Repeat Step 4 as often as you like.

Figure 61-1 shows a partial view of the characters in the Webdings font. The row number corresponds to the character number. You can enter these characters from the keyboard by using the numeric keypad. For example, to enter the character shown in row 105, hold down the Alt key while you type **105** on the numeric keypad. For codes less than 100, enter a leading zero. Make sure that the cell (or character) is formatted using the correct font.

CAUTION

If you plan to share your workbook with others, be careful about using nonstandard fonts (fonts that don't ship with Windows). If the font you specified isn't available on your colleague's system, Excel attempts to substitute the closest match. But it's not always successful.

The CHAR function works with only the first 255 characters in the font. Unicode fonts contain many additional characters, which cannot be displayed by using the CHAR function. However, you can create a simple VBA function procedure that mimics the Excel CHAR function — but works with character values greater than 255:

1. Press Alt+F11 to open the Visual Basic Editor window.

2. In the Project window, double-click the item that corresponds to your workbook.

3. Choose Insert ⇨ Module to insert a VBA module.

4. Type the following lines of code in the VBA module:

   ```
   Function CHAR2(code)
       CHAR2 = ChrW(code)
   End Function
   ```

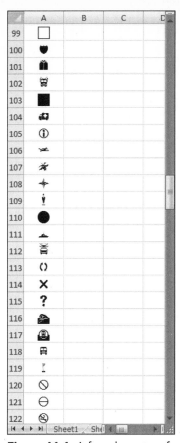

Figure 61-1: A few characters from the Webdings font.

After performing these steps, you can use the CHAR2 function in your formula. For example, the following formula displays a superscript 5 character:

```
=CHAR2(8309)
```

You can also access these characters (and determine their value) by using the Symbol dialog box. (See Tip 62 for more about using special characters.) The Symbol dialog box displays the code in hexadecimal. The CODE2 function accepts only a decimal argument, so you can convert it using the HEX2DEC function. For example, I learned from the Symbol dialog box that the hexadecimal code for a chessboard pawn character is 265F. To display this character, use this formula:

```
=CHAR2(HEX2DEC("265F"))
```

NOTE

The character displays correctly regardless of the font used in the cell.

Entering Special Characters

The Excel Symbol dialog box is useful for locating and inserting special characters into a cell (see Figure 62-1). You access this dialog box by choosing Insert ⇨ Text ⇨ Symbol.

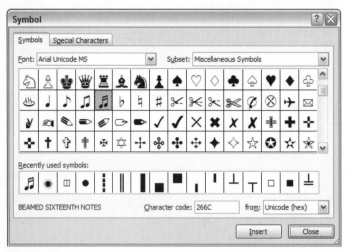

Figure 62-1: Characters in the Miscellaneous Symbols subset of the Arial Unicode MS font.

On the Symbols tab, you select a font from the Font drop-down list. For most fonts, you can also select a subset of the font from the Subset drop-down list. Select the character you want and click the Insert button. Insert additional characters if you like, or click Close to close the dialog box.

NOTE

If you insert a character from a particular font, Excel continues to display that same character, regardless of the font applied to the cell. For the largest selection of characters, use the Arial Unicode MS font.

If you use a particular character frequently, you might prefer to make it more accessible. You can do this by using Excel's AutoCorrect feature. The following instructions make the beamed eighth-notes character (it's selected in Figure 62-1) easy to access:

1. Select an empty cell.

2. Choose Insert ⇨ Text ⇨ Symbol, and use the Symbol dialog box to locate the character you want to use. In this case, the symbol is character code 266B, located in the Miscellaneous Symbols subset of the Arial Unicode MS font.

3. Insert that symbol into the cell by clicking the Insert button.

4. Click Close to close the Symbol dialog box.

5. Press Ctrl+C to copy the character in the active cell.

6. Choose Office ⇨ Excel Options to display the Excel Options dialog box, click the Proofing tab, and then click the AutoCorrect Options button to display the AutoCorrect dialog box. Or, just press Alt+TA.

7. In the AutoCorrect dialog box, click the AutoCorrect tab.

8. In the Replace field, enter a character sequence, such as **(m)**.

9. Activate the With field and press Ctrl+V to paste the special character.

10. Click OK to close the AutoCorrect dialog box.

After you perform these steps, Excel substitutes the musical-note symbol whenever you type (m). When you select a replacement string, choose a character sequence that you don't normally type. Otherwise, you might find that Excel is making the substitution when you don't want it to happen. Remember that you can always press Ctrl+Z to override an AutoCorrect entry.

Using Named Styles

Throughout the years, one of the most underused features in Excel has been named styles. It seems that the Excel designers set out to make this feature more visible, and in Excel 2007 the Style gallery is difficult to miss. It's on the Home ➪ Cells tab.

Named styles make it very easy to apply a set of predefined formatting options to a cell or range. In addition to saving time, using named styles helps to ensure a consistent look across your worksheets.

A style can consist of settings for up to six different attributes (which correspond to the tabs in the Format Cells dialog box):

- Number format
- Alignment (vertical and horizontal)
- Font (type, size, and color)
- Borders
- Fill (background color)
- Protection (locked and hidden)

The real power of styles is apparent when you change a component of a style. All cells that use that named style automatically incorporate the change. Suppose that you apply a particular style to a dozen cells scattered throughout your worksheet. Later, you realize that these cells should have a font size of 14 points rather than 12 points. Rather than change each cell, simply edit the style definition. All cells with that particular style change automatically.

Using the Style Gallery

Excel comes with dozens of predefined styles, and you apply these styles in the Style gallery (located in the Home ➪ Styles group). Figure 63-1 shows the predefined styles in the Style gallery. To apply a style to the selected cell or range, just click the style. Notice that this gallery provides a preview. When you hover your mouse over a style, it's temporarily applied to the selection so that you can see the effect. To make it permanent, just click the style.

After you apply a style to a cell, you can apply additional formatting to it by using any formatting method discussed in this chapter. Formatting modifications that you make to the cell don't affect other cells that use the same style.

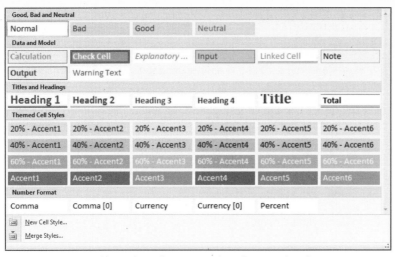

Figure 63-1: Use the Style gallery to work with named styles.

Modifying an Existing Style

To change an existing style, choose Home ⇨ Styles ⇨ Cell Styles. Right-click the style you want to modify and choose Modify from the shortcut menu. Excel displays the Style dialog box, shown in Figure 63-2. In this example, the Style dialog box shows the settings for the Normal style — which is the default style for all cells. (The style definitions vary, depending on which document theme is active.)

Figure 63-2: Use the Style dialog box to modify named styles.

Part III

Here's a quick example of how you can use styles to change the default font used throughout your workbook:

1. Choose Home ⇨ Styles ⇨ Cell Styles. Excels displays the list of styles for the active workbook.

2. Right-click Normal in the Styles list and choose Modify. Excel displays the Style dialog box, with the current settings for the Normal style.

3. Click the Format button. Excel displays the Format Cells dialog box.

4. Click the Font tab and choose the font and size that you want as the default.

5. Click OK to return to the Style dialog box.

6. Click OK again to close the Style dialog box.

The font for all cells that use the Normal style changes to the font that you specified. You can change any formatting attributes for any style.

Creating New Styles

In addition to using the built-in Excel styles, you can create your own styles. This flexibility can be quite handy because it enables you to apply your favorite formatting options very quickly and consistently.

To create a new style, follow these steps:

1. Select a cell and apply all the formatting that you want to include in the new style. You can use any of the formatting that's available in the Format Cells dialog box.

2. After you format the cell to your liking, choose Home ⇨ Styles ⇨ Cell Styles, and choose New Cell Style. Excel displays its Style dialog box, along with a proposed generic name for the style. Note that Excel displays the words `By Example` to indicate that it's basing the style on the current cell.

3. Enter a new style name in the Style Name box. The check boxes display the current formats for the cell. By default, all check boxes are checked.

4. If you don't want the style to include one or more format categories, remove the check marks from the appropriate boxes.

5. Click OK to create the style and to close the dialog box.

After you perform these steps, the new custom style is available when you choose Home ⇨ Styles ⇨ Cell Styles. Custom styles are available only in the workbook in which they were created. To copy your custom styles, see the section that follows.

NOTE

The Protection option in the Styles dialog box controls whether users can modify cells for the selected style. This option is effective only if you also turned on worksheet protection, by choosing Review ⇨ Changes ⇨ Protect Sheet.

Merging Styles from Other Workbooks

It's important to understand that custom styles are stored with the workbook in which they were created. If you created some custom styles, you probably don't want to go through all the work to create copies of those styles in each new Excel workbook. A better approach is to merge the styles from a workbook in which you previously created them.

To merge styles from another workbook, open both the workbook that contains the styles you want to merge and the workbook into which you want to merge styles. From the workbook into which you want to merge styles, choose Home ⇨ Styles ⇨ Cell Styles and choose Merge Styles. Excel displays the Merge Styles dialog box, which shows a list of all open workbooks. Select the workbook that contains the styles you want to merge, and click OK. Excel copies styles from the workbook you selected into the active workbook.

You might want to create a master workbook that contains all your custom styles so that you always know which workbook to merge styles from.

Adding a Background Image to a Worksheet

Most of the time, simpler is better. But, in some cases, you might want to spiff up a worksheet with something fancy. One way to do that is to apply a background image. A background image in Excel is similar to the wallpaper that you might display on your Windows desktop or an image used as the background for a Web page.

Figure 64-1 shows an example of a worksheet that contains an appropriate background image — money, for a financial services company.

Figure 64-1: You can add almost any image file as a worksheet background image, but some images work better than others.

 NOTE

Before you get too excited about this feature, remember this caveat: The graphical background on a worksheet is for on-screen display only — it isn't printed when you print the worksheet.

To add a background to a worksheet, choose Page Layout ➪ Page Setup ➪ Background. Excel displays a dialog box that enables you to select a graphics file. (All common graphics file formats are supported.) When you locate a file, click Insert. Excel tiles the image across your worksheet. Some images are specifically designed to be tiled, such as the one shown in Figure 64-1. This type of image is often used for Web page backgrounds, and it creates a seamless background.

You also want to turn off the gridline display because the gridlines show through the image. Some backgrounds make viewing text difficult, so you might want to use a solid background color for cells that contain text. Use the Home ⇨ Font ⇨ Fill Color control to change the background color of cells.

Part IV

Basic Formulas and Functions

The ability to create formulas is what makes a spreadsheet a spreadsheet. In this part, you'll find formula-related tips that can make your workbooks more powerful than ever.

Tips and Where to Find Them

Using Formula AutoComplete

A new feature in Excel 2007 is Formula AutoComplete. When you type an equal sign and the first letter of a function in a cell, Excel displays a drop-down list box that contains all the functions that begin with that letter. You also see a ScreenTip with a brief description for the function (see Figure 65-1).

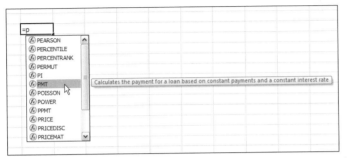

Figure 65-1: When you begin to enter a function, Excel lists available functions that begin with the typed letters.

When the AutoComplete list is displayed, you can continue typing (to narrow the number of items displayed in the list) or use the arrow keys to select the function from the list. After you select a function, press Tab (or double-click) to insert the function and its opening parenthesis into the cell.

NOTE

In addition to displaying function names, the Formula AutoComplete feature lists names and table references.

After you press Tab to insert the function, Excel displays another ScreenTip, which shows the arguments for the function (see Figure 65-2). The bold argument is the argument you are currently entering. Arguments shown in brackets are optional.

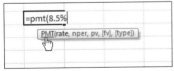

Figure 65-2: A function argument is displayed in a ScreenTip.

Notice that ScreenTips contain hyperlinks. (The hyperlinks appear when you move the mouse pointer over the function name or the arguments.) Click the hyperlink for the function name, and you can read the Help topic for the function. Clicking an argument hyperlink selects that argument in the cell. Also notice that you can drag the ScreenTip to a different location if it's in your way.

Part IV

Knowing When to Use Absolute References

When you create a formula that refers to another cell or range, the cell or range reference can be relative or absolute. A *relative* cell reference adjusts to its new location when the formula is copied and pasted. An *absolute* cell reference does not change, even when the formula is copied and pasted elsewhere. An absolute reference is specified with two dollar signs; for example:

```
=$A$1
=SUM($A$1:$F$24)
```

A relative reference, on the other hand, does not use dollar signs:

```
=A1
=SUM(A1:F24)
```

The majority of cell and range references you will ever use are relative references. In fact, Excel creates relative cell references in formulas except when the formula includes cells in different worksheets or workbooks. When do you use an absolute reference? The answer is simple: The only time you even need to *think* about using an absolute reference is if you plan to copy the formula.

The easiest way to understand this concept is with an example. Figure 66-1 shows a simple worksheet. The formula in cell D2, which multiplies the quantity by the unit price, is

```
=B2*C2
```

	A	B	C	D	E
1	Item	Quantity	Unit Price	Total	
2	Chair	4	$125.00	$500.00	
3	Desk	4	$695.00		
4	Lamp	3	$39.95		
5					
6					
7					

Sheet1

Figure 66-1: Copying a formula that contains relative references.

This formula uses relative cell references. Therefore, when the formula is copied to the other cells in the column, the references adjust in a relative manner. For example, copy the formula to cell D3 and it becomes

```
=B3*C3
```

What if the cell references in D2 contain absolute references, like this?

```
=$B$2*$C$2
```

In this case, copying the formula to the cells below produces incorrect results. The formula in cell D3 is exactly the same as the formula in cell D2.

Now extend the example to calculate sales tax. The sales tax rate is stored in cell B7 (see Figure 66-2). In this situation, the formula in cell D2 is

```
=B2*C2*$B$7
```

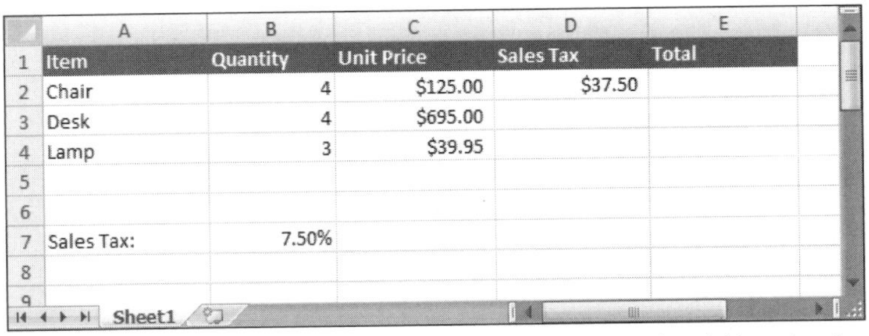

	A	B	C	D	E
1	Item	Quantity	Unit Price	Sales Tax	Total
2	Chair	4	$125.00	$37.50	
3	Desk	4	$695.00		
4	Lamp	3	$39.95		
5					
6					
7	Sales Tax:	7.50%			
8					
9					

Figure 66-2: Formula references to the sales tax cell should be absolute.

The quantity is multiplied by the price, and the result is multiplied by the sales tax rate stored in cell B7. Notice that the reference to B7 is an absolute reference. (You want that because you don't want the reference to change when the formula is copied.) When the formula in D2 is copied to the cells below, cell D3 contains this formula:

```
=B3*C3*$B$7
```

The references to cells B2 and C2 are adjusted, but the reference to cell B7 is not — which is exactly what you want.

Part IV

Knowing When to Use Mixed References

In the previous tip, I discuss absolute versus relative cell references. This tip covers an additional type of cell reference: In a *mixed cell reference,* either the column or the row is absolute (and therefore doesn't change when the formula is copied and pasted). Mixed cell references aren't used often, but as you see in this tip, in some situations, using mixed references makes your job much easier.

Whereas an absolute cell reference contains two dollar signs, a mixed cell reference contains, by comparison, only one dollar sign. Here are two examples of mixed references:

```
=$A1
=A$1
```

In the first example, the column part of the reference (A) is absolute and the row part (1) is relative. In the second example, the column part of the reference is relative and the row part is absolute.

Figure 67-1 shows a worksheet demonstrating a situation in which using mixed references is the best choice.

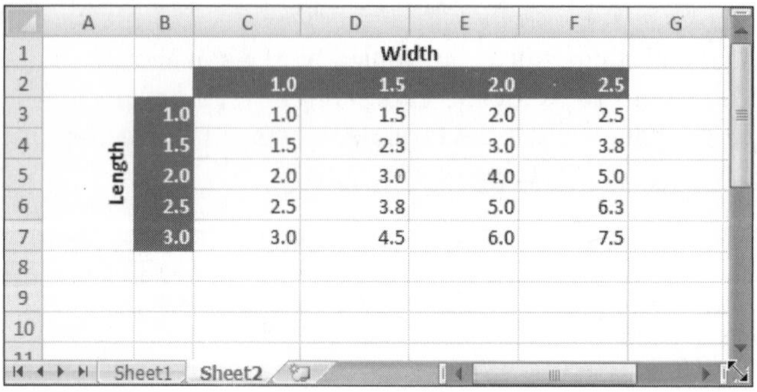

Figure 67-1: Using mixed cell references.

The formulas in the table calculate the area for various lengths and widths. Here's the formula in cell C3:

```
=$B3*C$2
```

Notice that both cell references are mixed. The reference to cell B3 uses an absolute reference for the column ($B), and the reference to cell C2 uses an absolute reference for the row ($2). As a result, this formula can be copied down and across, and the calculations are correct. For example, the formula in cell F7 is

```
=$B7*F$2
```

If C3 used either absolute or relative references, copying the formula would produce incorrect results.

Changing the Type of a Cell Reference

In Tips 66 and 67, I discuss absolute, relative, and mixed cell references. This tip describes an easy way to change the type of reference used when creating a formula.

You can enter nonrelative references (absolute or mixed) manually by simply typing dollar signs in the appropriate positions of the cell address. Or, you can use a handy shortcut: the F4 key. After you enter a cell reference when creating a formula, you can press F4 repeatedly to have Excel cycle through all four reference types.

For example, if you enter =A1 to start a formula, pressing F4 converts the cell reference to =$A$1. Pressing F4 again converts it to =A$1. Pressing it again displays =$A1. Pressing it one more time returns to the original =A1. Keep pressing F4 until Excel displays the type of reference you want.

NOTE

When you name a cell or range, Excel uses (by default) an absolute reference for the name. For example, if you give the name SalesForecast to A1:A12, the Refers To field in the Define Name dialog box lists the reference as $A$1:$A$12, which is almost always what you want. If you copy a cell that has a named reference in its formula, the copied formula contains a reference to the original name.

Converting a Vertical Range to a Table

Often, tabular data is imported into Excel as a single column. Figure 69-1 shows an example. Column A contains name and address information, and each "record" consists of five rows.

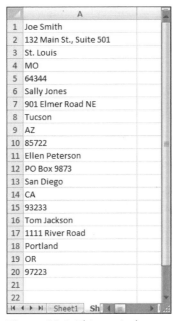

	A
1	Joe Smith
2	132 Main St., Suite 501
3	St. Louis
4	MO
5	64344
6	Sally Jones
7	901 Elmer Road NE
8	Tucson
9	AZ
10	85722
11	Ellen Peterson
12	PO Box 9873
13	San Diego
14	CA
15	93233
16	Tom Jackson
17	1111 River Road
18	Portland
19	OR
20	97223
21	
22	

Figure 69-1: This vertical range of data needs to be converted to a table.

Excel doesn't provide a direct way to convert such a range to a more usable table. But a few clever formulas will do the job. Insert the following formulas in range C1:G1:

```
C1:  =INDIRECT("A" & ROW()*5-4)
D1:  =INDIRECT("A" & ROW()*5-3)
E1:  =INDIRECT("A" & ROW()*5-2)
F1:  =INDIRECT("A" & ROW()*5-1)
G1:  =INDIRECT("A" & ROW()*5-0)
```

After you enter the formulas, copy them to the rows below to accommodate the amount of data in column A. Figure 69-2 shows the result.

Part IV

	A	B	C	D	E	F	G
1	Joe Smith		Joe Smith	132 Main St., Suite 501	St. Louis	MO	64344
2	132 Main St., Suite 501		Sally Jones	901 Elmer Road NE	Tucson	AZ	85722
3	St. Louis		Ellen Peterson	PO Box 9873	San Diego	CA	93233
4	MO		Tom Jackson	1111 River Road	Portland	OR	97223
5	64344						
6	Sally Jones						
7	901 Elmer Road NE						
8	Tucson						
9	AZ						
10	85722						
11	Ellen Peterson						
12	PO Box 9873						
13	San Diego						
14	CA						
15	93233						
16	Tom Jackson						
17	1111 River Road						
18	Portland						
19	OR						
20	97223						

Figure 69-2: Five formulas in columns C:G convert the original data into a table.

These formulas assume that the original data begins in cell A1 and that the conversion formulas begin in row 1. In addition, these formulas assume that each record consists of five rows. If your data uses fewer or more rows, you need to use fewer or more formulas — one for each row. In addition, you need to modify the formulas accordingly. For example, if each record consists of only three rows of data, the formulas are

```
C1: =INDIRECT("A" & ROW()*3-2)
D1: =INDIRECT("A" & ROW()*3-1)
E1: =INDIRECT("A" & ROW()*3-0)
```

Using AutoSum Tricks

Just about every Excel user knows about the AutoSum button. This command is so popular that Excel 2007 puts it in two Ribbon locations: in the Home ⇨ Editing group and in the Formulas ⇨ Function Library group.

Just click the button, and Excel analyzes the data surrounding the active cell and proposes a SUM formula. If the proposed range is correct, click the AutoSum button again (or press Enter), and the formula is inserted. If you change your mind, press Esc.

If Excel incorrectly guesses the range to be summed, just select the correct range to be summed and press Enter. It's easy and painless.

Following are some additional tricks related to AutoSum:

- The AutoSum button can insert other types of formulas. Notice the little arrow on the right side of that button? Click it, and you see four other functions: AVERAGE, COUNT, MAX, and MIN. Click one of those items, and the appropriate formula is proposed. You also see a More Functions item, which simply displays the Insert Function dialog box — the same one that appears when you choose Formulas ⇨ Function Library ⇨ Insert Function (or click the `fx` button to the left of the formula bar).

- If you need to enter a similar SUM formula into a range of cells, simply select the entire range before you click the AutoSum button. In this case, Excel inserts the functions for you without asking you — one formula in each of the selected cells. In Figure 70-1, the range to be summed is D4:G15, so I selected an additional row and column: D4:H16. Clicking the AutoSum buttons puts formulas in row 16 and column H.

- To sum both across and down a table of numbers, select the range of numbers plus an additional column to the right and an additional row at the bottom. Click the AutoSum button, and Excel inserts the formulas that add the rows and the columns.

- A more efficient way to access AutoSum is to use your keyboard. Pressing Alt+= has exactly the same effect as clicking the AutoSum button.

- If you're working with a table (created by using Insert ⇨ Tables ⇨ Table) using the AutoSum button after selecting the row below the table inserts a Total row for the table and creates formulas that use the SUBTOTAL function rather than the SUM function. The SUBTOTAL function sums only the visible cells in the table, which is useful if you filter the data.

- Unless you applied a different number format to the cell that will hold the SUM formula, AutoSum applies the same number format as the first cell in the range to be summed.

- To create a SUM formula that uses only *some* of the values in a column, select the cells to be summed and then click the AutoSum button. Excel inserts the SUM formula in the first empty cell below the selected range. The selected range must be a contiguous group of cells — a multiple selection isn't allowed.

Part IV

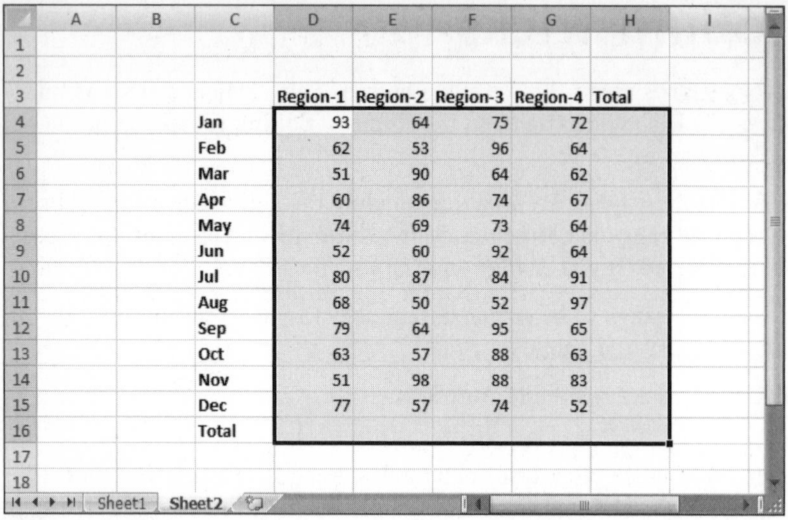

	A	B	C	D	E	F	G	H	I
1									
2									
3				Region-1	Region-2	Region-3	Region-4	Total	
4			Jan	93	64	75	72		
5			Feb	62	53	96	64		
6			Mar	51	90	64	62		
7			Apr	60	86	74	67		
8			May	74	69	73	64		
9			Jun	52	60	92	64		
10			Jul	80	87	84	91		
11			Aug	68	50	52	97		
12			Sep	79	64	95	65		
13			Oct	63	57	88	63		
14			Nov	51	98	88	83		
15			Dec	77	57	74	52		
16			Total						
17									
18									

Sheet1 Sheet2

Figure 70-1: Using AutoSum to insert SUM formulas for rows and columns.

Using the Status Bar Selection Statistics Feature

I'm always surprised when I encounter Excel users who have never noticed the handy selection statistics field on the status bar. When you select a range that contains values, Excel displays information about the selected range on the status bar, which is at the bottom of the Excel window. As you can see in Figure 71-1, the selected cells have an average value of 305.7, the number of selected cells is 30, and the sum of the values is 9,171.

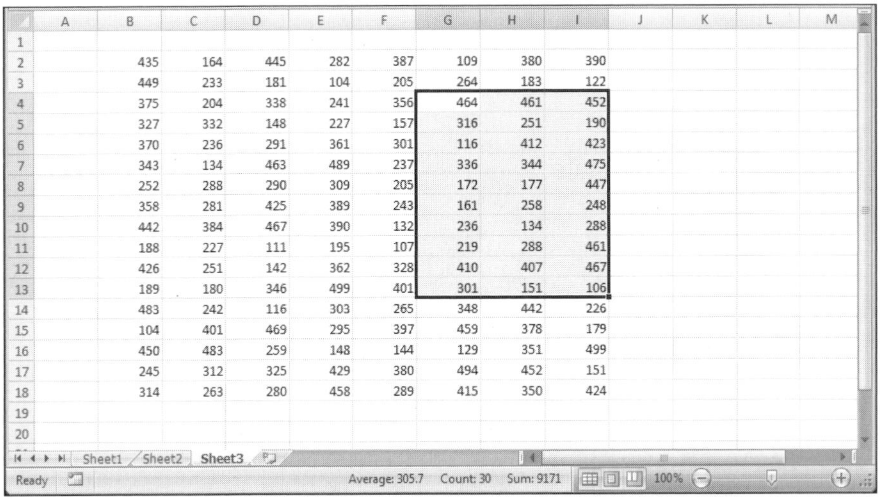

Figure 71-1: Excel displays information about the selected cells on the status bar.

If you prefer to see some other statistic relating to the selection, right-click the text on the status bar and make your selection from the shortcut menu (see Figure 71-2). Your choices are any or all of the following:

- Average
- Count
- Numerical Count
- Minimum
- Maximum
- Sum

If you prefer not to see any selection statistics, just remove the check mark from all six options.

Figure 71-2: Excel offers a choice of six statistics about the selected range.

When using this feature, remember that cells that contain text are ignored, except when the Count option is selected.

Converting Formulas to Values

If you have a range of cells that contain formulas, you can quickly convert these cells to values only (that is, the result of each formula). In fact, Excel 2007 makes this common operation easier than ever. In previous versions, you had to display the Paste Special dialog box, but that's no longer required.

Here's how to convert a range of formulas to their current values:

1. Select the range. It can include formula cells as well as nonformula cells.

2. Press Ctrl+C to copy the range.

3. Choose Home ⇨ Clipboard ⇨ Paste ⇨ Paste Values.

4. Press Esc to cancel Copy mode.

Each of the formulas in the selected range is replaced with its current value.

If you want to put the formula results in a different location, just select a different cell before you perform Step 3. The original formulas remain intact, but the new range contains the formula results.

Transforming Data without Using Formulas

Often, you have a range of cells containing data that must be transformed in some way. For example, you might want to increase all values by 5 percent. Or, you might need to divide each value by 2. This tip describes how to perform addition, subtraction, multiplication, and division on a range of values without using any formulas.

The following steps assume that you have values in a range and you want to increase all values by 5 percent. For example, the range can contain a price list and you're raising all prices by 5 percent:

1. Activate any empty cell and enter **1.05**. You will multiply the values by this number, which results in an increase of 5 percent.

2. Press Ctrl+C to copy that cell.

3. Select the range to be transformed. It can include values, formulas, or text.

4. Choose Home ⇨ Clipboard ⇨ Paste ⇨ Paste Special to display the Paste Special dialog box.

5. In the Paste Special dialog box, click the Multiply option.

6. Click OK.

7. Press Esc to cancel Copy mode.

The values in the range are multiplied by the copied value (1.05). Formulas in the range are modified accordingly. Assume that the range originally contained this formula:

```
=SUM(B18:B22)
```

After you perform the Paste Special operation, the formula is converted to

```
=(SUM(B18:B22))*1.05
```

This technique is limited to the four basic math operations: add, subtract, multiply, and divide.

Transforming Data by Using Temporary Formulas

In Tip 73, I describe how to perform simple mathematical transformations on a range of numeric data. This tip describes the much more versatile method of transforming data, by using temporary formulas.

Figure 74-1 shows a worksheet with names in column A. These names are in all upper-case, and the goal is to convert them to proper case (only the first letter of each name is uppercase).

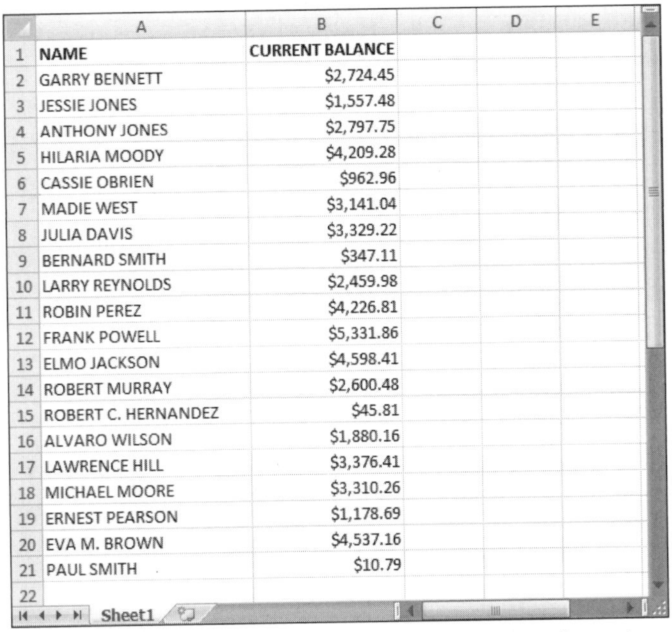

	A	B	C	D	E
1	NAME	CURRENT BALANCE			
2	GARRY BENNETT	$2,724.45			
3	JESSIE JONES	$1,557.48			
4	ANTHONY JONES	$2,797.75			
5	HILARIA MOODY	$4,209.28			
6	CASSIE OBRIEN	$962.96			
7	MADIE WEST	$3,141.04			
8	JULIA DAVIS	$3,329.22			
9	BERNARD SMITH	$347.11			
10	LARRY REYNOLDS	$2,459.98			
11	ROBIN PEREZ	$4,226.81			
12	FRANK POWELL	$5,331.86			
13	ELMO JACKSON	$4,598.41			
14	ROBERT MURRAY	$2,600.48			
15	ROBERT C. HERNANDEZ	$45.81			
16	ALVARO WILSON	$1,880.16			
17	LAWRENCE HILL	$3,376.41			
18	MICHAEL MOORE	$3,310.26			
19	ERNEST PEARSON	$1,178.69			
20	EVA M. BROWN	$4,537.16			
21	PAUL SMITH	$10.79			
22					

Sheet1

Figure 74-1: The goal is to transform the names in column A to proper case.

Follow these steps to transform the data in column A:

1. Create a temporary formula in an unused column. For this example, enter this formula in cell C2:

   ```
   =PROPER(A2)
   ```

2. Copy the formula down the column to accommodate all cells to be transformed.

3. Select the formula cells (in column C).

4. Press Ctrl+C.

Part IV

5. Select the original data cells (in column A).

6. Choose Home ⇨ Clipboard ⇨ Paste ⇨ Paste Values. The original data is replaced with the transformed data (see Figure 74-2).

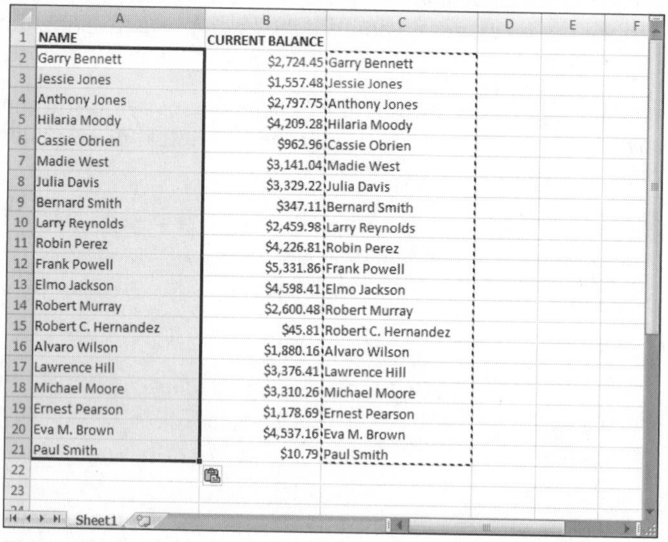

Figure 74-2: The formula results from column C replace the original data.

7. Press Esc to cancel Copy mode.

8. When you're satisfied that the transformation happened as you intended, you can delete the temporary formulas in column C.

You can adapt this technique for just about any type of data transformation you need. The key, of course, is constructing the proper transformation formula in Step 1.

Deleting Values While Keeping Formulas

A common type of spreadsheet model contains input cells (which are changed by the user), and formula cells that work with those input cells. If you want to delete all the values in the input cells but keep the formulas intact, here's a simple way to do it:

1. Select the range that you want to work with. If you want to delete all nonformula value cells on the worksheet, just select any single cell.

2. Choose Home ⇨ Editing ⇨ Find & Select ⇨ Go To Special. This step displays the Go To Special dialog box.

3. In the Go To Special dialog box, select the Constants option and then select Numbers.

4. Click OK, and the nonformula numeric cells are selected.

5. Press Delete to delete the values.

If you need to delete the value cells on a regular basis, you can specify a name for the input cells. After completing Step 4, choose Formula ⇨ Defined Names ⇨ Define Name to display the New Name dialog box. Enter a name for the selected cells — something like InputCells is a good choice. Click OK to close the New Name dialog box and create the name.

After naming the input cells, you can select the named cells directly by using the Name box — the drop-down list to the left of the formula bar.

Summing Across Sheets

Formulas can work with cells in other worksheets. You just need to precede the cell reference with the sheet name and an exclamation point. For example, the following formula adds 12 to the value in cell C1 on Sheet2:

```
=Sheet2!C1+12
```

What if you need to calculate the sum of all values in C1 on sheets Sheet2 through Sheet6? This formula does the job:

```
=SUM(Sheet2:Sheet6!C1)
```

In this case, the colon separates the first sheet name and the last sheet name. To create such a formula by pointing, follow these steps:

1. Activate the cell that will contain the formula, and type **=SUM(**.
2. Click the sheet tab for the first sheet (in this case, Sheet2), and select the cell (in this case, C1).
3. Press Shift, and click the sheet tab for the last sheet (in this case, Sheet6).
4. Press Enter, and the formula is entered into the cell.

In Step 2, you can select a multicell range rather than a single cell. For example, this formula returns the sum of C1:F12 on all sheets from Sheet2 through Sheet6:

```
=SUM(Sheet2:Sheet6!C1:F12)
```

And now, I show you an interesting trick that I learned from reading the Excel newsgroups. If you want to sum the same cell on all sheets except the active sheet, just enter a formula like this:

```
=SUM('*'!C1)
```

The asterisk serves as a wildcard character that's interpreted to mean "all sheets except this one." When you press Enter after typing this formula, Excel converts the formula to use the actual sheet names. It even works if the active sheet is in the middle of other sheets. For example, if a workbook has six sheets and you enter the preceding formula in a cell on Sheet3, Excel creates the following formula:

```
=SUM(Sheet1:Sheet2!C1,Sheet4:Sheet6!C1)
```

It gets even better. Enter the following formula to find the sum of cell C1 on all sheets that begin with the characters *Region:*

```
=SUM('Region*'!C1)
```

Excel might convert this formula to something like this:

```
=SUM(Region1:Region4!C1)
```

You can also use the ? wildcard character, which indicates any single character. For example, when you enter the formula that follows, Excel creates a formula that sums the value only on Sheet1 through Sheet9 (sheet names that contain a single numeric digit):

```
=SUM('Sheet?'!C1)
```

This trick isn't limited to the SUM function. It works with other functions, such as AVERAGE, MIN, and MAX.

Dealing with Function Arguments

Excel has dozens of useful functions, and each of them has its own, unique set of arguments. You probably memorize the arguments for functions you use frequently, but what about the other functions?

The best way to insert a function is to use the Insert Function dialog box. Display this dialog box by using any of these methods:

- Click the Insert Function button, located in the Formulas ⇨ Function Library group.
- Click the fx button to the left of the formula bar.
- Press Shift+F3.

If you don't know the name of the function you need, you can search for it by entering some text in the Search for a Function field and clicking the Go button (see Figure 77-1). After you identify the function, click OK, and you see the Function Arguments dialog box, which guides you through the function's arguments, as shown in Figure 77-2.

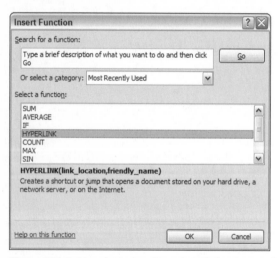

Figure 77-1: Use the Insert Function dialog box to help find the function you need.

By the way, if you're entering a function manually (without the assistance of the Insert Function dialog box), you can press Ctrl+A to display the Function Arguments dialog box. This key combination works only if you haven't yet entered any arguments for the function.

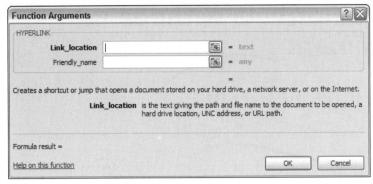

Figure 77-2: The Function Arguments dialog box helps you enter arguments for a function.

In some cases, you might want to insert "dummy" arguments for a function — placeholders that will be filled in later. This strategy is useful if you don't yet know the cell references that will be used. To insert argument names as placeholders, press Ctrl+Shift+A after you type the function's name. Excel uses the argument's names as arguments. For example, if you press Ctrl+Shift+A while entering the VLOOKUP function, Excel inserts the following:

```
=VLOOKUP(lookup_value,table_array,col_index_num,range_lookup)
```

The formula, of course, returns an error, so you need to replace the dummy arguments with actual values or cell references.

Part IV

Annotating a Formula without Using a Comment

The Excel comment feature is a great way to annotate your formulas. Just right-click the cell and choose Insert Comment from the shortcut menu. You can then describe the formula any way you like inside the comment.

This tip describes another, less obtrusive, way to annotate a formula. The trick involves Excel's rarely used N function. (This function is included in Excel primarily for compatibility with Lotus 1-2-3 files.) The N function takes one argument, and this argument is converted to a value. When the argument is a text string, the N function returns 0. You can take advantage of this and modify the formula so that it uses the N function.

Consider this simple formula:

```
=A4*.075
```

You can modify the formula to contain a comment. Because the N function returns 0, the comment has no effect on the value returned by the formula:

```
=A4*.275+N("27.5% represents the anticipated tax rate")
```

Making an Exact Copy of a Range of Formulas

When you copy a cell that contains a formula, Excel adjusts all the relative cell references. Assume that cell D1 contains this formula:

```
=A1*B1
```

When you copy this cell, the two cell references are changed relative to the destination. If you copy D1 to D12, for example, the copied formula is

```
=A12*B12
```

Sometimes, you might prefer to make an exact copy of a formula. One way is to convert all the cell references to absolute references (for example, change =A1*B1 to =$A$1*$B$1). Another way is to (temporarily) remove the equal sign from the formula, which converts the formula to text. Then you can copy the cell and manually insert the equal sign into the original formula and the copied formula.

What if you have a large range of formulas and you want to make an exact copy of those formulas? Editing each formula is tedious and error-prone. Here's a trick that accomplishes the task.

For the following steps, assume that you want to copy the formulas in A1:D10 on Sheet1 and make an exact copy in A13:D22, also on Sheet1:

1. Insert a new (temporary) worksheet after the sheet that contains the formulas to be copied. Assume that this sheet is named Sheet2.

2. Select the source range (A1:D10, in this example).

3. Group the source sheet with the empty sheet. To do this, press Ctrl while you click the sheet tab for the temporary sheet. Excel displays [Group] on the title bar to remind you that you've grouped sheets.

4. Choose Home ➪ Editing ➪ Fill ➪ Fill Across Worksheets, and then choose the All option in the Fill Across Worksheets dialog box.

5. Ungroup the sheets by clicking the sheet tab for Sheet2.

6. In Sheet2, the copied range is selected. Choose Home ➪ Clipboard ➪ Cut (or press Ctrl+X).

7. Activate cell A13 (in Sheet2) and press Enter to paste the cut cells. A13:D22 is then selected.

8. Regroup the sheets by Ctrl+clicking the sheet tab for Sheet1.

9. Choose Home ⇨ Editing ⇨ Fill ⇨ Fill Across Worksheets again.

10. Activate Sheet1, and you find that A13:D22 contains an exact replica of the formulas in A1:D10. You can then delete Sheet2 because it has served its purpose and is no longer needed.

Monitoring Formula Cells from Any Location

If you have a large spreadsheet model, you might find it helpful to monitor the values in a few key cells as you change various input cells. The Watch Window feature makes this sort of task very simple. Using the Watch Window, you can keep an eye on any number of cells, regardless of which worksheet or workbook is active.

To display the Watch Window, choose Formulas ⇨ Formula Auditing ⇨ Watch Window. To watch a cell, click the Add Watch button in the Watch Window, and then specify the cell in the Add Watch dialog box. When the Add Watch dialog box is displayed, you can select a range or press Ctrl and click individual cells.

Figure 80-1 shows the Watch Window, with several cells being monitored.

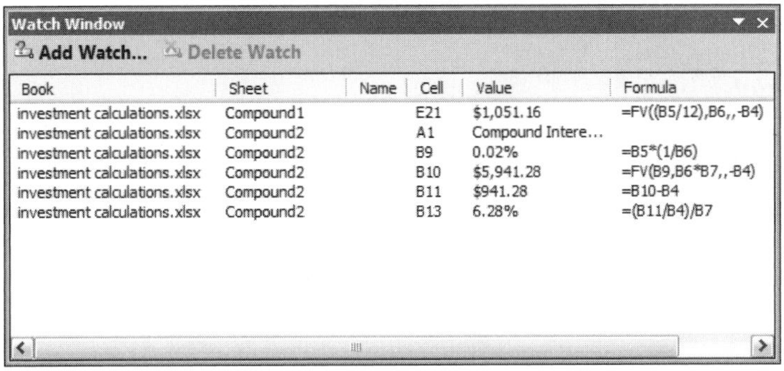

Book	Sheet	Name	Cell	Value	Formula
investment calculations.xlsx	Compound1		E21	$1,051.16	=FV((B5/12),B6,,-B4)
investment calculations.xlsx	Compound2		A1	Compound Intere...	
investment calculations.xlsx	Compound2		B9	0.02%	=B5*(1/B6)
investment calculations.xlsx	Compound2		B10	$5,941.28	=FV(B9,B6*B7,,-B4)
investment calculations.xlsx	Compound2		B11	$941.28	=B10-B4
investment calculations.xlsx	Compound2		B13	6.28%	=(B11/B4)/B7

Figure 80-1: Using the Watch Window to monitor the value of formula cells.

You can customize the display in the Watch Window by doing any of the following:

- Click and drag a border to change the size of the window.
- Drag the window to an edge of the Excel window, and it becomes docked rather than free floating.
- Click and drag the borders in the header to change the width of the columns displayed. By dragging a column border all the way to the left, you can hide the column.
- Click and drag any of the header borders to increase or decrease the width of the column.
- Click one of the headers to sort the contents by that column.

Part IV

Displaying and Printing Formulas

When you enter a formula into a cell, Excel displays the calculated value of the formula. To view a formula, activate the cell, and Excel shows the formula on the formula bar.

To view all your formulas, switch to Formula view. The easiest way to switch to this mode is to press Ctrl+`. (That's the accent character, usually located above the Tab key.) Excel then displays the formulas rather than their results. In addition, you can also see which cells are referenced by the selected formula because Excel displays those cells with a colored border. In Figure 81-1, C14 is the selected cell, and it references cells C2 and C13, which are displayed with a colored border.

	A	B	C	D
1		Last Year	This Year	Difference
2	January	9032	8233	=C2-B2
3	February	9375	8656	=C3-B3
4	March	9494	9252	=C4-B4
5	April	9647	8773	=C5-B5
6	May	9946	8458	=C6-B6
7	June	10476	8318	=C7-B7
8	July	10341	8698	=C8-B8
9	August	10035	8412	=C9-B9
10	September	10515	8206	=C10-B10
11	October	10042	8451	=C11-B11
12	November	9757	8842	=C12-B12
13	December	9423	9140	=C13-B13
14		=SUM(B2:B13)	=SUM(C2:C13)	
15				
16				

Figure 81-1: Excel's Formula view displays the formulas rather than their results.

In Formula view, you can use all Excel commands, and even modify the formulas.

In practice, you might find that Formula view isn't very useful. Although Excel widens the columns, you can see an entire formula only if it's very short. And, if you print the sheet in Formula view, you usually end up with a meaningless mess.

To document a worksheet by printing its formulas, your best bet is to locate a VBA macro to do the job. This simple no-frills VBA procedure makes a list of all formulas on the active worksheet:

```
Sub ListFormulas()
    On Error Resume Next
    Set FormulaCells = Range("A1").SpecialCells(xlFormulas, 23)
    If FormulaCells Is Nothing Then Exit Sub
    Set FormulaSheet = ActiveWorkbook.Worksheets.Add
    Row = 1
    For Each Cell In FormulaCells
        With FormulaSheet
            Cells(Row, 1) = Cell.Address(False, False)
```

```
            Cells(Row, 2) = " " & Cell.Formula
            Cells(Row, 3) = Cell.Value
            Row = Row + 1
        End With
    Next Cell
End Sub
```

To use this macro, press Alt+F11 to activate the Visual Basic Editor. Select your workbook in the Project window, and choose Insert ⇨ Module to insert a new VBA module. Type the code exactly as it appears. To execute the macro, activate the sheet that has the formulas, press Alt+F8, select ListFormulas from the macro list, and click Run. Figure 81-2 shows an example of the output from this macro. The first column contains the address of the formula, the second column contains the formula, and the third column shows the current result of the formula.

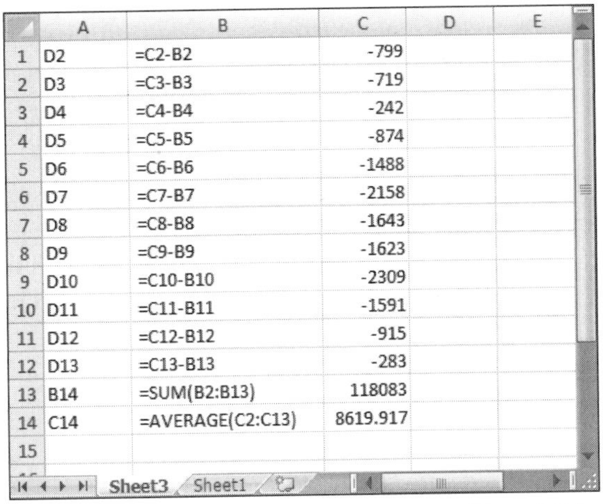

	A	B	C	D	E
1	D2	=C2-B2	-799		
2	D3	=C3-B3	-719		
3	D4	=C4-B4	-242		
4	D5	=C5-B5	-874		
5	D6	=C6-B6	-1488		
6	D7	=C7-B7	-2158		
7	D8	=C8-B8	-1643		
8	D9	=C9-B9	-1623		
9	D10	=C10-B10	-2309		
10	D11	=C11-B11	-1591		
11	D12	=C12-B12	-915		
12	D13	=C13-B13	-283		
13	B14	=SUM(B2:B13)	118083		
14	C14	=AVERAGE(C2:C13)	8619.917		
15					

Sheet3 / Sheet1

Figure 81-2: A list of formulas generated by a VBA macro.

Avoiding Error Displays in Formulas

Sometimes a formula returns an error, such as #REF! or #DIV/0!. Usually, you want to know when a formula error occurs, but in some cases you might prefer to simply avoid displaying the error messages. Figure 82-1 shows an example.

	A	B	C	D	E	F
1	Month	Total Sales	No. Reps	Average		
2	Jan	1,783,300	9	198,144		
3	Feb	2,433,921	12	202,827		
4	Mar	2,873,092	14	205,221		
5	Apr	2,998,017	14	214,144		
6	May			#DIV/0!		
7	Jun			#DIV/0!		
8	Jul			#DIV/0!		
9	Aug			#DIV/0!		
10	Sep			#DIV/0!		
11	Oct			#DIV/0!		
12	Nov			#DIV/0!		
13	Dec			#DIV/0!		
14						
15						

Sheet1

Figure 82-1: The formulas in column D display an error if the data is missing.

Column D contains formulas that calculate the average sales volume. For example, cell D2 contains this formula:

```
=B2/C2
```

Using the ISERROR Function

As you can see, the formula displays an error if the cells used in the calculation are empty. If you prefer to hide those error values, you can do so by using an IF function to check for an error.

For this example, change the formula in cell D1 to

```
=IF(ISERROR(B2/C2),"",B2/C2)
```

The ISERROR function returns TRUE if its argument evaluates to an error. In such a case, the IF function returns an empty string. Otherwise, the IF function returns the calculated value. As you see in Figure 82-2, when this formula is copied down the column, the result is a bit more visually pleasing.

	A	B	C	D	E	F
1	Month	Total Sales	No. Reps	Average		
2	Jan	1,783,300	9	198,144		
3	Feb	2,433,921	12	202,827		
4	Mar	2,873,092	14	205,221		
5	Apr	2,998,017	14	214,144		
6	May					
7	Jun					
8	Jul					
9	Aug					
10	Sep					
11	Oct					
12	Nov					
13	Dec					
14						

Figure 82-2: Using an IF function to hide error values.

You can adapt this technique to any formula. The original formula serves as the argument for the ISERROR function, and it repeats as the last argument of the IF function:

```
=IF(ISERROR(OriginalFormula),"",OriginalFormula)
```

By the way, you can put anything you like as the second argument for the ISERROR function. (It doesn't have to be an empty string.) For example, you can make it a cell reference.

Using the new IFERROR Function

If your workbook will be used only by people who have Excel 2007, you might prefer to use the new IFERROR function. This function takes two arguments: The first argument is the expression that's checked for an error, and the second is the value to return if the formula evaluates to an error. The formula presented in the preceding section can be rewritten as

```
=IFERROR(B2/C2,"")
```

Using this function has two advantages:

- Writing error-checking formulas is easier because IFERROR does the work of both the IF function and the ISERROR function.

- The expression is evaluated only one time, which can result in faster recalculation times.

Keep in mind that because IFERROR is new to Excel 2007, it doesn't work with previous versions of Excel.

Part IV

Using Goal Seeking

Many Excel worksheets are set up to do what-if analysis. For example, you might have a sales projection worksheet that allows you to answer questions such as "What is the total profit if sales increase by 20 percent?" If you set up your worksheet properly, you can change the value in one cell to see what happens to the profit cell.

Excel offers a useful tool that can best be described as what-if analysis in reverse. If you know what a formula result *should* be, Excel can tell you the value that you need to enter in an input cell to produce that result. In other words, you can ask a question such as "How much do sales need to increase to produce a profit of $1.2 million?"

Figure 83-1 shows a simple worksheet that calculates mortgage loan information. This worksheet has four input cells (C4:C7) and four formula cells (C10:C13).

	A	B	C	D	E	F	G
1		**Mortgage Loan Worksheet**					
2							
3		**Input Cells**					
4		Purchase Price:	$325,000				
5		Down Payment:	10%				
6		Loan Term (Months):	360				
7		Interest Rate (APR):	6.50%				
8							
9		**Result Cells**					
10		Loan Amount:	$292,500				
11		Monthly Payment:	$2,054				
12		Total Payments:	$739,520				
13		Total Interest:	$447,020				
14							
15							

Sheet1

Figure 83-1: Goal Seeker can tell you the value of an input cell that will result in a desired result.

Assume that you're in the market for a new home and you know that you can afford an $1,800 monthly mortgage payment. You also know that a lender can issue a fixed-rate mortgage loan for 6.50 percent, based on an 80 percent loan-to-value (that is, a 20 percent down payment). The question is "What is the maximum purchase price I can handle?" In other words, which value in cell C4 causes the formula in cell C11 to result in $1,800? One approach is to simply plug a bunch of values into cell C4 until C11 displays $1,800; however, Excel can determine the answer much more efficiently.

To answer this question, follow these steps:

1. Choose Date ➪ Data Tools ➪ What-If Analysis ➪ Goal Seek. Excel displays the Goal Seek dialog box.

2. Complete the three fields in the dialog box (shown in Figure 83-2) similar to forming a sentence: You want to set cell C11 to 1800 by changing cell C4. Enter this information in the dialog box by either typing the cell references or pointing with the mouse.

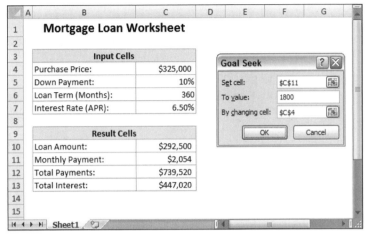

Figure 83-2: Enter the information in the Goal Seek dialog box, to the right of the mortgage loan worksheet.

3. Click OK to begin the goal-seeking process.

In less than a second, Excel displays the Goal Seek Status dialog box, which shows the target value and the value that Excel calculated. In this case, Excel finds an exact value. The worksheet now displays the found value in cell C4 ($284,779). As a result of this value, the monthly payment amount is $1,800. At this point, you have two options:

- Click OK to replace the original value with the found value.

- Click Cancel to restore your worksheet to the way it was before you chose the Goal Seek command.

This example is very simple. The power of goal seeking is more apparent when you're dealing with a complex model with many interrelated formulas.

Part IV

Understanding the Secret about Names

Most Excel users have at least a rudimentary understanding of named cells and named ranges. You can use the Formulas ➪ Defined Names ➪ Define Name command to provide a meaningful name to a cell or range. Then you can use those defined names in your formulas.

For example, if you give the name Sales to range A2:A13, you can write a formula such as =SUM(Sales). Just about every Excel user I know of refers to this concept as named ranges or named cells (even I did, in the first paragraph of this tip). This terminology isn't quite accurate, however.

Here's the secret to understanding names:

When you create a name, you're creating a named formula. Unlike a normal formula, a named formula doesn't exist in a cell. Rather, it exists in Excel's memory.

Although this revelation isn't exactly earth-shaking, keeping this "secret" in mind helps you understand some advanced naming techniques.

When you work with the New Name dialog box, the Refers To field contains the formula, and the Name field contains the formula's name. You'll find that the contents of the Refers To field always begin with an equal sign, which makes it a formula.

As you can see in Figure 84-1, the workbook contains a name (InterestRate) for cell B1 on Sheet1. The Refers To field lists the following formula:

```
=Sheet1!$B$1
```

Figure 84-1: Technically, the name InterestRate is a named formula, not a named cell.

Whenever you use the name InterestRate, Excel evaluates the formula named InterestRate and returns the result. For example, you might type this formula into a cell:

```
=InterestRate*1.05
```

When Excel evaluates this formula, it first evaluates the formula named InterestRate (which exists only in memory, not in a cell). Excel then multiplies the result of this named formula by 1.05 and displays the result. This cell formula, of course, is equivalent to the following formula, which uses the actual cell reference rather than the name:

```
=Sheet1!$B$1*1.05
```

Using Named Constants

This tip describes a useful technique that can remove some clutter from your worksheets: named constants.

Consider a worksheet that generates an invoice and calculates sales tax for a sales amount. The common approach is to insert the sales tax rate value into a cell and then use this cell reference in your formulas. To make things easier, you probably would name this cell something like SalesTax.

You can store your sales tax rate by using a name (and avoid using a cell). Figure 85-1 demonstrates the following steps:

1. Choose Formulas ➪ Defined Names ➪ Define Name to open the New Name dialog box.

2. Enter the name (in this case, SalesTax) into the Name field.

3. Click the Refers To field, delete its contents, and replace it with a simple formula, such as =**7.5%**.

4. Click OK to close the dialog box.

Figure 85-1: Defining a name that refers to a constant.

The preceding steps create a named formula that doesn't use any cell references. To try it out, enter the following formula into any cell:

```
=SalesTax
```

This simple formula returns .075, the result of the formula named SalesTax. Because this named formula always returns the same result, you can think of it as a *named constant.* And, you can use this constant in a more complex formula, such as this one:

```
=A1*SalesTax
```

SalesTax is a workbook-level name, so you can use it in any worksheet in the workbook.

A named constant can also consist of text. For example, you can define a constant for a company's name. You can use the New Name dialog box to create the following formula, named MSFT:

```
="Microsoft Corporation"
```

Then you can use a cell formula, such as this one:

```
="Annual Report: "&MSFT
```

This formula returns the text Annual Report: Microsoft Corporation.

 NOTE

Names that don't refer to ranges don't appear in the Name box or in the Go To dialog box (which appears when you press F5). This situation makes sense because these constants don't reside anywhere tangible. They do, however, appear in the Paste Name dialog box (which appears when you press F3). This does make sense, because you use these names in formulas.

As you might expect, you can change the value of the constant at any time by using the Name Manager dialog box (choose Formulas ⇨ Defined Names ⇨ Name Manager). Just click the Edit button to display the Edit Name dialog box. Then change the value in the Refers To field. When you close the dialog box, Excel uses the new value to recalculate the formulas that use this name.

Using Functions in Names

Tip 85 describes how to create a named constant. This tip, however, takes the concept one step further and describes how to use worksheet functions in your names.

Figure 86-1 shows an example of a named formula. In this case, the formula is named ThisMonth, and the actual formula is

```
=MONTH(TODAY())
```

Figure 86-1: Defining a named formula that uses worksheet functions.

The named formula uses two worksheet functions. The TODAY function returns the current date, and the MONTH function returns the month number of its date argument. Therefore, you can enter a formula such as the following into a cell and it returns the number of the current month. For example, if the current month is April, the following formula returns 4:

```
=ThisMonth
```

A more useful named formula returns the month name as text. To do so, create a formula named MonthName, defined this way:

```
=TEXT(TODAY(),"mmmm")
```

Now enter the following formula into a cell, and it returns the current month name as text. In the month of April, the formula returns the text April:

```
=MonthName
```

Here's another example of a named formula that uses a function. Create a formula with the name SumA, defined this way:

```
=SUM(Sheet1!$A:A$)
```

As you might expect, this named formula returns the sum of all values in column A.

NOTE

Note that the name is defined by using absolute references. This is critical. If you use relative references, the formula evaluates differently, depending on the location of the active cell.

Creating a List of Names

The Name Manager dialog box, shown in Figure 87-1, is a handy tool that displays a list of all names defined in the active workbook. Display this dialog box by choosing Formulas ⇨ Defined Names ⇨ Name Manager. Or, just press Ctrl+F3.

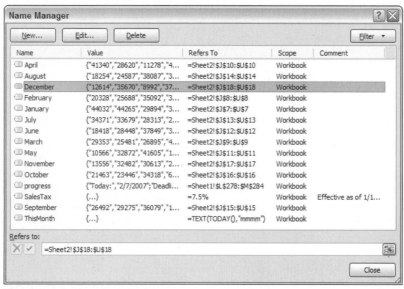

Figure 87-1: The Name Manager dialog box displays a sortable list of all names.

Suppose that you want to put a list of those names into a worksheet range, as a way to document your project. Although the Name Manager dialog box doesn't provide a way to paste a list of names, doing so is possible — you just need to know where to look.

The secret Paste List button is in the Paste Name dialog box. To display this dialog box, choose Formulas ⇨ Defined Names ⇨ Use in Formula ⇨ Paste Name. Or, press F3. Then click the Paste List button to create a list of names (and their definitions) starting at the active cell. Figure 87-2 shows the Paste Name dialog box, along with the list it created.

NOTE

If you display the Paste Name dialog box when you're editing a formula, the dialog box doesn't display the Paste List button.

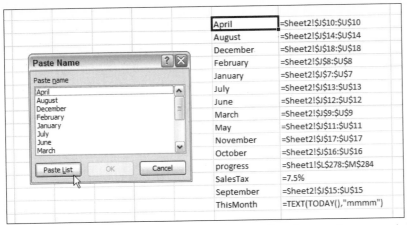

Figure 87-2: Use the Paste List button to create a list of names in your worksheet.

Using Dynamic Names

This tip describes a useful concept that can save you lots of time: the *dynamic named formula*, which is a named formula that refers to a range that isn't fixed in size. This idea can be difficult to grasp, so I provide a quick example.

Examine the worksheet shown in Figure 88-1. This sheet contains a listing of sales by month, through the month of May.

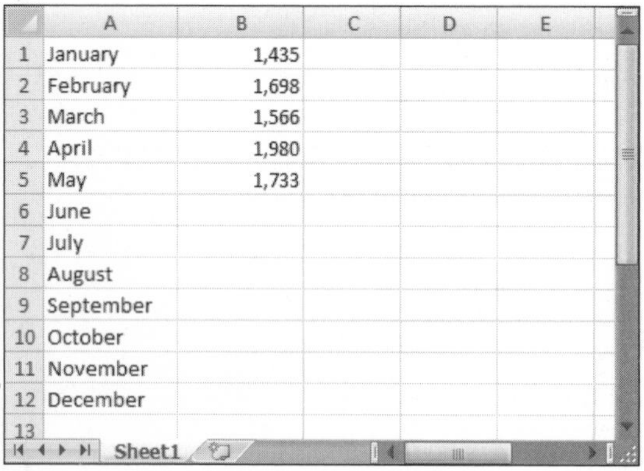

Figure 88-1: You can use a dynamic named formula to represent the sales data in column B.

Suppose that you want to create a name (SalesData) for the data in column B and you don't want this name to refer to empty cells. In other words, the reference for the SalesData range changes each month as you add a new sales figure. You can, of course, use the Name Manager dialog box to change the range name definition each month. Or, you can create a dynamic named formula that changes automatically as you enter new data (or delete existing data).

To create a dynamic named formula, start by re-creating the worksheet shown in Figure 88-1. Then follow these steps:

1. Select Formulas ⇨ Defined Names ⇨ Define Name to display the New Name dialog box.

2. Enter **SalesData** in the Name field.

3. Enter the following formula in the Refers To field (see Figure 88-2):

   ```
   =OFFSET(Sheet1!$B$1,0,0,COUNTA(Sheet1!$B:$B),1)
   ```

4. Click OK to close the New Name dialog box.

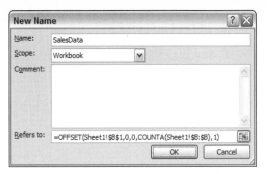

Figure 88-2: Creating a dynamic named formula.

The preceding steps create a named formula that uses the Excel OFFSET and COUNTA functions to return a range that changes, based on the number of non-empty cells in column B. To try out this formula, enter the following formula into any cell not in column B:

```
=SUM(SalesData)
```

This formula returns the sum of the values in column B. To verify that the name refers to only the nonblank cells, try this formula:

```
=ROWS(SalesData)
```

The formula returns 5, the number of rows in the range. Add more data or delete data, and you see that that SalesData name adjusts according.

Note that SalesData isn't displayed in the Name box and doesn't appear in the Go To dialog box. You can, however, open the Go To dialog box and type **SalesData** to select the range.

NOTE

This formula works only for data that doesn't contain gaps. In this example, if cell B3 is empty, the SalesData name doesn't include the last value in the column.

At this point, you might be wondering about the value of this exercise. After all, a simple formula such as the following does the same job, without the need to define a formula:

```
=SUM(B:B)
```

One of the most common uses for a dynamic named formula is for setting up data to be used in a chart. You can use this technique to create a chart with a data series that adjusts automatically as you enter new data:

```
=Sheet1!$E$1:$K$490
```

Part IV

In Excel 2007, a chart's data adjusts automatically if the data is in a table (specified by choosing Insert ⇨ Tables ⇨ Table), but creating a dynamic name is useful if you want to chart continually changing data that's not in a table.

CROSS-REFERENCE

For more on charts, turn to Part VII.

Creating Worksheet-Level Names

Normally, when you name a cell or range, you can use that name in all worksheets in the workbook. For example, if you create a name, RegionTotal, that refers to the cell M32 on Sheet1, you can use this name in any formula in any worksheet. This name is a *workbook-level* name (or a *global* name). By default, all cell and range names are workbook-level names.

Suppose that you have several worksheets in a workbook and you want to use the same name (such as RegionTotal) on each sheet. In this case, you should create worksheet-level names (sometimes referred to as *local* names).

To define the worksheet-level name RegionTotal, activate the worksheet in which you want to define the name and choose Formulas ⇨ Defined Names ⇨ Define Name. The New Name dialog box then appears. In the Names field, enter the name in the Name field, and use the Scope drop-down list to select the sheet in which the name is valid. Figure 89-1 shows a worksheet-level name being created.

New Name	? X
Name:	RegionTotal
Scope:	Region3 ▾
Comment:	
Refers to:	=Region3!$E$12
	OK Cancel

Figure 89-1: Creating a worksheet-level name.

You can also create a worksheet-level name by using the Name box (located to the left of the Formula bar). Select the cell or range you want named, click in the Name box, and type the name, preceded by the sheet name and an exclamation point. Press Enter to create the name. Here's an example of a worksheet-level name:

```
Region3!RegionTotal
```

If the worksheet name contains at least one space, enclose the worksheet name in apostrophes, like this:

```
'Western Region'!RegionTotal
```

When you write a formula that uses a worksheet-level name on the sheet in which you defined it, you don't need to include the worksheet name in the range name. (The Name box doesn't display the worksheet name, either.) If you use the name in a formula on a *different* worksheet, however, you must use the entire name (sheet name, exclamation point, and name).

The Name Manager dialog box clearly identifies each name by its scope (see Figure 89-2). If the scope of a name isn't Workbook, the dialog box lists the sheet on which the name is defined.

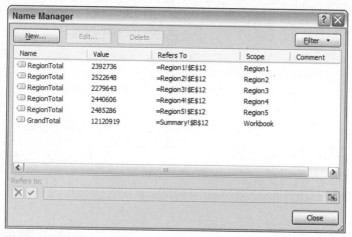

Figure 89-2: The Name Manager makes it easy to distinguish between workbook-level names and worksheet-level names.

NOTE

Only the worksheet-level names on the current sheet appear in the Name box. Similarly, only worksheet-level names in the current sheet appear in the list when you open the Paste Name dialog box (by pressing F3).

Working with Pre-1900 Dates

According to Excel, the world began on January 1, 1900. If you work with historical information, you might have noticed that Excel doesn't recognize pre-1900 dates. For example, if you enter `July 4, 1776` into a cell, Excel interprets it as text, not a date.

Unfortunately, the only way to work with pre-1900 dates is to enter the date into a cell as text. The problem, however, is that you can't perform any manipulation on dates recognized as text. For example, you can't change its numeric formatting, you can't determine which day of the week this date occurred on, and you can't calculate the date that occurs seven days later.

To be able to sort by dates that precede 1900, enter the year, month, and day into separate cells. Figure 90-1 shows a simple example.

	A	B	C	D	E
1	**President Birthdays**				
2					
3	**President**	**Year**	**Month**	**Day**	
4	James A. Garfield	1831	11	19	
5	William McKinley	1843	1	29	
6	William Henry Harrison	1773	2	9	
7	Franklin D. Roosevelt	1882	1	30	
8	Warren G. Harding	1865	11	2	
9	Zachary Taylor	1784	11	24	
10	Abraham Lincoln	1809	2	12	
11					
12					

Figure 90-1: To allow sorting by pre-1900 dates, enter the year, month, and day into separate cells.

To sort the presidents by birthday, first do an ascending sort on column D, and then an ascending sort on column C, and, finally, an ascending sort on column B. The result is shown in Figure 90-2.

	A	B	C	D	E
1	**President Birthdays**				
2					
3	**President**	**Year**	**Month**	**Day**	
4	William Henry Harrison	1773	2	9	
5	Zachary Taylor	1784	11	24	
6	Abraham Lincoln	1809	2	12	
7	James A. Garfield	1831	11	19	
8	William McKinley	1843	1	29	
9	Warren G. Harding	1865	11	2	
10	Franklin D. Roosevelt	1882	1	30	
11					
12					
13					

Figure 90-2: The presidents sorted by birthday, after performing three sorts.

Part IV

NOTE

I created an Excel add-in, XDATE, which contains a number of functions that make it possible to work with pre-1900 dates. You can download a free copy from my Web site: `www.j-walk.com/ss`.

Working with Negative Time Values

Because Excel stores dates and times as numeric values, you can add or subtract one from the other. Figure 91-1 shows a simple example that tracks the number of hours worked. The total is calculated in cell B8 by using this formula (and formatted using the [h]:mm number format):

```
=SUM(B2:B6)
```

Cell B9 uses the following formula to calculate the amount of time required to make up a 40-hour work week:

```
=(40/24)-B8
```

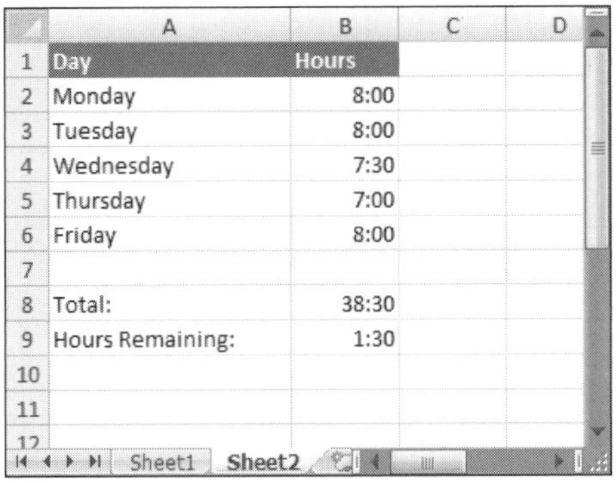

	A	B	C	D
1	Day	Hours		
2	Monday	8:00		
3	Tuesday	8:00		
4	Wednesday	7:30		
5	Thursday	7:00		
6	Friday	8:00		
7				
8	Total:	38:30		
9	Hours Remaining:	1:30		
10				
11				
12				

Sheet1 Sheet2

Figure 91-1: Cell B8 displays the time left in a 40-hour workweek.

If the number of hours worked exceeds 40 hours, the formula in cell B9 returns a negative number. But, as you can see in Figure 91-2, Excel can't deal with a negative time value.

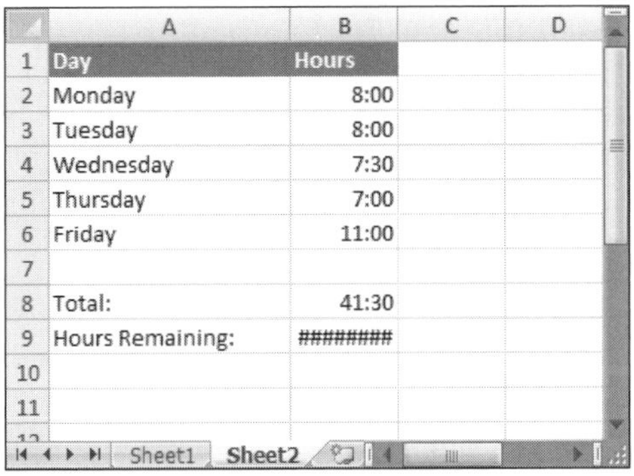

	A	B	C	D
1	Day	Hours		
2	Monday	8:00		
3	Tuesday	8:00		
4	Wednesday	7:30		
5	Thursday	7:00		
6	Friday	11:00		
7				
8	Total:	41:30		
9	Hours Remaining:	########		
10				
11				
12				

Sheet1 Sheet2

Figure 91-2: Excel displays a series of hash marks for negative time values.

Part IV

By default, Excel uses a date system that begins with January 1, 1900. A negative time value generates a date-time combination that falls before this date, which is invalid.

One solution is to use the optional 1904 date system, which assigns the date serial number 1 to January 2, 1904. Choose Office ⇨ Excel Options to display the Excel Options dialog box. Click the Advanced tab, and select the Use 1904 Date System check box. Your negative times are now displayed correctly, as shown in Figure 91-3.

	A	B	C	D
1	Day	Hours		
2	Monday	8:00		
3	Tuesday	8:00		
4	Wednesday	7:30		
5	Thursday	7:00		
6	Friday	11:00		
7				
8	Total:	41:30		
9	Hours Remaining:	-1:30		
10				
11				

Sheet1 Sheet2

Figure 91-3: Switching to the 1904 date system causes negative times to display properly.

CAUTION

Be careful if your workbook contains links to other workbooks that don't use the 1904 date system. In such a case, the mismatch of date systems can cause erroneous results.

Part  V

Useful Formula Examples

In this part, you'll find many formula examples. Some are useful as is. Others can be adapted to your own needs.

Tips and Where to Find Them

Calculating Holidays

Determining the date for a particular holiday can be tricky. Some holidays, such as New Year's Day and Independence Day (U.S.), are no-brainers because they always occur on the same date. For these kinds of holidays, you can simply use the DATE function. For example, to calculate New Year's Day (which always falls on January 1) for a specific year stored in cell A1, you can enter this function:

```
=DATE(A1,1,1)
```

Other holidays are defined in terms of a particular occurrence of a particular weekday in a particular month. For example, Labor Day in the U.S. falls on the first Monday in September.

The formulas that follow all assume that cell A1 contains a year (for example, 2008). Notice that because New Year's Day, Independence Day, Veterans Day, and Christmas Day all fall on the same days of the year, their dates can be calculated by using the simple DATE function.

New Year's Day

This holiday always falls on January 1:

```
=DATE(A1,1,1)
```

Martin Luther King Jr. Day

This holiday occurs on the third Monday in January. The following formula calculates Martin Luther King Jr. Day for the year in cell A1:

```
=DATE(A1,1,1)+IF(2<WEEKDAY(DATE(A1,1,1)),7-WEEKDAY(DATE(A1,1,1))
+2,2-WEEKDAY(DATE(A1,1,1)))+((3-1)*7)
```

Presidents' Day

Presidents' Day occurs on the third Monday in February. This formula calculates Presidents' Day for the year in cell A1:

```
=DATE(A1,2,1)+IF(2<WEEKDAY(DATE(A1,2,1)),7-WEEKDAY(DATE(A1,2,1))
+2,2-WEEKDAY(DATE(A1,2,1)))+((3-1)*7)
```

Easter

Calculating the date for Easter is difficult because of the complicated manner in which Easter is determined. Easter Day is the first Sunday after the next full moon occurs after the vernal equinox. I found these formulas to calculate Easter on the Web. I have no idea how they work. They don't work if your workbook uses the 1904 date system (refer to Tip 91):

```
=DOLLAR(("4/"&A1)/7+MOD(19*MOD(A1,19)-7,30)*14%,)*7-6
```

This one is slightly shorter, but equally obtuse:

```
=FLOOR("5/"&DAY(MINUTE(A1/38)/2+56)&"/"&A1,7)-34
```

Memorial Day

The last Monday in May is Memorial Day. This formula calculates Memorial Day for the year in cell A1:

```
=DATE(A1,6,1)+IF(2<WEEKDAY(DATE(A1,6,1)),7-WEEKDAY(DATE(A1,6,1))
+2,2-WEEKDAY(DATE(A1,6,1)))+((1-1)*7)-7
```

Notice that this formula calculates the first Monday in June and then subtracts 7 from the result, to return the last Monday in May.

Independence Day

The Independence Day holiday always falls on July 4:

```
=DATE(A1,7,4)
```

Labor Day

Labor Day occurs on the first Monday in September. This formula calculates Labor Day for the year in cell A1:

```
=DATE(A1,9,1)+IF(2<WEEKDAY(DATE(A1,9,1)),7-WEEKDAY(DATE(A1,9,1))
+2,2-WEEKDAY(DATE(A1,9,1)))+((1-1)*7)
```

Columbus Day

The Columbus Day holiday occurs on the second Monday in October. The following formula calculates Columbus Day for the year in cell A1:

```
=DATE(A1,10,1)+IF(2<WEEKDAY(DATE(A1,10,1)),7-WEEKDAY(DATE(A1,10,1))
+2,2-WEEKDAY(DATE(A1,10,1)))+((2-1)*7)
```

Veterans Day

The Veterans Day holiday always falls on November 11:

```
=DATE(A1,11,11)
```

Thanksgiving Day

Thanksgiving Day is celebrated on the fourth Thursday in November. This formula calculates Thanksgiving Day for the year in cell A1:

```
=DATE(A1,11,1)+IF(5<WEEKDAY(DATE(A1,11,1)),7-WEEKDAY(DATE(A1,11,1))
+5,5-WEEKDAY(DATE(A1,11,1)))+((4-1)*7)
```

Christmas Day

Christmas Day always falls on December 25:

```
=DATE(A1,12,25)
```

Calculating a Weighted Average

The Excel AVERAGE function returns the average (or mean) of a range of data. Often, users need to calculate a weighted average. You can search all day, and you won't find a function to do the calculation. You can, however, calculate a weighted average by creating a formula that uses the SUMPRODUCT and the SUM function.

Figure 93-1 shows a simple worksheet that contains 30 days of gasoline prices. For example, the price was $2.48 for the first four days. Then it decreased to $2.41 for two days. The price then dipped to $2.39 for three days, and so on.

	A	B	C	D
1	Gas Prices For January			
2				
3		Price	No. Days	
4		2.48	4	
5		2.41	2	
6		2.39	3	
7		2.35	1	
8		2.34	1	
9		2.41	2	
10		2.37	2	
11		2.42	4	
12		2.41	3	
13		2.47	8	
14				
15	Average:	2.405		
16	Wt. Avg:	2.428		
17				

Figure 93-1: The formula in cell B16 calculates the weighted average of the gas prices.

Cell B15 contains a formula that uses the AVERAGE function:

```
=AVERAGE(B4:B13)
```

If you think about it, this formula doesn't return an accurate result. Rather, the prices must be weighted by factoring in the number of days that each price was in effect. In other words, a weighted average is the appropriate type of calculation.

The following formula, in cell B16, does the job:

```
=SUMPRODUCT(B4:B13,C4:C13)/SUM(C4:C13)
```

This formula multiplies each price by its corresponding number of days and then adds all those products. The result is then divided by the number of days. You can easily adapt this formula for other types of weighted average calculations.

Calculating a Person's Age

Calculating a person's age is a bit tricky because the calculation depends on not only the current year but also the current day. And then you have to consider the complications resulting from leap years.

In this tip, I present three methods to calculate a person's age. These formulas assume that cell B1 contains the date of birth and that cell B2 contains the current date.

Method 1

The following formula subtracts the date of birth from the current date and divides by 365.25. The INT function then eliminates the decimal part of the result:

```
=INT((B2-B1)/365.25)
```

This formula isn't 100 percent accurate because it divides by the average number of days in a year. For example, consider a child who is exactly one year old. This formula returns 0, not 1.

Method 2

A more accurate way to calculate age uses the YEARFRAC function:

```
=INT(YEARFRAC(B2, B1))
```

The YEARFRAC function is normally used in financial calculations, but it works just fine for calculating ages. This function calculates the fraction of the year represented by the number of whole days between two dates. Using the INT function gets rid of the fraction and returns an integer.

Method 3

The third method for calculating age uses the DATEDIF function. This undocumented function isn't described in the Excel Help system:

```
=DATEDIF(B1,B2,"Y")
```

If you're a stickler for accuracy, here's another version:

```
=DATEDIF(B1,B2,"y") & " years, "&DATEDIF(B1,B2,"ym") &
" months, "&DATEDIF(B1,B2,"md") & " days"
```

This function returns a text string, like this:

```
33 years, 8 months, 17 days
```

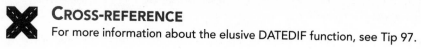 **CROSS-REFERENCE**

For more information about the elusive DATEDIF function, see Tip 97.

Ranking Values with an Array Formula

Often, computing the rank order for the values in a range of data is helpful. For example, if you have a worksheet containing the annual sales figures for your sales staff, you might want to know how each person ranks, from highest to lowest.

If you've used the Excel RANK function, you might have noticed that the ranks produced by this function don't handle ties the way that you might like. For example, if two values are tied for third place, the RANK function gives both of them a rank of 3. You might prefer to assign each an average (or midpoint) of the ranks — in other words, a rank of 3.5 for both values tied for third place.

Figure 95-1 shows a worksheet that uses two methods to rank a column of values. The first method (column C) uses the Excel RANK function. Column D uses array formulas to compute the ranks. The range B2:B16 is named Sales.

	A	B	C	D	E
1	Sales Person	Sales Amount	Excel's RANK Function	Array Formula	
2	Martin	312,000	1	1	
3	Jackson	305,000	2	2	
4	Ferlinghetti	145,000	3	3.5	
5	Kendricks	145,000	3	3.5	
6	Bassinger	126,000	5	5	
7	Everett	123,000	6	6	
8	Gomez	121,000	7	7	
9	Isaacs	102,000	8	8	
10	Childs	101,000	9	9	
11	Anthony	98,000	10	11	
12	Hernandez	98,000	10	11	
13	Galworthy	98,000	10	11	
14	Marx	89,000	13	13	
15	Adams	74,000	14	14	
16	Bennett	25,000	15	15	
17					
18					

Sheet1

Figure 95-1: Ranking data with the Excel RANK function and with array formulas.

The following line is the array formula in cell D2, which is copied to the cells below it:

```
=SUM(1*(B5<=Sales))-(SUM(1*(B5=Sales))-1)/2
```

NOTE

An array formula is a special type of formula that works with internal arrays of data. When you enter an array formula, you must press Ctrl+Shift+Enter (not just Enter) to indicate that it's an array formula. Excel displays curly braces around the formula to remind you that it's an array formula.

Part V

Notice that two people are tied for third place. The RANK function assigns each person a rank of 3, but the array formula gives each one a rank of 3.5. Also, three people are tied for tenth place. The RANK function gives each one a rank of 10. The array formula, on the other hand, gives these three people a rank of 11, which is the midpoint of 10, 11, and 12.

Converting Inches to Feet and Inches

If you ever need to convert inches to feet and inches, you'll quickly understand the merits of the metric system. Converting inches to feet and inches is basically a division problem, in which you need to pay attention to the remainder (leftover inches).

The following formula assumes that cell A1 contains a value that represents inches. The formula displays the result in feet and inches (for example, if A1 contains 43, the result is 3'7"):

```
=TEXT(INT(A1/12),"#,##0")&"' "&MOD(A1,12)&""""
```

This formula returns a text string, so you can't perform mathematical operations on the result. If you want to convert a feet-and-inches text string back to inches, this formula does the job (it assumes that cell A1 contains a string such 9'11"):

```
=(LEFT(A1,FIND("'",A1)-1)+((MID(A1,FIND("'",A1)+1,LEN(A1)-
FIND("'",A1)-1))/12))*12
```

 NOTE
These formulas work with positive inches only.

Figure 96-1 shows these formulas in use.

	A	B	C	D	E
1	**Inches**	**Feet & Inches**	**Back to Inches**		
2	43	3' 7"	43		
3	12	1' 0"	12		
4	1	0' 1"	1		
5	600	50' 0"	600		
6	632	52' 8"	632		
7	12.5	1' 0.5"	12.5		
8	36.25	3' 0.25"	36.25		
9	119	9' 11"	119		
10					
11					

Figure 96-1: Converting inches to feet and inches and then back to inches.

Part V

Using the DATEDIF Function

In Tip 94, I present a formula that uses the DATEDIF function, which calculates the difference between two dates and expresses the result in terms of months, days, or years.

This useful function, which isn't documented in the Help system, is one of the little Excel mysteries. Although the Excel 2000 Help system has an entry for DATEDIF, it's not documented in earlier or later versions.

The old Lotus 1-2-3 spreadsheet introduced DATEDIF, and Excel likely included the function for compatibility purposes. But, for some reason, Microsoft doesn't want to acknowledge its existence. Lawyers are probably somehow involved in this mystery.

In any case, this tip describes the DATEDIF function and tells you what Microsoft isn't willing to tell you. The syntax for the DATEDIF function is

```
=DATEDIF(Date1,Date2,Interval)
```

Date1 and Date2 are standard dates (or a reference to a cell that contains a date). Date1 must be earlier (or equal to) Date2. The third argument, Interval, is a text string that specifies the unit of time that will be returned.

Valid interval codes are described in this list:

- **m:** The number of complete months between Date1 and Date2.
- **d:** The number of days between Date1 and Date2.
- **y:** The number of complete years between Date1 and Date2.
- **ym:** The number of months between Date1 and Date2. This interval excludes years, so it works as though the two dates are in the same year.
- **yd:** The number of days between Date1 and Date2. This interval excludes years, so it works as though Date1 and Date2 are in the same year.
- **md:** The number of days between Date1 and Date2. This interval excludes both month and year, so it works as though Date1 and Date2 are in the same month and the same year.

Figure 97-1 shows a few examples of using the DATEDIF function with each of its possible interval arguments.

	A	B	C	D	E	
1	Date1	Date2	Interval	Result	Explanation	
2	12/2/2005	9/21/2007	m	21	Complete months	
3	12/2/2005	9/21/2007	d	658	Total days	
4	12/2/2005	9/21/2007	y	1	Complete years	
5	12/2/2005	9/21/2007	ym	9	Months (ignoring years)	
6	12/2/2005	9/21/2007	yd	42	Days (ignorng years)	
7	12/2/2005	9/21/2007	md	19	Days (ignoring years and months)	
8						
9						
10						

H ◄ ► H   Sheet1   Sheet2   Sheet3

Figure 97-1: Examples of using the DATEDIF function.

Counting Characters in a Cell

This tip contains formula examples that count characters in a cell.

Counting Specific Characters in a Cell

The following formula counts the instances of *B* (uppercase only) in the string in cell A1:

```
=LEN(A1)-LEN(SUBSTITUTE(A1,"B",""))
```

This formula works by using the SUBSTITUTE function to create a new string (in memory) that has all instances of *B* removed. Then the length of this string is subtracted from the length of the original string. The result reveals the number of occurrences of *B* in the original string.

The comparison is case sensitive. So, for example, if cell A1 contains the text *Bubble Chart*, the formula returns 1.

The following formula is a bit more versatile. It counts the number of *B*s (both upper- and lowercase) in the string in cell A1.

```
=LEN(A1)-LEN(SUBSTITUTE(UPPER(A1),"B",""))
```

If cell A1 contains the text `Bubble Chart`, the formula returns 3.

Counting the Occurrences of a Substring in a Cell

The following formula works with more than one character. It returns the number of occurrences of a particular substring (contained in cell B1) within a string (contained in cell A1). The substring can consist of any number of characters:

```
=(LEN(A1)-LEN(SUBSTITUTE(A1,B1,"")))/LEN(B1)
```

For example, if cell A1 contains the text *Blonde On Blonde* and B1 contains the text *Blonde*, the formula returns 2.

The comparison is case sensitive, so if B1 contains the text *blonde*, the formula returns 0. The following formula is a modified version that performs a case-insensitive comparison:

```
=(LEN(A1)-LEN(SUBSTITUTE(UPPER(A1),UPPER(B1),"")))/LEN(B1)
```

Numbering Weeks

Everyone knows that a year consists of 52 weeks. So, for any given day, you should be able to determine the week number, right? The question seems simple, but in real life, it's a bit more complicated.

The Excel WEEKNUM function seems like the ticket. This function accepts a date and returns the week number. It also assumes that the week containing January 1 is the first week of the year. Therefore, the first week of the year can consist of as few as one day (for example, 2011) or as many as seven days (for example, 2006).

The Excel WEEKNUM function doesn't conform to the International Standards Organization (ISO) standard. According to the ISO standard:

- A week always begins on a Monday and ends on a Sunday.

- Week 1 is the week that contains the year's first Thursday.

This definition means that, in some years, the first days of the year might have the week number 52 or 53. (They're in a week in the preceding calendar year).

 NOTE

The Excel WEEKNUM function uses an optional second argument. If this second argument is 2, weeks are assumed to begin on Monday rather than on Tuesday. However, using this option still doesn't make the WEEKNUM function correspond to the ISO standard.

The following formula, which was created by Laurent Longre, returns the ISO week number for the date in cell A1:

```
=1+INT((A1-DATE(YEAR(A1+4-WEEKDAY(A1+6)),1,5)+
WEEKDAY(DATE(YEAR(A1+4-WEEKDAY(A1+6)),1,3)))/7)
```

Figure 99-1 compares three ways to calculate the week number:

- Use the Excel WEEKNUM function (with Sunday as the week start day).

- Use the Excel WEEKNUM function (with Monday as the week start day).

- Use the ISO week number formula.

	A	B	C	D
1	Date	Excel WEEKNUM	Excel WEEKNUM,2	ISO Week Number
2	Saturday, January 01, 2011	1	1	52
3	Sunday, January 02, 2011	2	1	52
4	Monday, January 03, 2011	2	2	1
5	Tuesday, January 04, 2011	2	2	1
6	Wednesday, January 05, 2011	2	2	1
7	Thursday, January 06, 2011	2	2	1
8	Friday, January 07, 2011	2	2	1
9	Saturday, January 08, 2011	2	2	1
10	Sunday, January 09, 2011	3	2	1
11	Monday, January 10, 2011	3	3	2
12	Tuesday, January 11, 2011	3	3	2
13	Wednesday, January 12, 2011	3	3	2
14	Thursday, January 13, 2011	3	3	2
15	Friday, January 14, 2011	3	3	2
16	Saturday, January 15, 2011	3	3	2
17	Sunday, January 16, 2011	4	3	2
18	Monday, January 17, 2011	4	4	3
19	Tuesday, January 18, 2011	4	4	3
20	Wednesday, January 19, 2011	4	4	3
21	Thursday, January 20, 2011	4	4	3
22	Friday, January 21, 2011	4	4	3
23	Saturday, January 22, 2011	4	4	3

Sheet1

Figure 99-1: Three ways to calculate a week number.

Using a Pivot Table Rather than Formulas

The Excel pivot table feature is incredibly powerful, and you can often create pivot tables in lieu of creating formulas. This tip describes a simple problem and provides three different solutions.

Figure 100-1 shows a range of data that contains student test scores. The goal is to calculate the average score for all students plus the average score for each gender.

	A	B	C
1	**Student**	**Score**	**Gender**
2	Anne	90	Female
3	Billy	96	Male
4	Chuck	87	Male
5	Darlene	75	Female
6	Ella	84	Female
7	Frank	89	Male
8	George	85	Male
9	Hilda	97	Female
10	Ida	77	Female
11	John	93	Male
12	Keith	89	Male
13	Larry	77	Male
14	Mary	85	Female
15	Nora	100	Female
16	Opie	71	Male
17	Peter	89	Male
18	Quincy	83	Male
19	Rhoda	91	Female
20	Sally	87	Female
21	Tim	97	Male
22	Ubella	83	Female
23	Vince	86	Male
24	Walter	83	Male
25	Xavier	78	Male
26	Yolanda	100	Female
27	Zola	84	Female
28			

Sheet1

Figure 100-1: What's the best way to calculate the average test score for males versus females?

Inserting Subtotals

The first solution involves automatically inserting subtotals. For you to be able to use this method, the data must be sorted by the column that will trigger the subtotaling. In this case, you need to sort by the Gender column. Follow these steps:

1. Select any cell in column C.

2. Right-click, and choose Sort ➪ Sort A To Z from the shortcut menu.

3. Choose Data ⇨ Outline ⇨ Subtotal, to display the Subtotal dialog box.

4. In the Subtotal dialog box, specify At Each Change in Gender, Use Function Average, and Add Subtotal to Score.

The result of adding subtotals is shown in Figure 100-2. Notice that Excel also creates an outline, so you can hide the details and view just the summary.

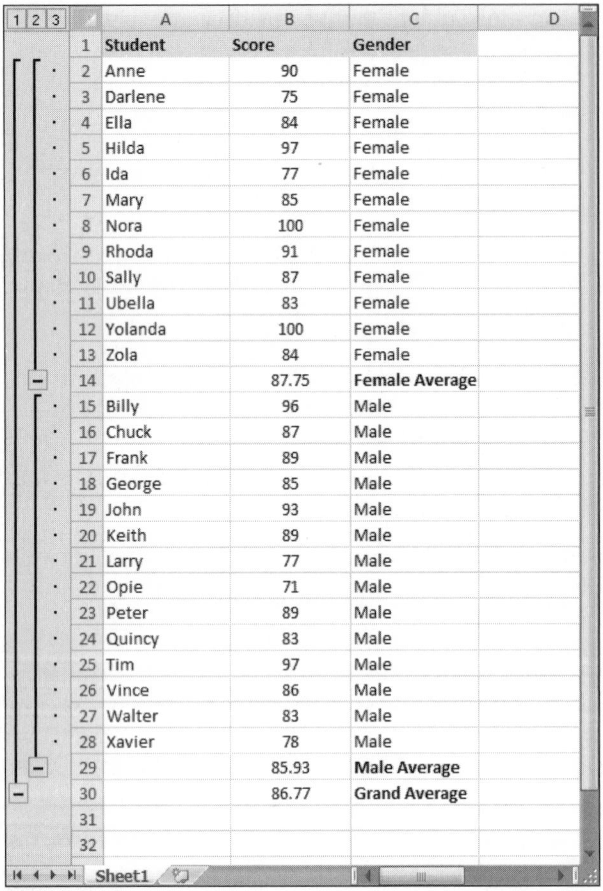

	A	B	C	D
1	Student	Score	Gender	
2	Anne	90	Female	
3	Darlene	75	Female	
4	Ella	84	Female	
5	Hilda	97	Female	
6	Ida	77	Female	
7	Mary	85	Female	
8	Nora	100	Female	
9	Rhoda	91	Female	
10	Sally	87	Female	
11	Ubella	83	Female	
12	Yolanda	100	Female	
13	Zola	84	Female	
14		87.75	**Female Average**	
15	Billy	96	Male	
16	Chuck	87	Male	
17	Frank	89	Male	
18	George	85	Male	
19	John	93	Male	
20	Keith	89	Male	
21	Larry	77	Male	
22	Opie	71	Male	
23	Peter	89	Male	
24	Quincy	83	Male	
25	Tim	97	Male	
26	Vince	86	Male	
27	Walter	83	Male	
28	Xavier	78	Male	
29		85.93	**Male Average**	
30		86.77	**Grand Average**	
31				
32				

Figure 100-2: Excel adds subtotals automatically.

The formulas inserted by Excel use the SUBTOTAL function, with 1 as the first argument (1 represents average). Here are the formulas:

```
=SUBTOTAL(1,B2:B13)
=SUBTOTAL(1,B15:B28)
=SUBTOTAL(1,B2:B28)
```

Using Formulas

Another method of creating averages is to use formulas. The formula to calculate the average of all students is simple:

```
=AVERAGE(B2:B27)
```

To calculate the average of the genders, you can take advantage of the AVERAGEIF function (available only in Excel 2007) to create these formulas:

```
=AVERAGEIF(C2:C27,"Female",B2:B27)
=AVERAGEIF(C2:C27,"Male",B2:B27)
```

Using a Pivot Table

A third method of averaging the scores is to create a pivot table. Many users avoid creating pivot tables because they consider this feature too complicated. As you can see, it's simple to use:

1. Select any cell in the data range, and choose Insert ⇨ Tables ⇨ PivotTable, to display the Create PivotTable dialog box.

2. In the dialog box, verify that Excel selected the correct data range, and specify a cell on the active worksheet as the location. Cell E1 is a good choice.

3. Click OK, and Excel displays the PivotTable Field List.

4. In the PivotTable Field List, drag the Gender item to the Row Labels section, at the bottom.

5. Drag the Score item to the Values section.

6. Excel creates the pivot table but displays the SUM function rather than the average. To change the summary function that's used, right-click any of the values in the pivot table and choose Summarize Data By ⇨ Average from the shortcut menu.

Figure 100-3 shows the pivot table.

 NOTE

Unlike a formula-based solution, a pivot table doesn't update itself automatically if the data changes. If the data changes, you must refresh the pivot table. Just right-click any cell in the pivot table and choose Refresh from the shortcut menu.

The pivot table in this example is extremely simple — but it's also extremely easy to create. Pivot tables can be much more complex, and they can summarize massive amounts of data in just about any way you can think of — without using any formulas.

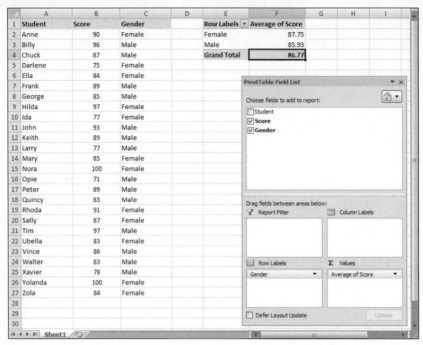

Figure 100-3: This pivot table calculates the averages without using formulas.

Expressing a Number As an Ordinal

You might need to express a value as an ordinal number. For example, `Today is the 21st day of the month`. In this case, the number 21 is converted to an ordinal number by appending the characters *st* to the number. Excel doesn't have a number format to do this, but you can do it by using a formula.

The specific characters appended to a number (*st*, *nd*, *rd*, or *th*) depend on the number. The pattern is a little convoluted, making the construction of a formula tricky. Most numbers use the *th* suffix. Exceptions occur for numbers that end with 1, 2, or 3 — except if the preceding number is a 1 (numbers that end with 11, 12, or 13). These rules might seem fairly complex, but you can translate them into an Excel formula.

The following formula converts the number in cell A1 (assumed to be an integer) to an ordinal number:

```
=A1&IF(OR(VALUE(RIGHT(A1,2))={11,12,13}),"th",IF(OR(VALUE(RIGHT(A1))={1,2,3}),
CHOOSE(RIGHT(A1),"st","nd","rd"),"th"))
```

This formula is rather complicated, so it might help to examine its components. Basically, the formula works this way:

1. If the last two digits of the number consist of 11, 12, or 13, use *th*.

2. If Rule 1 doesn't apply, check the last digit. If the last digit is 1, use *st*. If the last digit is 2, use *nd*. If the last digit is 3, use *rd*.

3. If neither Rule 1 nor Rule 2 applies, use *th*.

Figure 101-1 shows the formula in use.

 NOTE

The formula returns a text string, not a number. Therefore, you can't use the result in any numerical calculations.

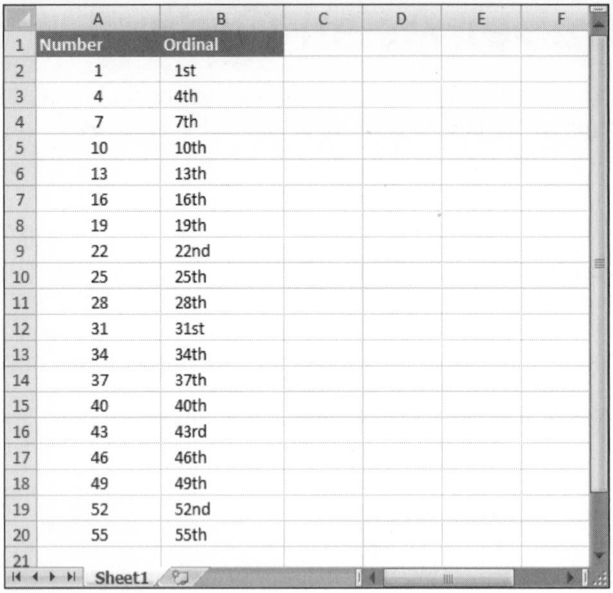

	A	B	C	D	E	F
1	Number	Ordinal				
2	1	1st				
3	4	4th				
4	7	7th				
5	10	10th				
6	13	13th				
7	16	16th				
8	19	19th				
9	22	22nd				
10	25	25th				
11	28	28th				
12	31	31st				
13	34	34th				
14	37	37th				
15	40	40th				
16	43	43rd				
17	46	46th				
18	49	49th				
19	52	52nd				
20	55	55th				
21						

Sheet1

Figure 101-1: Using a formula to express a number as an ordinal.

Extracting Words from a String

The formulas in this tip are useful for extracting words from text contained in a cell. For example, you can use a formula to extract the first word in a sentence.

Extracting the First Word of a String

To extract the first word of a string, a formula must locate the position of the first space character and then use this information as an argument for the LEFT function. The following formula does that:

```
=LEFT(A1,FIND(" ",A1)-1)
```

This formula returns all the text before the first space in cell A1. However, the formula has a slight problem: It returns an error if the text in cell A1 contains no space characters, because it consists of a single word. A slightly more complex formula solves the problem by using the new IFERROR function to display an empty string if an error occurs:

```
=IFERROR(LEFT(A1,FIND(" ",A1)-1),"")
```

If you need for the formula to be compatible with earlier versions of Excel, you can't use IFERROR. Therefore, use an IF function and an ISERR function to check for the error:

```
=IF(ISERR(FIND(" ",A1)),A1,LEFT(A1,FIND(" ",A1)-1))
```

Extracting the Last Word of a String

Extracting the last word of a string is more complicated because the FIND function works only from left to right. Therefore, the problem rests with locating the last space character. The following formula, however, solves this problem. The formula returns the last word of a string (all the text following the last space character):

```
=RIGHT(A1,LEN(A1)-FIND("*",SUBSTITUTE(A1," ","*",LEN(A1)-LEN
(SUBSTITUTE(A1," ","")))))
```

This formula, however, has the same problem as the first formula in the preceding section: It fails if the string doesn't contain at least one space character. The solution is to use the IFERROR function and return the entire contents of cell A1 if an error occurs:

```
=IFERROR(RIGHT(A1,LEN(A1)-FIND("*",SUBSTITUTE(A1," ","*",
LEN(A1)-LEN(SUBSTITUTE(A1," ","")))),A1)
```

Part V

The following formula is compatible with all versions of Excel:

```
=IF(ISERR(FIND(" ",A1)),A1,RIGHT(A1,LEN(A1)-FIND("*",SUBSTITUTE
(A1," ","*",LEN(A1)-LEN(SUBSTITUTE(A1," ","")))))
```

Extracting All Except the First Word of a String

The following formula returns the contents of cell A1, except for the first word:

```
=RIGHT(A1,LEN(A1)-FIND(" ",A1,1))
```

If cell A1 contains 2008 Operating Budget, the formula returns Operating Budget.

This formula returns an error if the cell contains only one word. The following version uses the IFERROR function to avoid the error; the formula returns an empty string if the cell doesn't contain multiple words:

```
=IFERROR(RIGHT(A1,LEN(A1)-FIND(" ",A1,1)),"")
```

This version is compatible with all versions of Excel:

```
=IF(ISERR(FIND(" ",A1)),"",RIGHT(A1,LEN(A1)-FIND(" ",A1,1)))
```

Parsing Names

Suppose that you have a list of people's names in a single column. You have to separate these names into three columns: one for the first name, one for the middle name or initial, and one for the last name. This task is more complicated than you might initially think, because not every name in the column has a middle name or middle initial. However, you can still do it.

NOTE

This task becomes a lot more complicated if the list contains names with titles (such as Mrs. or Dr.) or names followed by additional details (such as Jr. or III). In fact, the following formulas don't handle these complex cases. However, they still give you a significant head start if you're willing to do a bit of manual editing to handle the special cases.

The following formulas all assume that the name appears in cell A1.

You can easily construct a formula to return the first name:

```
=LEFT(A1,FIND(" ",A1)-1)
```

This formula returns the last name:

```
=RIGHT(A1,LEN(A1)-FIND("*",SUBSTITUTE(A1," ","*",LEN(A1)-
LEN(SUBSTITUTE(A1," ","")))))
```

The following formula extracts the middle name (if any). It assumes that the first name is in B1 and the last name is in D1:

```
=IF(LEN(B1&D1)+2>=LEN(A1),"",MID(A1,LEN(B1)+2,LEN(A1)-LEN(B1&D1)-2))
```

As you can see in Figure 103-1, the formulas work fairly well. A few problems occurred, however — notably, names that contain either one word or more than three words. But, as I mention earlier in this tip, you can clean these cases up manually.

NOTE

In many cases, you can avoid formulas and use the Excel Data ➪ Data Tools ➪ Text to Columns command to parse strings into their component parts. Selecting this command displays the Excel Convert Text to Columns Wizard, which consists of a series of dialog boxes that walk you through the steps to convert a single column of data into multiple columns. Generally, you want to select the Delimited option (in Step 1) and use Space as the delimiter (in Step 2).

	A	B	C	D	E
1	**Full Name**	**First**	**Middle**	**Last**	
2	Mark P. Johnson	Mark	P.	Johnson	
3	Lisa Smith	Lisa		Smith	
4	J.R. Robins	J.R.		Robins	
5	A. Baxter	A.		Baxter	
6	Roger Theodore Burnside	Roger	Theodore	Burnside	
7	John P. Van Williams	John	P. Van	Williams	
8	Mr. Paul Rockingham	Mr.	Paul	Rockingham	
9	Madonna	#VALUE!	#VALUE!	#VALUE!	
10	Joseph Roberts	Joseph		Roberts	
11	Henry Jackson, Jr.	Henry	Jackson,	Jr.	
12					
13					

Sheet1

Figure 103-1: This worksheet uses formulas to extract the first name, middle name (or initial), and last name from a list of names in column A.

Removing Titles from Names

If you have a list of names, you might need to remove titles (such as Mr., Ms., or Mrs.) from them. You might want to perform this operation before you parse the name, as described in Tip 103.

You can use the following formula to remove three common titles (Mr., Ms., and Mrs.) from a name; for example, if cell A1 contains Mr. Fred Mertz, the formula returns Fred Mertz:

```
=IF(OR(LEFT(A1,2)="Mr",LEFT(A1,3)="Mrs",LEFT(A1,2)="Ms"),
RIGHT(A1,LEN(A1) -FIND("",A1)),A1)
```

This formula tests for three conditions. If you need to test for more, just add arguments to the OR function.

Generating a Series of Dates

If you work with time-based data, you might want to insert a series of dates into a worksheet. For example, in a sales tracking application, you might want to enter a series of dates for a sales quarter — making sure, of course, to skip dates that occur during weekends.

Using the AutoFill Feature

The most efficient way to enter a series of dates doesn't require any formulas — just use the Excel AutoFill feature to insert a series of dates. Enter the first date, and then drag the cell's fill handle while pressing the right mouse button (right-drag the cell's fill handle). Release the mouse button and choose a command from the shortcut menu (see Figure 105-1).

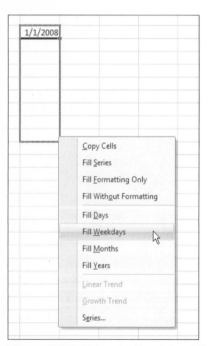

Figure 105-1: Using the Excel AutoFill feature to create a series of dates.

In some situations, you need to enter two dates before you use the AutoFill. For example, if you want to enter a series of dates that represent consecutive Mondays, you need to enter the first two dates of the series. Then select both dates, right-click, and choose Fill Days from the shortcut menu.

Using Formulas

Another way to enter a series of dates is to use formulas. The advantage of using formulas (rather than the AutoFill feature) to create a series of dates is that you can change the first date and the others are updated automatically. Enter the starting date into a cell, and then use formulas (copied down the column) to generate the additional dates.

The following examples assume that you entered the first date of the series into cell A1 and the formula into cell A2. You can then copy this formula down the column as many times as needed.

To generate a series of dates separated by seven days, use this formula:

```
=A1+7
```

To generate a series of dates separated by one month, use this formula:

```
=DATE(YEAR(A1),MONTH(A1)+1,DAY(A1))
```

To generate a series of dates separated by one year, use this formula:

```
=DATE(YEAR(A1)+1,MONTH(A1),DAY(A1))
```

To generate a series of weekdays only (no Saturdays or Sundays), use the following formula. It assumes that the date in cell A1 isn't a weekend day:

```
=IF(WEEKDAY(A1)=6,A1+3,A1+1)
```

Determining Specific Dates

This tip contains a number of useful formulas that return a specific date.

Determining the Day of the Year

January 1 is the first day of the year, and December 31 is the last day. What about all those days between them? The following formula returns the day of the year for a date stored in cell A1:

```
=A1-DATE(YEAR(A1),1,0)
```

For example, if cell A1 contains the date February 16, 2007, the formula returns 47 because that date is the 47th day of the year.

The following formula returns the number of days remaining in the year from a particular date (assumed to be in cell A1):

```
=DATE(YEAR(A1),12,31)-A1
```

 NOTE
When you enter either of these formulas, Excel automatically applies date formatting to the cell. You need to apply a nondate number format to view the result as a number.

Determining the Day of the Week

If you need to determine the day of the week for a date, the WEEKDAY function does the job. The WEEKDAY function accepts a date argument and returns an integer between 1 and 7 that corresponds to the day of the week. The following formula, for example, returns 3 because the first day of the year 2008 falls on a Tuesday:

```
=WEEKDAY(DATE(2008,1,1))
```

The WEEKDAY function uses an optional second argument that specifies the day numbering system for the result. If you specify 2 as the second argument, the function returns 1 for Monday, 2 for Tuesday, and so on. If you specify 3 as the second argument, the function returns 0 for Monday, 1 for Tuesday, and so on.

NOTE
You can also determine the day of the week for a cell that contains a date by applying a custom number format. A cell that uses the following custom number format displays the day of the week, spelled out:

dddd

Keep in mind that the cell really contains the full date, not just the day number.

Determining the Date of the Most Recent Sunday

The formula in this section returns the most recent specified day. You can use the following formula to return the date for the previous Sunday. If the current day is Sunday, the formula returns the current date. The result is a date serial number (you need to format the cell to display as a readable date):

```
=TODAY()-MOD(TODAY()-1,7)
```

To modify this formula to find the date of a day other than Sunday, change the 1 to a different number between 2 (for Monday) and 7 (for Saturday).

Determining the First Day of the Week after a Date

The following formula returns the specified day of the week that occurs after a particular date. For example, you can use this formula to determine the date of the first Monday after July 4, 2008.

The formula assumes that cell A1 contains a date and that cell A2 contains a number between 1 and 7 (1 for Sunday, 2 for Monday, and so on):

```
=A1+A2-WEEKDAY(A1)+(A2<WEEKDAY(A1))*7
```

If cell A1 contains July 4, 2008, and cell A2 contains 2 (for Monday), the formula returns July 7, 2008. It's the first Monday after July 4, 2008 (which is a Friday).

Determining the *n*th Occurrence of a Day of the Week in a Month

You might need a formula to determine the date for a particular occurrence of a weekday. Suppose that your company payday falls on the second Friday of each month and that you need to determine the paydays for each month of the year. The following formula makes this type of calculation:

```
=DATE(A1,A2,1)+A3-WEEKDAY(DATE(A1,A2,1))+(A4-(A3>=WEEKDAY
(DATE(A1,A2,1))))*7
```

Part V

This formula assumes that

- Cell A1 contains a year.

- Cell A2 contains a month.

- Cell A3 contains a day number (1 for Sunday, 2 for Monday, and so on).

- Cell A4 contains the occurrence number (for example, 2 to select the second occurrence of the weekday specified in cell A3).

If you use this formula to determine the date of the second Friday in June 2008, it returns June 13, 2008.

Determining the Last Day of a Month

To determine the date that corresponds to the last day of a month, you can use the DATE function. However, you need to increment the month by 1 and use a day value of 0. In other words, the "0th" day of the next month is the last day of the current month.

The following formula assumes that a date is stored in cell A1. The formula returns the date that corresponds to the last day of the month:

```
=DATE(YEAR(A1),MONTH(A1)+1,0)
```

You can use a variation of this formula to determine how many days comprise a specified month. The following formula returns an integer that corresponds to the number of days in the month for the date in cell A1 (make sure that you format the cell as a number, not as a date):

```
=DAY(DATE(YEAR(A1),MONTH(A1)+1,0))
```

Determining a Date's Quarter

For financial reports, you might find it useful to present information in terms of quarters. The following formula returns an integer between 1 and 4 that corresponds to the calendar quarter for the date in cell A1:

```
=ROUNDUP(MONTH(A1)/3,0)
```

This formula divides the month number by 3 and then rounds up the result.

Displaying a Calendar in a Range

This tip describes how to create a "live" calendar in a range of cells. Figure 107-1 shows an example. If you change the date that's displayed at the top of the calendar, the calendar recalculates to display the dates for the month and year.

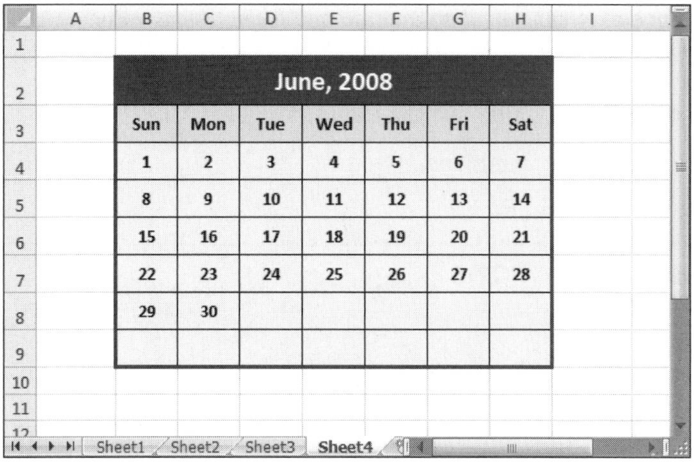

	A	B	C	D	E	F	G	H	I
1									
2		June, 2008							
3		Sun	Mon	Tue	Wed	Thu	Fri	Sat	
4		1	2	3	4	5	6	7	
5		8	9	10	11	12	13	14	
6		15	16	17	18	19	20	21	
7		22	23	24	25	26	27	28	
8		29	30						
9									
10									
11									
12									

Sheet1 / Sheet2 / Sheet3 \ **Sheet4**

Figure 107-1: This calendar was created with a complex array formula.

To create this calendar in the range B2:H9, follow these steps:

1. Select B2:H2, and then merge the cells by clicking the Merge and Center button on the Formatting toolbar.

2. Enter a date into the merged range. The day of the month isn't important, so change the format of the cell to a custom format that doesn't display the day: mmmm, yyyy.

3. Enter the abbreviated day names in the range B3:H3.

4. Select B4:H9, and then enter the following array formula without the line breaks. *Remember:* To enter an array formula, press Ctrl+Shift+Enter (not just Enter):

```
=IF(MONTH(DATE(YEAR(B2),MONTH(B2),1))<>MONTH(DATE(YEAR(B2),MONTH(B2),
1)-(WEEKDAY(DATE(YEAR(B2),MONTH(B2),1))-1)+
{0;1;2;3;4;5}*7+{1,2,3,4,5,6,7}-1),"",DATE(YEAR(B2),MONTH(B2),1)
-(WEEKDAY(DATE(YEAR(B2),MONTH(B2),1))-1)
+{0;1;2;3;4;5}*7+{1,2,3,4,5,6,7}-1)
```

5. Format the range B4:H9 to use this custom number format, which displays only the day: d.

6. Adjust the column widths, and format the cells the way you like.

Change the date and year, and the calendar updates automatically. After creating this calendar, you can copy the range to any other worksheet or workbook.

Part V

Various Methods of Rounding Numbers

Rounding numbers is a common task, and Excel provides quite a few functions that round values in various ways.

You must understand the difference between *rounding* a value and *formatting* a value. When you format a number to display a specific number of decimal places, formulas that refer to that number use the actual value, which might differ from the displayed value. When you round a number, formulas that refer to that value use the rounded number.

Table 108-1 summarizes the Excel rounding functions.

TABLE 108-1   EXCEL ROUNDING FUNCTIONS

Function	What It Does
CEILING	Rounds a number up (away from zero) to the nearest specified multiple
DOLLARDE	Converts a dollar price, expressed as a fraction, into a decimal number
DOLLARFR	Converts a dollar price, expressed as a decimal, into a fractional number
EVEN	Rounds up (away from zero) positive numbers to the nearest even integer; rounds down (away from zero) negative numbers to the nearest even integer
FLOOR	Rounds down (toward zero) a number to the nearest specified multiple
INT	Rounds down a number to make it an integer
MROUND	Rounds a number to a specified multiple
ODD	Rounds up (away from zero) numbers to the nearest odd integer; rounds down (away from zero) negative numbers to the nearest odd integer
ROUND	Rounds a number to a specified number of digits
ROUNDDOWN	Rounds down (toward zero) a number to a specified number of digits
ROUNDUP	Rounds up (away from zero) a number to a specified number of digits
TRUNC	Truncates a number to a specified number of significant digits

The following sections provide examples of formulas that use various types of rounding.

Rounding to the Nearest Multiple

The MROUND function is useful for rounding values to the nearest multiple. For example, you can use this function to round a number to the nearest 5. The following formula returns 135:

```
=MROUND(133,5)
```

Rounding Currency Values

Often, you need to round currency values. For example, a calculated price might be a number like $45.78923. In such a case, you want to round the calculated price to the nearest penny. This process might sound simple, but you can round this type of value in one of three ways:

- Round it up to the nearest penny.
- Round it down to the nearest penny.
- Round it to the nearest penny (the rounding can be up or down).

The following formula assumes that a dollar-and-cents value is in cell A1. The formula rounds the value to the nearest penny. For example, if cell A1 contains $12.421, the formula returns $12.42.

```
=ROUND(A1,2)
```

If you need to round up the value to the nearest penny, use the CEILING function. The following formula rounds up the value in cell A1 to the nearest penny (if, for example, cell A1 contains $12.421, the formula returns $12.43):

```
=CEILING(A1,0.01)
```

To round down a dollar value, use the FLOOR function. The following formula, for example, rounds down the dollar value in cell A1 to the nearest penny (if cell A1 contains $12.421, the formula returns $12.42):

```
=FLOOR(A1,0.01)
```

To round up a dollar value to the nearest nickel, use this formula:

```
=CEILING(A1,0.05)
```

Part V

Using the INT and TRUNC Functions

On the surface, the INT and TRUNC functions seem similar. Both convert a value to an integer. The TRUNC function simply removes the fractional part of a number. The INT function rounds down a number to the nearest integer, based on the value of the fractional part of the number.

In practice, INT and TRUNC return different results only when using negative numbers. For example, the following formula returns –14.0:

```
=TRUNC(-14.2)
```

The next formula returns –15.0 because –14.2 is rounded down to the next lower integer:

```
=INT(-14.2)
```

The TRUNC function takes an additional (optional) argument that's useful for truncating decimal values. For example, the following formula returns 54.33 (the value truncated to two decimal places):

```
=TRUNC(54.3333333,2)
```

Rounding to *n* Significant Digits

In some situations, you might need to round a value to a particular number of significant digits. For example, you might want to express the value 1,432,187 in terms of two significant digits (that is, as 1,400,000). The value 84,356 expressed in terms of three significant digits is 84,300.

If the value is a positive number with no decimal places, the following formula does the job. This formula rounds the number in cell A1 to two significant digits. To round to a different number of significant digits, replace the 2 in this formula with a different number:

```
=ROUNDDOWN(A1,2-LEN(A1))
```

For nonintegers and negative numbers, the solution is a bit trickier. The following formula provides a more general solution that rounds the value in cell A1 to the number of significant digits specified in cell A2. This formula works for positive and negative integers and nonintegers:

```
=ROUND(A1,A2-1-INT(LOG10(ABS(A1))))
```

For example, if cell A1 contains 1.27845 and cell A2 contains 3, the formula returns 1.28000 (the value, rounded to three significant digits).

Rounding Time Values

You might need to create a formula that rounds a time to a particular number of minutes. For example, you might need to enter your company's time records rounded to the nearest 15 minutes. This tip presents examples of various ways to round a time value.

The following formula rounds the time in cell A1 to the nearest minute:

```
=ROUND(A1*1440,0)/1440
```

This formula works by multiplying the time by 1440 (to get total number of minutes). This value is passed to the ROUND function, and the result is divided by 1440. For example, if cell A1 contains 11:52:34, the formula returns 11:53:00.

The following formula is similar, except that it rounds the time in cell A1 to the nearest hour:

```
=ROUND(A1*24,0)/24
```

If cell A1 contains 5:21:31, the formula returns 5:00:00.

The following formula rounds the time in cell A1 to the nearest 15 minutes (quarter of an hour):

```
=ROUND(A1*24/0.25,0)*(0.25/24)
```

In this formula, 0.25 represents the fractional hour. To round a time to the nearest 30 minutes, change 0.25 to 0.5, as in the following formula:

```
=ROUND(A1*24/0.5,0)*(0.5/24)
```

Returning the Last Nonblank Cell in a Column or Row

Suppose that you update a worksheet frequently by adding new data to its columns. You might need a way to reference the last value in a particular column (the value most recently entered).

Figure 110-1 shows an example. New data is entered daily, and the goal is to create a formula that returns the last value in column C.

	A	B	C	D	E	F
1	Date	Amount	Running Total			
2	6/1/2007	659	659			
3	6/2/2007	561	1,220			
4	6/3/2007	682	1,902			
5	6/4/2007	651	2,553			
6	6/5/2007	774	3,327			
7	6/6/2007	630	3,957			
8	6/7/2007	549	4,506			
9	6/8/2007	667	5,173			
10	6/9/2007					
11	6/10/2007					
12	6/11/2007					
13	6/12/2007					
14	6/13/2007					
15	6/14/2007					
16	6/15/2007					
17	6/16/2007					
18	6/17/2007					
19	6/18/2007					
20						

Figure 110-1: Use a formula to return the last nonempty cell in column C.

If column C contains no empty cells, the solution is relatively simple:

```
=INDEX(C:C,COUNTA(C:C))
```

This formula uses the COUNTA function to count the number of nonempty cells in column C. This value is used as the second argument for the INDEX function. For example, if the last value is in row 76, COUNTA returns 76, and the INDEX function returns the 76th value in the column.

If the column has one or more empty cells interspersed, which happens frequently, the preceding formula doesn't work because the COUNTA function doesn't count the empty cells. The following array formula returns the contents of the last nonempty cell in the first 500 rows of column C:

```
=INDEX(C1:C500,MAX(ROW(C1:C500)*(C1:C500<>"")))
```

NOTE

Press Ctrl+Shift+Enter (not just Enter) to enter an array formula.

You can, of course, modify the formula to work with a column other than column C. To use a different column, change the four column references from C to whatever column you need. If the last nonempty cell occurs in a row beyond row 500, you need to change the two instances of 500 to a larger number. The fewer rows referenced in the formula, the faster the calculation speed.

The following array formula is similar to the previous formula, but it returns the last non-empty cell in a row (in this case, row 1):

```
=INDEX(1:1,MAX(COLUMN(1:1)*(1:1<>"")))
```

To use this formula for a different row, change the three 1:1 row references to correspond to the correct row number.

Part V

Using the COUNTIF Function

The Excel COUNT and COUNTA functions are useful for basic counting, but sometimes you need more flexibility. This tip contains many examples of the powerful Excel COUNTIF function, useful for counting cells based on various types of criteria.

These formulas all work with a range named Data, so you need to adjust the formulas to refer to your own range. As you can see in Table 111-1, the criteria argument proves quite flexible. You can use constants, expressions, functions, cell references, and even wildcard characters (* and ?).

TABLE 111-1   COUNTIF FORMULAS

Formula	Number of Cells or Values It Returns
=COUNTIF(Data,12)	Cells containing the value 12
=COUNTIF(Data,"<0")	Cells containing a negative value
=COUNTIF(Data,"<>0")	Cells not equal to 0
=COUNTIF(Data,">5")	Cells greater than 5
=COUNTIF(Data,A1)	Cells equal to the contents of cell A1
=COUNTIF(Data,">"&A1)	Cells greater than the value in cell A1
=COUNTIF(Data,"*")	Cells containing text
=COUNTIF(Data,"???")	Text cells containing exactly three characters
=COUNTIF(Data,"budget")	Cells containing the single word budget and nothing else (not case sensitive)
=COUNTIF(Data,"*budget*")	Cells containing the text budget anywhere within the text (not case sensitive)
=COUNTIF(Data,"A*")	Cells containing text that begins with the letter A (not case sensitive)
=COUNTIF(Data,TODAY())	Cells containing the current date
=COUNTIF(Data,">"&AVERAGE(Data))	Cells with a value greater than the average
=COUNTIF(Data,">"&AVERAGE(Data)+STDEV(Data)*3)	Values exceeding three standard deviations above the mean

Formula	Number of Cells or Values It Returns
`=COUNTIF(Data,3)+COUNTIF(Data,-3)`	Cells containing the value 3 or –3
`=COUNTIF(Data,TRUE)`	Cells containing logical TRUE
`=COUNTIF(Data,TRUE)+` `COUNTIF(Data,FALSE)`	Cells containing a logical value (TRUE or FALSE)
`=COUNTIF(Data,"#N/A")`	Cells containing the #N/A error value

Counting Cells That Meet Multiple Criteria

Tip 111 presents examples of formulas that use the COUNTIF function. Those formulas are useful for counting cells that match a single criterion. The formula examples in this tip are useful when you need to count cells only if two or more criteria are met. These criteria can be based on the cells that are being counted or based on a range of corresponding cells.

 NEW

Some of these formulas use the new Excel 2007 COUNTIFS function. For compatibility purposes, I also present an alternative formula that works with previous version of Excel.

Using "And" Criteria

The And criterion counts cells if all specified conditions are met. A common example is a formula that counts the number of values that fall within a numerical range. For example, you might want to count cells that contain a value greater than 0 and less than or equal to 12. Any cell that has a positive value less than or equal to 12 is included in the count.

The following formula, which works only in Excel 2007, counts the cells in a range named Data that fall between 0 and 12:

```
=COUNTIFS(Data,">=0",Data,"<=12")
```

Arguments for the COUNTIFS function always come in pairs. This formula has two sets of paired arguments: The first argument in each pair is the range of interest, and the second argument is the criterion. Values are counted if they meet *all* criteria specified by each argument pair.

For compatibility with previous versions of Excel, use this formula:

```
=COUNTIF(Data,">0")-COUNTIF(Data,">12")
```

This formula counts the number of values that are greater than 0 and then subtracts the number of values that are greater than 12. The result is the number of cells that contain a value greater than 0 and less than or equal to 12.

Creating this type of formula can be confusing because the formula refers to the condition ">12" even though the goal is to count values that are less than or equal to 12. An alternative technique is to use an array formula, such as the following one (you might find creating this type of formula easier):

```
=SUM((Data>0)*(Data<=12))
```

NOTE
When you enter an array formula, you press Ctrl+Shift+Enter, not just Enter.

Figure 112-1 shows a simple worksheet that I use for some of the examples that follow. This sheet shows sales data categorized by Month, SalesRep, and Type. The worksheet contains named ranges that correspond to the labels in Row 1.

	A	B	C	D	E
1	Month	SalesRep	Type	Amount	
2	January	Albert	New	85	
3	January	Albert	New	675	
4	January	Brooks	New	130	
5	January	Cook	New	1350	
6	January	Cook	Existing	685	
7	January	Brooks	New	1350	
8	January	Cook	New	475	
9	January	Brooks	New	1205	
10	February	Brooks	Existing	450	
11	February	Albert	New	495	
12	February	Cook	New	210	
13	February	Cook	Existing	1050	
14	February	Albert	New	140	
15	February	Brooks	New	900	
16	February	Brooks	New	900	
17	February	Cook	New	95	
18	February	Cook	New	780	
19	March	Brooks	New	900	
20	March	Albert	Existing	875	
21	March	Brooks	New	50	
22	March	Brooks	New	875	
23	March	Cook	Existing	225	
24	March	Cook	New	175	
25	March	Brooks	Existing	400	
26	March	Albert	New	840	
27	March	Cook	New	132	
28					

Sheet1 / Sheet2

Figure 112-1: This worksheet demonstrates various counting techniques that use multiple criteria.

Sometimes, the counting criteria are based on cells other than the cells being counted. You might, for example, want to count the number of sales that meet the following criteria:

- Month is January, and
- SalesRep is Brooks, and
- Amount is greater than 1000

The following formula (for Excel 2007 only) uses three sets of paired arguments to return the count:

```
=COUNTIFS(Month,"January",SalesRep,"Brooks",Amount,">1000")
```

For compatibility with previous versions of Excel, use the following formula to count the number of items that meet all three criteria:

```
=SUMPRODUCT((Month="January")*(SalesRep="Brooks")*(Amount>1000))
```

NOTE

If your data is in a table (created by choosing Insert ➪ Tables ➪ Table), you can use filtering to display only the rows that meet multiple And criteria. Figure 112-2 shows the data filtered to show only the January sales for Brooks that exceed 1000. I also added a Total Row to this table, which displays the count. However, filtering cannot be used for Or criteria, which is discussed next.

	A	B	C	D
1	Month	SalesRep	Type	Amount
7	January	Brooks	New	1350
9	January	Brooks	New	1205
28	Count			2
29				
30				
31				

Sheet1 / Sheet2

Figure 112-2: Using table filtering to count rows that meet multiple And criteria.

Using "Or" Criteria

To count cells by using an Or criterion, you can sometimes use multiple COUNTIF functions. The following formula, for example, counts the number of instances of 1, 3, and 5 in the range named Data:

```
=COUNTIF(Data,1)+COUNTIF(Data,3)+COUNTIF(Data,5)
```

You can also use the COUNTIF function in an array formula. The following array formula, for example, returns the same result as the previous formula:

```
=SUM(COUNTIF(Data,{1,3,5}))
```

If you base your Or criteria on cells other than the cells being counted, the COUNTIF function doesn't work. Refer to Figure 112-1. Suppose that you want to count the number of sales that meet one of the following criteria:

- Month is January, or
- SalesRep is Brooks, or
- Amount is greater than 1000

The following array formula returns the correct count:

```
=SUM(IF((Month="January")+(SalesRep="Brooks")+(Amount>1000),1))
```

Combining "And" and "Or" Criteria

You can combine And and Or criteria when counting. Perhaps you want to count sales that meet the following criteria:

- Month is January, and
- SalesRep is Brooks, or
- SalesRep is Cook

This array formula returns the number of sales that meet the criteria:

```
=SUM((Month="January")*IF((SalesRep="Brooks")+(SalesRep="Cook"),1))
```

Part V

Counting Nonduplicated Entries in a Range

In some situations, you might need to count the number of nonduplicated entries in a range. Figure 113-1 shows an example. Column A has a list of animals, and the goal is to count the number of different animals in the list. The formula in cell B2 returns 8, which is the number of nonduplicated animals. This formula (an array formula, by the way) is

```
=SUM(1/COUNTIF(A1:A10,A1:A10))
```

 NOTE
When you enter an array formula, press Ctrl+Shift+Enter (not just Enter). Excel surrounds the formula with braces to remind you that it's an array formula.

	A	B	C	D
1	dog			
2	cat	8	different animals	
3	monkey			
4	pig			
5	cow			
6	horse			
7	chicken			
8	monkey			
9	horse			
10	lizard			
11				

Sheet1

Figure 113-1: Use an array formula to count the number of nonduplicated entries in a range.

This formula is one of those "Internet classics" that is passed around on various Web sites and newsgroups. Credit goes to David Hager, who first came up with the formula.

The preceding array formula works fine unless the range contains one or more empty cells. The following modified version of this array formula uses the new IFERROR function to overcome this problem:

```
=SUM(IFERROR(1/COUNTIF(A1:A10,A1:A10),0))
```

The preceding formulas work with both values and text. If the range contains only numeric values or blank cells (but no text), you can use the following formula (which isn't an array formula) to count the number of nonduplicated values:

```
=SUM(N(FREQUENCY(A1:A10,A1:A10)>0))
```

Calculating Single-Criterion Conditional Sums

The Excel SUM function is easily the most commonly used function. But sometimes you need more flexibility than the SUM function provides. The SUMIF function is useful when you need to compute conditional sums. For example, you might need to calculate the sum of just the negative values in a range of cells.

The examples in this tip demonstrate how to use the SUMIF function for conditional sums by using a single criterion.

These formulas are based on the worksheet shown in Figure 114-1, which is set up to track invoices. Column F contains a formula that subtracts the date in column E from the date in column D. A negative number in column F indicates that the payment is past due. The worksheet uses named ranges that correspond to the labels in row 1.

	A	B	C	D	E	F
1	InvoiceNum	Office	Amount	DateDue	Today	Difference
2	AG-0145	Oregon	$5,000.00	10/18/2007	11/21/2007	-34
3	AG-0189	California	$450.00	11/5/2007	11/21/2007	-16
4	AG-0220	Washington	$3,211.56	11/14/2007	11/21/2007	-7
5	AG-0310	Oregon	$250.00	11/16/2007	11/21/2007	-5
6	AG-0355	Washington	$125.50	11/20/2007	11/21/2007	-1
7	AG-0409	Washington	$3,000.00	11/26/2007	11/21/2007	5
8	AG-0581	Oregon	$2,100.00	12/9/2007	11/21/2007	18
9	AG-0600	Oregon	$335.39	12/9/2007	11/21/2007	18
10	AG-0602	Washington	$65.00	12/14/2007	11/21/2007	23
11	AG-0633	California	$250.00	12/16/2007	11/21/2007	25
12	TOTAL		$14,787.45			26
13						

Sheet1

Figure 114-1: A negative value in column F indicates a past-due payment.

Summing Only Negative Values

The following formula returns the sum of the negative values in column F. In other words, it returns the total number of past-due days for all invoices (for this worksheet, the formula returns –63):

```
=SUMIF(Difference,"<0")
```

The SUMIF function can use three arguments. Because you omit the third argument, the second argument ("<0") applies to the values in the Difference range.

Summing Values Based on a Different Range

The following formula returns the sum of the past-due invoice amounts (in column C):

```
=SUMIF(Difference,"<0",Amount)
```

Part V

This formula uses the values in the Difference range to determine whether the corresponding values in the Amount range contribute to the sum.

Summing Values Based on a Text Comparison

The following formula returns the total invoice amounts for the Oregon office:

```
=SUMIF(Office,"=Oregon",Amount)
```

Using the equal sign is optional. The following formula has the same result:

```
=SUMIF(Office,"Oregon",Amount)
```

To sum the invoice amounts for all offices except Oregon, use this formula:

```
=SUMIF(Office,"<>Oregon",Amount)
```

Summing Values Based on a Date Comparison

The following formula returns the total invoice amounts that have a due date of November 26, 2007, or later:

```
=SUMIF(DateDue,">="&DATE(2007,11,26),Amount)
```

Notice that the second argument for the SUMIF function is an expression. The expression uses the DATE function, which returns a date. Also, the comparison operator, enclosed in quotation marks, is concatenated (using the & operator) with the result of the DATE function.

The following formula returns the total invoice amounts that have a future due date (including today):

```
=SUMIF(DateDue,">="&TODAY(),Amount)
```

Calculating Multiple-Criterion Conditional Sums

Tip 114 contains summing examples that use a single comparison criterion. The examples in this tip involve summing cells based on multiple criteria. Because the SUMIF function doesn't work with multiple criteria, you need to use an array formula.

Figure 115-1 shows the sample worksheet again, for your reference. The formulas in this tip, of course, can be adapted to your own worksheets.

	A	B	C	D	E	F
1	InvoiceNum	Office	Amount	DateDue	Today	Difference
2	AG-0145	Oregon	$5,000.00	10/18/2007	11/21/2007	-34
3	AG-0189	California	$450.00	11/5/2007	11/21/2007	-16
4	AG-0220	Washington	$3,211.56	11/14/2007	11/21/2007	-7
5	AG-0310	Oregon	$250.00	11/16/2007	11/21/2007	-5
6	AG-0355	Washington	$125.50	11/20/2007	11/21/2007	-1
7	AG-0409	Washington	$3,000.00	11/26/2007	11/21/2007	5
8	AG-0581	Oregon	$2,100.00	12/9/2007	11/21/2007	18
9	AG-0600	Oregon	$335.39	12/9/2007	11/21/2007	18
10	AG-0602	Washington	$65.00	12/14/2007	11/21/2007	23
11	AG-0633	California	$250.00	12/16/2007	11/21/2007	25
12	TOTAL		$14,787.45			26
13						

Figure 115-1: This worksheet demonstrates summing based on multiple criteria.

Using "And" Criteria

Suppose that you want to get a sum of the invoice amounts that are past due and associated with the Oregon office. In other words, the value in the Amount range is summed only if both of these criteria are met:

- The corresponding value in the Difference range is negative.

- The corresponding text in the Office range is "Oregon".

The following formula, which uses the new SUMIFS function, does the job:

```
=SUMIFS(Amount,Difference,"<0",Office,"Oregon")
```

The first argument of the SUMIFS function is the range to be summed. Subsequent arguments come in pairs: the range on which the criterion is based, followed by the actual criterion.

If you plan to share your work with someone who uses an earlier version of Excel, you can't use the SUMIFS function. The following formula returns the same result:

```
=SUMPRODUCT(1*(Difference<0),1*(Office="Oregon"),Amount)
```

Part V

Using "Or" Criteria

Suppose that you want to get a sum of past-due invoice amounts, or ones associated with the Oregon office (regardless of their past-due status). In other words, the value in the Amount range is summed if either of the following criteria is met:

- The corresponding value in the Difference range is negative.
- The corresponding text in the Office range is `"Oregon"`.

This type of sum requires an array formula:

```
=SUM(IF((Office="Oregon")+(Difference<0),1,0)*Amount)
```

A plus sign (+) joins the conditions, and you can include more than two conditions.

 NOTE
When you enter an array formula, remember to press Ctrl+Shift+Enter.

Using "And" and "Or" Criteria

Things get a bit tricky when your criteria consists of both And and Or operations. For example, you might want to sum the values in the Amount range when both of the following conditions are met:

- The corresponding value in the Difference range is negative.
- The corresponding text in the Office range is `"Oregon"` or `"California"`.

Notice that the second condition consists of *two* conditions, joined with Or. The following array formula does the trick:

```
=SUM((Difference<0)*IF((Office="Oregon")+(Office="California"),1)*Amount)
```

Looking Up an Exact Value

The Excel VLOOKUP and HLOOKUP formulas are useful if you need to return a value from a table (in a range) by looking up another value.

The classic example of a lookup formula involves an income tax rate schedule (see Figure 116-1). The tax rate schedule shows the income tax rates for various income levels. The following formula (in cell B3) returns the tax rate for the income value in cell B2:

```
=VLOOKUP(B2,D2:F7,3)
```

	A	B	C	D	E	F
1				Income is Greater Than or Equal To...	But Less Than or Equal To...	Tax Rate
2	Enter Income:	$45,500		$0	$2,650	15.00%
3	The Tax Rate is:	31.00%		$2,651	$27,300	28.00%
4				$27,301	$58,500	31.00%
5				$58,501	$131,800	36.00%
6				$131,801	$284,700	39.60%
7				$284,701		45.25%
8						

Sheet1

Figure 116-1: Using VLOOKUP to look up a tax rate.

The tax table example demonstrates that VLOOKUP and HLOOKUP don't require an exact match between the value to be looked up and the values in the lookup table. In some cases, though, you might require a perfect match. For example, when looking up an employee number, you require a perfect match for the number.

To look up only an exact value, use the VLOOKUP (or HLOOKUP) function with the optional fourth argument set to FALSE.

Figure 116-2 shows a worksheet with a lookup table that contains employee numbers (column D) and employee names (column E). The formula in cell B3, which follows, looks up the employee number entered in cell B2 and returns the corresponding employee name:

```
=VLOOKUP(B2,D1:E11,2,FALSE)
```

Because the last argument for the VLOOKUP function is FALSE, the function returns a value only if an exact match is found. If the value isn't found, the formula returns #N/A. This is exactly what you want to happen, of course, because returning an approximate match for an employee number makes no sense. Also, notice that the employee numbers in column D aren't in ascending order. If the last argument for VLOOKUP is FALSE, the values don't need to be in ascending order.

	A	B	C	D	E	F
1				Employee Number	Employee Name	
2	Employee No.:	1101		873	Charles K. Barkley	
3	Employee Name:	Melinda Hindquest		1109	Francis Jenikins	
4				1549	James Brackman	
5				1334	Linda Harper	
6				1643	Louise Victor	
7				1101	Melinda Hindquest	
8				1873	Michael Orenthal	
9				983	Peter Yates	
10				972	Sally Rice	
11				1398	Walter Franklin	
12						

Sheet1

Figure 116-2: This lookup table requires an exact match.

If you prefer to see something other than #N/A when the employee number isn't found, you can use the IFERROR function to test for the #N/A result (using the ISNA function) and substitute a different string. The following formula displays the text "Not Found" rather than #N/A:

```
=IFERROR(VLOOKUP(B2,D1:E11,2,FALSE),"Not Found")
```

The IFERROR function is new to Excel 2007, so if your workbook must be compatible with earlier versions, use this formula:

```
=IF(ISERROR(VLOOKUP(B2,D1:E11,2,FALSE)),"Not Found",
VLOOKUP(B2,D1:E11,2,FALSE))
```

Performing a Two-Way Lookup

A two-way lookup identifies the value at the intersection of a column and a row. This tip describes two methods to perform a two-way lookup.

Using a Formula

Figure 117-1 shows a worksheet with a range that displays product sales by month. To retrieve sales for a particular month and product, the user enters a month in cell B1 and a product name in cell B2.

	A	B	C	D	E	F	G	H
1	Month:	July			Widgets	Sprockets	Snapholytes	Combined
2	Product:	Sprockets		January	2,892	1,771	4,718	9,381
3				February	3,380	4,711	2,615	10,706
4	Month Offset:	8		March	3,744	3,223	5,312	12,279
5	Product Offset:	3		April	3,221	2,438	1,108	6,767
6	Sales:	3,337		May	4,839	1,999	1,994	8,832
7				June	3,767	5,140	3,830	12,737
8				July	5,467	3,337	3,232	12,036
9				August	3,154	4,895	1,607	9,656
10				September	1,718	2,040	1,563	5,321
11				October	1,548	1,061	2,590	5,199
12				November	5,083	3,558	3,960	12,601
13				December	5,753	2,839	3,013	11,605
14				Total	44,566	37,012	35,542	117,120
15								

Sheet1

Figure 117-1: This table demonstrates a two-way lookup.

To simplify the process, the worksheet uses the following named ranges:

Name	Refers To
Month	B1
Product	B2
Table	D1:H14
MonthList	D1:D14
ProductList	D1:H1

The following formula (in cell B4) uses the MATCH function to return the position of the Month within the MonthList range. For example, if the month is January, the formula returns 2 because January is the second item in the MonthList range (the first item is a blank cell, D1):

```
=MATCH(Month,MonthList,0)
```

The formula in cell B5 works similarly but uses the ProductList range:

```
=MATCH(Product,ProductList,0)
```

The final formula, in cell B6, returns the corresponding sales amount. It uses the INDEX function with the results from cells B4 and B5:

```
=INDEX(Table,B4,B5)
```

You can, of course, combine these formulas into a single formula, as shown here:

```
=INDEX(Table,MATCH(Month,MonthList,0),MATCH(Product,ProductList,0))
```

 NOTE
You can use the Lookup Wizard add-in to create this type of formula (see Figure 117-2). The Lookup Wizard add-in is distributed with Excel. Press Atl+TI to display the Add-Ins dialog box and install the add-in. After you install the Lookup Wizard add-in, you access it by choosing Formulas ⇨ Solutions ⇨ Lookup.

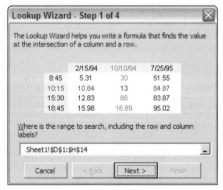

Figure 117-2: The Lookup Wizard add-in can create a formula that performs a two-way lookup.

Using Implicit Intersection

The second method to accomplish a two-way lookup is quite a bit simpler, but it requires that you create a name for each row and column in the table.

A quick way to name each row and column is to select the table and choose Formulas ⇨ Defined Names ⇨ Create From Selection. After creating the names, you can use a simple formula to perform the two-way lookup, such as

```
=Sprockets July
```

This formula, which uses the range intersection operator (a space), returns July sales data for Sprockets.

Performing a Two-Column Lookup

Some situations might require a lookup based on the values in two columns. Figure 118-1 shows an example.

	A	B	C	D	E	F	G
1	**Make:**	Jeep		**Make**	**Model**	**Code**	
2	**Model:**	Grand Cherokee		Chevy	Blazer	C-094	
3	**Code:**	J-701		Chevy	Tahoe	C-823	
4				Ford	Explorer	F-772	
5				Ford	Expedition	F-229	
6				Isuzu	Rodeo	I-897	
7				Isuzu	Trooper	I-900	
8				Jeep	Cherokee	J-983	
9				Jeep	Grand Cherokee	J-701	
10				Nissan	Pathfinder	N-231	
11				Toyota	4Runner	T-871	
12				Toyota	Land Cruiser	T-981	
13							
14							
15							
16							

Sheet1

Figure 118-1: This workbook performs a lookup by using information in two columns (D and E).

The lookup table contains automobile makes and models and a corresponding code for each one. The technique described here allows you to look up the value based on the car's make and model.

The worksheet uses named ranges, as shown in this table:

Range	Name
F2:F12	Code
B1	Make
B2	Model
D2:D12	Range1
E2:E12	Range2

The following array formula displays the corresponding code for an automobile make and model:

```
=INDEX(Code,MATCH(Make&Model,Range1&Range2,0))
```

 NOTE
When you enter an array formula, press Ctrl+Shift+Enter (not just Enter).

This formula works by concatenating the contents of Make and Model and then searching for this text in an array consisting of the corresponding concatenated text in Range1 and Range2.

An alternative approach is to create a new two-column lookup table, as shown in Figure 118-2. This table contains the same information as the original table, but column H contains the data from columns D and E, concatenated.

	A	B	C	D	E	F	G	H	I
1	Make:	Jeep		Make	Model	Code		MakeModel	Code
2	Model:	Grand Cherokee		Chevy	Blazer	C-094		ChevyBlazer	C-094
3	Code:	J-701		Chevy	Tahoe	C-823		ChevyTahoe	C-823
4				Ford	Explorer	F-772		FordExplorer	F-772
5	J-701			Ford	Expedition	F-229		FordExpedition	F-229
6				Isuzu	Rodeo	I-897		IsuzuRodeo	I-897
7				Isuzu	Trooper	I-900		IsuzuTrooper	I-900
8				Jeep	Cherokee	J-983		JeepCherokee	J-983
9				Jeep	Grand Cherokee	J-701		JeepGrand Cherokee	J-701
10				Nissan	Pathfinder	N-231		NissanPathfinder	N-231
11				Toyota	4Runner	T-871		Toyota4Runner	T-871
12				Toyota	Land Cruiser	T-981		ToyotaLand Cruiser	T-981

Figure 118-2: Avoid a two-column lookup by combing two columns into one.

After you create this new table, you can use a simpler formula to perform the lookup:

```
=VLOOKUP(Make&Model,H1:I12,2)
```

Performing a Lookup By Using an Array

If your lookup table is small, you might be able to avoid using a table altogether and store the lookup information in an array. This tip describes a typical lookup problem that uses a standard lookup table — and an alternative method that uses an array.

Using a Lookup Table

Figure 119-1 shows a worksheet with student test scores. The range E2:F6 (named GradeList) displays a lookup table used to assign a letter grade to a test score.

	A	B	C	D	E	F
1	Student	Score	Grade		Score	Grade
2	Adams	36	F		0	F
3	Baker	68	D		40	D
4	Camden	50	D		70	C
5	Dailey	77	C		80	B
6	Gomez	92	A		90	A
7	Hernandez	100	A			
8	Jackson	74	C			
9	Maplethorpe	45	D			
10	Paulson	60	D			
11	Ramirez	89	B			
12	Sosa	99	A			
13	Thompson	91	A			
14	Wilson	59	D			
15						

grade lookup

Figure 119-1: Looking up letter grades for test scores.

Column C contains formulas that use the VLOOKUP function and the lookup table to assign a grade based on the score in column B. The formula in C2, for example, is

```
=VLOOKUP(B2,GradeList,2)
```

Using an Array

When the lookup table is small (as in this example), you can use a literal array in place of the lookup table. This action can remove a bit of clutter on your worksheet. The following formula, for example, returns a letter grade without using a lookup table. Rather, the information in the lookup table is hard-coded into an array constant. Note the use of curly braces to indicate the array, and note the use of semicolons to separate "rows:"

```
=VLOOKUP(B2,{0,"F";40,"D";70,"C";80,"B";90,"A"},2)
```

Another approach, which uses a more legible formula, is to use the LOOKUP function with two array arguments:

```
=LOOKUP(B2,{0,40,70,80,90},{"F","D","C","B","A"})
```

Using the INDIRECT Function

To make a formula more flexible, you can use the Excel INDIRECT function to create a range reference. This rarely used function accepts a text argument that resembles a range reference and then converts the argument to an actual range reference. When you understand how this function works, you can use it to create more powerful interactive spreadsheets.

Specifying rows indirectly

Figure 120-1 shows a simple example that uses the INDIRECT function. The formula in cell E5 is

```
=SUM(INDIRECT("B"&E2&":B"&E3))
```

	A	B	C	D	E	F	G
1	Month	Sales					
2	Jan	45,983		First Row:	2		
3	Feb	47,335		Last Row:	4		
4	Mar	53,900					
5	Apr	54,962		SUM:	147,218		
6	May	56,932					
7	Jun	56,598					
8	Jul	58,054					
9	Aug	55,701					
10	Sep	53,786					
11	Oct	49,412					
12	Nov	47,641					
13	Dec	51,032					
14							
15							

Figure 120-1: Using the INDIRECT function to sum user-supplied rows.

Notice that the argument for the INDIRECT function uses the concatenation operator to build a range reference by using the values in cells E2 and E3. So, if E2 contains 2 and E3 contains 4, the range reference evaluates to this string:

```
"B2:B4"
```

The INDIRECT function converts that string to an actual range reference, which is then passed to the SUM function. In effect, the formula returns

```
=SUM(B2:B4)
```

When you change the values in E2 or E3, the formula is updated to display the sum of the specified rows.

Specifying worksheet names indirectly

Figure 120-2 shows another example, this time using a worksheet reference.

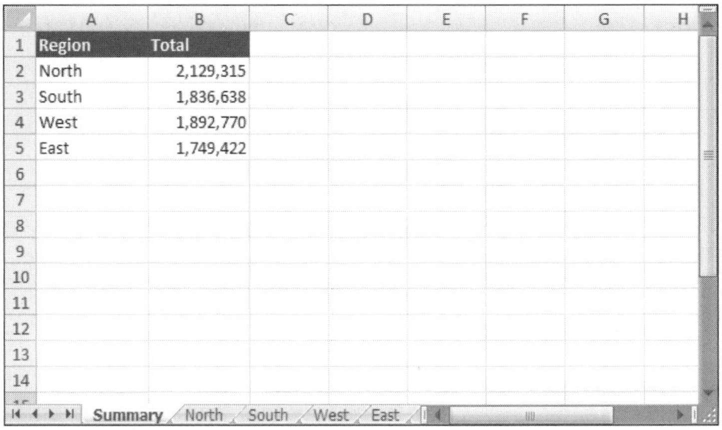

	A	B	C	D	E	F	G	H
1	Region	Total						
2	North	2,129,315						
3	South	1,836,638						
4	West	1,892,770						
5	East	1,749,422						
6								
7								
8								
9								
10								
11								
12								
13								
14								

Summary / North / South / West / East

Figure 120-2: Using the INDIRECT function to create references.

Column A, on the Summary worksheet, contains text that corresponds to other worksheets in the workbook. Column B contains formulas that reference these text items. For example, the formula in cell B2 is

```
=SUM(INDIRECT(A2&"!F1:F10"))
```

This formula concatenates the text in A2 with a range reference. The INDIRECT function evaluates the result and converts it to an actual range reference. The result is equivalent to this formula:

```
=SUM(North!F1:F10)
```

That formula is copied down the column. Each formula returns the sum of range F1:F10 on the corresponding worksheet.

Making a cell reference unchangeable

Another use for the INDIRECT function is to create a reference to a cell that never changes. For example, consider this simple formula, which sums the values in the first 12 rows of column A:

```
=SUM(A1:A12)
```

If you insert a new row 1, Excel changes the formula to

```
=SUM(A2:A13)
```

Part V

In other words, the formula adjusts so that it continues to refer to the original data (and it no longer sums the first 12 rows of column A). To prevent Excel from changing the cell references, use the INDIRECT function:

```
=SUM(INDIRECT("A1:A12"))
```

This formula *always* returns the sum of the first 12 rows in column A.

Creating Megaformulas

This tip describes a method of combining several intermediate formulas to create a single long formula (a *megaformula*). In the past, you might have seen some lengthy formulas that were virtually incomprehensible. Here, you learn how they were created.

The goal is to create a single formula that removes the middle name (for example, *Billy Joe Shaver* becomes *Billy Shaver*.) Figure 121-1 shows a worksheet with some names, plus six columns of intermediate formulas that accomplish the goal. Notice that the formulas aren't perfect; they can't handle a single-word name.

	A	B	C	D	E	F	G	H
1	Bob Smith	Bob Smith	4	#VALUE!	4	Bob	Smith	Bob Smith
2	Mike A. Jones	Mike A. Jones	5	8	8	Mike	Jones	Mike Jones
3	Jim Ray Johnson	Jim Ray Johnson	4	8	8	Jim	Johnson	Jim Johnson
4	Tom Alvin Jacobs	Tom Alvin Jacobs	4	10	10	Tom	Jacobs	Tom Jacobs
5	John Q. Public	John Q. Public	5	8	8	John	Public	John Public
6	R.J Smith	R.J Smith	4	#VALUE!	4	R.J	Smith	R.J Smith
7	R. Jay Smith	R. Jay Smith	3	7	7	R.	Smith	R. Smith
8	Tim Jones	Tim Jones	4	#VALUE!	4	Tim	Jones	Tim Jones
9	Billy Joe Shaver	Billy Joe Shaver	6	10	10	Billy	Shaver	Billy Shaver
10								
11								
12								

Sheet1

Figure 121-1: Removing the middle names and initials requires six intermediate formulas — or one megaformula.

The formulas are listed in Table 121-1.

TABLE 121-1   INTERMEDIATE FORMULAS

Cell	Intermediate Formula	What It Does
B1	=TRIM(A1)	Removes excess spaces
C1	=FIND(" ",B1,1)	Locates the first space
D1	=FIND(" ",B1,C1+1)	Locates the second space, if any
E1	=IFERROR(D1,C1)	Uses the first space if no second space exists
F1	=LEFT(B1,C1)	Extracts the first name
G1	=RIGHT(B1,LEN(B1)-E1)	Extracts the last name
H1	=F1&G1	Concatenates the two names

With a bit of work, you can eliminate all intermediate formulas and replace them with a single megaformula. You do so by creating all the intermediate formulas and then editing the final result formula (in this case, the formula in column H) by replacing each cell reference with a copy of the formula in the cell that's referred to. Fortunately, you can use the Clipboard to copy and paste the formulas rather than type them over again. Keep repeating this process until cell H1 contains nothing other than references to cell A1. You end up with the following megaformula in one cell:

```
=LEFT(TRIM(A1),FIND(" ",TRIM(A1),1))&
RIGHT(TRIM(A1),LEN(TRIM(A1))-
IFERROR(FIND(" ",TRIM(A1),FIND(" ",TRIM(A1),1)+1),
FIND(" ",TRIM(A1),1)))
```

When you're satisfied that the megaformula works, you can delete the columns that hold the intermediate formulas because they're no longer used.

If you're still not clear about this process, take a look at the step-by-step procedure:

1. Examine the formula in H1. This formula contains two cell references (F1 and G1):

   ```
   =F1&G1
   ```

2. Activate cell G1 and copy the contents of the formula (without the equal sign) to the Clipboard.

3. Activate cell H1 and replace the reference to cell G1 with the Clipboard contents. Now cell H1 contains the following formula:

   ```
   =F1&RIGHT(B1,LEN(B1)-E1)
   ```

4. Activate cell F1 and copy the contents of the formula (without the equal sign) to the Clipboard.

5. Activate cell H1 and replace the reference to cell F1 with the Clipboard contents. Now the formula in cell H1 is

   ```
   =LEFT(B1,C1)&RIGHT(B1,LEN(B1)-E1)
   ```

6. Now cell H1 contains references to three cells (B1, C1, and E1). The formulas in those cells replace each of the references to those cells.

7. Replace the reference to cell E1 with the formula in E1. The result is

   ```
   =LEFT(B1,C1)&RIGHT(B1,LEN(B1)-IFERROR(D1,C1))
   ```

8. Copy the formula from D1 and replace the references to cell D1. The formula now looks like this:

   ```
   =LEFT(B1,C1)&RIGHT(B1,LEN(B1)-IFERROR(FIND(" ",B1,C1+1),C1))
   ```

9. The formula has three references to cell C1. Replace each of those references with the formula contained in cell C1. The formula in cell H1 is

```
=LEFT(B1,FIND(" ",B1,1))&RIGHT(B1,LEN(B1)-IFERROR(FIND(" ",B1,FIND
(" ",B1,1)+1),FIND(" ",B1,1)))
```

10. Finally, replace the seven references to cell B1 with the formula in cell B1. The result is

```
=LEFT(TRIM(A1),FIND(" ",TRIM(A1),1))&
RIGHT(TRIM(A1),LEN(TRIM(A1))-
IFERROR(FIND(" ",TRIM(A1),FIND(" ",TRIM(A1),1)+1),
FIND(" ",TRIM(A1),1)))
```

Notice that the formula in cell H1 now contains references only to cell A1. The megaformula is complete, and it performs exactly the same tasks as all the intermediate formulas (which you can now delete).

You can, of course, adapt this technique to your own needs. A nice byproduct is that a single megaformula often calculates faster than a series of formulas does.

 NOTE

While you're replacing the cell references with formula text, make sure that the formula continues to display the correct result. In some situations, you might need to enclose the copied formula in parentheses.

Part VI

Conversions and Mathematical Calculations

This part provides you with a variety of handy measurement conversion tables and several calculations that you might find useful as you work away in Excel 2007.

Tips and Where to Find Them

Converting Between Measurement Systems

You know the distance from New York to London in miles, but your European office needs the numbers in kilometers. What's the conversion factor?

The Excel CONVERT function can convert between a variety of measurements in these categories:

- Weight and mass
- Distance
- Time
- Pressure
- Force
- Energy
- Power
- Magnetism
- Temperature
- Liquid measures

 NEW

In previous versions of Excel, the CONVERT function required the Analysis ToolPak add-in. In Excel 2007, this useful function is built in.

The CONVERT function requires three arguments: the value to be converted, the from-unit, and the to-unit. For example, if cell A1 contains a distance expressed in miles, use this formula to convert miles to kilometers:

```
=CONVERT(A1,"mi","km")
```

The second and third arguments are unit abbreviations, which are listed in the Help system. Some abbreviations are commonly used, but others aren't. And, of course, you must use the *exact* abbreviation. Furthermore, the unit abbreviations are case sensitive, so the following formula returns an error:

```
=CONVERT(A1,"Mi","km")
```

The CONVERT function is even more versatile than it seems. When using metric units, you can apply a multiplier. In fact, the first example I presented uses a multiplier. The unit abbreviation for the third argument is *m*, for meters. I added the kilo-multiplier — *k* — to express the result in kilometers.

In some situations, the CONVERT function requires some creativity. For example, what if you need to convert ten square yards to square feet? Neither of these units is available, but the following formula does the job:

```
=CONVERT(CONVERT(10,"yd","ft"),"yd","ft")
```

The nested instance of CONVERT converts ten yards into feet, and this result (30) is used as the first argument of the outer instance of the function. Similarly, to convert ten cubic yards into unit cubic feet, use this formula:

```
=CONVERT(CONVERT(CONVERT(10,"yd","ft"),"yd","ft"),"yd","ft")
```

Converting Temperatures

This tip presents formulas for conversion among three units of temperature: Fahrenheit, Celsius, and Kelvin.

Table 123-1 assumes that the temperature for conversion is in a cell named `temp`.

TABLE 123-1   TEMPERATURE CONVERSION FORMULAS

Type of Conversion	Formula
Fahrenheit to Celsius	=(temp-32)*(5/9)
Fahrenheit to Kelvin	=(temp-32)*(5/9)+273
Celsius to Fahrenheit	=(temp*1.8)+32
Celsius to Kelvin	=temp+273
Kelvin to Celsius	=temp-273
Kelvin to Fahrenheit	=((temp-273)*1.8)+32

Solving Right Triangles

This tip is for those who might be a bit rusty on their trigonometry skills.

A right triangle has six components: three sides and three angles. Figure 124-1 shows a right triangle with its parts labeled. Angles are labeled A, B, and C; sides are labeled Hypotenuse, Base, and Height. Angle C is always 90 degrees (or PI/2 radians). If you know any two of these components (excluding Angle C, which is always known), you can use formulas to solve for the others.

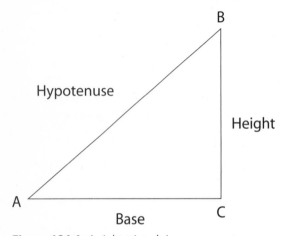

Figure 124-1: A right triangle's components.

The Pythagorean theorem states:

```
Height^2 + Base^2 = Hypotenuse^2
```

Therefore, if you know two sides of a right triangle, you can calculate the remaining side. The formula to calculate a right triangle's height (given the length of the hypotenuse and base) is

```
=SQRT((hypotenuse^2)-(base^2))
```

The formula to calculate a right triangle's base (given the length of the hypotenuse and height) is

```
=SQRT((hypotenuse^2)-(height^2))
```

The formula to calculate a right triangle's hypotenuse (given the length of the base and height) is

```
=SQRT((height^2)+(base^2))
```

Other useful trigonometric identities are

```
SIN(A) = Height/Hypotenuse
SIN(B) = Base/Hypotenuse
COS(A) = Base/Hypotenuse
COS(B) = Height/Hypotenuse
TAN(A) = Height/Base
SIN(A) = Base/Height
```

 NOTE

The Excel trigonometric functions all assume that the angle arguments are in radians. To convert degrees to radians, use the RADIANS function. To convert radians to degrees, use the DEGREES function.

If you know the height and base, you can use the following formula to calculate the angle formed by the hypotenuse and base (Angle A).

```
=ATAN(height/base)
```

The preceding formula returns radians. To convert to degrees, use this formula:

```
=DEGREES(ATAN(height/base))
```

If you know the height and base, you can use the following formula to calculate the angle formed by the hypotenuse and height (Angle B):

```
=PI()/2-ATAN(height/base)
```

The preceding formula returns radians. To convert to degrees, use this formula:

```
=90-DEGREES(ATAN(height/base))
```

Calculating Area, Surface, Circumference, and Volume

This tip contains formulas for calculating the area, surface, circumference, and volume for common two- and three-dimensional shapes.

Calculating the Area and Perimeter of a Square

To calculate the area of a square, square the length of one side. The following formula calculates the area of a square for a cell named `side`:

```
=side^2
```

To calculate the perimeter of a square, multiply one side by 4. The following formula uses a cell named `side` to calculate the perimeter of a square:

```
=side*4
```

Calculating the Area and Perimeter of a Rectangle

To calculate the area of a rectangle, multiply its height by its base. The following formula returns the area of a rectangle, using cells named `height` and `base`:

```
=height*base
```

To calculate the perimeter of a rectangle, multiply the height by 2 and add it to the width multiplied by 2. The following formula returns the perimeter of a rectangle, using cells named `height` and `width`:

```
=(height*2)+(width*2)
```

Calculating the Area and Perimeter of a Circle

To calculate the area of a circle, multiply the square of the radius by π. The following formula returns the area of a circle. It assumes that a cell named `radius` contains the circle's radius:

```
=PI()*(radius^2)
```

The radius of a circle is equal to one-half the diameter.

To calculate the circumference of a circle, multiply the diameter of the circle by π. The following formula calculates the circumference of a circle by using a cell named `diameter`:

```
=diameter*PI()
```

The diameter of a circle is the radius times 2.

Calculating the Area of a Trapezoid

To calculate the area of a trapezoid, add the two parallel sides, multiply by the height, and then divide by 2. The following formula calculates the area of a trapezoid, using cells named `parallel_side1`, `parallel_side2`, and `height`:

```
=((parallel_side1 + parallel_side2)*height)/2
```

Calculating the Area of a Triangle

To calculate the area of a triangle, multiply the base by the height and then divide by 2. The following formula calculates the area of a triangle, using cells named `base` and `height`:

```
=(base*height)/2
```

Calculating the Surface and Volume of a Sphere

To calculate the surface of a sphere, multiply the square of the radius by π, and then multiply by 4. The following formula returns the surface of a sphere, the radius of which is in a cell named radius:

```
=PI()*(radius^2)*4
```

To calculate the volume of a sphere, multiply the cube of the radius by 4 times π, and then divide by 3. The following formula calculates the volume of a sphere. The cell named radius contains the sphere's radius.

```
=((radius^3)*(4*PI()))/3
```

Calculating the Surface and Volume of a Cube

To calculate the surface area of a cube, square one side and multiply by 6. The following formula calculates the surface of a cube by using a cell named `side`, which contains the length of a side of the cube:

```
=(side^2)*6
```

To calculate the volume of a cube, raise the length of one side to the third power. The following formula returns the volume of a cube, by using a cell named side:

```
=side^3
```

Calculating the Surface and Volume of a Cone

The following formula calculates the surface of a cone (including the surface of the base). This formula uses cells named radius and height:

```
=PI()*radius*(SQRT(height^2+radius^2)+radius))
```

To calculate the volume of a cone, multiply the square of the radius of the base by π, multiply by the height, and then divide by 3. The following formula returns the volume of a cone, by using cells named radius and height:

```
=(PI()*(radius^2)*height)/3
```

Calculating the Volume of a Cylinder

To calculate the volume of a cylinder, multiply the square of the radius of the base by π, and then multiply by the height. The following formula calculates the volume of a cylinder, by using cells named radius and height:

```
=(PI()*(radius^2)*height)
```

Calculating the Volume of a Pyramid

Calculate the area of the base, and then multiply by the height and divide by 3. The following formula calculates the volume of a pyramid. It assumes cells named width (the width of the base), length (the length of the base), and height (the height of the pyramid).

```
=(width*length*height)/3
```

Solving Simultaneous Equations

This tip describes how to use formulas to solve simultaneous linear equations. The following example shows a set of simultaneous linear equations:

```
3x + 4y = 8
4x + 8y = 1
```

Solving a set of simultaneous equations involves finding the values for x and y that satisfy both equations. For this set of equations, the solution is

```
x = 7.5
y = -3.625
```

The number of variables in the set of equations must be equal to the number of equations. The preceding example uses two equations with two variables. Three equations are required in order to solve for three variables (x, y, and z).

The general steps for solving a set of simultaneous equations follow. See Figure 126-1, which uses the equations presented in the first paragraph of this tip.

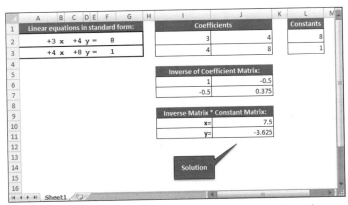

Figure 126-1: Using formulas to solve simultaneous equations.

1. Express the equations in standard form. If necessary, use basic algebra to rewrite the equations so that all variables appear on the left side of the equal sign. The following two equations are identical, but the second one is in standard form:

   ```
   3x -8 = -4y
   3x + 4y = 8
   ```

2. Place the coefficients in an n-by-n range of cells, where n represents the number of equations. In Figure 126-1, the coefficients are in the range I2:J3.

3. Place the constants (the numbers on the right side of the equal sign) in a vertical range of cells. In Figure 126-1, the constants are in the range L2:L3.

4. Use an array formula to calculate the inverse of the coefficient matrix. In Figure 126-1, the following array formula is entered into the range I6:J7. (Remember to press Ctrl+Shift+Enter to enter an array formula.)

```
=MINVERSE(I2:J3)
```

5. Use an array formula to multiply the inverse of the coefficient matrix by the constant matrix. In Figure 126-1, the following array formula is entered into the range J10:J11. This range holds the solution (x = 7.5, and y = −3.625).

```
=MMULT(I6:J7,L2:L3)
```

Solving Recursive Equations

A *recursive* equation is an equation in which a variable appears on both sides of the equal sign. The following equations are examples of recursive equations:

```
x = 1/(x+1)
x = COS(x)
x = SQRT(X+5)
x = 2^(1/x)
x = 5 + (1/x)
```

You can solve a recursive equation by using an intentional circular reference.

NOTE

This technique uses iterative calculations. By default, Excel doesn't perform iterative calculations, so you need to change a setting, by selecting the Enable Iterative Calculation check box on the Formulas tab of the Excel Options dialog box (see Figure 127-1).

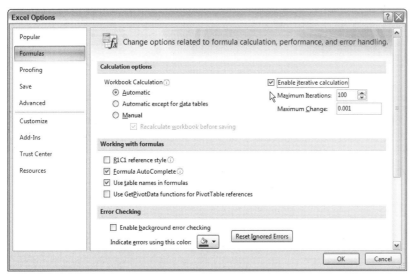

Figure 127-1: To solve a recursive equation, you must specify the Enable Iterative Calculation option.

The first step is to convert the recursive equation into a self-referencing formula. To solve the first equation, enter the following formula into cell A1:

```
=1/(A1+1)
```

The formula converges at 0.618033989, which is the value of x that satisfies the equation.

NOTE

Excel uses an iterative process to calculate the solution. The maximum number of iterations performed for each calculation is specified in Formulas tab of the Excel Options dialog box. You might need to press F9 several times before the solution stops changing.

Sometimes, this technique doesn't work. For example, the formula allows the possibility of a division-by-zero error. The solution is to check for an error. If the formula displays an error, modify the iterated value slightly. For example, the preceding formula can be rewritten using the new Excel 2007 IFERROR function:

```
=IFERROR(1/(A1+1),A1+0.01)
```

The following version of the formula is compatible with previous versions of Excel:

```
=IF(ISERR(1/(A1+1)),A1+0.01,1/(A1+1))
```

Figure 127-2 shows a worksheet that calculates several recursive equations in column B. The formulas in column D provide a check of the results. For example, the formula in column D2 is

```
=1/(B2+1)
```

Formulas in column E display the difference between the values in column B and column D. If the solution is correct, column E displays a zero (or a value very close to zero).

	A	B	C	D	E	F
1	Equation	Circular Ref Formula		Check	Difference	
2	x = 1/(x+1)	0.618033989		0.6180340	0.000000000	
3	x = COS(x)	0.739085133		0.7390851	0.000000000	
4	x = SQRT(X+5)	2.791287847		2.7912878	0.000000000	
5	x = 2^(1/x)	1.559610469		1.5596105	0.000000000	
6	x = 5 + (1/x)	5.192582404		5.1925824	0.000000000	
7						
8						

Figure 127-2: This workbook uses circular references to calculate several recursive equations.

Generating Random Numbers

Random numbers are often useful in spreadsheet applications. For example, you can fill a range with random numbers in order to test formulas. Or, you can generate random numbers to simulate various processes.

Excel provides several ways to generate random numbers.

Using the RAND Function

The Excel RAND function generates a uniform random number between 0 and 1. In other words, every number between 0 and 1 has an equal probability of being returned by the function.

If you need larger random numbers, just use a simple multiplication formula. The following formula, for example, generates a uniform random number between 0 and 1000:

```
=RAND()*1000
```

To limit the random number to whole numbers, use the ROUND function:

```
=ROUND((RAND()*1000),0)
```

Using the RANDBETWEEN Function

To generate uniform random integers between any two numbers, you can use the RANDBE-TWEEN function. The following formula, for example, generates a random number between 100 and 200:

```
=RANDBETWEEN(100,200)
```

In previous versions of Excel, the RANDBETWEEN function is available only when the Analysis Toolpak add-in is installed. For compatibility with previous versions (and to avoid using the add-in), use a formula like the following, where a represents the lower limit and b represents the upper limit:

```
=RAND()*(b-a)+a
```

To generate a random number between 40 and 50, use this formula:

```
=RAND()*(50-40)+40
```

Part VI

Using the Analysis Toolpak Add-In

Another way of getting random numbers into a worksheet is to use the Analysis Toolpak add-in. This tool can generate non-uniform random numbers. These numbers aren't generated by formulas, so if you want a new set of random numbers, you need to rerun the procedure.

Access the Analysis Toolpak add-in by choosing Data ⇨ Analysis ⇨ Data Analysis. If this command isn't available, install the Analysis Toolpak by using the Add-Ins dialog box. The easiest way to display this dialog box is to press Atl+TI.

In the Data Analysis dialog box, select the Random Number Generation option and click OK. The dialog box shown in Figure 128-1 appears.

Figure 128-1: The Random Number Generation dialog box.

Choose a distribution from the Distribution drop-down list, and then specify additional parameters (the parameters vary, depending on the distribution). Don't forget to specify the Output Range, which stores the random numbers.

Calculating Roots and a Remainder

Sometimes, you might need to figure out a complicated root of a value, or you might want to know a nondecimal remainder of a division. Excel can do that for you.

Calculating Roots

If you need to calculate the square root of a value, use the Excel SQRT function. The following formula, for example, calculates the square root of the value in cell A1:

```
=SQRT(A1)
```

What about other roots? You won't find a CUBEROOT function, and there's certainly isn't a FOURTHROOT function. The trick is to raise the number to the (1/root) power. For example, to calculate the cube root of the value in cell A1, use this formula:

```
=A1^(1/3)
```

To calculate the fourth root, use this formula:

```
=A1^(1/4)
```

Calculating a Remainder

When you divide two numbers, if the result isn't a whole number, you end up with a remainder. When Excel performs division, the result is a decimal value. How can you determine the remainder (if any) that results from a division?

The solution is to use the MOD function, which takes two arguments: the number and the divisor. The MOD function returns the remainder.

For example, if you have 187 books to be divided equally among 5 offices, how many will be left over? To get the answer (2), use this formula:

```
=MOD(187,5)
```

Calculating a Conditional Average

Excel makes it easy to calculate the average of a range of cells, by using the AVERAGE function. Excel 2007 includes two new functions for calculating conditional averages: AVERAGEIF and AVERAGEIFS. AVERAGEIF limits the result to cells that meet a single criterion. AVERAGEIFS allows you to specify multiple criteria.

For example, to calculate the average of only the positive values in A1:A30, use this formula:

```
=AVERAGEIF(A1:A30,">0",A1:A30)
```

Here's a trickier example. An instructor needs to calculate student grades by averaging a series of test scores and omitting the two lowest scores. Excel 2007 users can use the AVERAGEIFS function and create this formula (which assumes the scores are in a range named scores):

```
=AVERAGEIFS(scores, scores,"<>"&SMALL(scores,1), scores,"<>"&SMALL(scores,2))
```

Following is an alternative formula that works in all versions of Excel:

```
=(SUM(scores)-MIN(scores)-MAX(scores))/(COUNT(scores)-2)
```

Here's another examples that computes an average that ignores both the highest and lowest scores.

```
=AVERAGEIFS(scores,scores,"<>"&MAX(scores),scores,"<>"&MIN(scores))
```

Here's an alternative formula that's compatible with all versions of Excel:

```
=(SUM(scores)-MIN(scores)-MAX(scores))/(COUNT(scores)-2)
```

Part VII

Charts and Graphics

A well-conceived chart can make a range of incomprehensible numbers make sense. The tips in this part deal with various aspects of chart making.

Tips and Where to Find Them

Creating a Text Chart Directly in a Range

Tip 51 presents an example of the new Data Bars Conditional Formatting option, which enables you to create a simple bar chart directly in a range of cells. The Data Bars feature is handy, but it's not flexible. For example, it doesn't handle negative values well, and you have little control over the color. And, because it's a new feature, it's not compatible with versions before Excel 2007.

This tip describes another way to create a bar chart directly in a range. Figure 131-1 shows an example of a chart created by using formulas.

	A	B	C	D	E
1	Month	Units Sold		Chart	
2	January	834		========	
3	February	1,132		===========	
4	March	1,243		============	
5	April	1,094		==========	
6	May	902		=========	
7	June	1,543		===============	
8	July	1,654		================	
9	August	2,655		===========================	
10	September	2,081		=====================	
11	October	1,983		====================	
12	November	1,321		=============	
13	December	1,654		================	
14					

Sheet1 / Sheet2

Figure 131-1: A crude histogram created directly in a range of cells.

Column D contains formulas that feature the rarely used REPT function, which repeats a text string a specified number of times. For example, the following formula prints five asterisks:

```
=REPT("*",5)
```

In the example shown in Figure 131-1, cell D2 contains this formula, which was copied down the column:

```
=REPT("=",B2/100)
```

Notice that the formula divides the value in column B by 100. This is a way to scale the chart. After all, you don't really want to see 834 characters in a cell. For improved accuracy, you can include the ROUND function:

```
=REPT("=",ROUND(B2/100,0))
```

Part VII

Without the ROUND function, the formula simply *truncates* the result of the division (disregards the decimal part of the argument). For example, the value 1,654 in column B displays 16 characters in column D. Using ROUND rounds up the result to 17 characters.

You can use this type of graphical display in place of a column chart. As long as you don't require strict accuracy (because of rounding errors), this type of nonchart might fit the bill.

Figure 131-2 shows another example. The formulas in columns F and H graphically depict monthly budget variances by displaying a series of characters. You can then easily see which budget items are under or over budget. This "pseudo" bar chart example uses the character *n,* which appears as a small square in the Wingdings font.

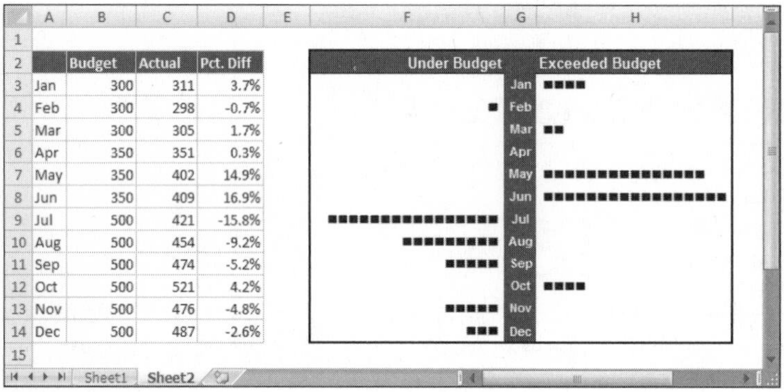

	A	B	C	D	E	F	G	H
1								
2		Budget	Actual	Pct. Diff		Under Budget		Exceeded Budget
3	Jan	300	311	3.7%			Jan	▪▪▪▪
4	Feb	300	298	-0.7%		▪	Feb	
5	Mar	300	305	1.7%			Mar	▪▪
6	Apr	350	351	0.3%			Apr	
7	May	350	402	14.9%			May	▪▪▪▪▪▪▪▪▪▪▪▪▪▪
8	Jun	350	409	16.9%			Jun	▪▪▪▪▪▪▪▪▪▪▪▪▪▪▪▪
9	Jul	500	421	-15.8%		▪▪▪▪▪▪▪▪▪▪▪▪▪▪▪▪	Jul	
10	Aug	500	454	-9.2%		▪▪▪▪▪▪▪▪▪	Aug	
11	Sep	500	474	-5.2%		▪▪▪▪▪	Sep	
12	Oct	500	521	4.2%			Oct	▪▪▪▪
13	Nov	500	476	-4.8%		▪▪▪▪▪	Nov	
14	Dec	500	487	-2.6%		▪▪▪	Dec	
15								

Sheet1 Sheet2

Figure 131-2: Using the Wingdings font to simulate a bar chart.

The key formulas are

```
F2: =IF(D2<0,REPT("n",ROUND(D2*-100,0)),"")
G2: =A2
H2: =IF(D2>0,REPT("n",ROUND(D2*100,0)),"")
```

For this example, follow these steps to set up the bar chart after entering the preceding formulas:

1. Assign the Wingdings font to cells F2 and H2.

2. Copy the formulas down columns F, G, and H to accommodate all the data.

3. Right-align the text in column E and adjust any other formatting.

Depending on the numerical range of your data, you might need to change the scaling. Experiment by replacing the 100 value in the formulas. You can substitute any character you like for the *n* in the formulas to produce a different character in the chart.

Selecting Elements in a Chart

An Excel chart consists of a number of different elements. For example, all charts contain a plot area and at least one data series. A chart can also contain elements such as a chart title, axes, and data labels. To work with a particular chart element, you need to select it — something that is often easier said than done.

Excel provides three ways to select a particular chart element:

- Use the mouse.
- Use the keyboard.
- Use the Chart Elements control.

Selecting with the Mouse

To select a chart element with your mouse, just click it. The chart element appears with small circles at the corners.

To ensure that you selected the chart element you intended to select, view the Chart Element control, by choosing Chart Tools ➪ Format ➪ Current Selection (see Figure 132-1).

When you move the mouse over a chart, a small "chart tip" displays the name of the chart element under the mouse pointer. When the mouse pointer moves over a data point, the chart tip also displays the value of the data point. See Figure 132-2 for an example.

NOTE

If these chart tips annoy you, you can turn them off. Choose Office ➪ Excel Options and click the Advanced tab in the Excel Options dialog box. Locate the Display section, and deselect either or both of the check boxes labeled Show Chart Element Names On Hover or Show Data Point Values On Hover.

Some chart elements (such as a series, legend, or data label) consist of multiple items. For example, a chart series element is made up of individual data points. To select a particular data point, click twice: First click the series to select it; then click the specific element within the series (for example, a column or a line chart marker). Selecting the element enables you to apply formatting to only a particular data point in a series.

You might find that some chart elements are difficult to select with the mouse. If you rely on the mouse for selecting a chart element, you might have to click it several times before the element you want is selected. Fortunately, Excel provides other ways to select a chart element, and it's worth your while to be familiar with them.

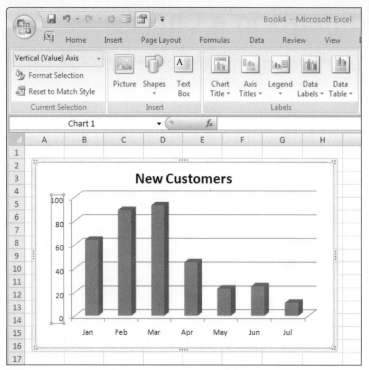

Figure 132-1: The Chart Element control displays the name of the selected chart element. In this example, Vertical (Value) Axis is selected.

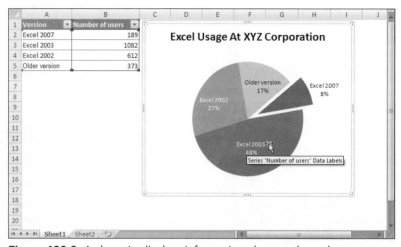

Figure 132-2: A chart tip displays information about a chart element.

Selecting with the Keyboard

When a chart is active, you can use the up-arrow and down-arrow keys on your keyboard to cycle among the chart's elements. Again, keep your eye on the Chart Elements control, to ensure that the selected chart element is what you think it is.

When a chart series is selected, use the left-arrow and right-arrow keys to select an individual item within the series. Similarly, when a set of data labels is selected, you can select a specific data label by pressing the left-arrow or right-arrow key. And, when a legend is selected, you can select individual elements within the legend by using the left-arrow or right-arrow keys.

Selecting with the Chart Element Control

The Chart Element control is located in the Chart Tools ➪ Format ➪ Current Selection group. This control displays the name of the selected chart element. Because it's a drop-down control, you can also use it to select a particular element in the active chart (see Figure 132-3).

This control lists only the top-level elements in the chart. To select an individual data point within a series, for example, you need to select the series and then use the left and right arrow keys (or your mouse) to select the data point.

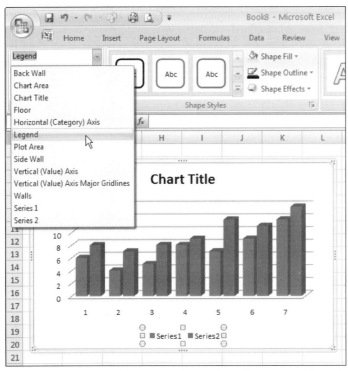

Figure 132-3: Using the Chart Element drop-down control to select a chart element.

NOTE
When a single data point is selected, the Chart Element control *will* display the name of the selected element, even though it's not available for selection in the drop-down list.

If you do a lot of work with charts, you might want to add the Chart Element control to your Quick Access Toolbar (QAT). That way, it's always visible regardless of which Ribbon tab is selected. To add the control to your QAT, right-click it and choose Add to Quick Access Toolbar.

Annotating a Chart

When you create a chart, you might want to provide some text annotation. Then you need to know how to add free-floating text to a chart. Before Excel 2007, adding text to a chart was amazingly simple: Select the chart and just start typing. When you finished, you pressed Enter to create a movable text box inside the chart.

That technique no longer works with Excel 2007. To add free-floating text to a chart, follow these steps:

1. Select the chart.

2. Choose Insert ⇨ Text ⇨ Text Box.

3. Click in the chart to create the text box.

4. Type your text.

When the text box is selected, you can apply formatting by using the tools in the Drawing Tools ⇨ Format tab. Figure 133-1 shows a chart that contains a text box with a fill color and shadow added.

 NOTE
If a chart is not selected when you perform Step 2, the text box is placed on top of the chart (not inside of the chart). If the text box is not inside of the chart, it does not move if you move the chart.

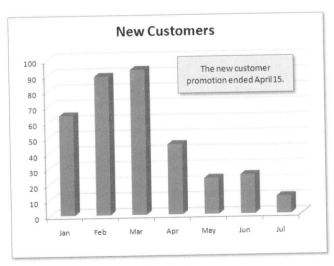

Figure 133-1: A text box in a chart.

Part VII

A chart can contain any number of text boxes, and you can move, resize, and format them any way you like.

 CROSS-REFERENCE

To find out how to link the text in a text box to a cell, see Tip 142.

Creating a Self-Expanding Chart

This tip describes how to create a chart that expands automatically when you add new data to a worksheet. Figure 134-1 illustrates the problem: The chart displays all data in the sheet. But when new data is entered, the chart series must be manually expanded to include the new data. It would be nice if Excel could do this automatically.

Figure 134-1: If this chart were self-expanding, it would update automatically when additional data is entered.

Creating a self-expanding chart is very simple in Excel 2007, thanks to its new table feature. If you need the workbook to be compatible with versions prior to Excel 2003, though, you can do a bit of setup work to make a self-expanding chart.

For Excel 2007 and Excel 2003

To create a self-expanding chart in Excel 2007, follow these simple steps:

1. Create your chart as usual.
2. Select any cell in the range that contains the data used by the chart.
3. Chose Insert ➪ Tables ➪ Tables to convert the range to a table.

That's all there is to it. Excel recognizes the data as a table, and data added to the table is shown in the chart.

NOTE
If you use Excel 2003, in Step 3 choose Data ➪ List ➪ Create List.

For Compatibility with Versions before Excel 2003

To make the chart self-expanding, you create named formulas and then substitute the names in the chart's Source Data dialog box. The following instructions refer to the chart shown earlier, in Figure 134-1.

First, create the named formulas:

1. Choose Formulas ⇨ Defined Names ⇨ Define Name to display the New Name dialog box.

2. In the Name field, type **Date**. In the Refers To field, enter this formula:

   `=OFFSET(Sheet1!$A$2,0,0,COUNTA(Sheet1!$A:$A)-1,1)`

3. Click OK to create the formula named Date.

   Note that the OFFSET function refers to the first category label (cell A2) and uses the COUNTA function to determine the number of labels in the column. Because column A has a heading in row 1, the formula subtracts 1 from the number.

4. Choose Formulas ⇨ Defined Names ⇨ Define Name to display the New Name dialog box.

5. Type **Sales** in the Name field and enter this formula in the Refers To field:

   `=OFFSET(Sheet1!$B$2,0,0,COUNTA(Sheet1!$B:$B)-1,1)`

6. Click OK to create the formula named Sales.

After you perform these steps, the workbook contains two new names: Date and Sales.

Next, modify the chart's SERIES formula so that it uses these names rather than range references. In other words, replace the reference to $A$2:$A$9 with `Date`, and replace the reference to $B$2:$B$9 with `Sales`.

1. Activate the chart and click any column. Excel displays the SERIES formula on the formula bar:

   `=SERIES(,Sheet1!$A$2:$A$9,Sheet1!$B$2:$B$9,1)`

2. Click the formula bar and edit the SERIES formula as follows:

   `=SERIES(,Sheet1!Date,Sheet1!Sales,1)`

3. Press Enter to change the SERIES formula for the chart.

After following these steps, you see that the chart expands when you add new data to the bottom of the list.

 NOTE

If your chart has more than one data series, you need to create an additional named formula for each series and then make sure that you update the series by using the Select Data Source dialog box.

Creating Combination Charts

Typically, a chart uses a single style: a column chart, a line chart, or a pie chart, for example. If your chart has more than one data series, you might want to display multiple styles within the same chart — a combination chart is just what you need. Figure 135-1 shows a combination chart. Projected sales are depicted by a line, and actual sales are depicted by columns.

Figure 135-1: This combination chart uses a line and columns.

You can search the Excel Ribbon all day and you won't find a command to create a combination chart. If you already created your chart (that has at least two data series), you can easily convert it to a combination chart. Follow these steps:

1. Click the series that you want to change.

2. Choose Chart Tools ⇨ Design ⇨ Type ⇨ Change Chart Type.

3. In the Change Chart Type dialog box, choose the icon that represents the chart type for the selected series.

The chart in Figure 135-1 started out as a standard column chart. A few mouse clicks later, one of the series (named Projected, in this case) is converted from columns to a line.

Figure 135-2 shows how far you can go with a combination chart. This chart combines five different chart types: Pie, Area, Column, XY, and Line. I can't think of any situation that would warrant such a chart, but it's an interesting demo.

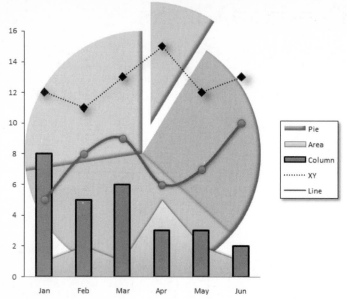

Figure 135-2: A five-way combination chart.

In some cases, you can't combine chart types. For example, you can't create a combination chart that involves a bubble chart or a 3-D chart. If you choose an incompatible chart type for the series, Excel lets you know.

If your chart plots data with drastically different scales, you might want to use a second value axis for one of the chart series. Select the series you want to change, and press Ctrl+1 to display the Format Data Series dialog box. Click the Series Options tab, and select the Secondary Axis option.

Figure 135-3 shows a combination chart that uses a secondary axis for the line series (Sales Staff).

Figure 135-3: This combination chart uses a second value axis.

Dealing with Missing Data in a Line Chart

When you create a line chart in Excel, missing data points (blank cells) aren't plotted, which leaves gaps in the chart. Excel provides two other ways of handling missing data:

- Treat the missing data as zero.

- Interpolate the data by connecting the line between the nonmissing data points.

Figure 136-1 shows the default behavior for missing data. The four missing data values aren't plotted. In some cases, you might want to use a different approach.

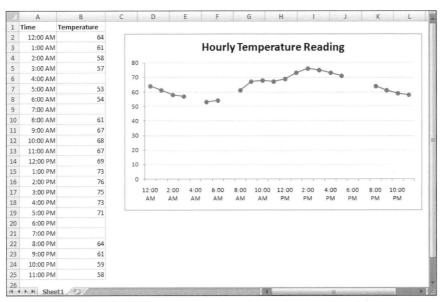

Figure 136-1: By default, Excel doesn't plot missing data in a line chart.

To change how Excel treats missing data, follow these steps:

1. Select the chart.

2. Choose Chart Tools ➪ Design ➪ Data ➪ Select Data to display the Select Data Source dialog box.

3. In the Select Data Source Dialog box, click the button labeled Hidden and Empty Cells, to display the Hidden and Empty Cell Settings dialog box (see Figure 136-2).

4. Make your selection, and click OK (twice).

Your choice applies to all data series in the selected chart. (This setting isn't global, for all charts.)

Figure 136-2: Use the Hidden and Empty Cell Settings dialog box to control how Excel handles missing data in a chart.

Figure 136-3 shows how these options look. The top chart uses the Zero option (which plots missing data as zero values), and the bottom chart uses the Connect Data Points with Line setting. In this example, connecting the missing data points with a line seems to be the better choice, given the data's time-based nature.

NOTE

You can also represent missing data with the formula =NA() rather than leave a cell blank. The chart connects the data points with a line for cells that contain this formula, regardless of the setting in the Hidden and Empty Cell Settings dialog box.

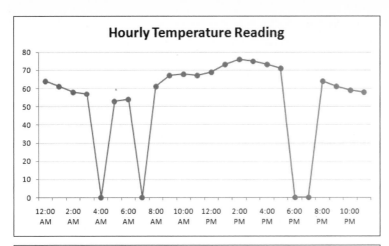

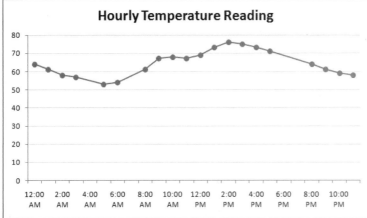

Figure 136-3: Two optional methods of dealing with missing data in a line chart.

Creating a Gantt Chart

A *Gantt chart* is a horizontal bar chart that's often used in project management applications. Although Excel doesn't support Gantt charts per se, creating a simple Gantt chart is fairly easy. The key is setting up your data properly.

Figure 137-1 shows a Gantt chart that depicts the schedule for a project that is in the range A2:C13. In the chart, the horizontal axis represents the total time span of the project, and each bar represents a project task. The viewer can quickly see the duration for each task and identify overlapping tasks.

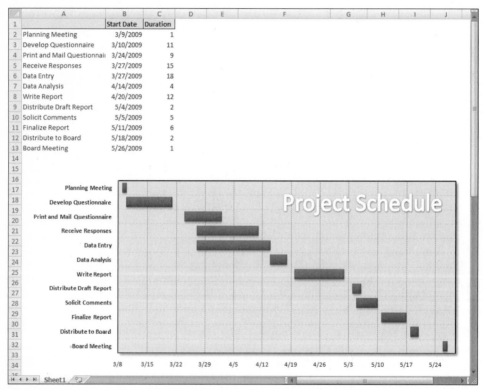

Figure 137-1: You can create a simple Gantt chart from a stacked bar chart.

Column A contains the task name, column B contains the corresponding start date, and column C contains the duration of the task, in days.

Follow these steps to create this chart:

1. Select the range A2:C13, choose Insert ➪ Charts ➪ Bar, and select the Stacked Bar Chart option.

2. Delete the legend.

3. Select the category (vertical) axis, and press Ctrl+1 to display the Format Axis dialog box.

4. In the Format Axis dialog box, click the Axis Options tab and specify Categories in Reverse Order to display the tasks in order, starting at the top. Choose Horizontal Axis Crosses at Maximum Category to display the dates at the bottom.

5. Select the Start Date data series, and display the Format Data Series dialog box.

6. In the Format Data Series dialog box, click the Fill tab and specify No Fill. Click the Border Color tab and specify No Line. These steps effectively hide the data series.

7. Select the value (horizontal) axis, and display the Format Axis dialog box.

8. In the Format Axis dialog box, adjust the Minimum and Maximum settings to accommodate the dates that you want to display on the axis. Unfortunately, you must enter these values as date serial numbers, not as actual dates. In this example, the minimum is 39880 (March 8, 2009) and the maximum is 39962 (May 29, 2009). Specify **7** for the Major Unit option, to display one-week intervals. Use the Number tab to specify a date format for the axis labels.

   Note: To determine the serial number for a date, enter the date into a cell, and then apply General number formatting to the cell.

9. Apply other formatting as desired.

Part VII

Creating a Thermometer-Style Chart

You're probably familiar with the thermometer-type display, which shows the percentage of a task that's completed. You can easily create this type of display in Excel. The trick involves creating a chart that uses a single cell (which holds a percentage value) as a data series.

Figure 138-1 shows a worksheet set up to track daily progress toward a goal: 1,000 new customers in a 15-day period. Cell B18 contains the goal value, and cell B19 contains a simple formula that calculates the sum. Cell B21 contains a formula that calculates the percentage progress of the goal:

```
=B19/B18
```

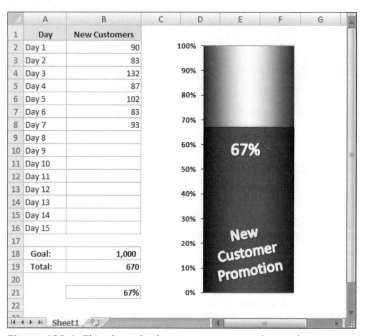

Figure 138-1: This chart displays progress toward a goal.

As you enter new data in column B, the formulas display the current results.

To make the thermometer chart, select cell B21 and create a column chart from that single cell. Notice the blank cell above cell B21. Without this blank cell, Excel uses the entire data block for the chart, not just the single cell. Because B21 is isolated from the other data, only the single cell is used.

Other changes are required:

- Select the horizontal category axis and press Delete, to remove the category axis from the chart.

- Remove the legend.

- Add data labels, by choosing Chart Tools ⇨ Layout ⇨ Data Labels. In the example, the data label displays 67%.

- In the Format Data Series dialog box (Series Options tab), set the Gap width to 0. This makes the column occupy the entire width of the plot area.

- Select the chart's vertical Value Axis and press Ctrl+1 to display the Format Value Axis dialog box. On the Axis Options tab, set the minimum to 0 and the maximum to 1.

- Select the chart's Plot Area, and apply a fill color by choosing Chart Tools ⇨ Format ⇨ Shape Styles ⇨ Shape Fill. The Plot Area is the "unfilled" area of the thermometer.

- If the chart doesn't have a title, add one by choosing Chart Tools ⇨ Layout ⇨ Labels ⇨ Title. Format the title and move it to the location you want. In the example, the chart title — New Customer Promotion — has been formatted to display at an angle.

- Make any other cosmetic adjustments to get the look you want. In the example, I used a gradient fill to give the column a three-dimensional look.

Part VII

Using Pictures in Charts

Excel makes it easy to incorporate a pattern, texture, or graphical file for elements in your chart. Figure 139-1 shows a chart that uses a photo as the background for a chart's Chart Area element.

Figure 139-1: The Chart Area contains a photo.

To display an image in a chart element, use the Fill tab in the element's Format dialog box. (Press Ctrl+1 to display this dialog box.) Select the Picture or Text Fill option, and then click the button that corresponds to the image source (File, Clipboard, or Clip Art). If you use the Clipboard button, make sure that you copied your image first. The other two options prompt you to supply the image.

Figure 139-2 shows two more examples: a pie chat that uses Office clip art as its fill, and a column chart that uses a shape, which was inserted on a worksheet and then copied to clipboard.

Using images in a chart offers unlimited potential for creativity. The key, of course, is to resist the temptation to go overboard. A chart's primary goal is to convey information, not to impress the viewer with your artistic skills. Also, remember that using images, especially photos, in charts can dramatically increase the size of your workbooks.

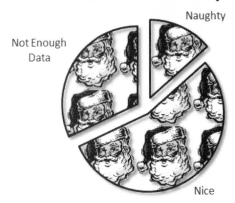

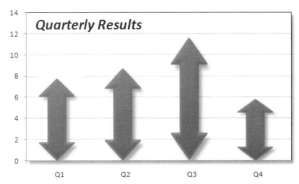

Figure 139-2: The top chart uses clip art, and the bottom chart uses a shape that was copied to the Clipboard.

Plotting Mathematical Functions

An Excel chart is a good way to display a mathematical or trigonometric function plot. This tip describes two function-plotting techniques:

- Plot a single-variable function by using a scatter chart.
- Plot a two-variable function by using a 3-D surface chart.

Plotting Single-Variable Mathematical Functions

A scatter chart (known as an XY chart in previous versions of Excel) displays a marker for each set of paired values. For example, Figure 140-1 shows a plot of the SIN function. The chart plots the calculated y value for values of x (expressed in radians) from −5 to +5 in increments of 0.5. Each pair of x and y values appears as a data point in the chart, and the points are connected by a line.

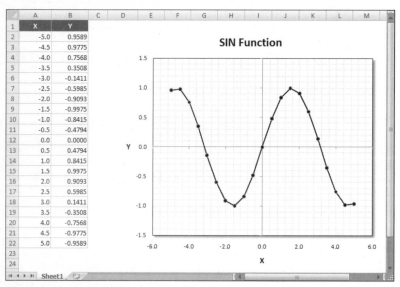

Figure 140-1: This chart plots the SIN(x).

The function is expressed as

```
y = SIN(x)
```

The corresponding formula in cell B2 (which is copied to the cells below) is

```
=SIN(A2)
```

To create this chart, follow these steps:

1. Select A1:B22.

2. Choose Insert ➪ Charts ➪ Scatter ➪ Scatter with Straight Lines and Markers.

3. Choose a chart layout that gives you the look you like, and then fine-tune it.

Change the values in column A to plot the function for different values of x. And, of course, you can use any single-variable formula you like in column B. Here are a few examples that make interesting plots:

```
=SIN(PI()*A2)*(PI()*A2)
=SIN(A2)/A2
=SIN(A2^3)*COS(A2^2)
=NORMDIST(A2,0,1,FALSE)
```

For more accurate charts, increase the number of plotted values and make the increments in column A smaller.

Plotting Two-Variable Mathematical Functions

You also can plot functions that use two variables. For example, the following function calculates a value of z for various values of two variables (x and y):

```
z = SIN(x)*COS(y)
```

Figure 140-2 shows a surface chart that plots the value of z for 21 x values ranging from -3 to 0 and for 21 y values ranging from 2 to 5. Both x and y use an increment of 0.15.

The x values are in A2:A22, and the y values are in B1:V1. The formula in cell B2, which is copied to the other cells in the table, is

```
= SIN($A2)*COS(B$1)
```

To create this chart, follow these steps:

1. Select A1:V22.

2. Choose Insert ➪ Charts ➪ Other Charts ➪ 3-D Surface.

3. Choose a chart layout that gives you the look you like, and then fine-tune it.

As long as the x and y values have equal increments, you can specify any two-variable formula you like. You might need to adjust the starting values and increment values for the x and y variables. For a smoother plot, use more x and y values with a smaller increment.

Part VII

	A	B	C	D	E	F	G	H	I	J	K	L	M	N	O	P	Q	R	S	T	U	V
1		0.0	0.2	0.4	0.6	0.8	1.0	1.2	1.4	1.6	1.8	2.0	2.2	2.4	2.6	2.8	3.0	3.2	3.4	3.6	3.8	4.0
2	0.0	0.00	0.00	0.00	0.00	0.00	0.00	0.00	0.00	0.00	0.00	0.00	0.00	0.00	0.00	0.00	0.00	0.00	0.00	0.00	0.00	0.00
3	0.2	0.20	0.19	0.18	0.16	0.14	0.11	0.07	0.03	-0.01	-0.05	-0.08	-0.12	-0.15	-0.17	-0.19	-0.20	-0.20	-0.19	-0.18	-0.16	-0.13
4	0.4	0.39																	-0.38	-0.35	-0.31	-0.25
5	0.6	0.56																	-0.55	-0.51	-0.45	-0.37
6	0.8	0.72																	-0.69	-0.64	-0.57	-0.47
7	1.0	0.84																	-0.81	-0.75	-0.67	-0.55
8	1.2	0.93																	-0.90	-0.84	-0.74	-0.61
9	1.4	0.99																	-0.95	-0.88	-0.78	-0.64
10	1.6	1.00																	-0.97	-0.90	-0.79	-0.65
11	1.8	0.97																	-0.94	-0.87	-0.77	-0.64
12	2.0	0.91																	-0.88	-0.82	-0.72	-0.59
13	2.2	0.81																	-0.78	-0.73	-0.64	-0.53
14	2.4	0.68																	-0.65	-0.61	-0.53	-0.44
15	2.6	0.52																	-0.50	-0.46	-0.41	-0.34
16	2.8	0.33																	-0.32	-0.30	-0.26	-0.22
17	3.0	0.14																	-0.14	-0.13	-0.11	-0.09
18	3.2	-0.06																	0.06	0.05	0.05	0.04
19	3.4	-0.26																	0.25	0.23	0.20	0.17
20	3.6	-0.44																	0.43	0.40	0.35	0.29
21	3.8	-0.61																	0.59	0.55	0.48	0.40
22	4.0	-0.76																	0.73	0.68	0.60	0.49

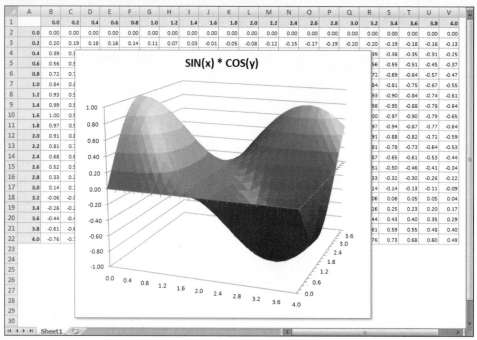

Figure 140-2: Using a 3-D surface chart to plot a function with two variables.

Here are some other formulas you can try:

```
=SIN(SQRT($A2^2 + B$1^2))
=SIN($A2)*COS($A2* B$1)
=COS($A2* B$1)
```

Displaying a Chart Slide Show

Although PowerPoint is a better choice for displaying a slide presentation, Excel can show a series of charts in full-screen mode. Excel certainly isn't as versatile as PowerPoint in this area, but it will do in a pinch.

You need to add a simple macro to your workbook. The following VBA macro displays each embedded chart (on the active worksheet) in Excel's Print Preview mode. To add this macro to your workbook, follow these steps:

1. Press Alt+F11 to activate the Visual Basic Editor.

2. In the Visual Basic Editor, double-click the workbook name in the Project window.

3. Choose Insert ⇨ Module to insert a new VBA module.

4. Type the following VBA code:

```
Sub EmbeddedChartSlideShow()
    Dim ChtObj As ChartObject
    Application.DisplayFullScreen = True
    For Each ChtObj In ActiveSheet.ChartObjects
        Application.ScreenUpdating = False
        ChtObj.Chart.PrintPreview
    Next ChtObj
    Application.DisplayFullScreen = False
End Sub
```

5. Press Alt+F11 to return to Excel.

To start the slide show, make sure that the active worksheet contains at least one chart. Then follow these steps:

1. Choose View ⇨ Macros ⇨ Macros to display the Macros dialog box (or press Alt+F8).

2. Select the Macro named EmbeddedChartSlideShow.

3. Click Run.

Excel displays the first chart in full-screen mode. Press Esc or Enter to advance to the next chart. After the last chart is displayed, the normal Excel screen is displayed.

Part VII

If your charts are located on chart sheets, use this macro:

```
Sub ChartSheetSlideShow()
    Dim Cht As Chart
    Application.DisplayFullScreen = True
    For Each Cht In ActiveWorkbook.Charts
        Application.ScreenUpdating = False
        Cht.PrintPreview
    Next Cht
    Application.DisplayFullScreen = False
End Sub
```

When this macro is executed, it displays all chart sheets in the active workbook.

Linking Chart Text to Cells

When you create a chart, you might like to have some of the chart's text elements linked to cells. That way, when you change the text in the cell, the corresponding chart element is updated. You can even link chart text elements to cells that contain a formula. For example, you might link the chart title to a cell that contains a formula that returns the current date.

You can create a link to a cell for the chart title, the vertical axis title, and the horizontal axis title.

1. Select the chart element that will contain the cell link.
2. Click the formula bar.
3. Type an equal sign (=).
4. Click the cell that will be linked to the chart element.

In addition, you can add a linked text box to a chart:

1. Select the chart.
2. Choose Insert ➪ Text ➪ Text Box.
3. Click inside the chart.
4. Click the formula bar.
5. Type an equal sign (=).
6. Click the cell that will be linked to the text box.

Figure 142-1 shows a chart that has links for the following elements: chart title, vertical axis title, horizontal axis title, and text box.

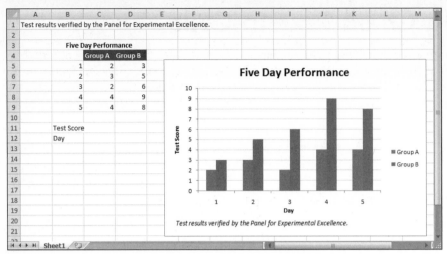

Figure 142-1: A chart with text elements linked to cells.

Creating a Chart Template

If you find that you're continually making the same types of customizations to your charts, you can probably save some time by creating a template. Many users avoid this feature because they think that it's too complicated. Creating a chart template is actually very simple.

To create a chart template, follow these steps:

1. Create a chart to serve as the basis for your template. The data you use for this chart isn't critical, but for best results, it should be typical of the data that you will eventually plot with your custom chart type.

2. Apply any formatting and customizations that you like. This step determines the appearance of the charts created from the template.

3. Activate the chart and choose Chart Tools ⇨ Design ⇨ Type ⇨ Save As Template. Excel displays its Save Chart Template dialog box.

4. Provide a name for the template and click Save.

Chart templates are stored by default in the following folder:

```
C:\Documents And Settings\<user name>Application
Data\Microsoft\Templates\Charts
```

To create a chart based on a template, follow these steps:

1. Select the data to be used in the chart.

2. Choose Insert ⇨ Charts ⇨ Other Charts ⇨ All Chart Types. Excel displays its Insert Chart dialog box.

3. On the left side of the Insert Chart dialog box, select Templates. Excel displays an icon for each custom template that has been created.

4. Click the icon that represents the template you want to use and click OK. Excel creates the chart based on the template you selected.

You can also apply a template to an existing chart. Select the chart and choose Chart Tools ⇨ Design ⇨ Change Chart Type.

Part VII

Saving a Chart As a Graphics File

Oddly, Excel doesn't provide a direct way to convert a chart into a standalone graphics file, such as a GIF or PNG file. In this tip, I present three methods for saving an Excel chart as a graphics file (one method uses a VBA macro).

Method 1: Paste the Chart into a Graphics Program

This method requires other software — namely, a graphics program. Select your chart and choose Home ⇨ Clipboard ⇨ Copy (or press Ctrl+C). Then access a document in your graphics program and choose Edit ⇨ Paste (or its equivalent command). Then you can save the file by using whichever graphics file format you like.

You might need to experiment to get optimal results. For example, you might need to copy the chart as a picture. To do so, select the chart, and then choose this (completely nonintuitive) command: Home ⇨ Clipboard ⇨ Paste ⇨ As Picture ⇨ Copy As Picture.

Method 2: Save As an HTML File

To convert all charts in a workbook to PNG files, save your workbook in HTML format and then locate the PNG files that are created. Follow these steps:

1. Save your workbook.

2. Choose Office ⇨ Save As.

3. In the Save As dialog box, choose Web Page (*.htm, *.html) from the Save As Type drop-down list.

4. Choose the Entire Workbook option.

5. Select a location for the file. (Your desktop is a good choice because it's easy to find.)

6. Provide a name for the file and click Save.

7. Close the workbook.

8. Open an Explorer window and locate the folder where you saved the file. In addition to the HTML file, you'll find a subdirectory with a name that corresponds to the filename with _files appended. Open that folder to see a PNG file that corresponds to each chart in your workbook.

 CAUTION

Save your workbook in a normal Excel file format first. The HTML version of your workbook should be considered a temporary version of your workbook. Excel 2007, unlike previous versions, doesn't support "round-tripping" with the HTML format. In other words, the HTML file doesn't preserve key information — such as formulas.

Method 3: Use a VBA Macro

This method uses a simple VBA macro that saves each chart on the active sheet as a GIF file.

To create the macro, press Alt+F11 to activate the Visual Basic Editor. Select your workbook in the Projects window, and choose Insert ⇨ Module to insert a new VBA module. Then type the following procedure into the module:

```
Sub SaveChartsAsGIF()
    Dim ChtObj As ChartObject
    Dim Fname As String
    For Each ChtObj In ActiveSheet.ChartObjects
        Fname = ThisWorkbook.Path & "\" & ChtObj.Name & ".gif"
        ChtObj.Chart.Export Filename:=Fname, FilterName:="gif"
  Next ChtObj
End Sub
```

After the macro is entered, press Alt+F11 to reactivate Excel. Then activate the worksheet that contains your charts. Press Alt+F8 to display the Macro dialog box. Select the SaveChartsAsGIF macro and click Run.

The procedure saves each chart in the active worksheet as a GIF file. (The chart's name is used as the filename.) The files are stored in the same folder as the workbook.

Making Charts the Same Size

If you have several embedded charts on a worksheet, you might want to make them all exactly the same size. Figure 145-1 shows a worksheet with four charts that would look better if they were all the same size and aligned.

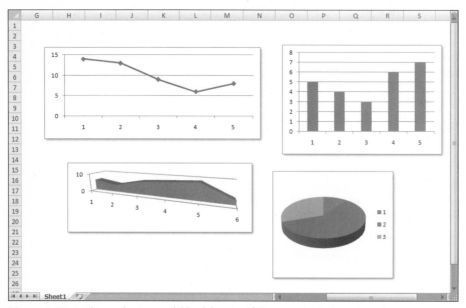

Figure 145-1: These charts would look better if they were all the same size.

To make all the charts the same size, first identify the chart that is already the size you want. In this case, you want to make all the charts the same size as the column chart in the upper right area.

1. Click the chart to select it.

2. Choose Chart Tools ⇨ Format. You see the Height and Width settings in the Size group.

3. Make a note of the Height and Width settings.

4. Ctrl+click the other three charts (so that all four are selected).

5. Choose Chart Tools ⇨ Format, enter the Height and Width settings that you noted in Step 3, and then click OK.

The charts are now exactly the same size.

You can align the charts manually, or you can use the Chart Tools ⇨ Format ⇨ Arrange ⇨ Align commands. Figure 145-2 shows the result.

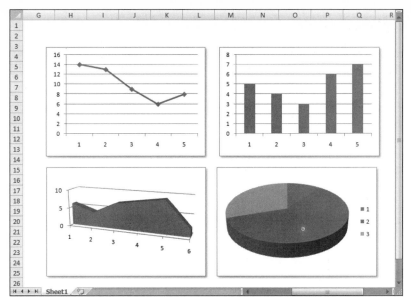

Figure 145-2: Four charts, resized and aligned.

Resetting All Chart Formatting

Excel 2007 provides you with many chart formatting options. You can select individual chart elements and apply all sorts of formatting: shadows, glows, bevels, fills, and outline styles, for example. Sometimes, it's easy to go overboard.

If you go overboard in formatting a chart element, you can undo your previous actions, although it's much easier to reset the chart element to its original state. Just right-click the element and choose Chart Tools ➪ Format ➪ Current Selection ➪ Reset to Match Style. Or, right-click the chart element and choose Reset to Match Style from the shortcut menu.

To reset all formatting changes in the entire chart, select the Chart Area before you choose the Reset to Match Style command.

Figure 146-1 shows a chart with way too much formatting. But, as you can see in Figure 146-2, even the gaudiest chart can be salvaged.

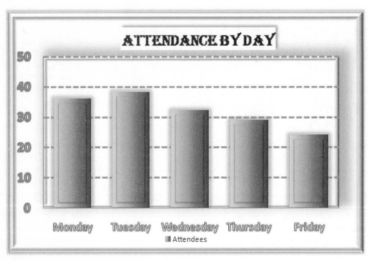

Figure 146-1: Formatting overload.

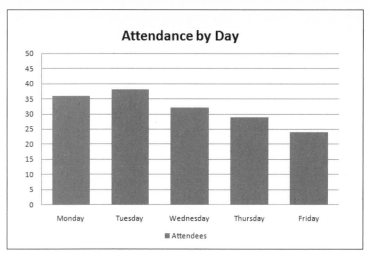

Figure 146-2: That's much better.

Freezing a Chart

Normally, an Excel chart uses data stored in a range. Change the data, and the chart is updated automatically. Usually, that's a good thing. But sometimes you want to "unlink" the chart from its data range to produce a *static* chart — a snapshot of a chart that never changes. For example, if you plot data generated by various what-if scenarios, you might want to save a chart that represents a baseline so that you can compare it with other scenarios. You can freeze a chart in two ways:

- Convert the chart to a picture.
- Convert the range references to arrays.

Converting a Chart into a Picture

To convert a chart to a static picture, follow these steps:

1. Create the chart as usual and format it the way you want.
2. Click the chart to activate it.
3. Choose Home ⇨ Clipboard ⇨ Paste ⇨ As Picture ⇨ Copy As Picture.
4. In the Copy Picture dialog box, accept the default settings and click OK.
5. Click any cell to deselect the chart.
6. Press Ctrl+V to paste the picture at the cell you selected in Step 5.

The result is a picture of the original chart. This chart can be edited as a picture, but not as a chart. In other words, you can no longer modify properties such as chart type and data labels. It's a dead chart — just what you wanted.

Converting Range References into Arrays

The other way to unlink a chart from its data is to convert the SERIES formula range references to arrays. Follow these steps:

1. Activate your chart.
2. Click the chart series. The formula bar displays the SERIES formula for the selected data series.
3. Click the formula bar.
4. Press F9, and then press Enter.

Repeat these steps for each series in the chart.

Figure 147-1 shows a pie chart that has been unlinked from its data range. Notice that the formula bar displays arrays, not range references. The original data is in A1:B6. The converted SERIES formula is

```
=SERIES(,{"Work","Sleep","Drive","Eat","Play Banjo","Other"},{8,7,2,1,3,3},1)
```

NOTE

Excel places a limit on the length of a series formula. Therefore, this method may not work if the series consists of a large number of data points.

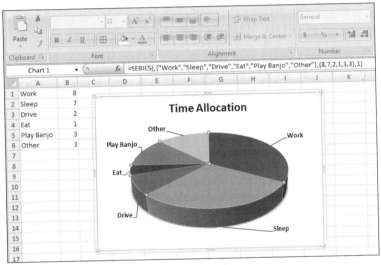

Figure 147-1: This chart isn't linked to a data range.

Selecting Objects on a Worksheet

Excel lets you place quite a few different types of objects on a worksheet: charts, shapes, and SmartArt, for example. To work with an object, you must select it. The easiest way to select a single object is to click it. What happens if you want to select multiple objects? For example, you might want to move several objects, delete them, or apply formatting.

Excel provides several ways to select multiple objects.

Ctrl+Click

Pressing the Ctrl key while you click objects is one way to select multiple objects.

The Selection and Visibility Pane

A new feature in Excel 2007 is the Selection and Visibility pane, shown in Figure 148-1. To display the Selection and Visibility pane, choose Home ⇨ Editing ⇨ Find & Select ⇨ Selection Pane.

The pane contains the name of each object on the active worksheet. Click an object name, and it's selected. Press Ctrl to select multiple objects. You can also use this window to hide objects — just click the little eyeball icon.

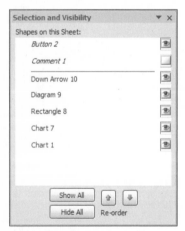

Figure 148-1: You can use the Selection and Visibility pane to easily select objects (if you know their names).

The Go to Special Dialog Box

To select all objects on a worksheet, choose Home ⇨ Editing ⇨ Find & Select ⇨ Go to Special. Then choose the Objects option in the Go to Special dialog box and click OK.

The Select Object Tool

Another way to select multiple objects is to use the Select Object tool (choose Home ⇨ Editing ⇨ Find & Select ⇨ Select Objects). When you choose this command, Excel goes into a special mode and the mouse pointer changes to an arrow. Click and drag to select all objects in a rectangular area.

Part VII

Making a Greeting Card

It's your boss's birthday, and you forgot to buy a birthday card! No problem. Follow these steps to create a do-it-yourself greeting card in a worksheet.

1. Start with an empty worksheet.

2. Select columns A and B, and then choose Home ⇨ Format ⇨ Cells ⇨ Column Width, and specify 47 as the column width.

3. Select rows 1 and 2, and then choose Home ⇨ Format ⇨ Cells ⇨ Row Height, and specify 365 as the row height.

4. Choose View ⇨ Workbook Views ⇨ Page Layout, to enter Page Layout view. You might want to use the Zoom control on right side of the status bar to reduce the size of the worksheet so you can see the four cells in the range A1:B2.

5. Choose Insert ⇨ Illustrations ⇨ Clip Art to display the Clip Art task pane.

6. Search for an appropriate word (for example, birthday), and locate a suitable clip art image.

7. Add the clip art image to the worksheet, and drag it to cell A1.

8. Click the green handle in the clip art image, and rotate it so the image is upside-down.

9. Type some text into cell B2, and format it any way you like. Centering vertically and horizontally is a good choice.

Your worksheet should look something like the one shown in Figure 149-1. You may need to tweak the row heights and column widths so range A1:B2 fills exactly one page.

Print the worksheet, and fold it once vertically and once horizontally. Voila! Instant (and cheap) greeting card.

Remember, it's the *thought* that counts.

Figure 149-1: Using Excel to create a greeting card.

Using Images As Line Chart Markers

When you create a Line chart (or a Scatter chart), you can choose from a few different marker styles. For added pizzazz, you might want to use a shape or a simple clip art image for your markers.

Figure 150-1 shows an example. This line chart uses a shape for its markers.

Figure 150-1: This line chart uses a shape for the line markers.

The procedure is simple:

1. Create a line chart, with markers.
2. Choose Insert ⇨ Illustrations ⇨ Shapes to add a shape to your worksheet.
3. Format the shape any way you like, and size it so that it's suitable for the chart.
4. Select the shape and press Ctrl+C.
5. Activate the chart, select the line series, and press Ctrl+V.

You can even use different shapes for each data point. The trick is to click the series once to select the entire series and then click a single data point marker. When you press Ctrl+V, only the selected marker is changed. Figure 150-2 shows a chart that uses two different shapes.

Figure 150-2: A line chart with two shapes for the line markers.

You can also use clip art for the line markers. For best results, use a relatively simple image. Figure 150-3 shows an example of a chart that uses a clip art image for line markers. Notice that I applied a shadow to the image before I pasted it.

Figure 150-3: A line chart with a clip art image for the line markers.

Changing the Shape of a Cell Comment

Cell comments are useful for a variety of purposes. But sometimes you just get tired of looking at the same old yellow rectangle. If you want your comment to get noticed, try changing the shape.

Figure 151-1 shows a normal cell comment. Figure 151-2 shows the same comment after it gets spiffed up a bit.

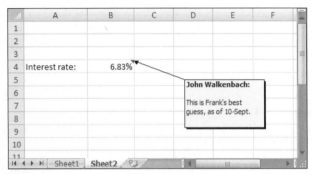

Figure 151-1: A typical cell comment.

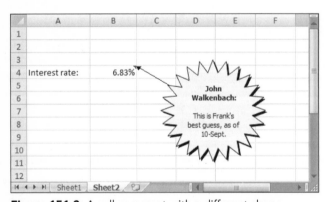

Figure 151-2: A cell comment with a different shape.

To change the shape of a cell comment, add a command to your Quick Access Toolbar (QAT):

1. Right-click the QAT and choose Customize Quick Access Toolbar. The Customization section of the Excel Options dialog box appears.

2. From the Choose Commands From drop-down list, select Drawing Tools ⇨ Format Tab.

3. In the list on the left, select Change Shape and then click the Add button.

4. Click OK to close the Excel Options dialog box.

After you complete these steps, your QAT has a new Change Shape icon.

To change the shape of a comment, make sure that it's visible. (Right-click the cell and choose Show/Hide Comments.) Then click the comment's border to select it as a shape (or, Ctrl+click the comment to select it as a shape). Click the Change Shape button on the QAT and choose a new shape for the comment from the Shape gallery.

Adding an Image to a Cell Comment

Most users don't realize it, but a cell comment can display an image. The image must reside in a file. In other words, you can't use shapes or clip art images that are copied to the Clipboard.

To add an image to a comment, follow these steps:

1. Make sure that the comment is visible. (Right-click the cell and choose Show/Hide Comments.)

2. Click the comment's border to select it as a shape (or, Ctrl+click the comment to select it as a shape).

3. Right-click the comment's border and choose Format Comment from the shortcut menu.

4. In the Format Comment dialog box, click the Colors and Lines tab.

5. Click the Color drop-down list and select Fill Effects.

6. In the Fill Effects dialog box, click the Picture tab and then click the Select Picture Button to specify a graphics file.

7. Click OK to close the Format Comment dialog box.

Figure 152-1 shows a comment that contains a picture.

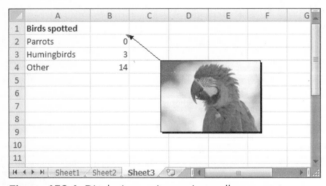

Figure 152-1: Displaying an image in a cell comment.

Part  VIII

Data Analysis and Lists

Much of the data contained in your worksheets is in the form of a list. In this part, you'll find tips that deal with lists and data analysis.

Tips and Where to Find Them

Using the Table Feature in Excel 2007

One significant new feature in Excel 2007 is tables. A *table* is a rectangular range of data that usually has a row of text headings to describe the contents of each column. Excel has always supported tables, of course, but the new implementation makes common tasks much easier to do — and makes the results a lot better looking. More important, the new table features might help eliminate some common errors. The problem, of course, is that many users will simply overlook this new feature.

Understanding What a Table Is

A *table* is simply a rectangular range of structured data. Each row in the table corresponds to a single entity. For example, a row can contain information about a customer, a bank transaction, an employee, or a product. Each column contains a specific piece of information. For example, if each row contains information about an employee, the columns can contain data, such as name, employee number, hire date, salary, or department. Tables typically have a header row at the top that describes the information contained in each column.

So far, I've said nothing new. Every previous version of Excel can work with this type of table. The magic happens when you tell Excel to convert a range of data into an "official" table. You do this by selecting any cell within the range and then choosing Insert ⇨ Tables ⇨ Table.

When you explicitly identify a range as a table, Excel can respond more intelligently to the actions you perform with that range. For example, if you create a chart from a table, the chart expands automatically as you add new rows to the table.

NOTE
Excel 2003 has a similar feature called a list. However, the Excel 2003 list feature is not nearly as versatile as an Excel 2007 table.

Range versus Table

What's the difference between a standard range and a table?

- Activating any cell in the table gives you access to a new Table Tools context tab on the Ribbon (see Figure 153-1).

- You can quickly apply background color and text color formatting by choosing from a gallery. This type of formatting is optional.

- Each column header contains a drop-down list, which you can use to sort the data or filter the table to hide specific rows.

- If you scroll down the sheet so that the header row disappears, the table headers replace the column letters in the worksheet header.

- Tables support calculated columns. A single formula in a column is automatically propagated to all cells in the column.

- Tables support structured references. Rather than use cell references, formulas can use table names and column headers. (See Tip 155.)

- The lower right corner of the lower right cell contains a small control that you can click and drag to extend the table's size, either horizontally (add more columns) or vertically (add more rows).

- Selecting rows and columns within the table is simplified.

Using a table has a few limitations:

- For some reason, when a workbook contains at least one table, Excel doesn't allow you to use the custom views feature (choose View ⇨ Workbook Views ⇨ Custom Views).

- You can't insert automatic subtotals within a table (by choosing Data ⇨ Outline ⇨ Subtotal).

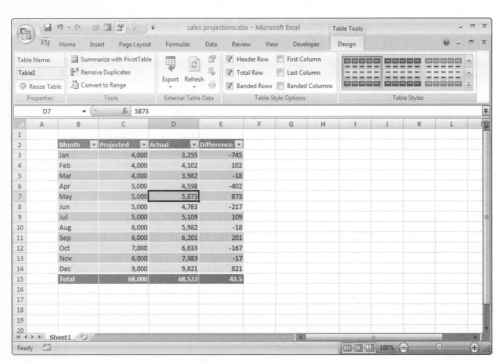

Figure 153-1: When a table is selected, Excel displays a context tab named Table Tools.

Creating a Table

Most of the time, you create a table from an existing range of data. Excel also allows you to create a table from an empty range so that you can fill in the details later. The following instructions assume that you already have a range of data that's suitable for a table:

1. Make sure that the range contains no completely blank rows or columns.

2. Activate any cell within the range.

3. Choose Insert ⇨ Tables ⇨ Table (or press Ctrl+T). Excel responds with its Create Table dialog box, shown in Figure 153-2. Excel tries to guess the range and whether the table has a header row. Most of the time, it guesses correctly. If not, make your corrections before you click OK.

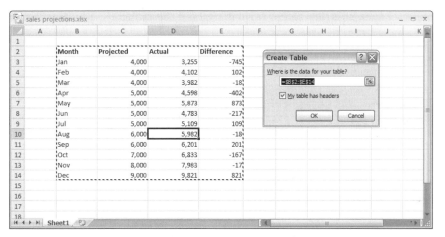

Figure 153-2: Use the Create Table dialog box to verify that Excel guessed the table dimensions correctly.

The range is converted to a table (and it uses the default table style) and the Table Tools context tab appears.

NOTE

Excel might guess the table's dimensions incorrectly if the table isn't separated from other information by at least one empty row or column. If Excel guesses incorrectly, just specify the exact range for the table in the Create Table dialog box. Or, click Cancel and rearrange your worksheet so that the table is separated from your other data by at least one blank row or column.

Part VIII

Working with Tables

Tip 153 presents a brief overview of the new table feature. This tip, on the other hand, provides a few pointers on working with tables.

Navigating in a Table

Selecting cells in a table works just like selecting cells in a normal range. One difference is apparent when you use the Tab key. Pressing Tab moves to the cell to the right, and when you reach the last column, pressing Tab again moves to the first cell in the next row.

Selecting Parts of a Table

When you move your mouse around in a table, you might notice that the pointer changes its shape. The pointer shapes help you select various parts of the table:

- **Select an entire column:** When you move the mouse to the top of a cell in the header row, the mouse pointer changes to a downward-pointing arrow. Click to select the data in the column. Click a second time to select the entire table column (including the header). You can also press Ctrl+spacebar (once or twice) to select a column.

- **Select an entire row:** When you move the mouse pointer to the left of a cell in the first column, the mouse pointer changes to a right-pointing arrow. Click to select the entire table row. You can also press Shift+spacebar to select a table row.

- **Select the entire table:** Move the mouse to the upper left part of the upper left cell. When the mouse pointer turns into a diagonal arrow, click to select the data area of the table. Click a second time to select the entire table (including the header row and the total row). You can also press Ctrl+A (once or twice) to select the entire table.

 NOTE
Right-clicking a cell in a table displays several selection options on the shortcut menu.

Adding New Rows or Columns

To add a new column to the end of a table, just activate a cell in the column to the right of the table and start entering the data. Excel automatically extends the table horizontally. Similarly, if you enter data in the row below a table, Excel extends the table vertically to include the new row.

An exception to automatically extending tables vertically is when the table is displaying a total row. If you enter data below the totals row, the table isn't extended.

To add rows or columns within the table, right-click and choose Insert from the shortcut menu. The Insert shortcut menu command displays additional menu items.

NOTE

When the cell pointer is in the lower right cell of a table, pressing Tab inserts a new row at the bottom.

When you move the mouse pointer to the resize handle in the lower right cell of a table, the mouse pointer turns into a diagonal line with two arrow heads. Click and drag down to add more rows to the table. Click and drag to the right to add more columns.

When you insert a new column, the header row displays a generic description, such as Column 1 or Column 2. Normally, you want to change these names to more descriptive labels.

Deleting Rows or Columns

To delete a row (or column) in a table, select any cell in the row (or column) to be deleted. If you want to delete multiple rows or columns, select them all. Then right-click and choose Delete ⇨ Table Rows (or Delete ⇨ Table Columns).

Moving a Table

To move a table to a new location in the same worksheet, move the mouse pointer to any of its borders. When the mouse pointer turns into a cross with four arrows, click and drag the table to its new location.

To move a table to a different worksheet (in the same workbook or in a different workbook):

1. Press Alt+A *twice* to select the entire table.

2. Press Ctrl+X to cut the selected cells.

3. Activate the new worksheet and select the upper left cell for the table.

4. Press Ctrl+V to paste the table.

Sorting and Filtering a Table

The header row of a table contains a drop-down arrow that, when clicked, displays sorting and filtering options (see Figure 154-1).

	A	B	C	D	E	F	G	H	I	J	K
1	Agent	Date Listed	Area	List Price	Bedrooms	Baths	SqFt	Type	Pool	Sold	
2	Adams	10/9/2007		Sort Smallest to Largest		2.5	1,510	Condo	FALSE	FALSE	
3	Adams	8/19/2007		Sort Largest to Smallest		2.5	1,862	Single Family	TRUE	FALSE	
4	Adams	4/28/2007		Sort by Color		3	1,905	Single Family	FALSE	FALSE	
5	Adams	7/19/2007				2.5	1,911	Single Family	FALSE	FALSE	
6	Adams	2/6/2007		Clear Filter From "Bedrooms"		2	1,552	Single Family	TRUE	TRUE	
7	Adams	8/1/2007		Filter by Color	▸	3	2,800	Single Family	TRUE	FALSE	
8	Adams	1/15/2007		Number Filters	▸	2.5	1,752	Single Family	FALSE	TRUE	
9	Jenkins	1/29/2007				5	4,696	Single Family	TRUE	FALSE	
10	Romero	4/4/2007		☑ (Select All)		5	4,800	Single Family	FALSE	FALSE	
11	Hamilton	2/24/2007		☑ 1		3	2,414	Single Family	TRUE	FALSE	
12	Randolph	4/24/2007		☑ 2		3	2,444	Single Family	TRUE	TRUE	
13	Adams	4/21/2007		☑ 3		3	2,207	Single Family	TRUE	TRUE	
14	Shasta	3/24/2007		☑ 4		2.5	2,620	Single Family	FALSE	FALSE	
15	Kelly	6/9/2007		☑ 5		2	1,971	Single Family	FALSE	FALSE	
16	Shasta	8/17/2007		☑ 6		3	3,109	Single Family	FALSE	FALSE	
17	Adams	6/6/2007				2.5	2,468	Condo	FALSE	FALSE	
18	Adams	2/8/2007				3	2,354	Condo	FALSE	TRUE	
19	Robinson	3/30/2007				3	3,000	Single Family	FALSE	TRUE	
20	Barnes	6/26/2007				2	1,800	Single Family	FALSE	FALSE	
21	Bennet	5/12/2007				3	2,041	Single Family	FALSE	TRUE	
22	Bennet	5/9/2007		OK	Cancel	3	1,940	Single Family	TRUE	FALSE	
23	Shasta	7/15/2007				3	3,927	Single Family	FALSE	FALSE	
24	Lang	5/3/2007	N. County			2.5	2,030	Condo	TRUE	FALSE	
25	Romero	1/28/2007	N. County	$369,900	4	3	1,988	Condo	FALSE	TRUE	
26	Bennet	6/26/2007	S. County	$229,900	3	2.5	1,580	Single Family	TRUE	FALSE	
27	Chung	7/8/2007	Central	$236,900	3	2	1,700	Single Family	FALSE	FALSE	
28	Chung	8/27/2007	Central	$339,900	4	2	2,238	Single Family	FALSE	FALSE	
29	Chung	4/21/2007	Central	$375,000	4	3	2,467	Single Family	TRUE	FALSE	

Sheet1

Figure 154-1: Each column in a table contains sorting and filtering options.

Using Formulas with a Table

This tip describes some new ways to use formulas with a table. The example uses a simple sales summary table with three columns: Month, Projected, and Actual, as shown in Figure 155-1. I entered the data and then converted the range to a table by using the Insert ⇨ Tables ⇨ Table command. Note that I didn't define any names, but the table is named `Table1` by default.

	A	B	C	D	E	F
1						
2		Month	Projected	Actual		
3		Jan	4,000	3,255		
4		Feb	4,000	4,102		
5		Mar	4,000	3,982		
6		Apr	5,000	4,598		
7		May	5,000	5,873		
8		Jun	5,000	4,783		
9		Jul	5,000	5,109		
10		Aug	6,000	5,982		
11		Sep	6,000	6,201		
12		Oct	7,000	6,833		
13		Nov	8,000	7,983		
14		Dec	9,000	9,821		
15						

Sheet1

Figure 155-1: A simple table with three columns.

Working with the Total Row

If you want to calculate the total projected and total actual sales, you don't even need to write a formula. Simply click a button to add a row of summary formulas to the table:

1. Activate any cell in the table.
2. Select the Table Tools ⇨ Design ⇨ Table Style Options ⇨ Total Row check box.
3. Activate a cell in the total row and select a summary formula from the drop-down list (see Figure 155-2). For example, to calculate the sum of the Actual column, select SUM from the drop-down list in cell D15. Excel creates this formula:

   ```
   =SUBTOTAL(109,[Actual])
   ```

For the SUBTOTAL function, `109` is an enumerated argument that represents SUM. The second argument for the SUBTOTAL function is the column name, in square brackets. Using the column name within brackets is a new way to create structured references within a table.

	A	B	C	D	E	F	G
1							
2		Month	Projected	Actual			
3		Jan	4,000	3,255			
4		Feb	4,000	4,102			
5		Mar	4,000	3,982			
6		Apr	5,000	4,598			
7		May	5,000	5,873			
8		Jun	5,000	4,783			
9		Jul	5,000	5,109			
10		Aug	6,000	5,982			
11		Sep	6,000	6,201			
12		Oct	7,000	6,833			
13		Nov	8,000	7,983			
14		Dec	9,000	9,821			
15		Total		68,522			
16				None			
17				Average			
18				Count			
19				Count Numbers			
20				Max			
21				Min			
22				Sum			
23				StdDev			
24				Var			
				More Functions...			

Sheet1

Figure 155-2: A drop-down list enables you to select a summary formula for a table column.

NOTE

You can toggle the total row display on and off by choosing Table Tools ⇨ Design ⇨ Table Style Options ⇨ Total Row. If you turn it off, the summary options you selected are remembered when you turn it back on.

Using Formulas within a Table

In many cases, you want to use formulas within a table. For example, in the table shown in Figure 155-1, you might want a column that shows the difference between the actual and projected amounts for each month. As you'll see, Excel 2007 makes this process very easy:

1. Activate cell E2 and type **Difference** for the column header. Excel automatically expands the table for you.

2. Move to cell E3 and type an equal sign to signify the beginning of a formula.

3. Press the left-arrow key to point to the corresponding value in the Actual column.

4. Type a minus sign and then press the left-arrow key twice to point to the corresponding value in the Projected column.

5. Press Enter to end the formula. The formula bar displays this formula:

```
=Table1[[#This Row],[Actual]]-Table1[[#This Row],[Projected]]
```

6. Excel also displays a smart tag, with one option: Overwrite All Cells in This Column with This Formula. If you click this option, the formula is propagated to the other cells.

Figure 155-3 shows the table with the new column.

	A	B	C	D	E	F
1						
2		Month	Projected	Actual	Difference	
3		Jan	4,000	3,255	-745	
4		Feb	4,000	4,102	102	
5		Mar	4,000	3,982	-18	
6		Apr	5,000	4,598	-402	
7		May	5,000	5,873	873	
8		Jun	5,000	4,783	-217	
9		Jul	5,000	5,109	109	
10		Aug	6,000	5,982	-18	
11		Sep	6,000	6,201	201	
12		Oct	7,000	6,833	-167	
13		Nov	8,000	7,983	-17	
14		Dec	9,000	9,821	821	
15		Total	68,000	68,522		
16						
17						

Sheet1

Figure 155-3: The Difference column contains a formula.

NOTE

Unfortunately, the formula created by pointing is overly complex. You really have no need to include the table name and the reference to This Row. You can edit the formula to make it much more understandable:

```
=[Actual]-[Projected]
```

Although the formula was entered into the first row of the table, that's not necessary. Anytime a formula is entered into an empty table column, you can specify that the formula be copied to all other cells in the column. If you need to edit the formula, you can also copy the edited formula to the other cells in the column.

The preceding set of steps used the column names to create the formula. Alternatively, you can enter the formula by using standard cell references. For example, you can enter the following formula in cell E3:

```
=D3-C3
```

If you type the cell references, Excel still gives you the opportunity to copy the formula to the other cells automatically.

Referencing Data in a Table

Excel 2007 adds some new ways to refer to data that's contained in a table: by using the table name and column headers. You don't need to create names for these items. The table itself has a name (for example, Table1), and you can refer to data within the table by using column headers.

You can, of course, use standard cell references to refer to data in a table, but the new method has a distinct advantage: The names adjust automatically if the table size changes by adding or deleting rows.

Refer to the table shown earlier, in Figure 155-1. This table was given the name Table1 when it was created. To calculate the sum of all data in the table, use this formula:

```
=SUM(Table1)
```

This formula always returns the sum of all the data, even if rows or columns are added or deleted. And, if you change the name of Table1, Excel automatically adjusts formulas that refer to that table. For example, if you rename Table1 as AnnualData (by using the Name Manager), the preceding formula changes to

```
=SUM(AnnualData)
```

Most of the time, you want to refer to a specific column in the table. The following formula returns the sum of the data in the Actual column:

```
=SUM(Table1[Actual])
```

Notice that the column name is enclosed in square brackets. Again, the formula adjusts automatically if you change the text in the column heading.

Even better, Excel provides some helpful assistance when you create a formula that refers to data within a table. Figure 155-4 shows the Formula AutoComplete feature helping to create a formula by showing a list of the elements in the table.

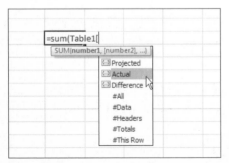

Figure 155-4: The Formula AutoComplete feature is useful when creating a formula that refers to data in a table.

Numbering Rows in a Table

If you have a table (created by choosing Insert ⇨ Tables ⇨ Table), you might want to number the rows in it. Figure 156-1 shows a table with an empty column labeled Number. The goal is to create a formula that displays the row number — and that remains correct even if table rows or added or deleted or if the table is filtered or sorted.

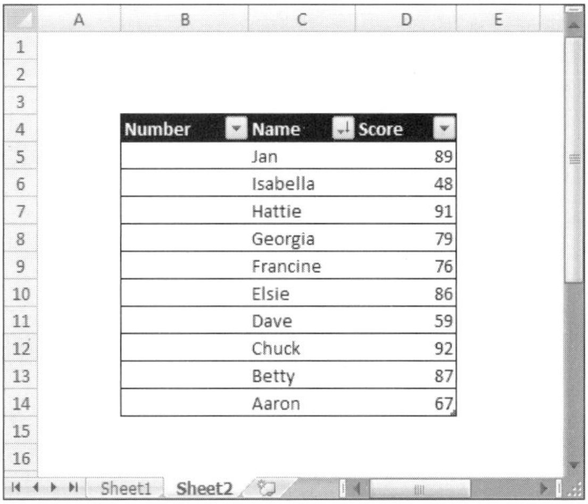

Figure 156-1: This table needs a row number in the first column.

The following formula, entered in column B5, does the job:

```
=SUBTOTAL(3,C$4:C4)
```

This formula uses the SUBTOTAL function with an argument of 3 (COUNTA). The formula returns the count of all cells in column D, starting with the header row and ending with the row that's one cell above the cell with the formula. Notice that the formula is in column C but references column D, to avoid a circular reference.

This formula continues to show consecutive row numbers if the table is sorted or filtered or if new rows are added or deleted.

Figure 156-2 shows the table after copying the formula to other cells in the column.

Part VIII

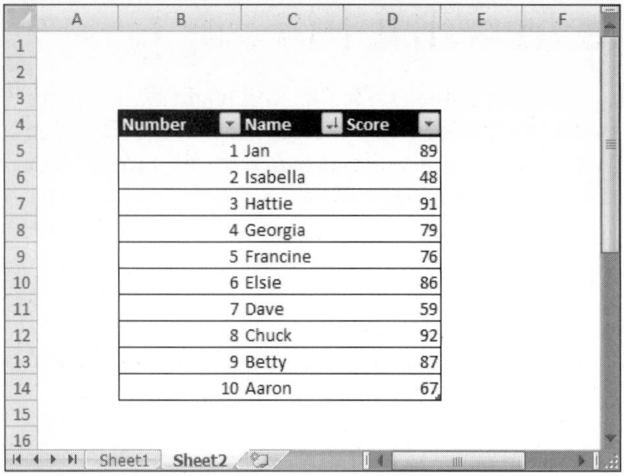

Figure 156-2: The table now has row numbers.

Figure 156-3 shows the table after filtering to show only rows in which the score is greater than 80. Notice that the Number column continues to show consecutive numbers.

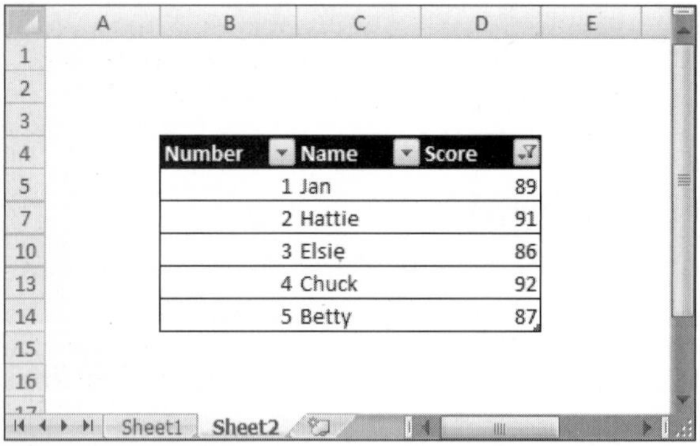

Figure 156-3: When rows are filtered, the first column still shows consecutive numbers.

Using Custom Views with Filtering

The Excel Filter feature is handy for hiding specific items in a list. For example, if you have a mailing list, you can choose to display only the rows in which the State column contains Montana. You can filter a list by using as many columns as you need, and the Custom option provides even more flexibility.

 CAUTION

For reasons known only to Microsoft, the View ⇨ Workbook Views ⇨ Custom Views command isn't available if your workbook contains a table (created by choosing Insert ⇨ Tables ⇨ Table). Therefore, this tip applies only to filtering done using a normal range of data.

To enable filtering of a range, select a cell in the range and choose Data ⇨ Sort & Filter ⇨ Filter. Excel displays drop-down arrows in the header row of the range. Use these drop-down arrows to filter the data.

Excel doesn't allow you to give a name to a particular set of filters. Therefore, if you tend to use several different filtering criteria for a particular list, you can waste a lot of time setting the filters manually.

The solution: The rarely used View ⇨ Workbook Views ⇨ Custom Views command. Here's how to do it:

1. Apply filtering to your range, and set the filters to your liking.

2. Select View ⇨ Workbook Views ⇨ Custom Views to display the Custom View dialog box.

3. Click the Add button to display the Add View dialog box, shown in Figure 157-1.

4. Provide a name for the view, and make sure that the Hidden Rows, Columns and Filter Settings check box is selected.

5. Click OK to close the Add View dialog box.

Repeat these steps for as many different Filter settings as you like. You might also want to create an unfiltered view, to display the list with no filtering applied.

Then, to apply a set of filter settings, choose View ⇨ Workbook Views ⇨ Custom Views and select the named view from the list.

Figure 157-1: Adding a custom view after applying a filter to a range.

Putting Advanced Filter Results on a Different Sheet

If you use Excel's Advanced Filter feature, you might have discovered that Excel is rather picky about where you choose to put the results.

Figure 158-1 shows an Advanced Filter operation in progress. Notice that the list range and the criteria range are on the active sheet (Sheet1), but the user has specified Sheet2 as the Copy To range. Clicking the OK button results in an error message: *You can only copy filtered data to the active sheet.*

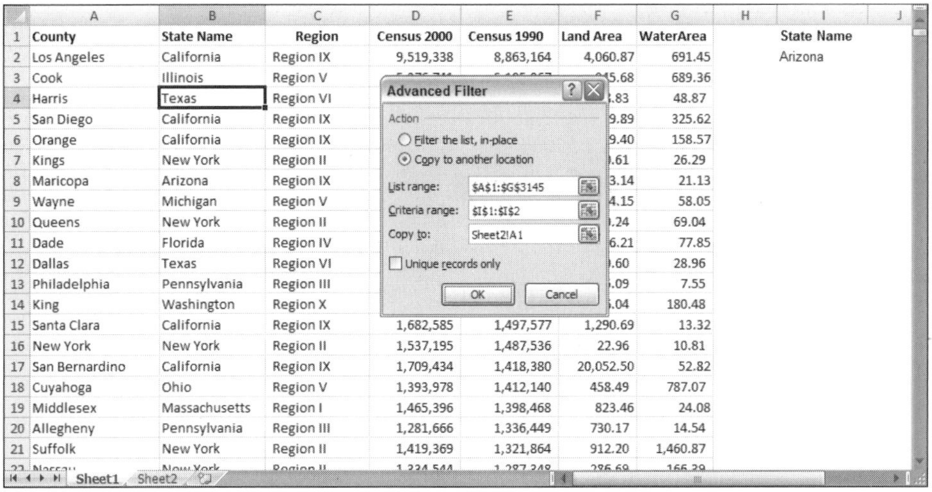

	A	B	C	D	E	F	G	H	I	J
1	County	State Name	Region	Census 2000	Census 1990	Land Area	WaterArea		State Name	
2	Los Angeles	California	Region IX	9,519,338	8,863,164	4,060.87	691.45		Arizona	
3	Cook	Illinois	Region V			5.68	689.36			
4	Harris	Texas	Region VI			.83	48.87			
5	San Diego	California	Region IX			9.89	325.62			
6	Orange	California	Region IX			9.40	158.57			
7	Kings	New York	Region II			.61	26.29			
8	Maricopa	Arizona	Region IX			3.14	21.13			
9	Wayne	Michigan	Region V			4.15	58.05			
10	Queens	New York	Region II			.24	69.04			
11	Dade	Florida	Region IV			6.21	77.85			
12	Dallas	Texas	Region VI			.60	28.96			
13	Philadelphia	Pennsylvania	Region III			.09	7.55			
14	King	Washington	Region X			.04	180.48			
15	Santa Clara	California	Region IX	1,682,585	1,497,577	1,290.69	13.32			
16	New York	New York	Region II	1,537,195	1,487,536	22.96	10.81			
17	San Bernardino	California	Region IX	1,709,434	1,418,380	20,052.50	52.82			
18	Cuyahoga	Ohio	Region V	1,393,978	1,412,140	458.49	787.07			
19	Middlesex	Massachusetts	Region I	1,465,396	1,398,468	823.46	24.08			
20	Allegheny	Pennsylvania	Region III	1,281,666	1,336,449	730.17	14.54			
21	Suffolk	New York	Region II	1,419,369	1,321,864	912.20	1,460.87			
22	Nassau	New York	Region II	1,334,544	1,287,248	286.69	166.29			

The Advanced Filter dialog box shows:

Action:
- ◯ Filter the list, in-place
- ◉ Copy to another location

List range: $A$1:$G$3145
Criteria range: $I$1:$I$2
Copy to: Sheet2!A1

☐ Unique records only

[OK] [Cancel]

Sheet1 Sheet2

Figure 158-1: Specifying a different sheet as the Copy To range causes an error.

Fortunately, you have a simple way around this meaningless limitation:

1. Start out on the sheet that will contain the results. If the list range and criteria range are on Sheet1 and you want the results on Sheet2, just activate Sheet2 when you choose the Data ➪ Sort & Filter ➪ Advanced Filter command.

2. To specify the List Range and Criteria Range settings, click the sheet tab for Sheet1 and select the ranges.

3. Enter a range on the active sheet (Sheet2) for the Copy To range.

Part VIII

Comparing Two Ranges with Conditional Formatting

A common task is comparing two lists of items. Doing it manually is far too tedious and error-prone, but Excel can make it easy. This tip describes a method that uses conditional formatting.

Figure 159-1 shows an example of two multicolumn lists of words. Applying conditional formatting can make the differences in the lists become immediately apparent. These list examples contain text, but this technique also works with numeric data.

The first list is in A2:B25, and this range is named OldList. The second list is in D2:E25, and the range is named NewList. The ranges were named by using the Formulas ⇨ Defined Names ⇨ Define Name command. Naming the ranges isn't necessary, but it makes them easier to work with.

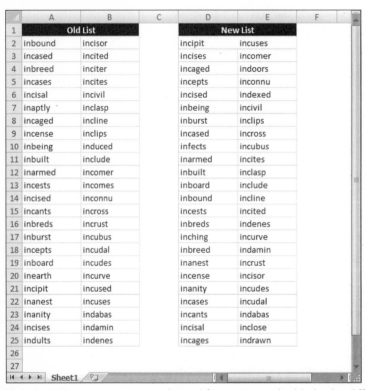

Figure 159-1: You can use conditional formatting to highlight the differences in these two ranges.

Start by formatting the old list:

1. Select the cells in the OldList range.

2. Choose Home ⇨ Conditional Formatting ⇨ New Rule to display the New Formatting Rule dialog box.

3. In the New Formatting Rule dialog box, click the option labeled Use a Formula to Determine Which Cells to Format.

4. Enter this formula in the dialog box (see Figure 159-2):

   ```
   =COUNTIF(NewList,A2)=0
   ```

5. Click the Format button and specify the formatting to apply when the condition is true. (A different fill color is a good choice.)

6. Click OK.

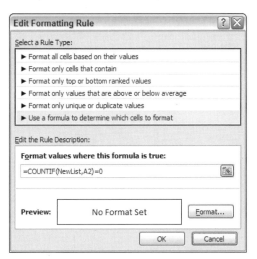

Figure 159-2: Applying conditional formatting.

The cells in the NewList range use a similar conditional formatting formula.

1. Select the cells in the NewList range.

2. Choose Home ⇨ Conditional Formatting ⇨ New Rule to display the New Formatting Rule dialog box.

3. In the New Formatting Rule dialog box, click the option labeled Use a Formula to Determine Which Cells to Format.

4. Enter this formula in the dialog box:

```
=COUNTIF(OldList,D2)=0
```

5. Click the Format button and specify the formatting to apply when the condition is true (a different fill color).

6. Click OK.

Figure 159-3 shows the result. Cells that are in the old list but not in the new list are highlighted. In addition, cells in the new list that aren't in the old list are highlighted in a different color.

Both these conditional formatting formulas use the COUNTIF function. This function counts the number of times a particular value appears in a range. If the formula returns 0, it means that the item doesn't appear in the range. Therefore, the conditional formatting kicks in and the cell's background color is changed.

NOTE

The cell reference in the COUNTIF function should always be the upper left cell of the selected range.

	A	B	C	D	E	F
1	Old List			New List		
2	inbound	incisor		incipit	incuses	
3	incased	incited		incises	incomer	
4	inbreed	inciter		incaged	indoors	
5	incases	incites		incepts	inconnu	
6	incisal	incivil		incised	indexed	
7	inaptly	inclasp		inbeing	incivil	
8	incaged	incline		inburst	inclips	
9	incense	inclips		incased	incross	
10	inbeing	induced		infects	incubus	
11	inbuilt	include		inarmed	incites	
12	inarmed	incomer		inbuilt	inclasp	
13	incests	incomes		inboard	include	
14	incised	inconnu		inbound	incline	
15	incants	incross		incests	incited	
16	inbreds	incrust		inbreds	indenes	
17	inburst	incubus		inching	incurve	
18	incepts	incudal		inbreed	indamin	
19	inboard	incudes		inanest	incrust	
20	inearth	incurve		incense	incisor	
21	incipit	incused		inanity	incudes	
22	inanest	incuses		incases	incudal	
23	inanity	indabas		incants	indabas	
24	incises	indamin		incisal	inclose	
25	indults	indenes		incages	indrawn	
26						
27						

Figure 159-3: Conditional formatting causes differences in the two lists to be highlighted.

Randomizing a List

This tip describes a quick method to randomize a list. It's like shuffling a deck of cards, where each row is a card.

Figure 160-1 shows a simple two-column list, arranged alphabetically by column A. The goal is to arrange the rows in random order.

	A	B	C	D
1	**Artist**	**DVD**		
2	Alanis Morissette	Jagged Little Pill, Live		
3	Alberta Hunter	My Castle's Rocking		
4	Animusic	Special Edition		
5	B.B. King	The Jazz Channel Presents B.B. King		
6	Blue Man Group	Audio		
7	Brian Setzer Orchestra	Live In Japan		
8	Cheryl Crow	Rockin' The Globe Live		
9	Dayna Kurtz	Postcards From Amsterdam		
10	Diana Krall	Live At The Montreal Jazz Festival		
11	Diana Krall	Live In Paris		
12	Eagles	Hell Freezes Over		
13	Eric Clapton	Live On Tour 2001		
14	Gillian Welch	The Revelator Collection		
15	J.J. Cale & Leon Russell	Sessions At The Paradise Studios		
16	James Taylor	Live At The Beacon Theatre		
17	John Prine	Live From Sessions At West 54th		
18	Joni Mitchell	Painting With Words And Music		
19	Joni Mitchell	Woman Of Heart And Mind		
20	Joni Mitchell	Refuge Of The Roads		
21	Joni Mitchell	Shadows And Light		
22	Keb' Mo'	Sessions At West 54th		
23	Keola Beamer	Ki Ho Alu		
24	King Crimson	Deja Vrooom		
25	Norah Jones	Live In 2004		
26	Norah Jones	Live In New Orleans		
27	Peter Frampton	Live In Detroit		
28	Randy Travis	Live: It Was Just A Matter Of Time		
29	Richard Thompson Band	Live In Providence		
30	Robert Earl Keen	Live From Austin TX		

Figure 160-1: This alphabetized list will be randomly arranged.

1. In cell C1, enter the column heading **Random**.

2. In cell C2, enter this formula:

   ```
   =RAND()
   ```

3. Copy C2 down the column to accommodate the number of rows in the list.

4. Activate any cell in column C and choose Home ⇨ Editing ⇨ Sort & Filter ⇨ Sort Smallest to Largest (or, right-click and choose the Sort command on the shortcut menu).

Now, every time you sort column C, the list is randomly rearranged. Figure 160-2 shows the randomized list.

Part VIII

	A	B	C	D
1	**Artist**	**DVD**	**Random**	
2	John Prine	Live From Sessions At West 54th	0.382404965	
3	Stevie Ray Vaughan	Live At The El Cmocambo	0.663194211	
4	Brian Setzer Orchestra	Live In Japan	0.009936048	
5	Sarah McLachlan	Mirrorball	0.406477471	
6	Townes Van Zandt	Houston 1988	0.297028135	
7	Alberta Hunter	My Castle's Rocking	0.916090891	
8	Joni Mitchell	Refuge Of The Roads	0.876414015	
9	Norah Jones	Live In 2004	0.87307617	
10	Keola Beamer	Ki Ho Alu	0.483741262	
11	Blue Man Group	Audio	0.815504986	
12	Eagles	Hell Freezes Over	0.265134234	
13	James Taylor	Live At The Beacon Theatre	0.907341954	
14	Joni Mitchell	Woman Of Heart And Mind	0.04153769	
15	Various	The Velvet Lounge	0.828428996	
16	Tom Petty	Playback	0.057197518	
17	Cheryl Crow	Rockin' The Globe Live	0.868644178	
18	Gillian Welch	The Revelator Collection	0.910348588	
19	Peter Frampton	Live In Detroit	0.852181977	
20	Keb' Mo'	Sessions At West 54th	0.953892265	
21	Randy Travis	Live: It Was Just A Matter Of Time	0.381051255	
22	Joni Mitchell	Shadows And Light	0.464031734	
23	Sade	Sade Live	0.041241646	
24	Various	Naxos Musical Journey: Bach	0.139186739	
25	Robert Earl Keen	Live From Austin TX	0.652025307	
26	Steely Dan	Two Against Nature	0.687751743	
27	Roy Orbison	Black & White Night	0.557246444	
28	Steve Goodman	Live From Austin City Limits And More	0.36276846	
29	Joni Mitchell	Painting With Words And Music	0.722790719	
30	Roger Waters	In The Flesh - Live	0.921234209	
31	Eric Clapton	Live On Tour 2001	0.042011847	

Sheet1

Figure 160-2: The list after being randomized.

Filling the Gaps in a Report

When you import data, you can end up with a worksheet that looks something like the one shown in Figure 161-1. This type of report formatting is common. As you can see, an entry in column A applies to several rows of data. If you sort this type of list, the missing data messes things up, and you can no longer tell who sold what.

	A	B	C	D	E
1					
2	Sales Rep	Month	Units Sold	Amount	
3	Jane K. Smith	Jan	152	35,027	
4		Feb	221	55,552	
5		Mar	233	57,072	
6	George Smothers	Jan	159	40,914	
7		Feb	108	22,243	
8		Mar	159	40,719	
9	Beth Ann Travers	Jan	221	55,388	
10		Feb	74	23,107	
11		Mar	142	33,606	
12	Dan Richardson	Jan	156	35,053	
13		Feb	112	32,365	
14		Mar	97	24,357	
15					

Sheet1 Sheet2

Figure 161-1: This report contains gaps in the Sales Rep column.

If your list is small, you can enter the missing cell values manually or by using a series of Home ⇨ Editing ⇨ Fill ⇨ Down commands. If you have a large list that's in this format, you need a better way of filling in those cell values. Here's how:

1. Select the range that has the gaps (A3:A14, in this example).

2. Choose Home ⇨ Editing ⇨ Find & Select ⇨ Go to Special to display the Go To Special dialog box.

3. In the Go To Special dialog box, select the Blanks option and click OK. This action selects the blank cells in the original selection.

4. On the formula bar, type an equal sign (=) followed by the address of the first cell with an entry in the column (**=A3,** in this example), and press Ctrl+Enter.

5. Reselect the original range and press Ctrl+C to copy the selection.

6. Choose Home ⇨ Clipboard ⇨ Paste ⇨ Paste Values to convert the formulas to values.

After you complete these steps, the gaps are filled in with the correct information, and your worksheet looks similar to the one shown in Figure 161-2. Now it's a more traditional list, and you can do whatever you like with it — including sorting.

Part VIII

	A	B	C	D	E
1					
2	**Sales Rep**	**Month**	**Units Sold**	**Amount**	
3	Jane K. Smith	Jan	152	35,027	
4	Jane K. Smith	Feb	221	55,552	
5	Jane K. Smith	Mar	233	57,072	
6	George Smothers	Jan	159	40,914	
7	George Smothers	Feb	108	22,243	
8	George Smothers	Mar	159	40,719	
9	Beth Ann Travers	Jan	221	55,388	
10	Beth Ann Travers	Feb	74	23,107	
11	Beth Ann Travers	Mar	142	33,606	
12	Dan Richardson	Jan	156	35,053	
13	Dan Richardson	Feb	112	32,365	
14	Dan Richardson	Mar	97	24,357	
15					
16					

Sheet1 Sheet2

Figure 161-2: The gaps are gone, and this list can now be sorted.

Creating a List from a Summary Table

You might be familiar with the Excel feature, which creates a summary table from a list. What happens if you want to perform the opposite operation? This tip describes how to create a list from a simple two-variable summary table.

The worksheet shown in Figure 162-1 shows the type of transformation I'm talking about. Range A1:E13 contains the original summary table: 48 data points. Columns G:I show part of a 48-row database table derived from the summary table. In other words, every value in the original summary table is converted to a row, which also contains the value's corresponding product name and month. This type of list is useful because it can be sorted and manipulated in other ways.

	A	B	C	D	E	F	G	H	I	J
1		North	South	East	West		Month	Region	Sales	
2	Jan	132	233	314	441		Jan	North	132	
3	Feb	143	251	314	447		Jan	South	233	
4	Mar	172	252	345	450		Jan	East	314	
5	Apr	184	290	365	452		Jan	West	441	
6	May	212	299	401	453		Feb	North	143	
7	Jun	239	317	413	457		Feb	South	251	
8	Jul	249	350	427	460		Feb	East	314	
9	Aug	263	354	448	468		Feb	West	447	
10	Sep	291	373	367	472		Mar	North	172	
11	Oct	294	401	392	479		Mar	South	252	
12	Nov	302	437	495	484		Mar	East	345	
13	Dec	305	466	504	490		Mar	West	450	
14							Apr	North	184	
15							Apr	South	290	
16							Apr	East	365	
17							Apr	West	452	
18							May	North	212	
19							May	South	299	
20							May	East	401	
21							May	West	453	
22							Jun	North	239	
23							Jun	South	317	
24							Jun	East	413	
25							Jun	West	457	
26							Jul	North	249	

Sheet1

Figure 162-1: Converting a summary table to a list.

The trick to creating this "reverse PivotTable" is to use a PivotTable. But before you can make use of this technique, you must add the PivotTable Wizard command to your Quick Access Toolbar (QAT). Excel 2007 still supports the PivotTable Wizard, but it's not available on the Ribbon. To gain access to the PivotTable Wizard, follow these steps:

1. Right-click the QAT, and choose Customize Quick Access Toolbar from the shortcut menu.

2. On the Customize tab of the Excel Options dialog box, choose Commands Not in the Ribbon from the drop-down list on the left.

3. Scroll down the list and select PivotTable and PivotChart Wizard from the list.

4. Click Add.

5. Click OK to close the Excel Options dialog box.

After you perform these steps, your QAT displays a new icon.

Now it's time to convert the summary table to a list. Keep in mind that, although the following steps are specific to the sample data shown here, you can easily modify the steps to work with your data. First, create the PivotTable:

1. Activate any cell in your summary table.

2. Click the PivotTable and PivotChart Wizard icon, which you added to your QAT.

3. In the PivotTable and PivotChart Wizard dialog box, select the Multiple Consolidation Ranges option and click Next.

4. In Step 2 of the PivotTable and PivotChart Wizard dialog box, choose the I Will Create the Page Fields option and click Next.

5. In Step 2b, specify a summary table range in the Range field (A1:E13 for the sample data) and click Add. Click Next to move on to Step 3 in the dialog box.

6. In Step 3, select a location for the PivotTable and click the Finish button. Excel creates a pivot table from the data and displays the PivotTable Field list.

7. In the PivotTable Field List, deselect the check boxes from the fields named Row and Column. This leaves the pivot table with only a data field: Sum of Value.

At this point, a small pivot table shows only the sum of all values (see Figure 162-2).

	A	B	C	D	E	F	G	H
1		North	South	East	West		Sum of Value	
2	Jan	132	233	314	441		17147	
3	Feb	143	251	314	447			
4	Mar	172	252	345	450			
5	Apr	184	290	365	452			
6	May	212	299	401	453			
7	Jun	239	317	413	457			
8	Jul	249	350	427	460			
9	Aug	263	354	448	468			
10	Sep	291	373	367	472			
11	Oct	294	401	392	479			
12	Nov	302	437	495	484			
13	Dec	305	466	504	490			
14								

Sheet1

Figure 162-2: This small pivot table can be expanded.

To finish up, double-click the cell that contains the total (17147, in this example). Excel creates a new sheet that displays the original data in the form of a table. Figure 162-3 shows part of this 48-row table.

The column headings display generic descriptions (Row, Column, and Value), so you probably want to change these headings to make them more descriptive.

	A	B	C	D	E	F
1	Row	Column	Value			
2	Jan	North	132			
3	Jan	South	233			
4	Jan	East	314			
5	Jan	West	441			
6	Feb	North	143			
7	Feb	South	251			
8	Feb	East	314			
9	Feb	West	447			
10	Mar	North	172			
11	Mar	South	252			
12	Mar	East	345			
13	Mar	West	450			
14	Apr	North	184			
15	Apr	South	290			
16	Apr	East	365			
17	Apr	West	452			
18	May	North	212			
19	May	South	299			
20	May	East	401			
21	May	West	453			
22	Jun	North	239			
23	Jun	South	317			
24	Jun	East	413			
25	Jun	West	457			

Sheet2 / Sheet1

Figure 162-3: The summary table has been successfully converted to a table.

Finding Duplicates by Using Conditional Formatting

You might find it helpful to identify duplicate values within a range of cells. For example, take a look at Figure 163-1. Are any of the values duplicated?

One approach to identifying duplicate values is to use conditional formatting. Then you can quickly spot duplicated cell values.

	A	B	C	D	E	F	G	H
1	1195	1993	1197	2892	2794	1330	2763	
2	1091	1313	1015	740	609	763	486	
3	2797	602	154	1175	2008	1544	2226	
4	2008	837	1908	468	1611	1561	125	
5	573	338	2123	54	2132	665	1123	
6	2136	793	2226	1681	1837	2443	2898	
7	119	2050	2894	2578	976	1865	1782	
8	277	416	1759	1356	2504	1196	1868	
9	916	1618	2008	346	734	2148	590	
10	2752	2832	2996	2868	2754	2855	574	
11	2846	1660	1878	2351	1349	1564	735	
12	2097	2125	2602	39	12	2771	2237	
13	90	641	1113	674	1364	2407	328	
14	1458	322	2463	1999	496	1348	2818	
15	2031	2041	307	2049	2008	1770	2416	
16	493	2569	1642	2924	2550	1040	370	
17	2866	2927	86	1709	1317	1851	1695	
18	1543	1815	1353	2366	1018	2430	1750	
19	419	2165	1522	1199	1481	2063	101	
20	2281	2603	1703	2971	2431	2722	457	
21	2775	1700	1297	1946	2875	2211	738	
22	2469	2446	2610	142	2418	854	336	
23								
24								

Sheet1 Sheet2

Figure 163-1: You can use conditional formatting to quickly identify duplicate values in a range.

Here's how to set up the conditional formatting

1. Select the cells in the range (in this example, A1:G22).

2. Choose Home ⇨ Conditional Formatting ⇨ New Rule to display the Conditional Formatting dialog box.

3. In the Conditional Formatting dialog box, select the option labeled Use a Formula to Determine Which Cells to Format.

4. For this example, enter this formula (change the range references to correspond to your own data):

```
=COUNTIF($A$1:$G$22,A1)>1
```

5. Click the Format button and specify the formatting to apply when the condition is true. (Changing the fill color is a good choice.)

6. Click OK.

Figure 163-2 shows the result. The six highlighted cells are the duplicated values in the range.

	A	B	C	D	E	F	G	H
1	1195	1993	1197	2892	2794	1330	2763	
2	1091	1313	1015	740	609	763	486	
3	2797	602	154	1175	2008	1544	2226	
4	2008	837	1908	468	1611	1561	125	
5	573	338	2123	54	2132	665	1123	
6	2136	793	2226	1681	1837	2443	2898	
7	119	2050	2894	2578	976	1865	1782	
8	277	416	1759	1356	2504	1196	1868	
9	916	1618	2008	346	734	2148	590	
10	2752	2832	2996	2868	2754	2855	574	
11	2846	1660	1878	2351	1349	1564	735	
12	2097	2125	2602	39	12	2771	2237	
13	90	641	1113	674	1364	2407	328	
14	1458	322	2463	1999	496	1348	2818	
15	2031	2041	307	2049	2008	1770	2416	
16	493	2569	1642	2924	2550	1040	370	
17	2866	2927	86	1709	1317	1851	1695	
18	1543	1815	1353	2366	1018	2430	1750	
19	419	2165	1522	1199	1481	2063	101	
20	2281	2603	1703	2971	2431	2722	457	
21	2775	1700	1297	1946	2875	2211	738	
22	2469	2446	2610	142	2418	854	336	
23								

Sheet1 Sheet2

Figure 163-2: Conditional formatting causes the duplicated cells to be highlighted.

You can extend this technique to identify entire rows within a list that are identical. The trick is to add a new column and use a formula that concatenates the data in each row. For example, if your list is in A2:G500, enter this formula in cell H2:

```
=A2&B2&C2&D2&E2&F2&G2
```

Copy the formula down the column and then apply the conditional formatting to the formulas in column H. In this case, the conditional formatting formula is

```
=COUNTIF($H$2:$H$500,H2)>1
```

Highlighted cells in column H indicate duplicated rows.

CROSS-REFERENCE
A new feature in Excel 2007 makes it easy to delete duplicate rows. See Tip 31.

Part VIII

Preventing Row or Column Insertions within a Range

If you have a list of data, you might require that the list maintain its integrity. Inserting a blank row or column within the list can cause serious problems because Excel no longer recognizes the complete list. For example, if you attempt to sort a list after inserting a new column within the list, not all the columns are sorted, and your data is transformed into a jumbled mess.

NOTE

If your data is in a table (created by choosing Insert ⇨ Tables ⇨ Table), inserting a blank row doesn't cause a problem. Excel continues to recognize the table, and it can still be sorted.

This tip describes how to prevent users from inserting new rows or columns within a list. When you protect a worksheet, you can specify any of several options that determine what the user can do. Figure 164-1 shows the Protect Sheet dialog box, which is displayed when you choose Review ⇨ Changes ⇨ Protect Sheet.

Figure 164-1: The Protect Sheet dialog box lets you specify what can be done when the worksheet is protected.

To prevent users from inserting rows or columns, you can protect the worksheet and make sure that the Insert Columns and Insert Rows options aren't selected. If you check all the other options, the worksheet works normally except for the inability to insert rows or columns.

For additional insurance, specify a password that will be required in order to unprotect the worksheet.

 NOTE
Keep in mind that worksheet password protection is not at all secure. Unprotecting a password-protected worksheet is a simple task.

Part VIII

Creating a Quick Frequency Tabulation

This tip describes a quick method for creating a frequency tabulation for a single column of data. Figure 165-1 shows a small part of a range that contains more than 20,000 rows of city and state data. The goal is to tally the number of times each state appears in the list.

Although you can tally the states in a number of ways, a PivotTable is the easiest choice for this task.

	A	B	C	D	E
1	City	State			
2	Stevenson Ranch	CA			
3	Woodbine	GA			
4	Federal Way	WA			
5	Memphis	TN			
6	Herculaneum	MO			
7	Riverside	CA			
8	Richmond	VA			
9	Williston	FL			
10	sacramento	CA			
11	Middletown	OH			
12	cincinnati	OH			
13	Oakland	NJ			
14	Corona	CA			
15	Freemont	CA			
16	Los Angeles	CA			
17	Grapevine	TX			
18	White Lake	MI			
19	New York	NY			
20	TEANECK	NJ			
21	Canby	OR			
22	Potomac	MD			
23	Los Angeles	CA			

Figure 165-1: You can use a PivotTable to generate a frequency tabulation for these state abbreviations.

Before you get started on this task, make sure that your data column has a heading. In this example, it's in cell B1.

Activate any cell in the column A or B and then follow these steps:

1. Choose Insert ➪ Tables ➪ PivotTable to display the Create PivotTable dialog box.

2. If Excel doesn't correctly identify the range, change the Table/Range setting.

3. Specify a location for the PivotTable.

4. Click OK. Excel creates an empty pivot table, and displays the PivotTable Field List.

5. In the Pivot Table Field List, drag the State field into the Row Labels section.

6. Drag the State field into the Values section.

Excel creates the pivot table, which shows the frequency of each state (see Figure 165-2).

	A	B	C	D	E	F	G	H
1	City	State			Row Labels ▼	Count of State		
2	Anchorage	AK			AK	113		
3	Juneau	AK			AL	204		
4	Anchorage	AK			AR	104		
5	Nome	AK			AZ	363		
6	Fairbanks	AK			CA	3150		
7	Anchorage	AK			CO	408		
8	Anchorage	AK			CT	388		
9	Sitka	AK			DC	84		
10	Juneau	AK			DE	96		
11	Anchorage	AK			FL	1001		
12	Anchorage	AK			GA	577		
13	Homer	AK			HI	71		
14	Palmer	AK			IA	115		
15	Anchorage	AK			ID	106		
16	Anchorage	AK			IL	954		
17	Anchorage	AK			IN	348		
18	Dutch Harbor	AK			KS	160		
19	Anchorage	AK			KY	138		
20	Anchorage	AK			LA	193		
21	Juneau	AK			MA	603		
22	Anchorage	AK			MD	517		
23	Anchorage	AK			ME	74		
24	Anchorage	AK			MI	652		
25	Little Rock	AK			MN	348		
26	Homer	AK			MO	300		
27	Anchorage	AK			MS	77		
28	Anchorage	AK			MT	56		
29	Juneau	AK			NC	523		
30	Anchorage	AK			ND	30		

Sheet1　Sheet2　Sheet3

Figure 165-2: A quick pivot table shows the frequency of each state abbreviation.

This pivot table can be sorted, and (as shown in Figure 165-3) you can even create a pivot chart to display the counts graphically. Just select any cell in the pivot table, and choose PivotTable Tools ➪ Options ➪ PivotChart.

Part VIII

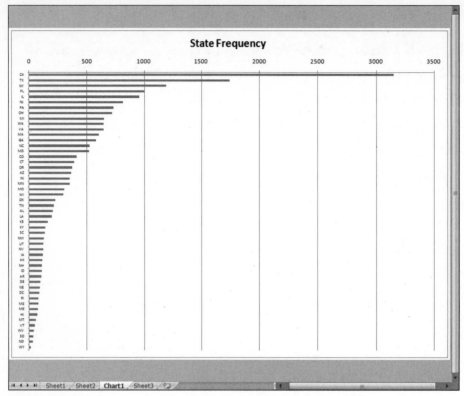

Figure 165-3: A few mouse clicks creates a chart from the pivot table.

Controlling References to Cells within a Pivot Table

If you work with pivot tables, you've probably noticed that if you write a formula that refers to a cell within the pivot table, the cell reference is converted automatically to a GETPIVOTDATA function with a number of arguments. Figure 166-1 shows an example. The formula in cell J7 is a simple reference to cell G6 in the pivot table. But rather than display the simple formula, Excel converts it to

```
=GETPIVOTDATA("Location",$E$1,"Location","Washington","Sex","Male",
"Location2","Western Region")
```

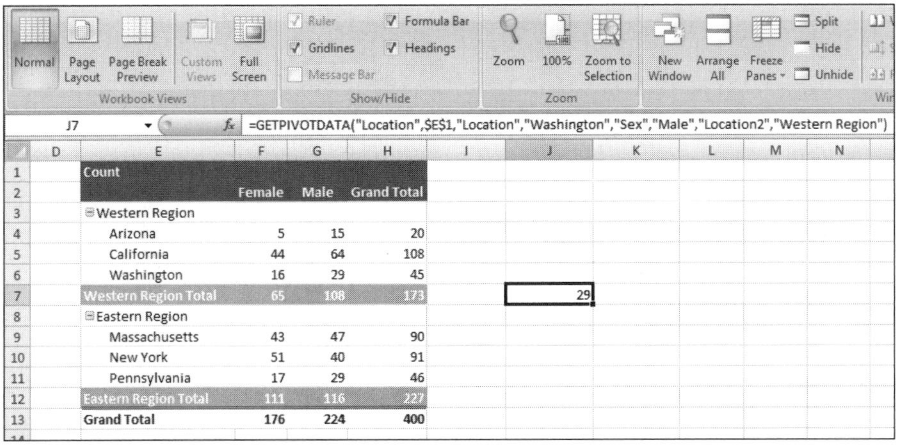

Figure 166-1: A formula that references a cell in a pivot table might result in a complex formula.

This type of referencing ensures that your formulas still return the correct result if the structure of the pivot table is changed. If you prefer to avoid this automatic conversion, don't use the pointing technique when creating formulas that reference cells in a pivot table.

You can also turn off the Generate GetPivotData option, by choosing PivotTable Tools ⇨ Options ⇨ PivotTable ⇨ Options ⇨ Generate GetPivotData.

The Generate GetPivotData button is a toggle. Click it once, and Excel stops generating GETPIVOTTABLE formulas. Click it again, and Excel starts generating those formulas again. This command doesn't affect existing formulas.

Grouping Items by Date in a Pivot Table

One of the more useful features of a pivot table is the ability to combine items into groups. Grouping items is simple: Select them, and choose PivotTable Tools ⇨ Options ⇨ Group ⇨ Group Selection.

You can go a step further, though. When a field contains dates, Excel can create groups automatically. Many users overlook this helpful feature. Figure 167-1 shows a portion of a table that has two columns of data: Date and Sales. This table has 730 rows and covers dates between January 1, 2006 and December 31, 2007. The goal is to summarize the sales information by month.

	A	B	C	D	E
1	Date	Sales			
2	1/1/2006	1,277			
3	1/2/2006	1,255			
4	1/3/2006	1,454			
5	1/4/2006	1,223			
6	1/5/2006	1,314			
7	1/6/2006	1,496			
8	1/7/2006	1,472			
9	1/8/2006	1,124			
10	1/9/2006	1,210			
11	1/10/2006	1,516			
12	1/11/2006	1,831			
13	1/12/2006	1,902			
14	1/13/2006	2,193			
15	1/14/2006	2,111			
16	1/15/2006	2,034			
17	1/16/2006	1,763			
18	1/17/2006	1,783			
19	1/18/2006	1,938			
20	1/19/2006	2,167			
21	1/20/2006	2,171			
22	1/21/2006	1,990			
23	1/22/2006	1,930			

data

Figure 167-1: You can use a PivotTable to summarize the sales data by month.

Figure 167-2 shows part of a pivot table (in columns D:E) created from the data. Not surprisingly, it looks exactly like the input data because the dates haven't been grouped.

To group the items by month, right-click any cell in the Date column and select Group from the shortcut menu. You see the Grouping dialog box, shown in Figure 167-3. In the list box, select Months and Years, and verify that the starting and ending dates are correct. Click OK.

The Date items in the PivotTable are grouped by years and by months (as shown in Figure 167-4).

	A	B	C	D	E	F
1	Date	Sales		Row Labels	Sum of Sales	
2	1/1/2006	1,276		1/1/2006	1,276	
3	1/2/2006	1,254		1/2/2006	1,254	
4	1/3/2006	1,454		1/3/2006	1,454	
5	1/4/2006	1,223		1/4/2006	1,223	
6	1/5/2006	1,314		1/5/2006	1,314	
7	1/6/2006	1,496		1/6/2006	1,496	
8	1/7/2006	1,472		1/7/2006	1,472	
9	1/8/2006	1,123		1/8/2006	1,123	
10	1/9/2006	1,209		1/9/2006	1,209	
11	1/10/2006	1,516		1/10/2006	1,516	
12	1/11/2006	1,831		1/11/2006	1,831	
13	1/12/2006	1,902		1/12/2006	1,902	
14	1/13/2006	2,193		1/13/2006	2,193	
15	1/14/2006	2,111		1/14/2006	2,111	
16	1/15/2006	2,033		1/15/2006	2,033	
17	1/16/2006	1,763		1/16/2006	1,763	
18	1/17/2006	1,783		1/17/2006	1,783	
19	1/18/2006	1,938		1/18/2006	1,938	
20	1/19/2006	2,167		1/19/2006	2,167	
21	1/20/2006	2,171		1/20/2006	2,171	
22	1/21/2006	1,990		1/21/2006	1,990	
23	1/22/2006	1,930		1/22/2006	1,930	
24	1/23/2006	1,826		1/23/2006	1,826	
25	1/24/2006	2,188		1/24/2006	2,188	
26	1/25/2006	2,214		1/25/2006	2,214	
27	1/26/2006	2,261		1/26/2006	2,261	

data

Figure 167-2: The pivot table, before grouping by months and years.

Figure 167-3: Use the Grouping dialog box to group items in a pivot table.

NOTE

If you select only Months in the Grouping list box, months in different years are combined. For example, the June item would display sales for both 2006 and 2007.

Part VIII

	A	B	C	D	E	F	G
1	Date	Sales		Row Labels	Sum of Sales		
2	1/1/2006	1,276		⊟ 2006			
3	1/2/2006	1,254		Jan	55,871		
4	1/3/2006	1,454		Feb	45,939		
5	1/4/2006	1,223		Mar	71,628		
6	1/5/2006	1,314		Apr	33,622		
7	1/6/2006	1,496		May	52,666		
8	1/7/2006	1,472		Jun	39,214		
9	1/8/2006	1,123		Jul	98,412		
10	1/9/2006	1,209		Aug	172,987		
11	1/10/2006	1,516		Sep	204,222		
12	1/11/2006	1,831		Oct	233,281		
13	1/12/2006	1,902		Nov	287,693		
14	1/13/2006	2,193		Dec	323,478		
15	1/14/2006	2,111		⊟ 2007			
16	1/15/2006	2,033		Jan	324,873		
17	1/16/2006	1,763		Feb	323,230		
18	1/17/2006	1,783		Mar	360,528		
19	1/18/2006	1,938		Apr	327,765		
20	1/19/2006	2,167		May	348,106		
21	1/20/2006	2,171		Jun	310,023		
22	1/21/2006	1,990		Jul	320,517		
23	1/22/2006	1,930		Aug	312,808		
24	1/23/2006	1,826		Sep	325,165		
25	1/24/2006	2,188		Oct	316,037		
26	1/25/2006	2,214		Nov	316,829		
27	1/26/2006	2,361		Dec	302,125		
28	1/27/2006	2,156		Grand Total	5,507,019		
29	1/28/2006	2,267					
30	1/29/2006	1,883					

Figure 167-4: The pivot table, after grouping by months and years.

Notice that the Grouping dialog box contains other time-based units. For example, you can group the data into quarters. Figure 167-5 shows the data grouped by quarters and years.

	A	B	C	D	E	F
1	Date	Sales		Row Labels	Sum of Sales	
2	1/1/2006	1,276		⊟ 2006		
3	1/2/2006	1,254		Qtr1	173,438	
4	1/3/2006	1,454		Qtr2	125,502	
5	1/4/2006	1,223		Qtr3	475,621	
6	1/5/2006	1,314		Qtr4	844,452	
7	1/6/2006	1,496		⊟ 2007		
8	1/7/2006	1,472		Qtr1	1,008,631	
9	1/8/2006	1,123		Qtr2	985,894	
10	1/9/2006	1,209		Qtr3	958,490	
11	1/10/2006	1,516		Qtr4	934,991	
12	1/11/2006	1,831		Grand Total	5,507,019	
13	1/12/2006	1,902				
14	1/13/2006	2,193				
15	1/14/2006	2,111				

Figure 167-5: The PivotTable, after grouping by quarters and years.

Part IX

Working with Files

In this part, you'll find tips that deal with files — information that every Excel user should know (but many don't).

Tips and Where to Find Them

Working with the Recent Documents List

Recent versions of Excel provided a way to open recent documents quickly, but this feature was quite limited. In Excel 2007, Microsoft finally got it right.

Opening a Recent Document

When you click the Office button, Excel displays a list of files you've opened recently. Just click the filename, and it opens — assuming that it hasn't been renamed or moved since you last opened it.

Pinning a Document

Many users overlook the little pushpin icons displayed to the right of each document name (see Figure 168-1). If you click one of those icons, it turns green — and the file will always be on the Recent Documents list. In other words, it's a way of ensuring that a particular file will not get pushed off the list and replaced by more recent documents.

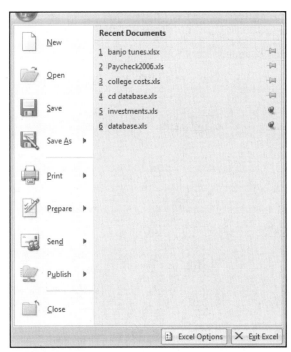

Figure 168-1: Click a pushpin icon to ensure that a file is always displayed in the Recent Documents list.

Part IX

Changing the Number of Recent Documents Displayed

You can customize the number of files shown in the Recent Documents list, from 0 to 50. To change the number of files displayed in the Recent Documents list, choose Office ⇨ Excel options and click the Advanced tab in the Excel Options dialog box. Specify in the Display section the number of files to display in the list.

Removing Files from the Recent Documents List

In some situations, you might prefer to clear some or all items from the Recent Documents list. If you set the number of files to 0, the list appears empty. However, the filenames are still stored and reappear if you change the number.

To permanently delete one or more files from the Recent Documents list, you can edit the Windows Registry:

1. Click the Windows Start button, and choose Run.

2. Type **regedit** to launch the Registry Editor.

3. In the Registry Editor, navigate to the following key:

   `HKEY_CURRENT_USER\Software\Microsoft\Office\12.0\Excel\File MRU`

   You see a list of all files in your Recent Documents list.

4. To remove a single item, click it and press Del. To remove all items, click the File MRU key and press Del.

You need to restart Excel in order for the changes to be apparent.

Understanding the Excel 2007 File Formats

Perhaps one of the most confusing aspects of Excel is the nearly overwhelming number of file formats that it can read and write. With the introduction of Excel 2007, things got even more confusing because it has quite a few new file formats.

Recognizing the Excel 2007 File Formats

Excel's new file formats are

- **XLSX:** A workbook file that doesn't contain macros
- **XLSM:** A workbook file that contains macros
- **XLTX:** A workbook template file that doesn't contain macros
- **XLTM:** A workbook template file that contains macros
- **XLSA:** An add-in file
- **XLSB:** A binary file similar to the old XLS format but able to accommodate the new features
- **XLSK:** A backup file

With the exception of XLSB, these are all *open* XLM file formats, which means that other applications can read and write these types of files.

NOTE

The XML files are zip-compressed text files. If you rename one of these files so that it has a ZIP extension, you can examine the contents by using any of several zip file utilities — including the zip file support built into Windows.

The Office 2007 Compatibility Pack

Normally, those who use an earlier version of Excel can't open workbooks saved in the new Excel 2007 file formats. But, fortunately, Microsoft has released the free Compatibility Pack for Office 2003 and Office XP.

An Office 2003 or Office XP user who installs the Compatibility Pack can open files created in Office 2007 and also save files in Office 2007 format. The Office programs that are affected are Excel, Word, and PowerPoint.

To download the Compatibility Pak, search the Web for **Office 2007 Compatibility Pack**.

Part IX

Saving a File for Use with an Older Version of Excel

To save a file for use with an older version of Excel, choose Office ⇨ Save As and select one of these options from the Save As Type drop-down list:

- **Excel 97-2003 Workbook (*.xls):** If the file will be used by someone who has Excel 97, Excel 2000, Excel 2002, or Excel 2003

- **Microsoft Excel 5.0/95 Workbook (*.xls):** If the file will be used by someone who has Excel 5 or Excel 95

When you save a file by using one of these file formats, Excel displays its Compatibility Checker dialog box. This dialog box lists all potential compatibility problems.

 NOTE

If the workbook will be used only by someone who has installed the Office 2007 Compatibility Pack, you don't need to save it by using an earlier file format. However, it's a good idea to run the Compatibility Checker to make sure that you're not using features that aren't supported by earlier versions of Excel. To check potential compatibility problems in the active workbook, choose Office ⇨ Prepare ⇨ Run Compatibility Checker.

Importing a Text File into a Worksheet Range

If you need to insert a text file into a specific range in a worksheet, you might think that your only choice is to import the text into a new workbook (by choosing Office ⇨ Open) and then to copy the data and paste it to the range where you want it to appear. However, you can do it in a more direct way.

Figure 170-1 shows a small CSV (*comma separated value*) file. The following instructions describe how to import this file, named `monthly.csv`, beginning at cell C4.

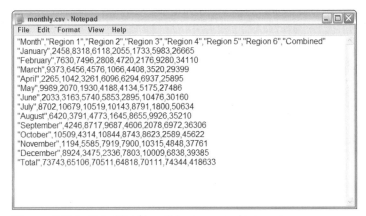

Figure 170-1: This CSV file will be imported into a range.

1. Choose Data ⇨ Get External Data ⇨ From Text to display the Import Text File dialog box.

2. Navigate to the folder that contains the text file.

3. Select the file from the list, and then click the Import button to display the Text Import Wizard.

4. Use the Text Import Wizard to specify how the data will be imported. For a CSV file, specify Delimited, with a Comma Delimiter.

5. Click the Finish button. Excel displays the Import Data dialog box.

6. In the Import Data dialog box, click the Properties button to display the External Data Range Properties dialog box.

7. In the External Data Range Properties dialog box, deselect the Save Query Definition check box, and click OK to return to the Import Data dialog box.

8. In the Import Data dialog box, specify the location for the imported data. (It can be a cell in an existing worksheet or a new worksheet.)

9. Click OK, and Excel imports the data (see Figure 170-2).

NOTE

You can ignore Step 7 if the data you're importing will be changing. By saving the query definition, you can quickly update the imported data by right-clicking any cell in the range and choosing Refresh Data.

	A	B	C	D	E	F	G	H	I	J	K
9											
10											
11											
12			Month	Region 1	Region 2	Region 3	Region 4	Region 5	Region 6	Combined	
13			January	2458	8318	6118	2055	1733	5983	26665	
14			February	7630	7496	2808	4720	2176	9280	34110	
15			March	9373	6456	4576	1066	4408	3520	29399	
16			April	2265	1042	3261	6096	6294	6937	25895	
17			May	9989	2070	1930	4188	4134	5175	27486	
18			June	2033	3163	5740	5853	2895	10476	30160	
19			July	8702	10679	10519	10143	8791	1800	50634	
20			August	6420	3791	4773	1645	8655	9926	35210	
21			September	4246	8717	9687	4606	2078	6972	36306	
22			October	10509	4314	10844	8743	8623	2589	45622	
23			November	1194	5585	7919	7900	10315	4848	37761	
24			December	8924	3475	2336	7803	10009	6838	39385	
25			Total	73743	65106	70511	64818	70111	74344	418633	
26											
27											
28											

Sheet1

Figure 170-2: This range contains data imported directly from a CSV file.

Getting Data from a Web Page

This tip describes three ways to capture data contained on a Web page:

- Paste a static copy of the information.
- Create a refreshable link to the site.
- Open the page directly in Excel.

Pasting Static Information

One way to get data from a Web page into a worksheet is to simply highlight the text in your browser, press Ctrl+C to copy it to the Clipboard, and then paste it into Excel. The results will vary, depending on what browser you use. If you use Microsoft Internet Explorer, the pasted results will probably look very similar to the original — complete with formatting, hyperlinks, and graphics.

If you use a browser other than Internet Explorer, choosing Home ➪ Clipboard ➪ Paste might put everything you copied from the Web page into a single cell — probably not what you want. The solution is to choose Home ➪ Clipboard ➪ Paste ➪ Paste Special and then select the HTML or Text option.

Pasting Refreshable Information

If you need to regularly access updated data from a Web page, create a Web query. Figure 171-1 shows a Web site that contains currency exchange rates. Note the three-column table.

These steps create a Web query that allows this information to be refreshed with a single mouse click:

1. Choose Data ➪ Get External Data ➪ From Web to display the New Web Query dialog box.

2. In the Address field, enter the URL of the Web site. For this example, the URL for the Web page shown in Figure 171-1 is

```
http://moneycentral.msn.com/investor/market/rates.asp
```

Notice that the New Web Query dialog box contains a minibrowser (Internet Explorer). You can click links and navigate the Web site until you locate the data you're interested in.

3. When a Web page is displayed in the New Web Query dialog box, you see one or more yellow arrows, which correspond to various elements in the Web page. Click an arrow, and it turns into a green check box, which indicates that the data in that element will be imported. You can import as many elements as you need. For this example, I clicked the arrow next to the rate table (see Figure 171-2).

4. Click the Import button to display the Import Data dialog box.

5. In the Import Data dialog box, specify the location for the imported data. (It can be a cell in an existing worksheet or a new worksheet.)

6. Click OK, and Excel imports the data (see Figure 171-3).

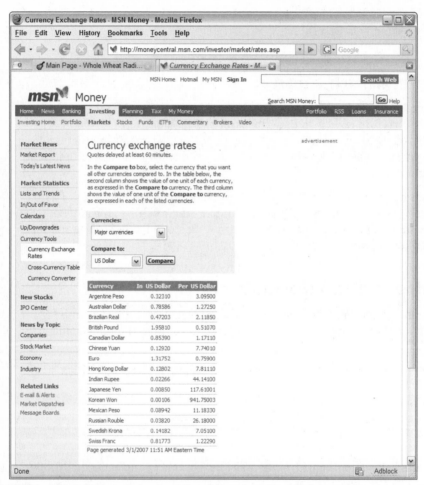

Figure 171-1: This site contains information that changes frequently.

By default, the imported data is a Web query. To refresh the information, right-click any cell in the imported range and choose Refresh Data from the shortcut menu.

If you don't want to create a refreshable query, specify it in Step 5 of the preceding step list. In the Import Data dialog box, click the Properties button and deselect the Save Query Definition check box.

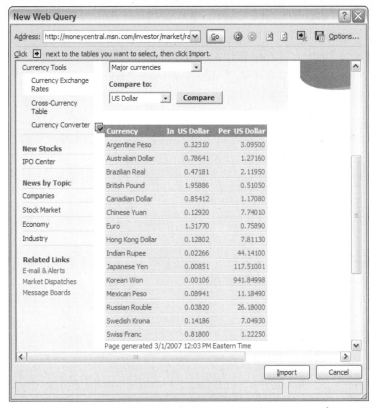

Figure 171-2: Using the New Web Query dialog box to specify the data to be imported.

	A	B	C	D	E	F
1						
2						
3			Currency	In US Dollar	Per US Dollar	
4			Argentine Peso	0.3231	3.095	
5			Australian Dollar	0.78641	1.2716	
6			Brazilian Real	0.47181	2.1195	
7			British Pound	1.95886	0.5105	
8			Canadian Dollar	0.85412	1.1708	
9			Chinese Yuan	0.1292	7.7401	
10			Euro	1.3177	0.7589	
11			Hong Kong Dollar	0.12802	7.8113	
12			Indian Rupee	0.02266	44.141	
13			Japanese Yen	0.00851	117.51001	
14			Korean Won	0.00106	941.84998	
15			Mexican Peso	0.08941	11.1849	
16			Russian Rouble	0.0382	26.18	
17			Swedish Krona	0.14186	7.0493	
18			Swiss Franc	0.818	1.2225	
19						
20						

Sheet3

Figure 171-3: The data, imported from a Web page.

Opening the Web Page Directly

Another way to get Web page data into a worksheet is to open the URL directly, by using Excel's Office ⇨ Open command. Just enter the complete URL into the File Name field and click Open. Figure 171-4 shows the MSN currency rate page open in Excel. As you can see, it contains quite a bit of extraneous information.

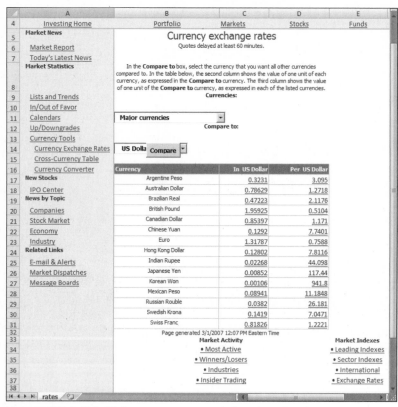

Figure 171-4: This Web page was opened directly in Excel.

Displaying a Workbook's Full Path

If you have lots of files open in Excel, you might need to know the full path of the active workbook. Oddly, Excel provides no direct way to get this information.

You can always issue the Office ➪ Save As command. Excel proposes that you save the file in its current directory. Even then, the Save As dialog box doesn't display the full path of the workbook. Another option is to enter the following formula into a cell:

```
=CELL("filename")
```

The formula displays the path, including the name of the worksheet that contains the formula.

The solution is simple — but certainly not intuitive. Just add the Document Location control to the Quick Access Toolbar (QAT). Figure 172-1 shows what this control looks like. Unfortunately, you can't change the width of this control, but if you click the displayed name, you can see the entire path.

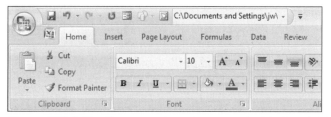

Figure 172-1: The Document Location control added to the QAT displays the full path of the active workbook.

To add this control to your QAT, follow these steps:

1. Right-click the QAT, and choose Customize Quick Access Toolbar.

2. In the Customize tab of the Excel Options dialog box, choose Commands Not in the Ribbon from the drop-down list on the left.

3. Scroll down the list and select Document Location.

4. Click the Add button to add the selected control to the QAT.

5. Click OK to close the Excel Options dialog box.

NOTE

Another way to view the path of the active workbook is to display the Document Properties panel (choose Office ➪ Prepare ➪ Properties). The Document Properties panel is displayed above the formula bar. Unfortunately, the Document Properties panel takes up quite a bit of space and can't be moved or resized.

Part IX

Saving a Preview of Your Workbook

If you have lots of workbooks, you may want to save a preview of each workbook to provide a visual clue when you use the Open dialog box. When you open a workbook (by using the Open dialog box), you have a number of options regarding how the files are displayed. You can change how the file display looks by clicking the arrow on the Views icon in the Open dialog box. You can choose from among these options:

- **Thumbnails:** Shows each filename with a large icon. (This option is more appropriate for graphical images.)

- **Tiles:** Shows each filename with an icon, along with the file type and size.

- **Icons:** Similar to Tiles, but the file type and size aren't displayed.

- **List:** Shows the filenames with no other information.

- **Details:** Shows the filenames, along with other information. You can sort the list by clicking any column header.

- **Properties:** Displays information about the selected file. If you entered any information in the Properties panel (displayed when you choose Office ➪ Prepare ➪ Properties), that information is also displayed.

- **Preview:** Displays a preview of the file (if you specified that option in the Advanced Properties dialog box). Figure 173-1 shows an example.

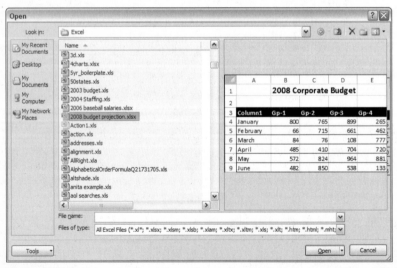

Figure 173-1: Using the Preview option can make it easier to locate workbooks.

The Preview option can be useful if you know what a workbook looks like but can't remember its filename. The option isn't all useful, however, if you don't remember to save the preview picture. Excel 2007 doesn't make it easy to save a preview picture. Here's the procedure:

1. Choose Office ➪ Prepare ➪ Properties to display the Document Properties pane.

2. Click the Document Properties drop-down list and choose Advanced Properties, which displays a dialog box.

3. Select the Save Preview Picture check box.

After you complete these steps, saving the file generates a picture of the upper left corner of the first sheet in the workbook. The picture is updated when the file is saved.

NOTE

If the workbook requires a password to open it, the preview isn't shown.

Unfortunately, Excel offers no way to enable this feature for all your workbooks. If you want a preview picture, you must specify it manually for each file. Or, you can create a book.xltx template that has the Save Preview Picture setting enabled.

CROSS-REFERENCE

Refer to Tip 12 for instructions on customizing the default workbook.

Part IX

Using Document Properties

If you have many Excel files — and have trouble keeping them organized — this tip might be helpful. You can specify a number of properties for each workbook file. The properties describe the workbook and can be useful when searching.

Figure 174-1 shows the Document Properties panel, located above the formula bar. To display this panel, choose Office ⇨ Prepare ⇨ Properties.

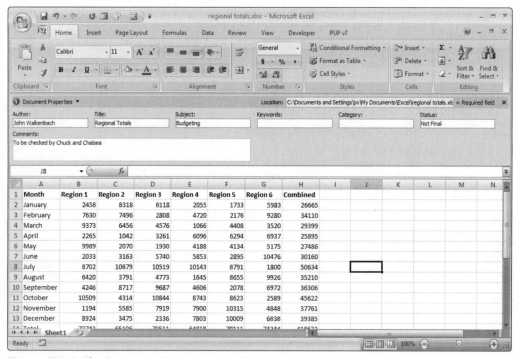

Figure 174-1: The Document Properties panel.

You can enter information in any of these fields:

- Author
- Title
- Subject
- Keywords
- Category
- Status
- Comments

When you open an Explorer window, you can specify which properties to display. Right-click the column header (which normally displays Name, Size, Type, and Data Modified). You see a number of additional file properties that you can display. Click the More option, and you get the Choose Details dialog box, shown in Figure 174-2. When these additional properties are displayed, you can sort the file list by any property.

Figure 174-2: Use the Windows Choose Details dialog box to specify which file properties to display in an Explorer window.

Part IX

Inspecting a Workbook

When you send an Excel workbook to someone (or post it on the Internet), you should invoke the Excel Document Inspector before you save for the last time. The Document Inspector checks for these types of content:

- Comments and annotations

- Document properties and personal information

- Custom XML data

- Headers and footers

- Hidden rows and columns

- Hidden worksheets

- Invisible content

To display the Document Inspector dialog box (shown in Figure 175-1), choose Office ⇨ Prepare ⇨ Inspect Document.

Figure 175-1: Use the Document Inspector to identify hidden information in your workbook.

When you click the Inspect button, Excel searches the workbook for the items that are selected in the dialog box. If any items are found, you can remove them all.

Unfortunately, this tool leaves much to be desired. For example, it doesn't provide you with any specific information or generate a report that contains the details. But, it's better than checking those items manually.

Finding the Missing No to All Button When Closing Files

Assume that you have a dozen or so workbooks open and you want to close Excel without saving any changes. Excel displays the dialog box shown in Figure 176-1. And it does it for every changed workbook that is open.

Figure 176-1: Excel displays this prompt for every unsaved file.

As you can see, this dialog box has a Yes to All button but lacks a No to All button. Here's the secret: Press Shift while you click the No button. That action functions exactly like clicking a No to All button — if one existed.

By the way, this tip works in many of the Windows dialog boxes as well. For example, if you're copying a group of files and some of the files already exist, Windows makes you verify your overwrite intentions. That dialog box also lacks a No to All button, but you can Shift+click the No button.

Getting a List of Filenames

You would think that putting a list of filenames into a worksheet range would be fairly straightforward: Just instruct Windows to generate a list of files for a directory, and then import the list into an Excel worksheet. Unfortunately, it's not that easy. Most users are surprised to discover that Windows doesn't provide a direct way to export a list of filenames to a file.

Perhaps the best solution is to write a VBA macro to create a list of files. The method described here doesn't require a macro. However, it does require that you go back in time and use an old-fashioned command line interface.

The following instructions assume that you want to generate a list of files contained in a directory named `c:\my files\excel\`:

1. Click the Windows Start button, and choose Run.

2. In the Run dialog box, type **cmd** and click OK. This step displays the Windows command shell.

3. Navigate to the directory that you're interested in by typing **cd**, followed by the full path. In this example, enter this line:

   ```
   cd c:\my files\excel
   ```

4. Type the following command and press Enter:

   ```
   dir > filelist.txt
   ```

Figure 177-1 shows what the command prompt window looks like as you work through the preceding set of steps.

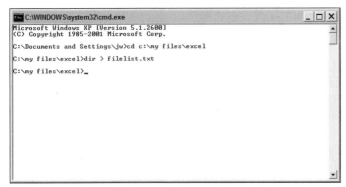

Figure 177-1: Using the Windows command prompt to generate a list of files.

Windows creates a file named `filelist.txt` in the current directory (the one you specified in Step 3). You can then use Excel's Office ⇨ Open command to import this file, which starts the File Import Wizard. (Make sure to specify fixed-width data.) Figure 177-2 shows some data that I imported.

	A	B	C	D
1	Volume in	drive C ha	s no label.	
2	Volume Se	rial Number	is F08D-900C	
3				
4	Directory	of C:\my f	iles\excel	
5				
6	3/1/2007	1:09 PM	<DIR>	.
7	3/1/2007	1:09 PM	<DIR>	..
8	11/17/2006	5:40 AM	15,385	2006 baseball salaries.xlsx
9	3/1/2007	12:04 PM	22,121	2008 budget projection.xlsx
10	6/23/2003	10:41 AM	411,648	3d data surface.xls
11	10/25/2005	12:05 PM	17,408	50states.xls
12	4/8/2005	11:56 AM	23,552	action.xls
13	1/21/2003	4:58 PM	35,328	background.xls
14	4/13/2006	6:41 AM	16,384	banjo strings.xls
15	7/21/2003	10:26 AM	56,320	bank accounts.xls
16	8/2/2002	8:48 AM	702,464	baseball stats.xls
17	5/7/2003	6:21 PM	28,672	budget.xls
18	1/29/2007	8:20 AM	11,710	budget.xlsx
19	11/11/2006	6:28 PM	24,154	bush approval charts.xlsx
20	6/27/2006	11:20 AM	95,776	climate data.xlsx
21	3/1/2007	1:09 PM	0	filelist.txt
22		14 File	(s) 1,460,92	2 bytes
23		2 Dir(	s) 68,652,879,87	2 bytes free
24				

Figure 177-2: This file listing was imported from a text file.

As you can see, the listing needs to be cleaned up a bit, but all the information is there, including the date, time, and size of each file.

NOTE

The DIR command has quite a few options. For example, you can get a list of the files in all subdirectories as well as the current directory. Search online for **DOS commands**, and you'll find lots of information about the DIR command.

Understanding Excel Passwords

Excel provides several ways to "protect" your work by using passwords. I use the word *protect* loosely because using passwords might offer a false sense of protection. You can enter a password in six places in Excel:

- **The Protect Sheet dialog box:** Open it by choosing Review ⇨ Changes ⇨ Protect Sheet.

- **The Protect Workbook dialog box:** Open it by choosing Review ⇨ Changes ⇨ Protect Workbook.

- **The Encrypt Document dialog box:** Open it by choosing Office ⇨ Prepare ⇨ Encrypt Document. Encrypting a document appears to have the same effect as protecting a workbook with a password by using the Protect Workbook dialog box.

- **The Protect Shared Workbook dialog box:** Open it by choosing Review ⇨ Changes ⇨ Protect and Share Workbook.

- **The Save Options dialog box:** Open it by choosing Office ⇨ Save As and then by choosing Tools ⇨ General Options in the Save As dialog box.

- **The Protection tab in the Project Properties dialog box:** Open it in the Visual Basic Editor by choosing Tools ⇨ VBAProject Properties.

Many users assume that password protection is a way to make their work secure, protecting all or parts of it from those who don't know the password. The truth is that anyone who knows the secret can crack any Excel passwords. And, even someone who doesn't know the secret can use a password-cracking service.

The moral of this story: If you're looking for a way to keep your data secure, assigning a password in Excel isn't the solution.

Part IX

Using Workspace Files

If you have a project that uses multiple workbooks, you probably get tired of opening the same files every time you work on the project.

The solution? Create a workspace file:

1. Open all the files used for your project.

2. Arrange the workbook windows the way you like them.

3. Choose View ⇨ Window ⇨ Save Workspace to display the Save Workspace dialog box.

4. Excel proposes the name `resume.xlw`, but you can specify any name you like. Just make sure that you use the XLW extension.

5. Click Save, and the workspace file is created.

After creating a workspace file, you can open it by choosing Office ⇨ Open. In the Open dialog box, specify Workspaces (`*.xlw`) in the Files of Type drop-down list.

NOTE

A workspace file contains *only* the filenames and window position information — not the workbooks.

CAUTION

Leave it to Microsoft to add a new feature that has the same name as an old feature. In Office 2007, you might encounter the term Document Workspace, which refers to a SharePoint services site and has absolutely nothing to do with Excel workspace files.

Customizing the My Places Bar

When you choose File ⇨ Open, the Open dialog box displays several icons along the left side (My Recent Documents, Desktop, and My Documents, for example). This panel is the *My Places bar.* Clicking an icon on the My Places bar displays that location and is usually much faster than navigating through directories.

It's not immediately obvious, but you can add new places to the My Places bar. To do so, follow these steps:

1. Navigate to the directory that you want to add.

2. Right-click the My Places bar, and choose Add *xxxx*, where *xxxx* represents the name of the current directory.

3. If you want, right-click the new icon and choose Rename to give it a more meaningful name.

Places that you add are also displayed on the My Places bar in the Save As dialog box. The My Places bar can hold up to 256 items.

Figure 180-1 shows the Open dialog box with some new additions to the My Places bar.

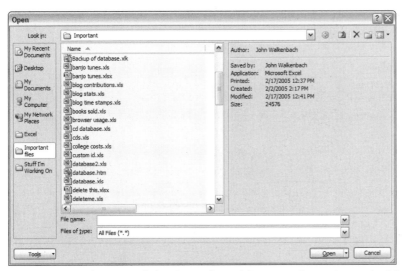

Figure 180-1: The Open dialog box, after adding new directories to the My Places bar.

To remove an item, right-click it and choose Remove. The standard My Places items, shown in this list, cannot be removed:

- My Recent Documents
- Desktop
- My Documents
- My Computer
- My Network Places

Part X

Printing

We haven't quite reached the paperless office yet, so it's still important to get your work on paper in a way that looks good. The tips in this part deal with printing and previewing your work.

Tips and Where to Find Them

Controlling What Gets Printed

This tip deals with some printing basics.

Displaying the Quick Print Button

No, your eyes don't deceive you. It's true that Excel 2007, by default, doesn't display a Print button on the Ribbon. The "normal" way of printing a document is to choose the Office ⇨ Print command.

If you like the idea of one-click printing, modify the Quick Access Toolbar (QAT):

1. Click the downward-pointing arrow to the right of the QAT.

2. Choose Quick Print.

After you complete these steps, the QAT displays a new icon. Click the icon, and Excel prints the entire contents of the active worksheet. But sometimes you want a bit more control over the documents you send to your printer. To find out how to get that additional control, keep reading.

Printing All Sheets

To print all sheets (worksheets and chart sheets), choose Office ⇨ Print (or press Ctrl+P) to display the Print dialog box. In the Print What section, select the Entire Workbook option, and then click OK.

Printing Specific Sheets

If you want to print only certain sheets in your workbook, press Ctrl and then click the sheet tabs of the sheets to be printed. Then choose Office ⇨ Print (or press Ctrl+P) to display the Print dialog box. In the Print What section, select the Active Sheet(s) option and click OK.

Setting the Print Area for a Worksheet

To print only a specific range on a worksheet, select the range, and then choose Page Layout ⇨ Page Setup ⇨ Set Print Area ⇨ Set Print Area.

The print area can also consist of a noncontiguous range (that is, a multiple selection). To select multiple ranges, press Ctrl while you select the range. Then choose Page Layout ⇨ Page Setup ⇨ Set Print Area ⇨ Set Print Area. Each range is printed beginning on a new page.

Part X

Another way to accomplish this task (without changing the sheet's print area) is to select the range or ranges to be printed. Then choose Office ⇨ Print (or press Ctrl+P) to display the Print dialog box. Select the Selection option in the Print What section of the Print dialog box, and click OK.

Printing Specific Pages

If you're printing a lengthy report, you might discover an error on one or more pages. You don't have to reprint the entire report after you correct any errors. You can print only specific pages by following these steps:

1. Choose Office ⇨ Print (or press Ctrl+P) to display the Print dialog box.

2. In the Print Range section, select the Page(s) option and enter the beginning and ending page numbers. For example, to print only page 25, type **25** in both the From field and the To field.

3. Click OK to print the specified pages.

If you're not sure which pages you need to print, choose Office ⇨ Print ⇨ Print Preview to preview the print job and determine the page numbers.

Displaying Repeating Rows or Columns on a Printout

You might be familiar with the Excel View ⇨ Window ⇨ Freeze Panes command, which you can use to specify rows or columns, or both, that will remain fixed while you scroll the worksheet.

The View ⇨ Window ⇨ Freeze Panes command has no effect on printed output. If you want your printout to display one or more fixed rows at the top and/or one or more fixed columns along the left, you need to set up this task separately:

1. Select Page Layout ⇨ Page Setup ⇨ Print Titles to display the Sheet tab of the Page Setup dialog box.

2. To specify one or more rows to repeat at the top, click the icon on the far right side of the Rows to Repeat at Top field, and then point to the rows in your worksheet.

3. To specify one or more columns to repeat on the left, click the icon on the far right side of the Columns to Repeat at Left field, and then point to the columns in your worksheet.

4. Click OK to close the Page Setup dialog box, and then print the worksheet.

Printing Noncontiguous Ranges on a Single Page

If you need to print several different ranges, Excel always starts printing each range on a separate sheet of paper. This tip describes a technique that allows you to print multiple ranges on a single page.

The trick involves creating a linked picture of each of the ranges to be printed and then arranging these pictures on a separate worksheet. Here's one way to create a linked picture:

1. Select the range.

2. Press Ctrl+C.

3. Activate a different cell.

4. Choose Home ➪ Clipboard ➪ Paste ➪ As Picture ➪ Paste Picture Link.

Fortunately, Excel has a much more efficient tool for the job: the Camera tool (which, for some reason, Microsoft keeps rather hidden).

Breaking Out the Camera Tool

To add the Camera tool to your Quick Access Toolbar (QAT), follow these steps:

1. Right-click the QAT and choose Customize Quick Access Toolbar to display the Customize tab of the Excel Options dialog box.

2. In the drop-down list on the left, choose Commands Not in the Ribbon.

3. Select Camera in the list.

4. Click Add to add the Camera tool to your QAT.

5. Click OK to close the Excel Options dialog box.

The Camera tool creates a linked picture of a range. Therefore, if the data in the linked range changes, the picture is updated automatically.

Figure 183-1 shows a worksheet. The goal is to print two ranges (A3:C10 and E13:G20) on a single page.

	A	B	C	D	E	F	G	H
1	**Call Volume Stats**							
2								
3	**Date**	**Calls**	**Weekday**		235	75	7	
4	3/1	175	Thursday		66	942	342	
5	3/2	266	Friday		571	57	476	
6	3/3	254	Saturday		66	630	947	
7	3/4	265	Sunday		211	157	434	
8	3/5	211	Monday		890	11	84	
9	3/6	190	Tuesday		681	778	616	
10	3/7	225	Wednesday		658	786	982	
11								
12								
13	978	533	838		**Date**	**Calls**	**Weekday**	
14	894	983	308		4/1	211	Sunday	
15	400	50	745		4/2	190	Monday	
16	908	160	506		4/3	225	Tuesday	
17	964	411	383		4/4	175	Wednesday	
18	768	230	283		4/5	266	Thursday	
19	134	462	809		4/6	254	Friday	
20	163	968	491		4/7	265	Saturday	
21								
22								

Sheet1

Figure 183-1: It's normally impossible to print ranges A3:C10 and E13:G20 on a single page.

Shooting with the Camera

The following steps show you how to use the Camera tool to print multiple ranges on one piece of paper:

1. Make sure that the Camera tool is available on your QAT. (Refer to the preceding steps if it's not.)

2. Insert a new worksheet (Sheet2) to hold the linked pictures.

3. Select A3:C10, and click the Camera tool.

4. Activate Sheet2 and click to insert the linked picture.

5. Return to the previous worksheet, select E13:G20, and click the Camera tool.

6. Activate Sheet2 and click to insert the linked picture.

7. Use your mouse to arrange the linked pictures any way you like. You might want to turn off the gridline display in the worksheet that holds the linked pictures.

Figure 183-2 shows the worksheet that contains the linked pictures. If the data in Sheet1 changes, the linked pictures are updated. When you print Sheet2, both ranges appear on the same page.

Part X

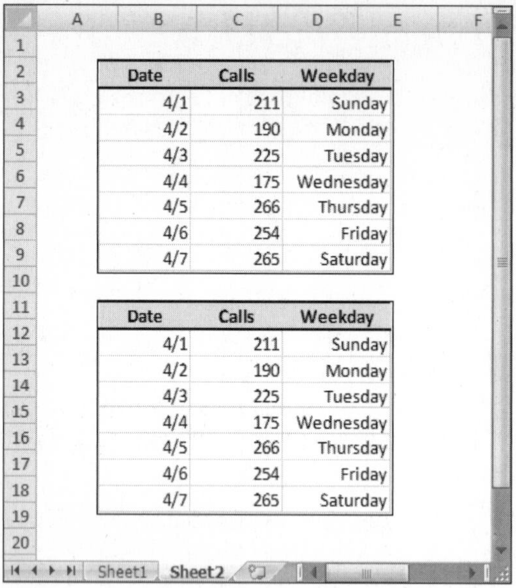

	A	B	C	D	E	F
1						
2		Date	Calls	Weekday		
3		4/1	211	Sunday		
4		4/2	190	Monday		
5		4/3	225	Tuesday		
6		4/4	175	Wednesday		
7		4/5	266	Thursday		
8		4/6	254	Friday		
9		4/7	265	Saturday		
10						
11		Date	Calls	Weekday		
12		4/1	211	Sunday		
13		4/2	190	Monday		
14		4/3	225	Tuesday		
15		4/4	175	Wednesday		
16		4/5	266	Thursday		
17		4/6	254	Friday		
18		4/7	265	Saturday		
19						
20						

Sheet1 / Sheet2

Figure 183-2: Using linked pictures makes it possible to print the two ranges on a single page.

Preventing Objects from Printing

You can place a wide variety of objects on a worksheet — charts, shapes, pictures, SmartArt, and controls (such as check boxes), for example. By default, all these objects are printed when you print the worksheet.

You can, of course, specify that a particular object *doesn't* print. However, the procedure varies with the type of object.

The following list describes how to keep a particular object from printing. In all cases, start by clicking the object to select it.

- **Chart:** Click the dialog box launcher in the Chart Tools ⇨ Format ⇨ Size group. (It's the tiny icon to the right of the word *Size*.) In the Size and Properties dialog box, click the Properties tab and deselect the Print Object check box.

- **SmartArt:** Click the dialog box launcher in the SmartArt Tools ⇨ Format ⇨ Size group. (It's the tiny icon to the right of the word *Size*.) In the Size and Properties dialog box, click the Properties tab and deselect the Print Object check box.

- **WordArt:** Click the dialog box launcher by choosing Drawing Tools ⇨ Format ⇨ Size group. (It's the tiny icon to the right of the word *Size*.) In the Size and Properties dialog box, click the Properties tab and deselect the Print Object check box.

- **Shape, Textbox, Picture, or Clipart:** Right-click the object and choose Size and Properties from the shortcut menu. In the Size and Properties dialog box, click the Properties tab and deselect the Print Object check box.

- **Form control:** (You insert it by choosing Developer ⇨ Controls ⇨ Insert ⇨ Form Controls.) Right-click the control and choose Format Control from the shortcut menu. In the Format Control dialog box, click the Properties tab and deselect the Print Object check box.

- **ActiveX control:** (You insert it by choosing Developer ⇨ Controls ⇨ Insert ⇨ ActiveX Controls.) Make sure that Excel is in Design mode. (Click the Developer ⇨ Controls ⇨ Design Mode button.) Right-click the control and choose Format Control from the shortcut menu. In the Format Control dialog box, click the Properties tab and deselect the Print Object check box.

Part X

Page-Numbering Tips

For lengthy printouts, you probably want to add page numbers to help keep the pages in order. Excel 2007 makes it easier than ever to work with page numbers, and this tip describes your options.

Applying Basic Page Numbering

To add page numbering, follow these steps:

1. Choose View ⇨ Workbook Views ⇨ Page Layout, to switch to Page Layout view.

   Notice that each page has a header at the top and a footer at the bottom. Each header and footer is divided into three sections: left, center and right.

2. Click the header or footer area where you want the page number to appear.

3. Choose Header & Footer Tools ⇨ Design ⇨ Page Number. Excel inserts a code that represents the page number.

4. Click any cell in the worksheet to see the actual page numbers.

In Step 3, the code that Excel adds simply inserts a number. You can add text to the page numbering code. For example, if you want your page numbers to read Page 3, type **Page** (followed by a space) before the code. This type of header or footer entry looks like this:

```
Page &[Page]
```

You might prefer to include the total number of pages so that the page numbering reads like this: Page 3 of 20. In Step 3, choose Header & Footer Tools ⇨ Design ⇨ Number of Pages to insert the code. You also need to enter the word *of*. The complete code looks like this:

```
Page &[Page] of &[Pages]
```

Changing the Starting Page Number

If your printout will be part of a larger report, you might want to begin page numbering with a number other than 1. To do so, follow these steps:

1. Click the dialog box launcher in the Page Layout ⇨ Page Setup group. (It's the tiny icon to the right of the words Page Setup.)

2. In the Page Setup dialog box, click the Page tab.

3. Enter the starting page number in the field labeled First Page Number.

NOTE

If you specify a starting page number other than 1, you probably don't want to use the `&[Pages]` code in your header or footer. If you do, you might see text that reads `Page 18 of 3`.

Previewing Page Breaks

If you print a lengthy document, you might be concerned about page breaks. For example, you probably don't want to end a page with a row of column headings for data that begins on the next page.

Excel offers three ways to see a preview of your work before printing the document.

Print Preview Mode

To get a preview of your printed output (one page at a time), choose Office ⇨ Print ⇨ Print Preview. You see a representation of how your work will look when it's printed.

If you click the Show Margins check box in the Preview window, Excel displays the margins and cell width indicators along the top. You can adjust the margins and the cell widths in Print Preview mode by dragging them. For example, if you notice that a single column of data is printed separately on a page, you can tweak the column widths so that the information doesn't extend to a new page on the right. Or, you can make the page margins smaller.

Print Preview mode is useful, but it displays only one page at a time — and you can't modify any cells.

Page Break Preview

Another way to view page breaks is in Page Break Preview mode. To enter Page Break Preview mode, choose View ⇨ Workbook Views ⇨ Page Break Preview. Or, click the Page Break Preview icon on the right side of the status bar.

Excel reduces the zoom factor of the sheet and also displays the page breaks and page numbers (see Figure 186-1).

In Page Break Preview mode, you can adjust the zoom factor to make the text larger or smaller. (Use the Zoom control on the Standard toolbar). You can make the text size 100 percent, and the overlaid page numbers will still appear. You can also adjust the page breaks by simply dragging the blue lines. Automatic page breaks are indicated by a dashed blue line; manual page breaks are indicated by a solid blue line.

To exit Page Break Preview mode, choose View ⇨ Workbook Views ⇨ Normal.

Page Layout View

Page Layout view, which is new to Excel 2007, provides the ultimate WYSIWYG (*what you see is what you get*) environment. To enter Page Layout view, choose View ⇨ Workbook Views ⇨ Page Layout. Or, click the Page Layout icon on the right side of the status bar.

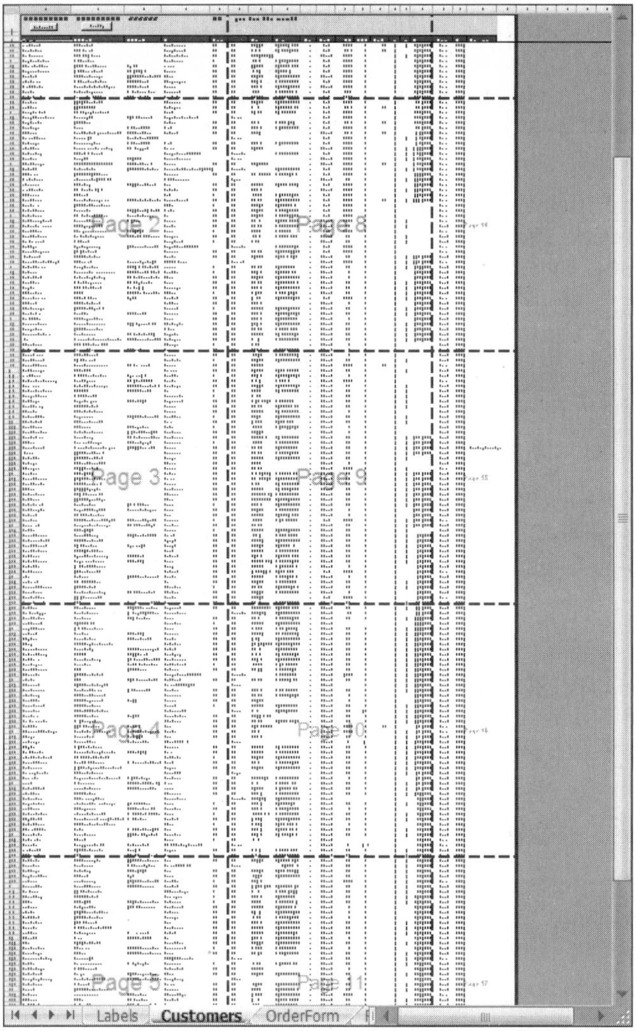

Figure 186-1: Page Break Preview mode shows multiple pages.

In addition to giving you a preview of the page breaks, Page Layout view shows headers and footers. The best part about Page Layout view is that the workbook is completely *live:* You can perform any action that you normally do. Some operations might be a bit slower, but you always know exactly how your pages will print.

Adding and Removing Page Breaks

Most Excel users just let Excel determine where page breaks fall. That situation might be acceptable most of the time, but sometimes you need to control page breaks. This tip describes how.

As you might have discovered, Excel handles page breaks automatically. After you print or preview your worksheet, Excel displays dashed lines to indicate where page breaks occur. Sometimes, however, you want to force a page break — either a vertical or horizontal one — so that the worksheet prints the way you want. For example, if your worksheet consists of several distinct sections, you might want to print each section on a separate sheet of paper.

Forcing a Page Break to Appear Where You Want It

To insert a horizontal page break line, move the cell pointer to the cell that will begin the new page and make sure to place the pointer in column A; if you don't, you'll insert a vertical page break and a horizontal page break. For example, if you want row 14 to be the first row of a new page, select cell A14. Then choose Page Layout ⇨ Breaks ⇨ Insert Page Break. Excel displays a dashed line to indicate the page break.

To insert a vertical page break line, move the cell pointer to the cell that will begin the new page, but in this case make sure that you place the pointer in row 1. Choose Page Layout ⇨ Breaks ⇨ Insert Page Break to create the page break.

Removing Page Breaks You've Added

To remove a manual page break, move the cell pointer to the first row beneath (or the first column to the right of) the manual page break, and then choose Page Layout ⇨ Breaks ⇨ Remove Page Break. (This command has an effect only when you place the cell pointer adjacent to a manual page break.)

To remove all manual page breaks in the worksheet, choose Page Layout ⇨ Breaks ⇨ Reset All Page Breaks. After you issue this command, the only page breaks that remain are those that occur naturally.

Saving to a PDF File

The Adobe PDF (Portable Document Format) file standard has become increasingly popular, for several reasons:

- PDF files can be read on many different platforms by using Adobe Acrobat Reader (a free product).

- The information looks the same, regardless of the computer or printer used.

- The document cannot be easily modified.

Excel 2007 finally includes a built-in option to save to a PDF file — sort of. I have to qualify that sentence because the support for PDF files doesn't ship with Office 2007. Rather, you download and install a free add-in from Microsoft. Apparently, this inconvenience is the result of some legal dispute. For whatever reason, Adobe has chosen to make Microsoft customers make the extra effort.

To download the PDF add-in for Office 2007, go to the following URL and search for **PDF**:

```
http://www.microsoft.com/downloads/
```

After you download and install the file, you have a new command: Office ➪ Save As ➪ PDF. Choosing this command displays the Publish As PDF dialog box, where you can specify the location for the file.

NOTE

In addition, several free (or low-cost) alternatives are available. Do a Web search for **PDF driver**, and you'll find lots of choices. When you install this driver, it appears in the Name drop-down list of printers that's displayed in the Print dialog box. Select the printer and click OK. You're prompted for a filename, and then the PDF driver creates the PDF file from your Excel worksheet.

Part X

Avoiding Printing Specific Rows

Excel makes it easy to print your work, but sometimes you might not want to print everything. For example, you might need to avoid printing certain rows in your worksheet if the rows contain confidential information or intermediate results that need not be printed.

This tip describes two ways to quickly hide and unhide rows.

Using a Custom View

One approach is to use a custom view of your worksheet. Start by unhiding the rows, to display the entire worksheet:

1. Choose View ➪ Workbook Views ➪ Custom Views to display the Custom Views dialog box

2. In the Custom Views dialog box, click Add, to display the Add View dialog box.

3. Specify a name for the view (such as **NormalView**), and make sure that the setting labeled Hidden Rows, Column and Filter Settings is enabled.

4. Click OK to save the view.

5. Hide the rows that you don't want to print.

6. Choose View ➪ Workbook Views ➪ Custom Views again.

7. Click Add, and specify a different name (such as **HiddenRows**).

After you create these two views, you can choose the View ➪ Workbook Views ➪ Custom Views command to quickly hide the rows before printing and to unhide the rows after printing.

If your workbook contains at least one table (created by choosing the Insert ➪ Tables ➪ Table command), the Custom Views command isn't available. In that case, you can create an outline, described next.

Using an Outline

The Group and Outline feature in Excel is a way to quickly toggle the hidden status of any number of rows. Figure 189-1 shows a simple example. In this case, rows 5, 10, 15, and 20 should not be printed.

	A	B	C	D	E	F	G	H	I
1		701	945	646	826	612	671		
2		592	682	531	982	781	643		
3		656	546	639	915	991	921		
4		989	598	595	863	595	877		
5	Total	2938	2771	2411	3586	2979	3112		
6		872	520	951	586	737	768		
7		917	793	545	690	811	688		
8		739	759	504	856	772	651		
9		723	710	741	540	564	837		
10	Total	3251	2782	2741	2672	2884	2944		
11		666	919	768	953	726	987		
12		592	660	567	692	944	745		
13		911	951	603	828	929	605		
14		839	788	749	832	848	586		
15	Total	3008	3318	2687	3305	3447	2923		
16		648	920	980	702	519	968		
17		893	794	795	581	829	514		
18		979	662	736	547	778	790		
19		850	505	620	752	581	759		
20	Total	3370	2881	3131	2582	2707	3031		
21									
22									

Sheet1

Figure 189-1: The goal is to prevent the Total rows from being printed.

To set up a simple worksheet outline for this example, follow these steps:

1. Select row 5.

2. Choose Data ⇨ Group ⇨ Group (or press Alt+Shift+right arrow).

3. Select row 10.

4. Press F4. (This key repeats the last command.)

5. Select row 15.

6. Press F4.

7. Select row 20.

8. Press F4.

The preceding steps create an outline of the data, and the outline symbols are displayed along the left side of the sheet. You can hide all grouped rows by clicking the small 1 (the number one) button at the top of the outline symbol area (see Figure 189-2).

After you print the sheet, click the 2 button to redisplay all the rows.

Part X

1 2		A	B	C	D	E	F	G	H
	1		701	945	646	826	612	671	
	2		592	682	531	982	781	643	
	3		656	546	639	915	991	921	
	4		989	598	595	863	595	877	
+	6		872	520	951	586	737	768	
	7		917	793	545	690	811	688	
	8		739	759	504	856	772	651	
	9		723	710	741	540	564	837	
+	11		666	919	768	953	726	987	
	12		592	660	567	692	944	745	
	13		911	951	603	828	929	605	
	14		839	788	749	832	848	586	
+	16		648	920	980	702	519	968	
	17		893	794	795	581	829	514	
	18		979	662	736	547	778	790	
	19		850	505	620	752	581	759	
+	21								
	22								
	23								

Sheet1

Figure 189-2: Use the outline controls to quickly hide the rows you don't want printed.

NOTE

If you don't like seeing the outline symbols, you can toggle them on and off by pressing Ctrl+8. The outline remains in effect even if the symbols are hidden.

Making Your Printout Fit on One Page

If you need to ensure that your printed output fits on a single page, you can spend time adjusting the font sizes — or you can let Excel do the work for you.

Figure 190-1 shows a worksheet in Page Layout view. This workbook will print on six pages.

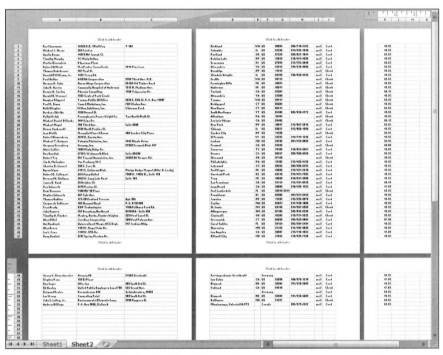

Figure 190-1: This worksheet will print on six pages.

To force Excel to print the entire worksheet on a single sheet, choose Page Layout ⇨ Scale To Fit, and specify 1 Page for the Width and 1 Page for the Height. Excel will shrink the output to your specifications. Figure 190-2 shows the worksheet after specifying these values.

Obviously, you need to consider the legibility of the printout. If you force too much information on a single sheet, it's printed so small that you need a magnifying glass to read it.

NOTE

The Page Layout ⇨ Scale To Fit settings affect the worksheet's Zoom level. These settings do not change the font size. To return to normal view, specify Automatic for the Width and Height settings.

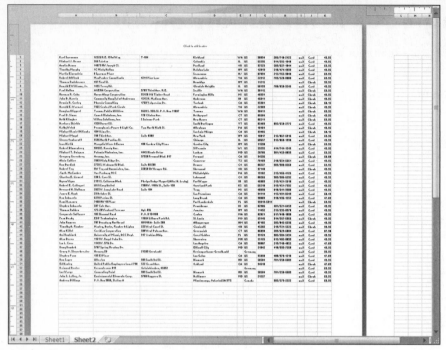

Figure 190-2: Excel shrunk the output to fit on a single page.

Printing the Contents of a Cell in a Header or Footer

The Excel Header and Footer options are fairly flexible, but you have no direct way to display the contents of a cell in a page header or footer. The solution is a simple VBA macro.

Figure 191-1 shows a worksheet with some values. Cell A1 contains a simple formula that calculates the sum of the values. The goal is to display the value in cell A1 in the center header of the page.

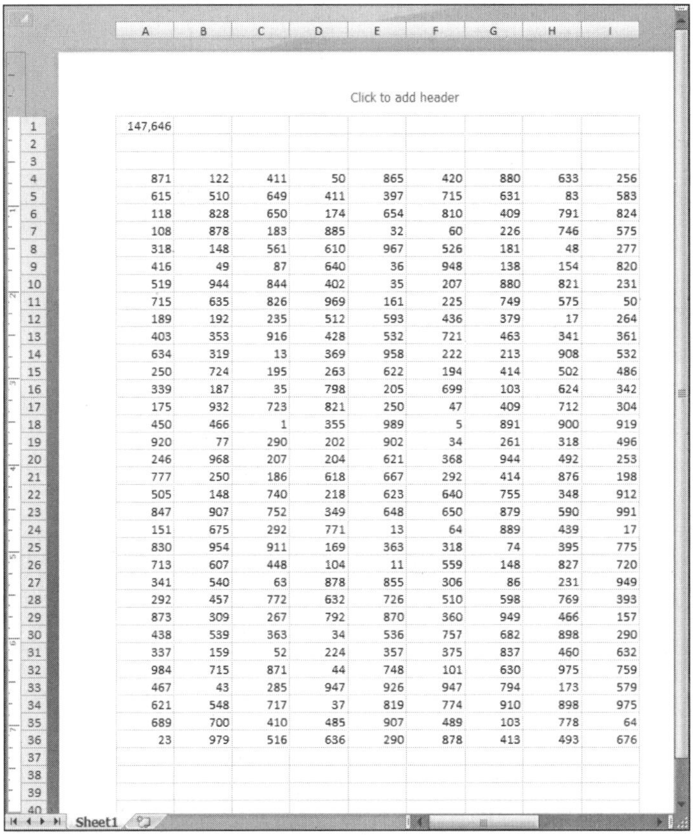

	A	B	C	D	E	F	G	H	I
1	147,646								
2									
3									
4	871	122	411	50	865	420	880	633	256
5	615	510	649	411	397	715	631	83	583
6	118	828	650	174	654	810	409	791	824
7	108	878	183	885	32	60	226	746	575
8	318	148	561	610	967	526	181	48	277
9	416	49	87	640	36	948	138	154	820
10	519	944	844	402	35	207	880	821	231
11	715	635	826	969	161	225	749	575	50
12	189	192	235	512	593	436	379	17	264
13	403	353	916	428	532	721	463	341	361
14	634	319	13	369	958	222	213	908	532
15	250	724	195	263	622	194	414	502	486
16	339	187	35	798	205	699	103	624	342
17	175	932	723	821	250	47	409	712	304
18	450	466	1	355	989	5	891	900	919
19	920	77	290	202	902	34	261	318	496
20	246	968	207	204	621	368	944	492	253
21	777	250	186	618	667	292	414	876	198
22	505	148	740	218	623	640	755	348	912
23	847	907	752	349	648	650	879	590	991
24	151	675	292	771	13	64	889	439	17
25	830	954	911	169	363	318	74	395	775
26	713	607	448	104	11	559	148	827	720
27	341	540	63	878	855	306	86	231	949
28	292	457	772	632	726	510	598	769	393
29	873	309	267	792	870	360	949	466	157
30	438	539	363	34	536	757	682	898	290
31	337	159	52	224	357	375	837	460	632
32	984	715	871	44	748	101	630	975	759
33	467	43	285	947	926	947	794	173	579
34	621	548	717	37	819	774	910	898	975
35	689	700	410	485	907	489	103	778	64
36	23	979	516	636	290	878	413	493	676
37									
38									
39									
40									

Figure 191-1: A simple VBA macro displays the contents of cell A1 in the page header.

To create the macro, follow these steps:

1. Make sure that the workbook's window isn't maximized.
2. Right-click the workbook window's title bar and choose View Code.

   The (empty) code module for the ThisWorkbook object is displayed in the Visual Basic Editor.

3. Type the following macro (see Figure 191-2):

```
Private Sub Workbook_BeforePrint(Cancel As Boolean)
    With ActiveSheet.PageSetup
    .CenterHeader = Sheets("Sheet1").Range("A1").Text'
    End With
End Sub
```

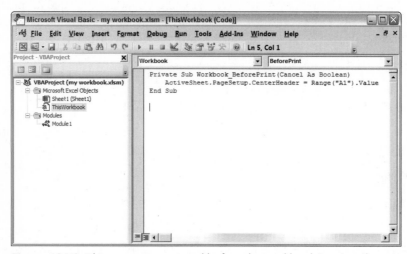

Figure 191-2: This macro is executed before the workbook is printed or previewed.

This macro is executed whenever the workbook is printed or previewed. The macro simply copies the contents of cell A1 (on Sheet1) into the center header. You can, of course, adjust the sheet name or range address so that the header displays the contents of a different cell.

To put the cell contents in a different header or footer position, substitute one of the following names for CenterHeader:

- LeftHeader
- RightHeader
- LeftFooter
- CenterFooter
- RightFooter

NOTE

If your workbook has an XLSX extension, you need to resave it with an XLSM extension. Otherwise, Excel will discard the macro.

Copying Page Setup Settings across Sheets

Each Excel worksheet has its own Print Setup options (orientation, margins, and headers and footers, for example). These options are specified in the Page Setup group on the Page Layout tab.

When you add a new sheet to a workbook, the sheet contains the default Page Setup settings. Here's an easy way to transfer the settings from one worksheet to additional worksheets:

1. Activate the sheet that contains the setup information you want. This is the *source* sheet.

2. Select the target sheets. Ctrl+click the sheet tabs of the sheets you want to update with the settings from the source sheet.

3. Click the dialog box launcher in the Page Layout ⇨ Page Setup group. It's the small icon to the right of the Page Setup group name. Clicking this icon displays the Page Setup dialog box.

4. When the Page Setup dialog box appears, click OK to close it.

5. Ungroup the sheets by right-clicking any selected sheet and choosing Ungroup Sheets from the shortcut menu.

The Page Setup settings of the source sheet are transferred to all the target sheets.

NOTE

Two settings located on the Sheet tab of the Page Setup dialog box are not transferred: Print Area and Print Titles. In addition, pictures in the header or footer are not transferred.

Part X

Printing Cell Comments

Normally, when you print a worksheet that contains cell comments, the comments are not printed. If you want to print the comments, follow these steps:

1. Click the dialog box launcher in the Page Layout ⇨ Page Setup group. It's the small icon to the right of the Page Setup group name. Clicking this icon displays the Page Setup dialog box.

2. In the Page Setup dialog box, click the Sheet tab.

3. Make your choice from the Comments drop-down control: At End of Sheet or As Displayed on Sheet (see Figure 193-1).

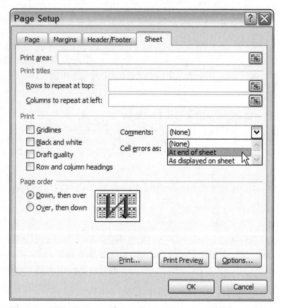

Figure 193-1: Specifying how to print cell comments.

4. Click OK to close the Page Setup dialog box. Or, click the Print button to print the worksheet.

Printing a Giant Banner

Excel really wasn't designed for this task, but if you need to print a giant banner — and you have no other way to do it — follow these instructions to create a workbook that prints one large character per page.

1. Start with a new workbook, and make sure that all other workbooks are closed.

2. Type your message, one character per cell, in column A.

3. Select the cells, and make the text bold and centered vertically and horizontally.

4. Set the font size to 409 (the largest allowable font).

5. Select column A, choose Home ➪ Cells ➪ Format ➪ Column Width, and set the column width to 84. Or, adjust as needed. Your goal is to make column A occupy an entire horizontal page.

6. Choose Page Layout ➪ Page Setup ➪ Margins ➪ Custom Margin to display the Margins tab of the Page Setup dialog box.

7. In the Page Setup dialog box, place a checkmark in both the Horizontally and the Vertically check boxes.

8. Choose View ➪ Workbook Views ➪ Page Layout to enter Page Layout view.

9. Use the Zoom control on the status bar to set the worksheet zoom to 10 percent. Then you can see many complete pages.

10. Use the Page Layout ➪ Scale To Fit ➪ Scale control to increase the scale factor to 150 percent. Adjust, if necessary, until each page displays a large character.

Make sure to look at your sheets in Print Preview mode before printing to ensure that each character is as large as possible on the page.

Figure 194-1 shows the word *Congrats* in Page Layout view.

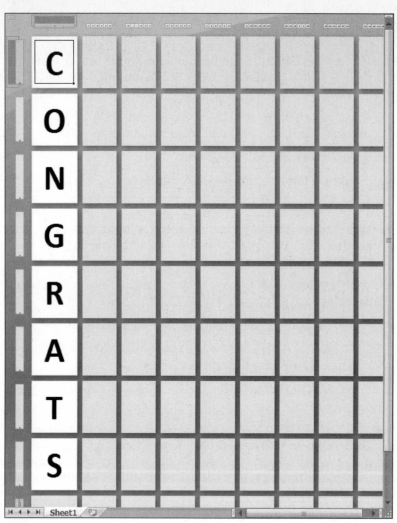

Figure 194-1: Printing one character per page to create a banner.

Part XI

Spotting, Fixing, and Preventing Errors

Just because your spreadsheet doesn't display an error value doesn't mean that it's accurate. The tips in this part will help you identify, fix, and prevent errors.

Tips and Where to Find Them

Using the Excel Error-Checking Features

If your worksheets use a lot of formulas, you might find it helpful to take advantage of the Excel automatic error-checking feature. You enable this feature on the Formulas tab of the Excel Options dialog box (see Figure 195-1). You turn error checking on or off by using the Enable Background Error Checking check box. In addition, you can specify which types of errors to check by selecting check boxes in the Error Checking Rules section.

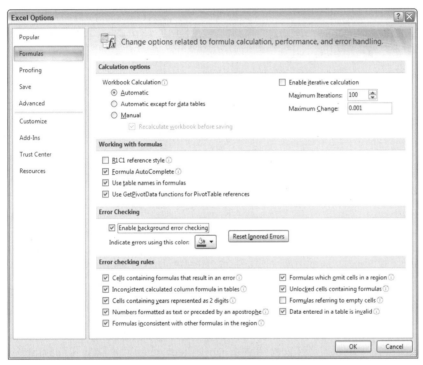

Figure 195-1: Excel can check your formulas for potential errors.

When error checking is turned on, Excel continually evaluates your worksheet, including its formulas. If a potential error is identified, Excel places a small triangle in the upper left corner of the cell. When the cell is activated, a smart tag appears. Clicking it provides you with some options. Figure 195-2 shows the options that appear when you click the smart tag in a cell that contains a #DIV/0! error. The options vary, depending on the type of error.

Part XI

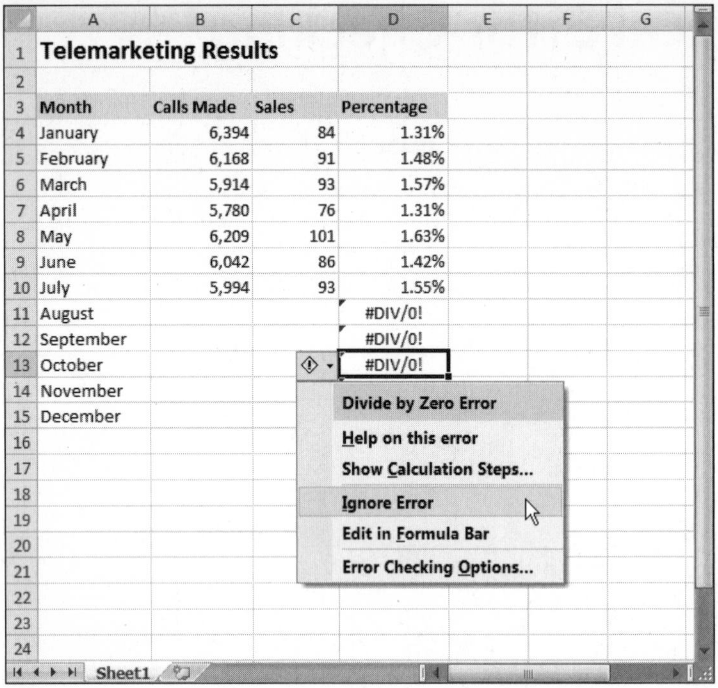

Figure 195-2: Clicking an error smart tag gives you a list of options.

In many cases, you choose to ignore an error by choosing the Ignore Error option, which eliminates the cell from subsequent error checks. However, all previously ignored errors can be reset so that they appear again. (Click the Reset Ignored Errors button in the Excel Options dialog box.)

You can choose the Formulas ⇨ Formula Auditing ⇨ Error Checking command to display a dialog box that displays each potential error cell in sequence, much like using a spell-checking feature. Figure 195-3 shows the Error Checking dialog box. Note that because it's a modeless dialog box, you can still access your worksheet when the Error Checking dialog box is displayed.

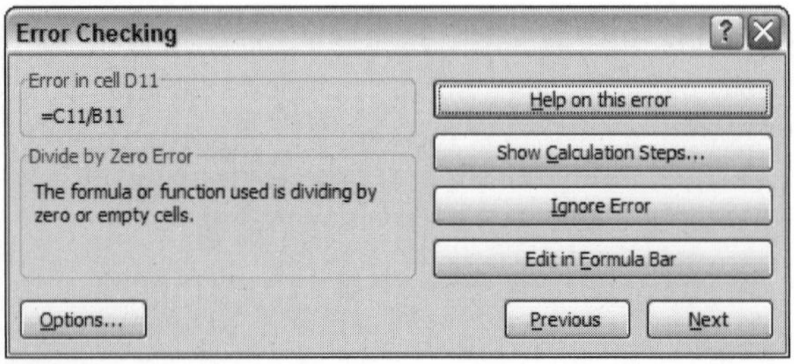

Figure 195-3: Using the Error Checking dialog box to cycle through potential errors identified by Excel.

CAUTION

Understand that the error-checking feature isn't perfect. In fact, it's not even close to perfect. In other words, you can't assume that you have an error-free worksheet simply because Excel doesn't identify any potential errors! Also, be aware that this error-checking feature doesn't catch a common type of error — overwriting a formula cell with a value.

Identifying Formula Cells

One common spreadsheet problem occurs when a formula is accidentally replaced with a value. This type of error is often difficult to locate, especially if your worksheet contains a large number of formulas. This tip describes two ways to quickly identify the formulas in a worksheet by highlighting them. Then, if you zoom out (make the cells appear very small), you might be able to spot gaps in groups of formulas.

Using Go To Special

This method of identifying formula cells is easy, but it's not dynamic. In other words, it's good for a one-time check:

1. Select any single cell in your worksheet.

2. Choose Home ⇨ Editing ⇨ Find & Select ⇨ Go to Special to display the Go to Special dialog box.

3. In the Go to Special dialog box, click the Formulas option, and make sure that all check boxes below it are selected.

4. Click OK. Excel selects all formula cells.

5. Click the Fill Color button on the Formatting toolbar. (Select any color that's not already being used.)

6. Use the Zoom control, and zoom your worksheet to a small percentage (25 percent is a good choice).

7. Check the sheet carefully, and look for any unshaded cells in a group of shaded cells. (It might be a formula that was overwritten by a value.)

If you didn't make any edits, you can click Undo (or press Ctrl+Z) to remove the fill colors you applied in Step 6.

Using Conditional Formatting

This method of identifying formula cells takes a bit of setup work, but it has a distinct advantage over the previous method: It's dynamic. Formula cells are identified immediately when they're entered.

To set up conditional formatting, follow these steps:

1. Choose Formulas ⇨ Defined Names ⇨ Define Name to display the New Name dialog box.

2. In the New Name dialog box, enter the following line in the Name field:

```
CellHasFormula
```

3. Enter the following formula in the Refers To field:

```
=GET.CELL(48,INDIRECT("rc",FALSE))
```

4. Click OK to close the New Name dialog box.

5. Select all cells to which you want to apply the conditional formatting. Generally, they comprise a range from A1 down to the lower right corner of the used area of the worksheet.

6. Choose Home ⇨ Conditional Formatting ⇨ New Rule to display the New Formatting Rule dialog box.

7. In the top part of the dialog box, select the option labeled Use a Formula to Determine Which Cells to Format.

8. Enter this formula in the bottom part of the dialog box (see Figure 196-1):

```
=CellHasFormula
```

Figure 196-1: Using conditional formatting to highlight formula cells.

9. Click the Format button to display the Format Cells dialog box. Select the type of formatting you want for the cells that contain a formula. An unused fill color is a good choice.

10. Click OK to close the Format Cells dialog box, and click OK again to close the New Formatting Rule dialog box.

After you complete these steps, every cell that contains a formula and is within the range you selected in Step 5 displays the formatting of your choice. In addition, if you enter a formula, the cell immediately displays the formatting. This formatting lets you easily identify a cell that should contain a formula but doesn't.

NOTE

The formula you enter in Step 3 is an XML macro. Consequently, you must save the workbook as a macro-enabled file (using an XLSM extension). If you save the workbook as an XLSX file, Excel deletes the CellHasFormula name.

Dealing with Floating-Point Number Problems

Excel users are often baffled by Excel's apparent inability to perform simple math. It's not the program's fault: Computers, by their nature, don't have infinite precision. Excel stores numbers in binary format by using 8 bytes, which can handle numbers with 15-digit accuracy. Some numbers can't be expressed precisely by using 8 bytes, so the number is stored as an approximation.

To demonstrate how this limitation might cause problems, enter the following formula into cell A1:

```
=(5.1-5.2)+1
```

The result should be 0.9. However, if you format the cell to display 15 decimal places, you discover that Excel calculates the formula with a result of 0.899999999999999 — a value that's *close to* 0.9, but certainly *not* 0.9. This result occurs because the operation in parentheses is performed first, and this intermediate result is stored in binary format by using an approximation. The formula then adds 1 to this value, and the approximation error is propagated to the final result.

In many cases, this type of error doesn't present a problem. However, if you need to test the result of that formula by using a logical operator, it might present a problem. For example, the following formula (which assumes that the previous formula is in cell A1) returns FALSE:

```
=A1=.9
```

One solution to this type of error is to use the Excel ROUND function. The following formula, for example, returns TRUE because the comparison is made by using the value in A1 rounded to one decimal place:

```
=ROUND(A1,1)=0.9
```

Here's another example of a precision problem. Try entering the following formula:

```
=(1.333-1.233)-(1.334-1.234)
```

This formula should return 0 but instead returns −2.22045E-16 (a number very close to zero).

If that formula were in cell A1, the following formula would return Not Zero:

```
=IF(A1=0,"Zero","Not Zero")
```

One way to handle these "very close to zero" rounding errors is to use a formula like this:

```
=IF(ABS(A1)<1E-6,"Zero","Not Zero")
```

This formula uses the less-than operator to compare the absolute value of the number with a very small number. This formula would return Zero.

Another option is to instruct Excel to change the worksheet values to match their displayed format. To do this, access the Excel Options dialog box and click the Advanced tab. Check the Set Precision as Displayed check box (which is located in the section named When Calculating This Workbook).

 CAUTION

Selecting the Precision as Displayed option changes the numbers in your worksheets to permanently match their appearance onscreen. This setting applies to all sheets in the active workbook. Most of the time, this option is not what you want. Make sure that you understand the consequences of using the Set Precision as Displayed option.

Removing Excess Spaces

A common type of error involves something that you can't even see: a space character. Consider the example shown in Figure 198-1. Cell B2 contains a formula that looks up the color in cell B1 and returns the corresponding code. The formula is

```
+++=VLOOKUP(B1,D1:E7,2,FALSE)
```

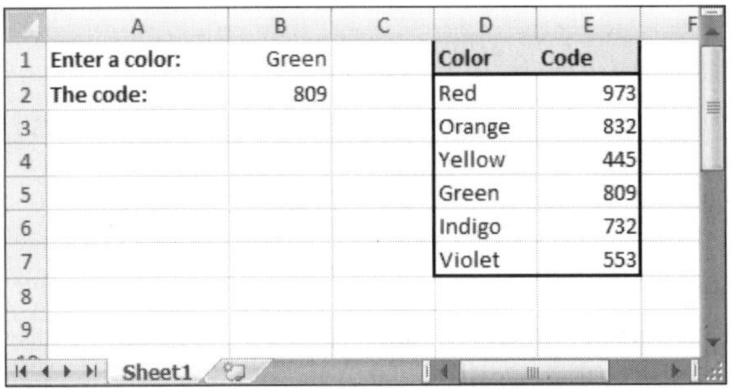

	A	B	C	D	E	F
1	Enter a color:	Green		Color	Code	
2	The code:	809		Red	973	
3				Orange	832	
4				Yellow	445	
5				Green	809	
6				Indigo	732	
7				Violet	553	
8						
9						

Figure 198-1: A simple lookup formula returns the code for a color entered in cell B1.

In Figure 198-2, the formula in cell B2 returns an error — indicating that Yellow wasn't found in the table. Hundreds of thousands of Excel users have spent far too much time trying to figure out why this sort of thing doesn't work. In this case, the answer is simple: Cell D4 doesn't contain the word *Yellow*. Rather, it contains the word *Yellow* followed by a space. To Excel, these text strings are completely different.

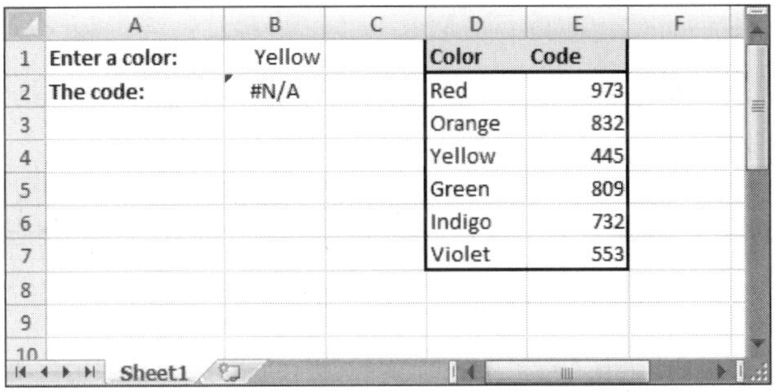

	A	B	C	D	E	F
1	Enter a color:	Yellow		Color	Code	
2	The code:	#N/A		Red	973	
3				Orange	832	
4				Yellow	445	
5				Green	809	
6				Indigo	732	
7				Violet	553	
8						
9						
10						

Figure 198-2: The lookup formula can't find the word *Yellow* in the table.

If your worksheet contains thousands of text entries — and you need to perform comparisons using that text — you might want to identify the cells that contain excess spaces and then fix those cells. The term *excess spaces* means a text entry that contains any of the following: one or more leading spaces, one or more trailing spaces, or two or more consecutive spaces.

Part XI

One way to identify this type of cell is to use conditional formatting.

To set up conditional formatting, follow these steps:

1. Select all text cells to which you want to apply conditional formatting.

2. Choose Home ⇨ Conditional Formatting ⇨ New Rule to display the New Formatting Rule dialog box.

3. In the top part of the dialog box, select the option labeled Use a Formula to Determine Which Cells to Format.

4. Enter a formula like the following in the bottom part of the dialog box:

   ```
   =A1<>TRIM(A1)
   ```

   Note: This formula assumes that cell A1 is the upper left cell in the selection. If that's not the case, substitute the address of the upper left cell in the selection you made in Step 1.

5. Click the Format button to display the Format Cells dialog box. Select the type of formatting you want for the cells that contain excess spaces. A yellow fill color is a good choice.

6. Click OK to close the Format Cells dialog box, and click OK again to close the New Formatting Rule dialog box.

After you complete these steps, every cell that contains excess spaces and is within the range you selected in Step 1 displays the formatting of your choice. You can then easily spot these cells and remove the spaces.

 NOTE

Because of the way the TRIM function works, the formula in Step 4 also applies the conditional formatting to all numeric cells. A slightly more complex formula that doesn't apply the formatting to numeric cells is

```
=IF(NOT(ISNONTEXT(A1)),A1<>TRIM(A1))
```

Viewing Names Graphically

If your worksheet has lots of range names, it might be helpful to identify the location of the ranges. Excel can help: Just zoom the worksheet to 39 percent or less (using the Zoom control on the status bar), and the names are displayed.

Figure 199-1 shows an example of a worksheet that has three named ranges: Monthly, Pmt_Breakdown, and Annual.

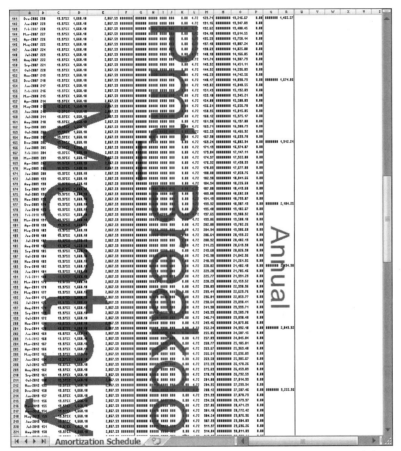

Figure 199-1: Excel displays the range names when you zoom a worksheet to 39 percent or less.

Locating Phantom Links

You might open a workbook and see a message like the one shown in Figure 200-1. If the workbook contains links, you expect to see this message. But sometimes this message appears even when a workbook contains no linked formulas.

Figure 200-1: The Excel way of asking whether you want to update links in a workbook.

To get rid of these phantom links, first try clicking the Edit Links button in the dialog box (or choose Office ⇨ Prepare ⇨ Edit Links to Files) to display the Edit Links dialog box. Then select each link and click Break Link. Save the workbook and reopen it.

If breaking the links doesn't solve the problem, the phantom link might be caused by an erroneous name. (Phantom links might be created when you copy a worksheet that contains names.) Choose Formulas ⇨ Defined Names ⇨ Name Manager and scroll through the list of names. If you see a name that refers to #REF!, delete the name. There's an excellent chance that your phantom link will disappear.

Understanding Displayed versus Actual Values

You might encounter a situation in which values in a range don't appear to add up correctly. For example, Figure 201-1 shows a worksheet with the following formula entered into each cell in the range B3:B5:

```
=1/3
```

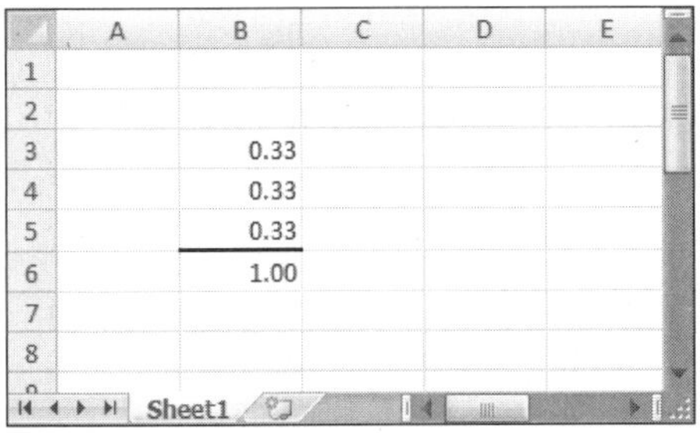

	A	B	C	D	E
1					
2					
3		0.33			
4		0.33			
5		0.33			
6		1.00			
7					
8					

Figure 201-1: A simple demonstration of numbers that appear to add up incorrectly.

Cell B6 contains the following formula:

```
=SUM(B3:B5)
```

All the cells are formatted to display with two decimal places. As you can see, the formula in cell B6 appears to display an incorrect result. (You might expect it to display 0.99.) The formula, of course, returns the correct result. The formula uses the actual values in the range B3:B5, not the displayed values.

You might be tempted to instruct Excel to use the displayed values. You do this by selecting the Set Precision As Displayed check box on the Advanced tab of the Excel Options dialog box. (Choose Office ➪ Excel Options to display this dialog box.)

Generally, using the Set Precision As Displayed check box isn't the best way to handle this type of problem. Checking the Set Precision As Displayed check box also affects normal values (not formulas) that have been entered into cells. For example, if a cell contains the value 4.68 and is displayed with no decimal places (that is, 5), selecting the Set Precision as Displayed check box converts 4.68 to 5.00. This change is permanent, and you can't restore the original value if you later deselect the Set Precision as Displayed check box.

A better approach is to use the Excel ROUND function to round the values to the number of decimal places you want. In the example shown here, the range B3:B5 would contain this formula:

```
=ROUND(1/3,2)
```

Summing the three values results in 0.99.

Part XI

Tracing Cell Relationships

In many worksheets, the cells might contain complex interrelationships. Trying to debug a formula can be easier if you understand two key concepts: cell precedents and cell dependents:

- **Cell precedents:** Applicable only to cells that contain a formula, a formula cell's precedents are all the cells that contribute to the formula's result. A *direct precedent* is a cell that you use directly in the formula. An *indirect precedent* is a cell that isn't used directly in the formula, but is used by a cell that you refer to in the formula.

- **Cell dependents:** These formula cells depend on a particular cell. A cell's dependents consist of all formula cells that use the cell. Again, the formula cell can be a *direct dependent* or an *indirect dependent*.

Identifying cell precedents for a formula cell often sheds light on why the formula isn't working correctly. Conversely, knowing which formula cells depend on a particular cell is also helpful. For example, if you're about to delete a formula, you might want to see whether it has any dependents.

Identifying Precedents

You can identify cells used by a formula in the active cell in a number of ways:

- **Press F2.** The cells that are used directly by the formula are outlined in color, and the color corresponds to the cell reference in the formula. This technique is limited to identifying cells on the same sheet as the formula.

- **Display the Go To Special dialog box** (choose Home ⇨ Editing ⇨ Find & Select ⇨ Go To Special). Select the Precedents option and then select either Direct Only (for direct precedents only) or All Levels (for direct and indirect precedents). Click OK, and Excel selects the precedent cells for the formula. This technique is limited to identifying cells on the same sheet as the formula.

- **Press Ctrl+[** to select all direct precedent cells on the active sheet.

- **Press Ctrl+Shift+{** to select all precedent cells (direct and indirect) on the active sheet.

- **Choose Formulas ⇨ Formula Auditing ⇨ Trace Precedents,** and Excel draws arrows to indicate the cell's precedents. Click this button multiple times to see additional levels of precedents. Choose Formulas ⇨ Formula Auditing ⇨ Remove Arrows to hide the arrows.

Figure 202-1 shows a worksheet with precedent arrows drawn to indicate the precedents for the formula in cell C13.

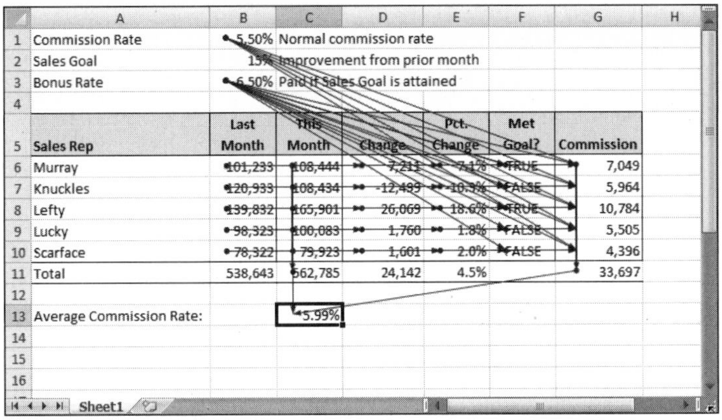

	A	B	C	D	E	F	G
1	Commission Rate	5.50%	Normal commission rate				
2	Sales Goal	15%	Improvement from prior month				
3	Bonus Rate	6.50%	Paid if Sales Goal is attained				
4							
5	Sales Rep	Last Month	This Month	Change	Pct. Change	Met Goal?	Commission
6	Murray	101,233	108,444	7,211	7.1%	TRUE	7,049
7	Knuckles	120,933	108,434	-12,499	-10.3%	FALSE	5,964
8	Lefty	139,832	165,901	26,069	18.6%	TRUE	10,784
9	Lucky	98,323	100,083	1,760	1.8%	FALSE	5,505
10	Scarface	78,322	79,923	1,601	2.0%	FALSE	4,396
11	Total	538,643	562,785	24,142	4.5%		33,697
12							
13	Average Commission Rate:		5.99%				

Figure 202-1: This worksheet displays arrows that indicate cell precedents for the formula in cell C13.

Identifying Dependents

You can identify formula cells that use a particular cell in a number of ways:

- **Display the Go to Special dialog box.** Select the Dependents option and then select either Direct Only (for direct dependents only) or All Levels (for direct and indirect dependents). Click OK. Excel selects the cells that depend on the active cell. This technique is limited to identifying cells on only the active sheet.
- **Press Ctrl+]** to select all direct dependent cells on the active sheet.
- **Press Ctrl+Shift+}** to select all dependent cells (direct and indirect) on the active sheet.
- **Choose Formulas ➪ Formula Auditing ➪ Trace Dependents,** and Excel draws arrows to indicate the cell's dependents. Click this button multiple times to see additional levels of dependents. Choose Formulas ➪ Formula Auditing ➪ Remove Arrows to hide the arrows.

Part XII

Basic VBA and Macros

Even if you know nothing about VBA and macros, you may find that some of the tips in this section whet your appetite to learn more. And, if you're just starting out with macros, you'll find some useful tips in this part.

Tips and Where to Find Them

Learning about Macros and VBA

The terms *macro* and *VBA* remain a mystery to most Excel users. This tip provides a broad overview to help you decide whether learning to create Excel macros would be useful.

What Is a Macro?

A *macro* is a sequence of instructions that automates some aspect of Excel so that you can work more efficiently and with fewer errors. You use the scripting language Visual Basic for Applications (VBA) to create macros. You might create a macro, for example, to format and print your month-end sales report. After the macro is developed, you can then execute the macro to perform many time-consuming procedures automatically.

You need not be a power user to create and use simple VBA macros. Casual users can simply turn on the Excel macro recorder: Excel records your actions and converts them into a VBA macro. When you execute this macro, Excel performs the actions again.

More advanced users can write code that tells Excel to perform tasks that can't be recorded. For example, you can write procedures that display custom dialog boxes, add new commands to the Excel menus, or process data in a series of workbooks.

What Can a Macro Do?

VBA is an extremely rich programming language with thousands of uses. The following list describes just a few things you can do with VBA macros:

- **Insert a text string or formula:** If you need to enter your company name into worksheets frequently, you can create a macro to do the typing (and even format the cell) for you. The Excel AutoCorrect feature can insert text, but it can't do any formatting.

- **Automate a procedure that you perform frequently:** For example, you might need to prepare a month-end summary. If the task is straightforward, you can develop a macro to do it for you.

- **Automate repetitive operations:** If you need to perform the same action in 12 different workbooks, you can record a macro while you perform the task once — and then let the macro repeat your action in the other workbooks.

- **Create a custom command:** For example, you can combine several Excel commands so that they're executed from a single keystroke or from a single mouse click.

- **Create a custom Quick Access Toolbar button:** You can customize the Excel QAT with your own buttons to execute macros that you write.

- **Create a simplified "front end" for users who don't know much about Excel:** For example, you can set up a foolproof data entry template.

- **Develop a new worksheet function:** Although Excel includes a wide assortment of built-in functions, you can create custom functions that can greatly simplify your formulas.

- **Create complete, macro-driven applications:** Excel macros can display custom dialog boxes and be executed from commands you add to the Ribbon.

- **Create custom add-ins for Excel:** Most add-ins that are shipped with Excel were created with Excel macros.

Recording a Macro

The easiest way to get started learning about Excel macros is to use the macro recorder to record a sequence of actions. Then you can play back the sequence — otherwise known as *running* the macro.

The following hands-on demonstration gives newcomers a feel for how macros work. This example demonstrates how to record a simple macro that inserts your name in the active cell.

Creating the Macro

To create the macro, follow these steps:

1. Activate an empty cell.

2. Click the Record Macro button on the left side of the status bar. Excel displays the Record Macro dialog box.

3. Enter a new single-word name for the macro, to replace the default Macro1 name. A good name is MyName.

4. Assign this macro to the shortcut key Ctrl+Shift+N by typing uppercase **N** in the edit box labeled Shortcut Key.

5. Click OK to close the Record Macro dialog box and begin recording your actions.

6. Type your name in the selected cell.

7. The macro is finished, so click the Stop Recording button on the status bar.

This macro is very simple. Most of the time, you record more actions than in this example.

Examining the Macro

The macro was recorded in a new VBA module named Module1. If you're interested, you can take a look at the instructions that were recorded. To view the code in this module, you must activate the Visual Basic Editor (VBE). Press Alt+F11 to toggle between the VBE and the Excel window.

In the VBE, the Project window displays a list of all open workbooks and add-ins. This list is displayed as a tree diagram, which you can expand or collapse. The code that you recorded previously is stored in Module1 in the current workbook. When you double-click Module1, the code in the module is displayed in a Code window.

Figure 204-1 shows the recorded macro, as displayed in the Code window.

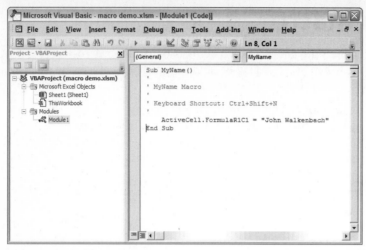

Figure 204-1: The MyName macro was generated by Excel's macro recorder.

Notice that Excel inserted some comments at the top of the procedure. This is some of the information that appeared in the Record Macro dialog box. These comment lines (which begin with an apostrophe) aren't necessary, and deleting them has no effect on how the macro runs.

Testing the Macro

Before you recorded this macro, you set an option that assigned the macro to the Ctrl+Shift+N shortcut key combination. To test the macro, return to Excel by pressing Alt+F11.

When Excel is active, activate a worksheet. (It can be in the workbook that contains the VBA module or in any other workbook.) Select a cell or range and press Ctrl+Shift+N. The macro immediately enters your name into the cell.

NOTE

In this example, notice that you selected the cell before you started recording your macro. This is important. If you select a cell while the macro recorder is turned on, the actual cell that you selected is recorded into the macro. In such a case, the macro always enters your name into that cell and the macro isn't a "general-purpose" macro.

Part XII

...os

...o execute it. This tip describes all the ways to exe-

...Box

...acro dialog box. For a macro to be available, the
...t be open. To display the Macro dialog box, choose
...+F8).

...205-1, displays the macros in a list. Just select the

...all available macros.

...ditor Window

...he Visual Basic Editor (VBE) — although it's cer-
...Press Alt+F11 to activate the VBE. Then locate
...ontains the macro. Place the cursor anywhere within
the macro code, and choose Run ⇨ Run Sub / UserForm (or press F5).

Use a Shortcut Key

When you begin recording a macro, the Record Macro dialog box gives you an opportunity to provide a shortcut key for the macro. If you later want to change the shortcut key or provide a shortcut key for a macro that doesn't have one, follow these steps:

1. Press Alt+F8 to display the Macro dialog box.

2. In the Macro dialog box, select the macro name from the list.

3. Click the Options button. Excel displays the Macro Options dialog box (see Figure 205-2).

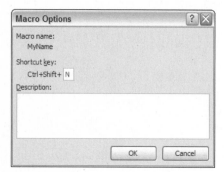

Figure 205-2: Assigning a shortcut key to a macro.

4. Specify the shortcut key and click OK to return to the Macro dialog box.

5. Click Cancel to close the Macro dialog box.

Assign the Macro to a Button

You can add a button to a worksheet and then execute a macro by clicking the button.

NOTE

To add a button to a worksheet, the Developer tab must be present. To display this tab, choose File ➪ Excel Options. In the Excel Options dialog box, select Personalize. Select the Show Developer Tab option in the Ribbon.

Perform these steps to add a button to your worksheet and to **assign a** macro to the button:

1. Choose Developer ➪ Controls ➪ Insert and click the Button control in the Form Controls section (see Figure 205-3).

2. Draw the button on the worksheet. Excel displays the Assign Macro dialog box.

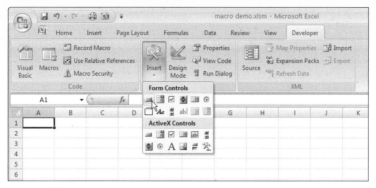

Figure 205-3: Adding a button to a worksheet.

3. In the Assign Macro dialog box, select the macro from the list.

4. Click OK to close the Assign Macro dialog box.

5. If you want to change the text that appears on the button, to make it descriptive, right-click the button, choose Edit Text from the shortcut menu, and make your changes.

After you complete these steps, clicking the button executes the assigned macro.

Assign the Macro to a Shape

You can also assign a macro to a shape object on a worksheet. Just right-click the shape and choose Assign Macro from the shortcut menu. Select the macro from the Assign Macro dialog box, and click OK.

After you perform these steps, clicking the shape runs the macro.

Add a Button to Your Quick Access Toolbar

Another way to execute a macro is to assign it to a button on the Quick Access Toolbar (QAT):

1. Right-click the QAT and choose Customize Quick Access Toolbar to display the Excel Options dialog box.

2. In the drop-down list on the left, choose Macros. A list of available macros is displayed.

3. Select the macro from the list and click Add.

4. Optionally, you can click the Modify button, select a different icon, and provide a different name for the QAT button (see Figure 205-4).

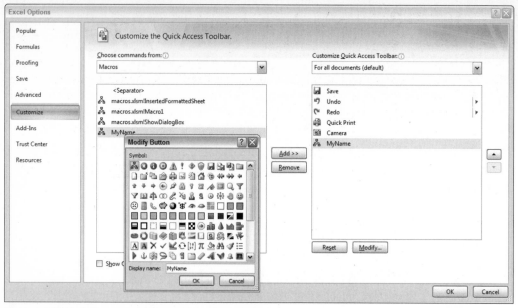

Figure 205-4: Selecting a different icon for a QAT button.

NOTE

When you assign a macro to a QAT button, the button works only when the workbook that contains the macro is active. An exception occurs if the macro is in your Personal Macro Workbook (see Tip 207) or in an add-in (see Tip 216).

Understanding Security Issues Related to Macros

Macro security was a key priority in developing Excel 2007. The reason is that macros are powerful — so powerful that they can do serious damage to your computer and even to other computers on your network. Unfortunately, lots of people in the world find it entertaining to see how much harm they can accomplish from their computer desks.

Security settings are specified in the Trust Center dialog box. Figure 206-1 shows the Macro Settings section of the Trust Center dialog box. To display this dialog box, follow these steps:

1. Choose Office ⇨ Excel Options.

2. In the Excel Options dialog box, click the Trust Center tab.

3. Click the Trust Center Settings button.

4. Click the Macro Settings tab.

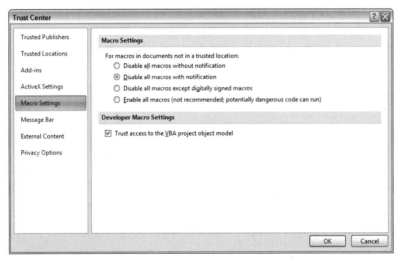

Figure 206-1: The Macro Settings section of the Trust Center dialog box.

By default, Excel uses the Disable All Macros with Notification option. With this setting in effect, if you open a workbook that contains macros (and the file isn't digitally "signed" or in a trusted location), the macros are disabled and Excel displays a security alert above the formula bar. If you're certain that the workbook comes from a trusted source, click Enable Content (and verify your decision in the subsequent dialog box) to enable the macros.

NOTE

If the Visual Basic Editor window is open when you open a workbook that contains macros, Excel doesn't display the security alert above the formula bar. Rather, it displays a dialog box with two buttons: Enable Macros and Disable Macros.

Perhaps the best way to handle macro security is to designate one or more folders as "trusted locations." All the workbooks in a trusted location are opened without a macro warning. You designate trusted folders in the Trusted Locations section of the Trust Center dialog box.

Using a Personal Macro Workbook

When you start recording a macro, the Record Macro dialog box prompts you for a location to store the macro (see Figure 207-1). Your choices are

- Personal Macro Workbook
- New Workbook
- This Workbook

Figure 207-1: The Record Macro dialog box lets you choose where to store the recorded macro.

Most user-created macros are designed for use in a specific workbook, but you might want to use some macros in all your work. You can store these general-purpose macros in the Personal Macro Workbook so that they are always available to you.

The Personal Macro Workbook is loaded whenever you start Excel. The file, named `personal.xlsb`, doesn't exist until you record a macro by using Personal Macro Workbook as the destination.

NOTE
The Personal Macro Workbook normally is in a hidden window (to keep it out of the way).

To record the macro in your Personal Macro Workbook, select the Personal Macro Workbook option in the Record Macro dialog box before you start recording. This is one of the options on the Store Macro In drop-down list.

If you store macros in the Personal Macro Workbook, you don't have to remember to open the Personal Macro Workbook when you load a workbook that uses macros. Excel automatically opens it.

If you made any changes to your Personal Macro Workbook, you're prompted to save the file when you close Excel.

Understanding Functions versus Subs

Excel VBA macros come in two distinct varieties: Sub procedures and Function procedures. This tip describes how they differ.

VBA Sub Procedures

You can think of a *Sub procedure* as a new command. You can have any number of Sub procedures in an Excel workbook. Figure 208-1 shows a simple VBA Sub procedure. When this code is executed, VBA inserts the current date into the active cell, formats it, makes the cell bold, and then adjusts the column width.

Figure 208-1: A simple VBA procedure.

Sub procedures always start with the keyword Sub, the macro's name, and then a pair of parentheses. The End Sub statement signals the end of the procedure. The lines between this keyword and statement comprise the procedure's code.

You execute a VBA Sub procedure in several ways. For example, you can press Alt+F8 and then select the macro from the Macros dialog box. For other ways to execute Sub procedures, see Tip 205.

NOTE

When you record a macro, it's always a Sub procedure.

VBA Functions

A second type of VBA procedure is a *Function* procedure, which always returns a single value (just as a worksheet function always returns a single value). A VBA Function procedure can be executed by other VBA procedures or used in worksheet formulas, just as you would use the built-in Excel worksheet functions.

Figure 208-2 shows the listing of a custom worksheet function and shows the Function procedure in use in a worksheet. This Function procedure, named CubeRoot, requires a single argument. CubeRoot calculates the cube root of its argument. A Function procedure looks much like a Sub procedure. Notice, however, that Function procedures begin with the keyword Function and end with an End Function statement.

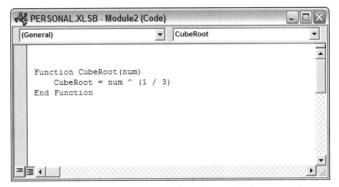

```
PERSONAL.XLSB - Module2 (Code)

(General)                              CubeRoot


   Function CubeRoot(num)
       CubeRoot = num ^ (1 / 3)
   End Function
```

Figure 208-2: A Function procedure that calculates a cube root.

Displaying Pop-Up Messages

You can easily display pop-up messages by using VBA, thanks to its handy MsgBox function. MsgBox is thoroughly described in the VBA Help system. This tip just provides a few examples of the versatility of this function.

Displaying the Time

The following macro, when executed, displays the current time, as shown in Figure 209-1:

```
Sub ShowTheTime()
    MsgBox "It's now " & Time
End Sub
```

Figure 209-1: Using MsgBox to display the time.

By using optional arguments for MsgBox, you can display custom text on the title bar and even add an icon. Figure 209-2 shows the result of executing the following macro:

```
Sub ShowTheTime2()
    MsgBox "It's now " & Time, vbInformation, "Wake up!"
End Sub
```

Figure 209-2: Using MsgBox to display the time, along with custom title bar text and an icon.

In this example, vbInformation is one of several built-in constants that you can use in the second argument of the MsgBox function. Table 209-1 lists all the MsgBox constants, along with brief descriptions.

TABLE 209-1   CONSTANTS USED FOR BUTTONS IN THE MSGBOX FUNCTION

Constant	Value	Description
vbOKOnly	0	Displays OK button only
vbOKCancel	1	Displays OK and Cancel buttons
vbAbortRetryIgnore	2	Displays Abort, Retry, and Ignore buttons
vbYesNoCancel	3	Displays Yes, No, and Cancel buttons
vbYesNo	4	Displays Yes and No buttons
vbRetryCancel	5	Displays Retry and Cancel buttons
vbCritical	16	Displays Critical Message icon
vbQuestion	32	Displays Warning Query icon
vbExclamation	48	Displays Warning Message icon
vbInformation	64	Displays Information Message icon
vbDefaultButton1	0	Indicates that first button is default
vbDefaultButton2	256	Indicates that second button is default
vbDefaultButton3	512	Indicates that third button is default
vbDefaultButton4	768	Indicates that fourth button is default

Asking a Question

The following macro displays the message shown in Figure 209-3. Notice that the message box has two buttons, which result from using the vbYesNo constant.

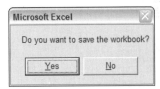

Figure 209-3: Using MsgBox to get a response from the user.

This macro uses a variable, Ans, to store the user's response (that is, clicking the Yes button or clicking the No button). It also uses an If statement to determine whether the Ans is Yes (represented as vbYes). If so, the workbook is saved. If Ans is not equal to vbYes, nothing happens:

```
Sub AskQuestion()
    Ans = MsgBox("Do you want to save the workbook?", vbYesNo)
    If Ans = vbYes Then ActiveWorkbook.Save
End Sub
```

Combining Buttons and Icons

The following example demonstrates how to combine the MsgBox constants by using the + operator. This message box, shown in Figure 209-4, displays two buttons and an icon. If the user clicks Yes, the procedure named ReformatHardDrive (not shown here) is executed:

```
Sub WarnUser()
  Ans = MsgBox("Your drive will be reformatted. Continue?", vbYesNo + vbCritical)
  If Ans = vbYes Then ReformatHardDrive
End Sub
```

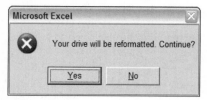

Figure 209-4: Using MsgBox to display buttons and an icon.

Getting Information from the User

Tip 209 presents a few MsgBox examples. This tip demonstrates other ways to get information from the user.

The VBA InputBox Function

The VBA InputBox function displays a field into which the user can enter information.

The following macro displays the dialog box shown in Figure 210-1. The user is prompted for a report title, and the macro then puts the text into cell A1 on the active sheet:

```
Sub GetTitle()
    Title = InputBox("Enter a title for the report.")
    Range("A1") = Title
End Sub
```

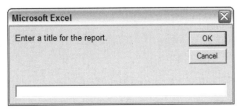

Figure 210-1: Using InputBox to get text.

The InputBox Method

The previous example used the VBA InputBox function. In addition, you can make use of the Excel InputBox method — which is similar to the InputBox function.

One advantage of using the InputBox method is that your macro can prompt for a range of cells. The user can then select the range, and the macro can work with those cells.

The following macro, when executed, displays the dialog box shown in Figure 210-2. When the user specifies a range and clicks OK, the VBA code erases the information in the range:

```
Sub EraseRange()
    Dim UserRange As Range
    DefaultRange = Selection.Address
    On Error GoTo Canceled
    Set UserRange = Application.InputBox _
        (Prompt:="Range to erase:", _
        Title:="Range Erase", _
```

```
        Default:=DefaultRange, _
        Type:=8)
    UserRange.Clear
    UserRange.Select
Canceled:
End Sub
```

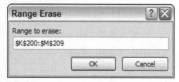

Figure 210-2: Using the InputBox method to get a range selection.

Running a Macro When a Workbook Is Opened

Excel is capable of monitoring a wide variety of events and executing a VBA macro when a particular event occurs. Here are just a few of the many events Excel can recognize:

- The workbook is opened.

- The workbook is saved.

- A new worksheet is added.

- A cell has been modified.

This tip focuses on one very useful event: the Workbook Open event. In many cases, it's useful to execute a macro as soon as a workbook is opened. That's the purpose of a Workbook_Open event-handler macro.

The Workbook_Open event-handler macro must be located in a specific place: the code module for the ThisWorkbook object. The easiest way to get to the code module for the ThisWorkbook object is to right-click the workbook's title bar and choose View Code from the shortcut menu (see Figure 211-1). Note that the workbook's title bar isn't visible when the workbook is maximized.

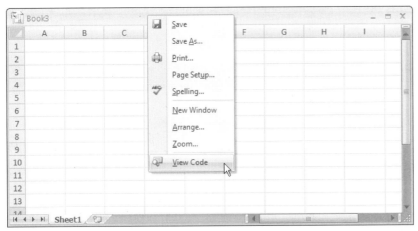

Figure 211-1: Using a shortcut menu to jump to the code module for the ThisWorkbook object.

In addition to being located in the proper place, a Workbook_Open event-handler macro must have a specific name: Workbook_Open.

Greeting the User by Name

The following macro runs when the workbook is opened. It simply displays a message box that greets the user by name (see Figure 211-2):

```
Private Sub Workbook_Open()
    MsgBox "Hello " & Application.UserName
End Sub
```

Figure 211-2: Greeting the user when the workbook is opened.

Keeping Track of the Number of Times a Workbook Is Opened

The following Workbook_Open macro uses the Windows registry to keep track of the number of times the workbook has been opened. Every time the macro runs, it updates the number and displays that number in a message box (see Figure 211-3):

```
Private Sub Workbook_Open()
'   Get setting from registry
    Counter = GetSetting("XYZ Corp", "Budget", "Count", 0)
    LastOpen = GetSetting("XYZ Corp", "Budget", "Opened", "")

'   Display the information
    Msg = "This file has been opened " & Counter & " times."
    Msg = Msg & vbCrLf & "Last opened: " & LastOpen
    MsgBox Msg, vbInformation, ThisWorkbook.Name

'   Update the information and store it
    Counter = Counter + 1
    LastOpen = Date & " " & Time
    SaveSetting "XYZ Corp", "Budget", "Count", Counter
    SaveSetting "XYZ Corp", "Budget", "Opened", LastOpen
End Sub
```

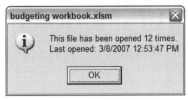

Figure 211-3: Displaying the number of times a workbook has been opened.

Creating a Usage Log

If you want to keep track of who opens a workbook, and at what time, add the following procedure to the ThisWorkbook code module:

```
Private Sub Workbook_Open()
    Open ThisWorkbook.Path & "\usage.log" For Append As #1
    Print #1, Application.UserName, Now
    Close #1
End Sub
```

When this procedure is executed, it appends the user's name and the current date and time to a text file. The file is stored in the workbook's directory and is named usage.log. If the text file doesn't exist, it is created. You can, of course, change the code so that the text file is written to a different directory.

 NOTE

A Workbook_Open procedure isn't executed if the workbook is opened with macros disabled.

Part XII

Creating Simple Worksheet Functions

Excel provides many worksheet functions, but sometimes you need something other than what's available by default. This tip provides a few examples of custom functions that can be used in worksheet formulas.

NOTE

Function procedures must be placed in a normal VBA module. If your workbook doesn't have any VBA modules, activate the Visual Basic Editor, select your workbook from the Project list, and choose Insert ⇨ Module.

Returning the User Name

The following USERNAME function simply displays the name of the user — the name listed on the General tab of the Options dialog box:

```
Function USERNAME()
    USERNAME = Application.USERNAME
End Function
```

Here's a worksheet formula that uses this function:

```
=USERNAME()
```

Determine Whether a Cell Contains a Formula

The following CELLHASFORMULA function accepts a single-cell argument and returns TRUE if the cell has a formula:

```
Function CELLHASFORMULA(cell) As Boolean
'    Returns TRUE if cell has a formula
    CELLHASFORMULA = cell.Range("A1").HasFormula
End Function
```

If a multicell range argument is passed to the function, the function works with the upper left cell in the range.

Returning a Worksheet Name

The following SHEETNAME function accepts a single argument (a range) and returns the name of the worksheet that contains the range:

```
Function SHEETNAME(rng) As String
'    Returns the sheet name for rng
     SHEETNAME = rng.Parent.Name
End Function
```

Returning a Workbook Name

The following function, WORKBOOKNAME, returns the name of the workbook:

```
Function WORKBOOKNAME() As String
'    Returns the workbook name of the cell
'    that contains the function
     WORKBOOKNAME = Application.Caller.Parent.Parent.Name
End Function
```

Reversing a String

The following REVERSETEXT function returns the text in a cell backward:

```
Function REVERSETEXT(text) As String
'    Returns its argument, reversed
     REVERSETEXT = StrReverse(text)
End Function
```

Extracting the Nth Element from a String

The EXTRACTELEMENT function extracts an element from a text string based on a specified separator character. Assume that cell A1 contains the following text:

```
123-456-789-9133-8844
```

The following formula returns the string 9133, which is the fourth element in the string. The string uses a hyphen (-) as the separator.

```
=EXTRACTELEMENT(A1,4,"-")
```

The EXTRACTELEMENT function uses three arguments:

- **Txt:** The text string from which you're extracting (can be a literal string or a cell reference)
- **n:** An integer that represents the element to extract
- **Separator:** A single character used as the separator

Here's the VBA code for the EXTRACTELEMENT function:

```
Function EXTRACTELEMENT(Txt, n, Separator) As String
'    Returns the nth element of a text string, where the
'    elements are separated by a specified separator character
     Dim AllElements As Variant
     AllElements = Split(Txt, Separator)
     EXTRACTELEMENT = AllElements(n - 1)
End Function
```

Making Excel Talk

This tip describes how to make Excel monitor a particular cell and give a verbal report using the text-to-speech feature when the value changes. The tip uses an event-handler macro — specifically, a macro named Worksheet_Calculate.

 CROSS-REFERENCE

See Tip 36 for more about using the text-to-speech options in Excel.

The Worksheet_Calculate macro must be placed in the code module for the worksheet that contains the cell that's being monitored. The easiest way to activate that code module is to right-click the sheet tab and choose View Code from the shortcut menu.

The following listing assumes that cell A1 contains a total and is the cell that's being monitored. The listing uses a different phrase for each of six conditions. For example, if cell A1 contains the value 1,050, Excel says "You're over the budget."

You can, of course, add as many conditions as you like and adjust the ranges for the conditions.

```
Private Sub Worksheet_Calculate()
    With Application.Speech
    Select Case Range("A1")
        Case Is < 600: .Speak "Way below the budget"
        Case 601 To 900: .Speak "Within the budget"
        Case 901 To 999: .Speak "Getting close to the budget"
        Case 1000: .Speak "You are exactly at the budget"
        Case 1001 To 1100: .Speak "You are over the budget"
        Case Is > 1100: .Speak "You are going to get fired"
    End Select
    End With
End Sub
```

Understanding Custom Function Limitations

Almost all users who start creating custom worksheet functions by using VBA make a fatal mistake: They try to get the function to do more than what is possible.

A worksheet function returns a value, and the function must be completely passive: In other words, the function cannot change anything on the worksheet.

For example, you might write a function like the following. This function takes one argument (a cell reference) and attempts to change the formatting of the cell. Although the following function contains perfectly valid VBA code, it does *not* make the referenced cell bold:

```
Function MakeBold(cell)
    If cell.Value > 100 Then
        cell.Font.Bold = True
    Else
        cell.Font.Bold = False
    End If
End Function
```

In many cases, you can use an event macro rather than a custom function. The following macro, located in the module for a worksheet, is executed whenever the sheet is calculated. If cell A1 contains a value greater than 100, the cell is made bold; otherwise, it isn't bold:

```
Private Sub Worksheet_Calculate()
    If Range("A1").Value > 100 Then
        Range("A1").Font.Bold = True
    Else
        Range("A1").Font.Bold = False
    End If
End Sub
```

 NOTE

This simple example is for illustration only. A more efficient solution is to use Excel's conditional formatting feature.

Executing a Ribbon Command with a Macro

This tip describes how to write VBA code that mimics clicking a command on the Excel Ribbon. For example, you can write a macro that executes the Home ⇨ Alignment ⇨ Align Text Left command.

To execute a Ribbon command, you must know the command's name. One way to find a command's name is to use the Customize tab of the Excel Options dialog box. Choose Office ⇨ Excel Options and click the Customize tab. Then locate the command in the list on the left and hover your mouse over the command. A ToolTip displays the command's name (in parentheses).

In Figure 215-1, for example, the ToolTip indicates that the command name for Home ⇨ Alignment ⇨ Align Text Left is AlignLeft. The following VBA macro, when executed, has the same effect as choosing the Home ⇨ Alignment ⇨ Align Text Left command:

```
Sub ExecuteAlignLeft()
    CommandBars.ExecuteMso "AlignLeft"
End Sub
```

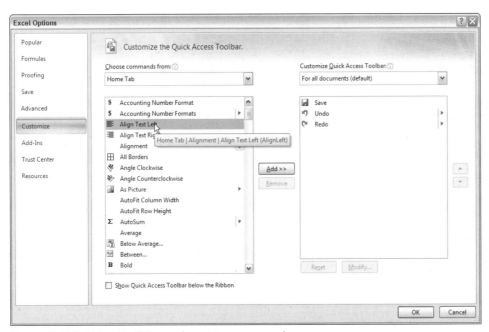

Figure 215-1: Using ToolTips to determine command names.

NOTE

You can download a workbook from the Microsoft site that lists all Excel Ribbon command names — more than 1,700 of them. Try this URL:

```
http://msdn.microsoft.com/office/tool/ribbon/
```

Here's another example that displays the Font tab of the Format Cells dialog box:

```
Sub ShowFontTab()
    CommandBars.ExecuteMso "FormatCellsFontDialog"
End Sub
```

Attempting to execute a command in an incorrect context generates an error. For example, if you execute the ShowFontTab macro when a chart series is selected, the macro generates a run-time error because that command isn't appropriate for a chart series. The following modified version displays a friendlier error message:

```
Sub ExecuteAlignLeft()
    On Error Resume Next
    CommandBars.ExecuteMso "FormatCellsFontDialog"
    If Err.Number <> 0 Then
        MsgBox "That command is not appropriate.", vbInformation
    End If
End Sub
```

Storing Custom Functions in an Add-In

If you create custom worksheet functions by using VBA, you have three choices regarding where to store the functions:

- **In the workbook in which you use them:** This choice is best for functions that are used in only one workbook.

- **In your Personal Macro Workbook:** This choice is good for functions used in multiple workbooks. The problem, however, is that the function name must be preceded by the name of the Personal Macro Workbook, as in this example:

  ```
  =PERSONAL.XLSB!MYFUNCTION(C16)
  ```

- **In an add-in:** If your functions will be used in multiple workbooks, this choice is the best one. If you need to make a change in the function, you need to make it in only one file. In addition, when a function is in an add-in, you need not precede the function name with the name of the add-in, as shown in this example:

  ```
  =MYFUNCTION(C16)
  ```

Follow these steps to create an add-in that contains your custom VBA functions:

1. Open a new workbook.
2. Copy all your functions to a VBA module in the new workbook. Make sure that they're in a standard VBA module, not in a code module for a sheet (for example, Sheet1) or for the workbook (ThisWorkbook).
3. Choose Office ➪ Save As to display the Save As dialog box.
4. In the Save As dialog box, select Excel Add-In (*.xlam) from the Save As Type drop-down list.
5. Enter a name for the add-in in the File Name field and specify a folder where you want to save the add-in. The default folder suggested by Excel is a good choice.
6. Click Save.
7. Close the workbook.

Next, install the add-in you just saved by using the Add-Ins dialog box. The easiest way to display this dialog box is to press Alt+TI. In the Add-Ins dialog box, click the Browse button and locate your new add-in. When the add-in is installed, you can use the Insert Function dialog box to insert your custom function when you create a formula. The custom functions appear in the User Defined category.

Using Add-Ins

Excel is a great program, but let's face it: Sometimes it just doesn't have the features you want. Fortunately, Excel's design allows you to use add-ins to enhance its capabilities and add new features.

Add-Ins That Ship with Excel

The following list of add-ins are included with Excel 2007. Some of these add-ins might not have been installed by default when you installed Excel. If you try to use one of these add-ins and it's not installed, a prompt asks whether you want to install it:

- **Analysis ToolPak:** Contains statistical and engineering tools, plus new worksheet functions. Access this add-in by choosing Data ➪ Analysis ➪ Data Analysis.

- **Analysis ToolPak – VBA:** Adds VBA functions for the Analysis ToolPak. Most users have no need for this add-in.

- **Conditional Sum Wizard:** Helps you to create formulas that add values based on a condition. Access this add-in by choosing Formulas ➪ Solutions ➪ Conditional Sum.

- **Euro Currency Tools:** Contains tools for converting and formatting the euro currency. Access this add-in by choosing Formulas ➪ Solutions ➪ Euro Formatting or Formulas ➪ Solutions ➪ Euro Conversion.

- **Internet Assistant VBA:** A tool for programmers that enables them to publish data to the Web. This add-in is for VBA programmers and isn't accessible from Excel.

- **Lookup Wizard:** Helps you to create formulas that look up data in a list. Access this add-in by choosing Formulas ➪ Solutions ➪ Lookup.

- **Solver Add-In:** Adds a tool that helps you to use a variety of numeric methods for equation solving and optimization. Access this add-in by choosing Data ➪ Analysis ➪ Solver.

 NOTE
You can download additional Excel add-ins from http://office.microsoft.com.

Installing Add-Ins

Most Excel add-ins are contained in an *.xla file — but those developed for Excel 2007 might have an *.xlam extension. To install an *.xla (or *.xlam) add-in, press Alt+TI to display the Add-Ins dialog box. Then, in the Add-Ins dialog box, click the Browse button and locate the *.xla (or *.xlam) file on your hard drive. The add-in name then appears in the list. (Make sure that it's checked.) Click OK to close the Add-Ins dialog box, and the add-ins that have a checkmark are available for use.

The Add-Ins dialog box lists all add-ins that Excel knows about. The add-ins in the list with check marks are currently installed. To uninstall an add-in, just remove the check mark.

NOTE

Most add-in files can also be opened by choosing Office ➪ Open. After an add-in is opened, however, you find that you can't choose Office ➪ Close to close it. The only way to remove the add-in is to close and restart Excel or write a macro to close the add-in.

When an add-in is opened, you may or may not notice anything different. In nearly every case, however, a change is made to the user interface. For example, when you install the Analysis ToolPak add-in, a new Ribbon command is available: Data ➪ Analysis ➪ Data Analysis. When you open my Power Utility Pak v7 add-in, you get a new Ribbon tab, named PUP v7.

NOTE

Most add-ins that were created before Excel 2007 modify the old Excel user interface. In other words, they add a new menu or toolbar. Because Excel 2007 doesn't have menus or toolbars, the user interface for these older add-ins appears on a new Ribbon tab, named Add-Ins.

Finding Add-Ins

The best way to find Excel add-ins that are suitable for a particular task is to search the Web, including the Excel newsgroups (available through www.groups.google.com). If you still can't find what you're looking for, try posting a question in one of the Excel newsgroups. Describe what functionality you're looking for. If such an add-in exists, someone will know about it and respond.

Part XII

Part XIII

Sources for Excel Information

This book contains lots of information, but it certainly doesn't cover everything. In this part, you'll find some helpful tips on where to find more information about Excel.

Tips and Where to Find Them

Searching the Internet for Help

This tip is probably the best one in the book. If you have a question about Excel, there's a 90 percent chance that you can find the answer by searching the Internet. The Web has dozens of excellent sites about Excel that provide tips, advice, examples, and downloads.

Many good search engine sites are available. My favorites are

- **Google:** `www.google.com`
- **A9:** `www.a9.com`
- **MSN:** `search.msn.com`

The key to a successful search is composing a good search phrase. Make sure that the phrase includes Excel, and then add other keywords that are likely to be present in the answer to your question. Enclose common phrases in quotes. For example, if you're having a problem with formatting in a PivotTable, use the search string **Excel "pivot table" formatting**.

The more you use the search sites, the better you get in composing effective search strings.

Using Excel Newsgroups

What if you had access to hundreds of thousands of answers to specific questions about Excel? Well, guess what? You do — all you need is an Internet connection, and you can find hundreds of thousands of answers in Usenet newsgroups.

The *Usenet* Internet service provides access to several thousand special interest groups that enable you to communicate with people who share common interests. A newsgroup works like a public bulletin board: You can post a message with your questions, and (usually) others reply to your message.

Newsgroups cover virtually every topic you can think of (and many that you haven't thought of). Typically, questions posted on a newsgroup are answered within 24 hours — assuming, of course, that you ask the questions in a manner that makes others want to reply.

Accessing Newsgroups by Using a Newsreader

You can use newsreader software to access the Usenet newsgroups. Many of these programs are available, but you probably already have one installed: Microsoft Outlook Express, which is installed with Internet Explorer. If you use Windows Vista, this program is named Windows Mail.

Microsoft maintains an extensive list of newsgroups, including quite a few devoted to Excel. If your Internet service provider doesn't carry the Microsoft newsgroups, you can access them directly from the Microsoft news server. (In fact, that's the preferred method.) You need to configure your newsreader software (not your Web browser) to access the news server at this address:

```
msnews.microsoft.com
```

Accessing Newsgroups by Using a Web Browser

As an alternative to using newsreader software, you can read and post to the Microsoft newsgroups directly from your Web browser. This option is often significantly slower than using standard newsgroup software and is best suited for situations in which newsgroup access is prohibited by network policies. Two options to access newsgroups using your browser are:

- **Access thousands of newsgroups at Google Groups:**

  ```
  http://groups.google.com
  ```

- **Access the Microsoft newsgroups (including Excel newsgroups) from this URL:**

  ```
  www.microsoft.com/communities/newsgroups/default.mspx
  ```

The following table lists the most popular English-language Excel newsgroups on the Microsoft news server (and also available at Google Groups).

Newsgroup	Topic
`microsoft.public.excel`	General Excel topics
`microsoft.public.excel.charting`	Building charts with Excel
`microsoft.public.excel.interopoledde`	OLE, DDE, and other cross-application issues
`microsoft.public.excel.macintosh`	Excel issues on the Macintosh operating system
`microsoft.public.excel.misc`	General topics that don't fit in one of the other categories
`microsoft.public.excel.newusers`	Help for newcomers to Excel
`microsoft.public.excel.printing`	Printing with Excel
`microsoft.public.excel.programming`	Programming Excel with VBA macros
`microsoft.public.excel.templates`	Spreadsheet Solutions templates and other XLT files
`microsoft.public.excel.worksheet.functions`	Worksheet functions

Searching Newsgroups

The fastest way to find a quick answer to a question is to search past newsgroup postings. Often, searching past newsgroup postings is an excellent alternative to posting a question to the newsgroup, because you can get the answer immediately. Unless your question is obscure, there's an excellent chance that it has already been asked and answered. The best source for searching newsgroup postings is Google Groups:

`http://groups.google.com`

How does searching work? Suppose that you have a problem identifying unique values in a range of cells. You can perform a search using the following keywords: **Excel**, **Range**, and **Unique**. The Google search engine probably will find dozens of newsgroup postings that deal with these topics.

If the number of results is too large, refine your search by adding search terms. Sifting through the messages might take a while, but you have an excellent chance of finding an answer to your question. In fact, I estimate that at least 90 percent of the questions posted in the Excel newsgroups can be answered by searching Google.

Browsing Excel-Related Sites

If you know where to look, you can find some very useful Web sites devoted to Excel. In this tip, I list a few of my favorites.

AJP Excel Information

http://www.andypope.info/

Andy Pope, based in the UK, has a great site with many creative Excel examples. My favorite section is Fun 'n' Funky.

Stephen Bullen's Excel Page

www.bmsltd.co.uk/excel

Stephen's Web site contains some fascinating examples of Excel code, including the section They Said It Couldn't Be Done.

Contextures

http://www.contextures.com/

Debra Dalgleish's site has dozens of useful tips and downloads — all nicely organized and easy to find.

Daily Dose of Excel

http://DailyDoseOfExcel.com

This frequently updated Web log was created by Dick Kusleika, with about a dozen contributors (including me). It covers a variety of topics, and readers can leave comments.

Excel Guru

http://excelguru.ca/

Ken Puls' site is designed to "help remove the mysteries of Excel." It's packed with useful articles and free downloads.

David McRitchie's Excel Pages

www.mvps.org/dmcritchie/excel/excel.htm

David's site is jam-packed with useful Excel information and is updated frequently.

Mr. Excel

www.MrExcel.com

Mr. Excel, also known as Bill Jelen, maintains an extensive site devoted to Excel. The site also features a message board.

Pearson Software Consulting

www.cpearson.com/excel.htm

This site, maintained by Chip Pearson, contains dozens of useful examples of VBA and clever formula techniques.

Jon Peltier's Excel Page

http://peltiertech.com/Excel

Those who frequent the `microsoft.public.excel.charting` newsgroup are familiar with Jon Peltier. He has an uncanny ability to solve practically any chart-related problem. His Web site contains many Excel tips and an extensive collection of charting examples.

Ron's Excel Page

http://www.rondebruin.nl/

Ron de Bruin, who is based in The Netherlands, has a site with many useful VBA examples, plus several free add-ins.

The Spreadsheet Page

http://www.j-walk.com/ss

My own Web site contains files to download, developer tips, spreadsheet jokes, and information about my books.

Index

Symbols and Numbers

continued

continued

continued

continued